Gendered Justice in the American West

Gendered Justice in the American West

WOMEN PRISONERS IN
MEN'S PENITENTIARIES

Anne M. Butler

University of Illinois Press
Urbana and Chicago

© 1997 by the Board of Trustees of the
University of Illinois
Manufactured in the United States of America
C   5   4   3   2   1

This book is printed on acid-free paper.

Library of Congress Cataloging-in-Publication Data
Butler, Anne M., 1938–
Gendered justice in the American West : women
prisoners in men's penitentiaries / Anne M. Butler.
     p.   cm.
Includes bibliographical references (p.) and index.
ISBN 0-252-02281-5 (cloth : acid-free paper)
1. Women prisoners—West (U.S.)—History.
2. Female offenders—West (U.S.) History.
3. Prisons—West (U.S.)—History.
4. Sex discrimination against women—West (U.S.)
History.
5. Sex discrimination in criminal justice
administration—West (U.S.)—History.
I. Title.
HV9475.W38B87   1997
365'.6'082—dc21   96-45886   CIP

For Jay

. . . to get the real story of a woman convict's life is not as easy as turning on a phonograph. . . . One must get it piecemeal, bit by bit, from time to time.
   —Kate Richards O'Hare
   Missouri State Penitentiary
   1917

Contents

Illustrations follow pages 48, 111, and 173

Abbreviations

ADC	Arkansas Department of Corrections, Pine Bluff, Arkansas
AHS	Arizona Historical Society, Tucson, Arizona
ASA	Arizona Department of Library, Archives, and Public Records, Phoenix, Arizona
ASHC	Arkansas State History Commission, Little Rock, Arkansas
CLDS	Church of Jesus Christ of Latter-day Saints History Department, Salt Lake City, Utah
CSA	Colorado State Archives and Public Records, Denver, Colorado
HFPRC	Historical Foundation of the Presbyterian and Reformed Churches, Montreat, North Carolina
ISA	Iowa State Archives, Des Moines, Iowa
ISL	Idaho State Library, Boise, Idaho
ISP	Idaho State Penitentiary, Boise, Idaho
KSHS	Kansas State Historical Society, Topeka, Kansas
LC	Library of Congress, Washington, D.C.
LSP	Louisiana State Penitentiary, Angola, Louisiana
MnHS	Minnesota Historical Society, St. Paul, Minnesota
MSA	Missouri State Archives, Jefferson City, Missouri
MtHS	Montana Historical Society, Helena, Montana
NA	National Archives, Washington, D.C.
NMSA	New Mexico State Records Center and Archives, Santa Fe, New Mexico
NSA	Nebraska State Archives, Lincoln, Nebraska
NSCMA	Nevada State, County, and Municipal Archives, Carson City, Nevada
NSL	Nevada State Library, Carson City, Nevada
NSP	Nebraska State Penitentiary, Lincoln, Nebraska
SDSA	South Dakota State Archives, Pierre, South Dakota
TSA	Texas State Library and Archives, Austin, Texas
UKKC	Kansas Collection, University of Kansas, Lawrence, Kansas

UM	Western Historical Manuscript Collection/Columbia and State Historical Society of Missouri, University of Missouri, Columbia, Missouri
UTBC	Barker Center for American History, University of Texas, Austin, Texas
WSAHD	Wyoming State Archives, Museums and Historical Department, Cheyenne, Wyoming

Preface

This work, a direct outgrowth of earlier research on the topic of prostitution, continues my interest in groups of women who lived in the American West during the late nineteenth and early twentieth centuries. At the outset of my first project, several knowledgeable persons steered me away from state penitentiary records as a source for information about prostitutes. They assured me that prostitution remained a matter for local jurisdictions, and that I should look for my subjects only in the county jails of the West. The conventional wisdom held that authorities reserved the state and territorial penitentiaries for male offenders.

That advice, although well intentioned, missed the mark. As my research progressed, I came across some county records that made note of women remanded to the state authorities. In several different states, western newspapers carried stories of prostitutes, usually convicted in sensational murder trials, sent to the main prison facility. Turning to penitentiary registers to trace those women, I found mounting evidence that homicidal prostitutes represented only some of the female inmates inside male prisons. In addition, lesser crimes than murder and manslaughter often accounted for the penitentiary imprisonment of women.

At some institutions, women inmates trickled in sporadically, while in others the female population rose as a constant over fifty years. While never a sizable portion of the prisoner population, women passed in an increasingly regular parade through the penitentiary gates. To limit the penal agencies considered, I centered my research on state penitentiaries built for and managed by men. Even after eliminating federal prisons, county jails, women's reformatories, industrial farms, and houses of correction, I found my numbers of women inmates climbing.

Just as the nineteenth-century West itself encompassed a mix of cultures, so did the women who went to prison. They came from among recent European immigrants and the American born. Within the western boundaries of my research, women inmates most generally represented African American, Euro American, and Hispanic American cultures. These three groups constitute those whose accounts make up this work.

The criminal records of two other important populations of western women—Native Americans and Asians—did not emerge from the documents. Perhaps this resulted from their residence in insular or remote situations, which typically kept the women from regular contact with Anglo law. Internal cultural practices may have been used to punish female lawbreakers inside communities reluctant to surrender their members to the jurisdictions of white society.

When Anglo arrest and trial procedures did involve Native American women, usually the mantle of federal authority, a jurisdiction outside the focus of this work, fell across the case. Richer information about imprisoned Native American women may be found by consulting federal government prison records. The occasional Native American woman, typically a mixed blood, sentenced to a state penitentiary appeared to be one working and living beyond the limits of the federally regulated reservation. In that circumstance, state and local governments assumed responsibility for prosecution. As indicated by the research in this study, the numbers of such women stayed exceedingly low.

Within the geographic area in this work, Asian women, always an extremely small percentage of the western population, simply did not appear regularly as defendants in Anglo courts. Before 1880, coercive prostitution, a feature of the early immigrant community, drew some women into justice of the peace courts, where charges of abduction by pimps and brothel owners were sorted out. After that date, the Chinese community increasingly took on family characteristics. Prostitution as an outcome for female emigration declined, and newcomers became home-centered wives caring for domestic duties. As Asian communities built their places in the West, the women remained aloof from much of the larger society by reason of language barriers, cultural choice, and the intense discrimination directed at them and their families. Given all these factors, Asian women rarely had either occasion or opportunity to commit felonies that attracted the Anglo legal system and thus did not appear in the prisons in this study.

Those western women who did enter penitentiaries spoke many languages—Spanish, Norwegian, French, English, Czech, German, Swedish—and prayed in many voices—Methodist, Congregational, Lutheran, Baptist, Mormon, Presbyterian, Catholic. They ranged in age from eleven to seventy; they included the single woman, the married, the divorced, the widowed. They came alone, with their spouses and partners, or carrying their children—both the born and the unborn. Some wrote movingly of their experiences, others were barely literate. A few came from homes of comfort, most were poor. Together, across a fifty-year span, they managed to leave their mark on the prison system.

The public record, which I pursued in approximately two dozen western repositories, gave witness to these women and their actions. Access to these records, however, proved complex. Despite advance preparations I made with various prison systems, the actual collection of information posed a challenge. In most states, my letter of inquiry bounced across many desks before happening into the hands of an interested official. It became apparent that not every agency had a clear notion of the whereabouts of records for women prisoners. When located, files were often a hodgepodge collection of odds and ends. Frequently documents in state archives required added research clearance from an administrator or warden, far removed from the repository and invariably totally uninformed about nineteenth-century materials, their condition or content.

In addition to state archives and historical societies, I conducted research inside three male penitentiaries. I took meals and slept overnight in one prison. At another I saw my letter of entry revoked by a local administrator, piqued because someone other than herself had given the research permission. One warden, passionate about his prison's history, provided an informative and detailed tour of the facility, including the cemetery, death-row holding cell, and execution chamber, before he produced the documents.

Some officials greeted me with suspicion, others were baffled, many were enthusiastic. I dealt with prison administrators eager to put the story of women into my hands and one whose hands shook almost uncontrollably as he tried to talk me out of my request. In one state, an assistant warden hesitated about honoring my written permission for access because he thought I might sell prisoner names to the *Reader's Digest* mailing list and inmates would be harassed by junk mail. I pointed out that if my nineteenth-century subjects remained alive by the late 1980s, they would probably be happy to receive any mail, even an advertisement. He countered by insisting that, regardless of the era of incarceration, a prisoner's name must never be revealed by penitentiary officials. Later the manager of records in that institution informed me that creditors routinely called the prison to confirm the whereabouts of debtors, inquiries that were freely answered.

In a different state, regulations allowed a researcher to see names of inmates but not medical histories, although both categories of information appeared on the same page in the prison register. A gracious state's attorney lifted the restraint after repeated phone calls from a willing but uncertain archivist. In another jurisdiction, a state's attorney accidentally granted me access to all past and current prison files. One female supervisor called the state capitol and successfully lobbied for me to enter the prison's locked records unit, an office reached by walking through the prisoners' infirmary. Another literally risked her job because she believed the history of women prisoners had been suppressed deliberately; the conduct of her superiors affirmed the soundness of her sentiment. I thank the many pressed and overworked public servants, professionals in an arena far different from my academic world, who gave me their time and critical assistance; especially I am indebted to these two necessarily anonymous women for their generosity and courage.

From all these reactions I realized that the history of a penitentiary remains a thorny subject for modern society. Current administrators often feel personally indicted by early conditions that show their state in an unbecoming light. The abuses of the nineteenth century act as a lightening rod drawing attention to the adverse prison circumstances of the twentieth. Obviously, political implications linger in today's halls of government as a result of past prison management. The reactions, both of encouragement and of obstruction, among prison officials fueled my sense that women constituted a part of western prison history but also a component in the modern debate. The shock of watching a guard conduct weapon searches on four African American children, ages six to nine, before visits with their imprisoned mothers solidified my conviction that this subject touches America's past, present, and future.

When I decided to make western women prisoners the focus of a monograph, I hoped to uncover lives from among the West's unknown daughters, for such anonymous women draw my scholarly interest. As the experiences of my research occurred and the stories of incarcerated women unfolded before me, I realized other aspects to this topic. First, the history of women incarcerated in western penitentiaries gives a gendered perspective to a larger regional statement about violence. Second, the management of women prisoners in the past links directly to the status of the female offender in modern society.

This project required many years to complete. During that time, I accumulated a wide range of scholarly debts. I acknowledge the contributions of the many, but retain sole responsibility for any error in my work. I thank Utah State University and Gallaudet University, especially Michael Karchmer, director of the research division, for monetary support.

Staff members at several public agencies facilitated my research; I thank all those who work in the repositories listed in the bibliography at the end of this book. Special thanks go to: Mario M. Einaudi at the Arizona Historical Society, Terry Harmon at the Kansas State Historical Society, Roger S. Thomas, former assistant warden of the Louisiana State Penitentiary, and Mrs. Eddie Williams at the Texas State Archives. My warm thanks to Elaine Way of the Old Montana Prison, who assisted me in gathering materials from that state, and David Moos, who helped in Texas. I am grateful to Cynde Georgen for the rich family material she sent about her great-grandmother, Jessie Carmon, and to the historical muses that arranged for our paths to cross.

I thank the exceptional students who passed through the offices of the *Western Historical Quarterly*—Steven Amerman, Todd Anderson, Bradley Birzer, Craig Breaden, Jared Farmer, James Feldman, Andrew Hardcastle,

John Heaton, Andrew Honker, Michael Lansing, Kelly May, Daniel Moos, Kathryn Morse, Jane Reilly, Brett Rushforth, Renée Sentilles. They performed numerous tasks and made many library jaunts with good cheer.

My former colleagues Donna Ryan and John S. Schuchman extended much-appreciated encouragement, long after I departed from their midst. I am indebted to my present excellent colleagues in the history department of Utah State University, where there exists an unusually kind spirit of collegial support. David Rich Lewis, associate editor at the *WHQ*, not only assumed extra work during my sabbatical but brightened all with his singular and wonderful wit. Ona Siporin, also a *WHQ* colleague and friend, reminded me of the importance of literary rigor and intellectual sensitivity, as she does with everything that we share.

Douglas D. Martin, the consummate teacher, seems never to weary of offering impeccable guidance and steady friendship; as always he demanded I hone my ideas more carefully. Glenda Riley was enthusiastic in her support for this topic, practical in her advice about the content, and constant in her friendship to its author. Clyde A. Milner II, senior editor at the *Western Historical Quarterly*, brings great gifts—originality of thought, administrative vision, academic generosity, and unparalleled humor—to our office; no one is his equal. I thank these three fine scholars for the way they have shaped my personal life and professional experience.

In my office, Barbara Stewart and, in the USU history department, Carolyn Doyle and Sally Okelberry, who prepared the manuscript, juggled an assortment of chores for me with a steady cheerfulness that diluted every crisis. The USU computer wizards, Paul Cook and Chris Okelberry, grounded me in the world of technology. At the Outer Banks of North Carolina, Bryan Belk repaired the equipment and saved my sanity after a computer disaster. At the University of Illinois Press, I thank my editors, Elizabeth Dulany who encourages my work and Patricia Hollahan who improves it.

Without my family, this work could not have been completed. My children—Dan and Karen, Kate and Joel—offered, as they always have, the best of life with their love, common sense, and laughter. My remarkable mother, Jean A. Posey, and my good-spirited brother and sister-in-law, Ed and Joan Oligney, kept watch over the Utah hearth, so that I could retreat to North Carolina for several months of writing. There, Amy, Hank, and Renata welcomed us into a merry world that eased the writing task into a beach-filled sabbatical memory of good times, family joy, and warm grandparenting. An undying affection for the West made Jennifer a willing listener when she visited. All these relationships and my scholarly work are enhanced by Jay, my partner in life and love. I could never thank him sufficiently for the way he sustains my well-being and his many contributions to this book; it is appropriately dedicated to him.

Gendered Justice in the American West

Introduction

America has always had a violent past and the frontier in a way has stood for this country at its most violent.[1]

Violence and the American West bond as equal partners in the historical discourse. One almost cannot speak of western history without taking into account the place and power of violence in the heritage of the West. Depictions of violence range from its glorification to its defense to its castigation to its analysis. Through each of these stages, the discussion of western violence resonates with a decidedly masculine tone. Male encounters—psychotic gunfighters versus stout-hearted lawmen, Indian warriors versus government soldiers, railroad laborers versus Asian workers, cattlemen versus sheepherders, indigenous Hispanics versus southwestern colonizers—dominate considerations of the violence of the West. Across smoke-filled horizons, men on horseback, men in breechclouts, men in uniform dart, crouch, run, and twist. Stampeding cattle, roaring six-shooters, dangling noos-

Belle Grose, Colorado State Penitentiary. Courtesy Division of State Archives and Public Records, Denver, Colo.

1

es, burning buildings—these serve as the accoutrements of the violent male westerner.

The historical literature, in all its forms, deals with these images of the West. Historians have approached this western element from many angles and suggested many explanations for its prevalence: The West had just the right amount of violence to bring about its settlement by whites. The West did not have much violence at all. We misunderstand violence in the West. There was good violence and bad violence. Only "bad" people in the West resorted to violence. People from the East brought violence to the West. People in the West responded with violence when people from the East threatened their homes. We assess western violence by impressionistic standards applied to the bizarre actions of a notorious few. Some men in the West lived by violence, but that is how they got what they wanted and became heroes. Westerners judged a man not by who he was but by what he could do—violence against minorities being just an unfortunate exception to this rule. Frontier violence was more or less honorable, the understandable outcome of the anxieties caused by conquering native-born populations.[2]

These themes appear in a wide range of literature. Their treatment and development vary from scholar to scholar and alter with the shifting tides of historical interpretation. Nonetheless, from the most romantic to the most erudite, they remain rigidly masculine.

It took historian Richard Maxwell Brown to suggest ideas that shifted the debate away from its male polestar. Brown talked about the dynamics of power in connection with violence, pointing out that violence, in all its forms, involves the strong against the weak, the abuser and the abused. In his consideration of the impact of violence on the nation as a whole Brown said: "violence has not been the action only of the roughnecks and racists among us but has been the tactic of the most upright and respected people."[3]

In this single observation, Richard Maxwell Brown expanded the boundaries of the violence debate to encompass not only all classes of American men but women as well. Perhaps, Brown reminded us, images of smoking guns and brawling men did not quite bring into focus the many faces touched by western violence. He made it clear that earlier definitions of violence need to be reorganized. Despite Brown's groundbreaking comment in 1969, scholars did not hasten to take up the subject of women and western violence.

In a region, fairly or unfairly, tied to a gun and grab history, the implications of violence—the exertion of physical and/or mental force so as to abuse or injure another—for western women remained unexplored. In 1982 Robert L. Griswold in *Family and Divorce in California, 1850–1890: Victorian Illusions and Everyday Realities* cast the subject in new terms and documented the way in which physical abuse emerged as a legitimate grievance in the dissolution of marriage. In 1984, Roger D. McGrath in *Gunfighters, Highwaymen and Vigilantes: Violence on the Frontier* returned the discussion to its more traditional masculine focus in his study on two Colorado towns. Although mainly concerned with men in the West, McGrath concluded "There is . . . a considerable body of evidence that indicates that women were generally free from crimes of all varieties and treated with great respect," and "Aurora and Bodie women, other than prostitutes, suffered little from crime or violence."[4] McGrath based his observations about violence on statistical use of public records. That marked an important departure from much earlier work, grounded mainly in heroics by justification. McGrath, however, overlooked for all classes and cultures the violence that eluded the public record but invaded women's private lives.

Paula Petrik affirmed Robert Griswold's findings in two articles, "If She Be Content: The Development of Montana Divorce Law, 1865–1907" and "Not a Love Story: Bordeaux vs. Bordeaux." Turning to divorce petitions for her evidence, Petrik showed that abused women often secretly tolerated domestic violence out of fear and shame, reluctantly revealing it when their court case needed added ballast. In a 1991 publication, *Divorce: An American Tradition,* Glenda Riley found that in the nineteenth-century West the divorce rate soared beyond other national regions, with women commonly charging verbal and physical abuse in their petitions. Griswold, Petrik, and Riley each pointed to the West and found elements of a violence we had barely considered. Their works suggest that if violence touched women with the resources to hire lawyers and to seek divorce perhaps it found its way into many other female lives as well.

Several years earlier, Richard White in "Outlaw Gangs of the Middle Border" had introduced yet another element to the subject of western violence, noting the southern heritage of many western outlaws and the antagonistic relationships that spilled into the West in the aftermath of the Civil War. In a later work, *"It's Your Misfortune and None of My Own,"* White referred to Texas and Oklahoma as "those southern wedges into the West," emphasizing in a range of western topics how easily one regional heritage bleeds into another.[5] In 1991 Richard Maxwell Brown, in *No Duty to Retreat: Violence and Values in American History and Society,* commented on the way that Civil War loyalties remained powerful factors in the social and political development of the nineteenth-century West. The conflicting sentiments of North and South found a new arena in the American West, where the struggle to encode values often took on violent hues. Both White and Brown suggested that to understand western violence, it is imperative to acknowledge that cultural diffusion did not halt at state borders.

It became increasingly clear that we needed to look beyond the gunfighter dressed in black and all his masculine counterparts for a fuller understanding of the nature of western violence. Unless we did, western violence would continue to be defined only by the silhouetted figures of warring males. If we adjust the angle of the historical lens away from this masculine center, other westerners—women and children—come into focus. We need to examine these western players more closely to appreciate how their lives added to the patterns within power relationships, a motif in which women have held a distinct disadvantage, especially in public forums.

Because, as Richard Maxwell Brown suggested, violence involved all classes of people, the search for women's experiences with violence can prove frustrating. Historical brutality—both mental and physical—wore well the mantle of secrecy, divorce actions notwithstanding. Among western Anglos, those with knowledge of community violence—law officers, attorneys, judges, physicians, clergymen, newspaper reporters—extended the cloak of discretion to a select group of citizens. Middle- and upper-class people enjoyed the financial means and social favor to hide offensive behaviors more skillfully than those who resided in the ethnic neighborhoods and vice districts, the streets and taverns of the West. Nonetheless, in the private space of all cultures and across economic lines, women witnessed, endured, and participated in violence, that "special" characteristic of the West.

To bind these subjects of western women and violence, this study turns to the state penitentiaries of the West. The text takes in nineteen states, ranging from the Mississippi River to the intermountain West. The Pacific Coast states of California, Oregon, and Washington have their own distinctive history and are excluded. Some may argue persuasively against such a dissecting point. Yet along the Pacific, the ocean coastlines and well-watered landscapes shaped a historical narrative that differed, in my view, from the inland West.

This is not to suggest that the region under consideration represented a physical and historical monolith. Rather, it divided along many lines—region into region, culture into culture, and then as many times again. Louisiana, one of the "Gateways to the West," differed in terrain, economics, and population from Montana. Early Montana bore little resemblance to Arizona. Hispanics of Arizona were not Mormons of Utah, European immigrants of South Dakota not former slaves of Texas. Yet a certain elasticity steadied the borders between these states from the river to the mountains. Competing for regional prominence, quarreling over land and water, standing together in opposition to economic domination from either coast, they rubbed cultural shoulders as they exchanged people and western ideas of identity. This dynamic kept these states connected like distant cousins, somewhat unacquainted with each other but related through inclusion in what came to be called "the western experience." Although there can be many definitions of "the West," this patchwork quilt of states is the one used here.

In the main, this study focuses on the years 1865 to 1915. With the conclusion of the Civil War, European and Asian immigrants and eastern-ers—both black and white—turned to the promise seen in western land. Their descent upon the West and the people who lived therein—Native Americans and Hispanics—unleashed a cyclone of societal forces. Truly the West absorbed the cultural baggage of the nation.

During this time period, the penitentiary mirrored much of the social, economic, and political struggle that accompanied western change. These years of unprecedented upheaval marked the era during which western courts frequently sentenced women, convicted of either misdemeanors or felonies, to serve their time in male prisons.

In part, the absence of separate female penal institutions in new juris-dictions accounted for such arrangements. By 1915, as the West settled into its twentieth-century ambiance, as civic-minded women wielded public influence, and as social reform escalated, most states ended the housing of female inmates inside male facilities under male administrators. Although many types of penal institutions existed in the West, this work examines only those state/territorial prisons built for and managed by men; federal facilities or women's reformatories remain outside the scope of the text.

Oddly, within a region known for its proud celebration of male pursuits, few spotlights and little fanfare have been directed at the masculine peni-tentiary. Yet, the penitentiary, a highly visible, well-defined, but seques-tered institution, embodied the maleness of the nineteenth-century Amer-ican West. Male convicts and guards came and went through its gates. Its routines revolved around the rigors of men's work. Breaking stone, mining coal, running machinery were the daily labors. Male voices—their cries and curses, occasionally their laughter and songs—echoed off cellblock walls. A masculine prison vocabulary labeled everything from "fresh fish" for a newcomer to "come-alongs" for handcuffs to "hard-boiled" for each oth-er. An occasional baseball team or prison band brought the touches of rec-reation. The aromas of cigars and pipes filled the air. The penitentiary ex-uded as much masculine presence as any cowboy campfire or military bivouac.

This study explicitly does not suggest that male prisoners escaped the harshness of penitentiary life or that all male administrators reveled in dishonesty and cruelty. Quite the opposite was true, and many accounts in this text document that assertion and capture the hardship of prison life for men. As in all human society, the interaction between jailer and jailed produced a complex set of behaviors, in which the contours of power assumed many shapes. In the penitentiary these shapes emerged within a distinctly masculine community.

Against this backdrop, the experiences of women prisoners stand in contrast and provide a gendered portrait of the violence of penitentiary life. This work argues that women, faced with distinct social, economic, and political disadvantages within the West generally, found inside male penitentiaries their womanhood exposed them to gender-specific physical and mental violence. Gender represented an additional penal burden for women inmates, who learned that violence in several forms colored every aspect of penitentiary life. When race and class adhered to gender, violence intensified for women inmates.

Ultimately, race, class, and gender, as elements within the penitentiaries, demonstrated that possible and actual violence surrounded and threatened all women in the West. While not every woman experienced personal violence, all lived in a western society where one might fall prey to its sudden attack, if the fates brought her inside a male penitentiary. That reality linked the few incarcerated females to the larger number of free women and underscored the importance of the penitentiary as a symbol of western violence far deeper than romantic images of the lone gunfighter, the reckless cowboy, the itinerant bandit.

Penitentiaries in the West have their own political heritage, one that provided the underpinnings for women's experiences. Yet western prisons, obviously, did not spring forth from a vacuum. Territorial and state penitentiaries in the American West both reflected national penal movements and charted their own regional course.

Their first impulses came from the rather loose agreement among Americans that the country needed prisons. Rising crime rates coupled with changing ideas about societal progress pushed the burgeoning new republic to consider its penal choices.[6] As a young America of the seventeenth and eighteenth centuries matured, it selected imprisonment—rather than public display—as the cornerstone of the national system of punishment for criminal behavior. While torture and execution before a watchful boulevard audience existed, they did not become a permanent component of punishment policy within the criminal justice system.

Early jails functioned as temporary detention centers for prisoners awaiting trial or execution. Once the judiciary extended confinement periods for felons, the small local jail could not handle the demands of long-term care for resident criminals. The decision to incarcerate, rather than summarily execute, thieves and murderers changed the locus of punishment from town and county jails to state penitentiaries. In addition, as American crime steadily swung upward, eastern states felt the need for larger and more substantial prisons to accommodate the increasing number of convicts.

Such decisions automatically increased the civic debate, rumbling through the country since its independence, about the nature of the American prison. As with most such discussions, disagreement prevailed among Americans as to the trend and tone expected inside penitentiaries. Those who cared about management policies, as well as the results produced by inmate incarceration, tended to divide into two camps. One group, drawing on values of the Philadelphia Quakers, endorsed prisoner isolation with a routine of labor, silence, and prayer in an environment of humane care, as an incentive to personal reformation. A second contingent supported a plan modeled on the New York prison at Auburn. There, in the early 1800s, administrators ignored religious considerations and looked to inflexible regimentation, corporal punishment, and hard work to convince prisoners of the folly of crime.

Each of these plans produced questionable results and neither halted the movement toward the penitentiary.[7] After 1830, the United States committed itself to the construction of state penitentiaries. As these penitentiaries, literally massive granite and stone monuments to the state's judicial presence and power, emerged in America's eastern communities, a correspondingly clear definition of the practices within and purpose of the institution did not develop. Attempts to segregate prisoners by crimes committed invariably collapsed because of overcrowding, a problem second only to the custom of housing juvenile offenders with adult criminals. As a result, prisons acquired reputations as arenas for barely controlled debauchery and corruption at every level. By 1844 the disorder within the penitentiaries was so evident that those determined to bring about better management and improved conditions formed activist groups such as the New York Prison Association. While prison reformers in every era proved to be articulate champions for improved conditions and inmate rehabilitation, they failed to galvanize the public to demand systematic, long-range, lasting change inside the penitentiary. Their successes, however, included keeping penology a part of American reform interest, maintaining a vigorous dialogue with proponents of harsher punishment practices, and forcing administrators to consider prison management alternatives.

In general though, most Americans seemed to overlook the fact that prisons flowered within the context of the social, economic, and political forces that so rapidly changed the American landscape of the nineteenth century. Huge demographic shifts, escalated by the end of slavery and the flood of immigration, coupled with the rise of America's industrial power, placed new demands on a prison system run more by expedience than policy. Left largely to administer itself, the American prison, despite professional efforts by some of its employees and the interest of reformers, followed a predictable route and emerged as a fearsome institution.

By 1870 pressures caused by the indiscriminate overcrowding of inmates characterized penology in all the major eastern cities. Inmates remained an average of twenty months in prisons that continued to mix young offenders with seasoned criminals. Complaints about this practice led to the reformatory movement, designed to stimulate rehabilitation by tempering the conditions faced by the youthful lawbreaker. Thirty years later, in another refashioning, the industrial prison, a walled ancillary to the American factory, arose. In an era of booming American business, this plan wedded inmate labor to private industry in a renewed effort to produce profit from corrections. Each of these initiatives was designed to control crime, divide criminals into treatment categories, enhance the meaning of prison time for the inmate, encourage productivity, and streamline expenses for the government. Due to poor planning, limited budgets, overlapping local authorities, and conflicting ideologies, each faltered and actually made American penology more complicated and unsatisfactory.

By the early twentieth century, crime continued to increase, prisons remained centers of corruption and mismanagement, and the American public showed less and less interest in the country's penal policy. Despite these trends, until 1904 the nation instituted no formal system for tracking crime or for gathering statistics about criminals and American prisons. A rising corps of professional law officers warned of a worsening crime rate and called for better maintenance of national records. Americans fretted about law and order, but failed to relate the passage of more criminal statutes and increased arrests to the rising crime figures. Individual states added to the murky situation by keeping their records in a haphazard or secretive manner, further obscuring the question of how penitentiaries dealt with their inmates.

In the latter decades of the nineteenth century and the first of the twentieth, a new crop of reformers, more and more of whom were women, lobbied for a series of ameliorative measures for prisons. These, part of the general reform impulse that swept the country during the Progressive Era, were seen as relief for the tensions inside the prisons and help for inmates returning to society. Better yet, in the eye of the reformer, were regulatory programs that intervened before a person entered the prison system. A combination of plans tried to address concerns about prison dynamics and give inmates a reason to cooperate with the forces of penal administration.

Probation, first used in Massachusetts in 1878, entitled a convicted offender to remain out of prison. The court placed the lawbreaker under the direct supervision of an officer of the court. The intent was to reduce prison populations and keep first-time offenders away from contact with mature criminals.

The pardon and parole system, adopted at an uneven pace across the country, gave inmates the chance to earn early discharge. A pardon, issued by the state governor, expunged the crime and restored the convict to the rights of citizenship, which for men included suffrage, although not all locales honored that provision for non-Anglos. Parole allowed an inmate to apply to a state board for release under supervision. Prisoners had to serve a specified portion of the sentence, compile good conduct records, and produce proof of outside employment to be eligible to request parole. If a parole was granted, prison boards required that a citizen in good standing accept responsibility for the parolee. Parents, spouses, attorneys, or future employers often filled this role for the recently released convict. Authorities monitored the former inmate's behavior, employment, and movements, requiring the submission of monthly reports after release. The duties of the custodial party diminished according to the conditions of the parole.

Less attractive to inmates was the use of the indeterminate sentence, by which penitentiary officials decided when a prisoner demonstrated the moral, mental, and physical transformation that warranted release. Intended to encourage inmates to concentrate on their personal reformation, the indeterminate sentence divided the responsibility for evaluating prisoner progress among several different prison administrators. In truth, inmates had little control over earning their release as the sentencing judge, board of pardons, and prison officials might all participate in decisions, often based on the most arbitrary and impressionistic evidence.

Perhaps most controversial in these procedures was "good time," a reward system by which inmates accrued days to be subtracted from the time left to serve. Since the program fell to the discretion and whim of prison guards, "good time" days could be painstakingly earned and then lost in the flicker of a moment. Inmates who might have amassed several weeks or months of credit could lose many days for the slightest infraction, real or imagined. On the other hand, favored prisoners or those with political connections might retain "good time" days even though their conduct did not conform with penitentiary regulations.

"Good time" and each of the larger reform plans came under criticism because of a lack of uniform application. While one judge might sentence a first offender to two years in the penitentiary, another gave ten years for the same crime. While one convict might win a parole in three months, another sentenced for the same offense served a full term. One prisoner on parole might be required to report back to the board for four months, while another sent monthly statements for several years. In all corners of the nation, these various plans took shape over many years and only after numerous legislative adjustments. As a result, the regulations that guided them varied greatly from state to state and shifted numerous times before they became fixtures in American penology.

Of course, beneath these many disparities lay the basic American confusion about the purpose of the penal code and the penitentiary. No one really seemed to agree if the prison existed to protect society, punish wrongdoers, and stop crime, or to rehabilitate inmates. Americans could not decide whether they expected the state to act out the private vengeance desired by the wronged party or impose a just punishment that drew its legitimacy from a just society. In an ongoing circular debate, politicians, social reformers, prison administrators, and prisoners themselves engaged these theoretical questions that surrounded crime and its consequences.

Although the West often seemed removed from such intellectual issues within American civil philosophy, these same basic concerns and forces fueled the development of western prisons. But other elements added to the western penal text. Along with the endemic problems of penology came a regional disorder among western politicians faced with launching comprehensive governmental offices simultaneously. An intense federal versus territorial/state rivalry, unclear jurisdictional distinctions, conflicting political agendas inside new communities, poorly selected prison sites, controversial inmate labor systems, diverse prisoner populations, and somewhat cavalier hiring of guards and personnel combined to give western penitentiaries—set by mountain and valley, desert and plain—their own peculiar history.

The architectural design of the facilities themselves stood as a variegated testament to the evolution of the western prison. Although territorial legislatures approved elaborate blueprints, several prisons—those of Nevada, Arizona, and Kansas among them—were little more than temporary stockades when opened. A few cells, usually about six by eight feet in size, and a main building with the kitchen, dining hall, guards' room, one or two common rooms, a small yard, a laundry, work shops, all partially enclosed by a wooden fence—such were the common descriptors of the early days of a western penitentiary. It required years of inmate labor before the imposing Gothic buildings and thick stone walls, so familiar in the East, rose in the West. Anamosa in Iowa, Laramie in Wyoming, Deer Lodge in Montana—each gradually took on a grandiose shape, built by the sweat of convict laborers who broke and dressed the stone. Inside the walls, the available yard space yielded to more and more buildings, as one warden added a chapel and a bath house, another new cells and a twine factory. Sometimes the arrangements spilled outside the walls, and the superintendent's house, the gardens, or a small building for women inmates stood just beyond the main gate.

If but a few prisoners rattled around in a new penitentiary, compliant territorial legislatures, such as Minnesota's in the late 1850s, revised the statutes, broadening the definition of who qualified for incarceration at the penitentiary.[8] Western penitentiaries also made room and board arrangements with the federal government and received a stipend for housing its prisoners. By these means, western prison cells filled promptly, for those who maintained facilities seldom wanted to watch over empty buildings, an embarrassing silent query as to the necessity of their own jobs.

Generally, western prisons tended to be overcrowded as they opened, the facility obsolete from the outset. Instability in the region's economy, transient populations, clashes between various ethnic and national groups helped a bustling judicial system to enlarge arrest and conviction rates. Inmate numbers quickly exceeded living space, prompting western prisons to seek more housing at a minimal financial investment. Under one popular scheme, authorities boarded inmates in neighboring penal institutions, rather than undertake expensive building campaigns at home. Using this arrangement, the Oklahoma Territory sent inmates to Kansas, Wyoming to Colorado.

Other plans represented the dual desire to incarcerate prisoners and return a profit to the state. Drawing on an established system of convict management, especially refined in Louisiana, the West introduced two or three variations. In an arrangement known as the contract system, private business owners hired convict labor and the state retained its responsibility to feed, clothe, and guard the inmates. Inmates worked in manufacturing businesses, inside the penitentiary and often alongside civilian employees of the contractor. Under another plan, called the lease system, a private citizen applied for permission to work the convicts away from the prison in outside camps. These arrangements that removed inmates from the direct supervision of public authority opened the door for numerous abuses. Most western states flirted at least briefly with some form of contractual agreements that left inmates under the care of private enterprise, a pattern that added to the unique history of western prisons.

Western prison administrators particularly cut their own path in matters of fiscal management, vacillating between this matter of allowing private contractors complete control of inmates and exercising legislative oversight. The former led to unchecked brutality, the latter to political corruption; often the two operated in tandem. Overall, a preoccupation with the economic merit of self-sustaining or profit-making prisons distracted western states from issues concerning government responsibility, purposes of the penitentiary, appropriate uses of convict labor, and the role of the West in the development of penology in the United States. In response to these unresolved dilemmas, western states relinquished their prisons to entrepreneurs or political appointees, with neither the training or the interest in professional standards for corrections. While an emerging corps of professional prison administrators championed humanitarian methods to bring about criminal reform, the West lagged behind, more inclined to devote attention to building facilities than harnessing their management. This produced western penitentiaries mired in every kind of legal and human violation, easy targets for widespread criticism, often as examples of the very worst in the American penal system.

Westerners, those who broke the law and those who administered it, believed that, regardless of outside opinion, conditions in the West differed significantly from those in the East. In 1870, N. A. M. Dudley, the superintendent of the state penitentiary at Huntsville, Texas, wrote glowingly of the "golden future just being opened to [Texas]," and of the "mighty and increasing flow of emigration now tiding in upon this vast territory, from almost every part of the old world."[9] Dudley believed that the swelling population, drawn from "nearly every" state in the Union, "the British Provinces," and "almost every part of Europe," guaranteed a surge in the number of convicts.[10] In his view, the western destiny of Texas demanded looking ahead to the many convicts who would fill state penal institutions.

Only the next year, a new superintendent, A. J. Bennett, argued that Texas smarted under an administrative disadvantage because it employed fewer guards per hundred convicts than did Massachusetts. The Bay State might have been the model of reformatory discipline, but its prisoners could not match those of the Lone Star State for a "desperate reputation abroad," Bennett boasted.[11] In 1874, J. K. P. Campbell, penitentiary inspector, continued the theme of a difference for western prisons, asserting that the "sterling advantages" of Texas naturally drew "respectable immigrants," as well as "the vagabond criminal class." Campbell used his "booming state" theory as the rationale for asking for two new prisons, one in western Texas and the other in the northeastern part of the state.[12] Western expansion continued to mean preparing for something bigger and better, in this case, convict numbers. Twenty years later, a former Texas convict attributed the crime of his inmate peers to their stress as unseasoned migrants, who in ignorance took up with rough western companions.[13] Obviously, not everyone agreed on the source of the western prisoners—whether reckless transients or homegrown rowdies—but they all knew the West had more criminals of a rougher character than the East.

This assumption of the regional distinctiveness of western criminals and their prisons did not confine itself to Texas. In the 1890s, in the prison at Rawlins, Wyoming, guards beat an easterner senseless and then hung him by his heels in the dark hole because the prisoner ridiculed the manhood of those from the West.[14] Other prisoners, native to the West, thought the brutalized and near-dead inmate a fool who had gotten what he deserved. In the same penitentiary, several ranchers, imprisoned for a vigilante lynching, repeated their crime by hanging an unpopular prisoner.[15] Prison officials responded to the event as many communities did on such occasions; they retreated behind closed doors during the hanging and asked few questions afterwards.[16] Whether it was justified or not, those connected to crime in the West believed western criminals to be different and the demands of the penitentiaries distinct from those of other regions.

Despite this sense of uniqueness, the administration of these far-flung western penal institutions followed the same troubled path in each of the states. After the United States assumed governance for western lands following the Mexican War, federal authorities viewed administering a prison system as only one of the mammoth tasks at hand. In this climate, political distractions impeded systematic policy development and set the early legislation off on an inconsistent course.

In the 1850s and 1860s, the U.S. Congress, especially through the Territorial Penitentiaries Act, unveiled its prison initiative for the western territories. The plan—to set in place a chain of western penal institutions, where U.S. marshals as wardens would oversee both territorial and federal offenders—fell far short of its goal. The huge fiscal burden and awkward logistics of long distance management, coupled with a relentless hostility between federal and territorial officials, led the United States to withdraw its financial and administrative support from territorial prisons throughout the 1870s. The federal government then concentrated on supervising a limited number of prisons, exclusively for federal offenders.[17]

The Deer Lodge, Montana, penitentiary serves as an example of the shifting administrative history of most western prisons. After the territory secured a modest appropriation for construction, Deer Lodge opened as a federal penitentiary in 1871. Within two years, by 1873, the federal government expressed the intention to retreat from its penal arrangements with Montana, as well as with Idaho, Colorado, and Wyoming. Oversight responsibility for the still incomplete facility at Deer Lodge and its twenty-one inmates transferred to the Montana Territory.

Not until 1884 did the territorial government, buttressed by an infusion of more federal dollars, move with purpose to finish the structure. This initiative proved woefully inadequate. Two years later administrators added more brick cells, but the prison, crippled from years of poor planning, inferior construction, and prisoner overcrowding, hardly noticed the improvements. In 1889, when Montana entered the Union, Deer Lodge, saddled with administrative and financial problems since its inception, became the state penitentiary and served as such until 1979.[18]

The reluctance of federal and state governments to invest in the establishment of solid prison systems from the outset helped pave the way for a clouded history for each institution. Confusion over uncertain and shifting policies rarely abated, encouraging disorder inside the walls and at the work farms across the West. Disputes, as well as geographic distance, between those at the prison and those holding the state purse strings kept the penitentiaries operating on unstable budgets.

In his 1871 report, Texas superintendent A. J. Bennett complained bitterly that the legislature of the previous year had failed to appropriate any money for the penitentiary. With a burst of passion unusual among administrators, Bennett asked about the prisoners, "Were they to go naked and barefooted, cold and exposed during the present inclement winter?"[19] Bennett's frustration with the ungenerous, apathetic legislature pinpointed one of the constant problems in prison management—institutional indifference, fostered by inconsistent policies, competing political goals, and slim state funding. That indifference marked the history of western prisons and created the environment into which the courts, without state penal institutions for women, sent female offenders.

A diverse literature focuses on the history of penitentiaries and the right of the state to punish. Little of it directly examines the American West, less investigates the case for women. Still, the work of several scholars provided the foundations for my thinking in this study.

In 1936 Blake McKelvey published *American Prisons: A Study in American Social History prior to 1915,* a classic in the historiography of prisons. McKelvey in an orderly and thoughtful fashion outlined the American response to the national problem of increasing convict numbers and escalating expenditures for maintenance. In his view, American prisons operated with three goals: to halt the corruption of inmates, to promote obedience and industry, and to reform the criminal mind. McKelvey suggested that across time geographic, industrial, and cultural factors shaped American penal trends. He also noted the difficulties of studying prison history in a comprehensive fashion, warning that factional rivalries and private ambition, the driving forces in penal management, inhibited research.

David Rothman in *The Discovery of Asylum* and *Conscience and Convenience* considered the history of the American penitentiary in an epic manner. The first book, published in 1971, melded the prison with other custodial institutions, as Rothman sought to explain how these agencies took shape within American society. They were, he concluded, a response to a disturbing sense of social disorder among Americans. His second volume, which appeared in 1980, addressed the success of reformers in introducing certain programs, such as the pardon and parole system, to manage criminals, both inside and outside the prison walls. Although critics argued that Rothman bypassed important social and economic components in his analysis, with these two publications he significantly elevated the importance of the history of American penology.

The most dramatic scholarship concerning the history of prisons and punishment came to the academic community by way of the French scholar Michel Foucault. Foucault's *Discipline and Punish: The Birth of the Prison* appeared in 1975 and within two years had been translated into English. More than twenty years after its first publication, Foucault's work remains pivotal for the student of the penitentiary, even though it reverberates more with the tones of the political philosopher than those of the historical researcher.

Foucault, moved by Marxist convictions, placed the transformation of punishment and the prison at the center of his wide-ranging treatise that touched on the exercise of power at both the macro and micro levels. One cannot ignore Foucault's convincing descriptions of the transformation of punishment from public spectacle to private torment, the shift from torture of the criminal body to control of the inmate mind. Nor can it be overlooked that Foucault wrote passionately on the structure and reasoning by which society organized around the concepts of personal discipline and formal punishment, a marriage of consent and force. In this discussion, Foucault delineated his perceptions of power relations, the falsity of humanitarianism, and the questionable nature of individualism, all subjects guaranteed to make Americans uneasy. Foucault dismissed the notion that social justice will correct social ills by describing reform as simply a rearrangement of power, designed to assure its better, not fairer, balance among the agents of society.

Although Foucault focused on European institutions and crafted his insights along philosophical lines, his themes about power dynamics, mental coercion, physical torture, corrective routines, architectural space, and the rituals of punishment mesh with the social and political environment of the nineteenth-century western prison. Further, Foucault's dichotomous simple folk, victims and players, cast into the turbulence of compliance and resistance suggest theoretical linkages to the experiences of women prisoners. Foucault has not been without critics, and his work is painfully dense and often contradictory. Nonetheless, his provocative thinking generated a substantial body of literature, a testimony to the complex thought he stimulated.[20] Above all, his boldly constructed ideas cannot be discounted, even among those who take an opposing view.

One such opposing view came from Michael Ignatieff in *A Just Measure of Pain: The Penitentiary in the Industrial Revolution, 1750–1850,* published in 1978. Ignatieff also tried to delineate the social processes by which society transformed its mechanisms of punishment. Concerned with the emergence of the modern philosophy of punishment, he argued that the penitentiary represented one institutional cog in the interlocking machinations that gave rise to a new industrial order. Like Foucault, Ignatieff examined state efforts to legitimatize its right to punish miscreants within the modern penitentiary. Unlike Foucault, Ignatieff, committed to the societal benefits that flow from informed progressivism, rejected the view of institutional hopelessness.

Turning to the literature of gender, one must consider the critically important works of four women scholars, Estelle B. Freedman, Nicole Hahn Rafter, Clarice Feinman, and Camille Naish. Estelle B. Freedman, author of *Their Sisters' Keepers: Women's Prison Reform in America, 1830–1930,* examined the role of female reformers in the context of women's changing status and sphere. Her assessment, grounded in feminist ideology, explained why separate women's prisons finally became a reality in the United States. Accordingly, her excellent book focused more directly on the women outside of prison rather than those incarcerated.

Nicole Hahn Rafter's *Partial Justice: Women in State Prisons, 1800–1935,* published in 1985, represents the historical work most germane to this study. It was Rafter who identified the race, class, and gender imperatives that shaped the prison life of American women. Rafter's work focused on the federal system and specifically on New York, Ohio, and Tennessee. She traced the way in which gender inequities and the powerful racism of the past led to the modern conditions of discrimination for women prisoners.

Clarice Feinman, in *Women in the Criminal Justice System,* published in 1986, mapped out the complex patterns resulting from a dual nature imposed on women by societal fiat. She argued that society's construction of a madonna/whore identity for women placed special hardships on those apprehended by the law. Feinman saw in this assigned bipolar nature of women, along with the myth of male chivalry, the explanation for the extreme punishments heaped on female offenders guilty of slight crimes.

In 1991 Camille Naish's *Death Comes to the Maiden: Sex and Execution* offered a wide assessment of women and the death penalty. Her work complemented Feinman's conclusion that male chivalry existed more in fancy than reality. Naish drew a parallel between the nineteenth-century American refusal to execute women with the equally trenchant denial of civic rights for female citizens. In Naish's view, masculine attitudes of "protecting" women worked especially well for the male-driven justice system, which could dispense liberty or punishment without concern for female social status or political power. Naish's ideas are particularly helpful in reconciling the seemingly contradictory decisions of the courts to punish some women mightily with prison terms but to accommodate others in matters of divorce and child custody. In her perception, the two actions emerge out of a single male attitude designed to maintain masculine power. Granted, her concept of male "beneficence" toward criminal females does not always fit comfortably into American prison history, where women of color seldom experienced any protection or leniency, even the paternalistic kind. Nonetheless, Naish's observations apply to western female prisoners, especially her insight that questions of guilt or innocence remained far less important than the desire to remove offending women from public view.

Each of these works brought organizing principles to the literature of prison history. I found their arguments persuasive and tried to examine prison documents using their ideas about the intent of state punishment and the realities of race, class, and gender dynamics as guides to my findings. Yet none of these authors specifically dealt with women—African American, Anglo, Hispanic, Native American, or Asian—of the American West, a region often defined by its myriad forms of violence.[21] Nor did these scholars focus on the social and political ramifications of placing women into male facilities. This study, then, seeks to bring together a number of components—the West, male penitentiaries, female inmates, and violence—and determine through a narrative account whether the bonded four illuminate some aspect of our western heritage that we have left shrouded.

Prison accounts offend our most basic democratic sensibilities, for neither justice or fairness emerge from the chronicle. Because of this, prison history, especially for women, often seems driven only by themes of oppressors and victims. Certainly, severe constraints existed. Not every prisoner, guilty or innocent, rose phoenixlike to defeat "the system."

To believe they could do so romanticizes the prison atmosphere. Penitentiaries symbolized and actualized the fault lines of power, a reality not open for debate in the nineteenth century. Inherent in prison administration was the intent to control inmates and to crush the rebel-minded. Inmate initiative and individuality had little place, and prison overseers stood prepared to eradicate it quickly and forcefully. In the face of an excessively uneven power structure, some inmates yielded, many died. Yet within the institutional procedures participants on both sides of the bars exercised choice. Granted, it was choice with limitation, but it layered the interactions beyond their obvious brutality.

Women reacted in varying manners to penitentiary conditions. Not all chose open rebellion. Not all cultivated a submissive manner. Some excelled at the dramatic statement, some at the cooperative posture. Some held dear the thought of waiting family and children who needed them. Some resisted for a time and then yielded, serving out their sentences quietly. Others chose escape through death. Many endured with a day-to-day stoicism until released.

Overall, women inmates designed survival strategies for themselves, using the tools of compliance and resistance. They acted on their own behalf and in concert with other women prisoners and males as well. Overt and covert, their individual actions coalesced into a demonstration of womanly will. Their collective response underscored the universal refusal of the human spirit to accept a justice without integrity.

Within the West, male penitentiaries from Montana to Texas, Louisiana to Minnesota, Nebraska to Nevada, Arizona to South Dakota faltered in the treatment of female inmates and then kept shoddy records about the women. Within the voluminous documents generated about each prison's operations, scant mention was made of women prisoners. Often the annual report of the warden completely ignored women inmates, only their names in the appended list of prisoners acknowledged their presence. Those who authored the official papers sidestepped a discussion about women as much as possible, choosing to focus on operational procedures and progress of male inmates. Some administrators used their energies to bury the latest scandal about misuse of prison funds, disappearance of supplies, or abuse of male inmates. Others tried to sort out the tangle left by predecessors, smooth over the most recent exposé. In either situation, women prisoners represented just one more potential for scandal, an opportunity for journalists and reformers to press home their opposition to prison management, while embarrassing incumbent politicians.

As a consequence, prison documents of the West present a dazzling array of uneven and inconsistent record keeping, where women were hidden under the weight of many other topics. Files on women inmates generally appeared to be kept by random spirits. An occasional folder yielded a complete trial transcript or handwritten letters from the woman convict. Most had only a few poorly labeled forms, pulled from a variety of public agencies. Even the information recorded when a prisoner entered the penitentiary was often only partially completed for women. Reconstructing the women's lives required tracking female prisoners through a variety of documents. From the annual and biennial summaries, prison registers, inmate files, discipline ledgers, pardon and parole applications, and investigative reports, western penitentiaries grudgingly and sparingly surrendered the history of women prisoners.

Within a large assortment of prison papers and documents, these women, seemingly the least significant of western citizens, managed to leave a path to their lives. In doing so, they gave voice to the painful meaning of their inmate days and the connections between violence and western womanhood. Their existence before incarceration, their crimes, the masculine world they entered, their frail health, their prison work, their responses, and above all, the daily violence they confronted—these formed some of their history, left by women prisoners for its placement in our western annals. These women deserve that place within the heritage of the West. After all, they walked through a hell on earth for it.

Notes

1. W. Eugene Hollon, *Frontier Violence: Another Look* (New York: Oxford University Press, 1974), p. vii.
2. These ideas are found in a number of studies that consider western violence. Among them are: Dane Coolidge, *Fighting Men of the West* (New York: Dutton, 1932); Wayne Gard, *Frontier Justice* (Norman: University of Oklahoma Press, 1949); Duncan Emrich, *It's an Old Wild West Custom* (New York: Vanguard Press, 1949); Eugene Cunningham, *Triggernometry: A Gallery of Gunfighters* (Caldwell, Idaho: Caxton Printers, 1956); Joe B. Frantz, "The Frontier Tradition: An Invitation to Violence," in Hugh Davis Graham and Ted Robert Gurr, eds., *Violence in America: Historical and Comparative Perspectives*, vol. 1: *A Report to the National Commission on the Causes and Prevention of Violence* (Washington: G.P.O., 1969), pp. 127–54; Philip D. Jordan, *Frontier Law and Order* (Lincoln: University of Nebraska Press, 1970); Hollon, *Frontier Violence;* and Roger D. McGrath, *Gunfighters, Highwaymen and Vigilantes: Violence on the Frontier* (Berkeley: University of California Press, 1984).
3. Richard Maxwell Brown, "Historical Patterns of Violence in America," in Graham and Gurr, *Violence in America*, p. 76.
4. McGrath, *Gunfighters, Highwaymen and Vigilantes*, pp. 161 and 251.
5. Richard White, *"It's Your Misfortune and None of My Own": A New History of the American West* (Norman: University of Oklahoma Press, 1991), p. 589.
6. Larry E. Sullivan, *The Prison Reform Movement: Forlorn Hope* (Boston: Twayne Publishers, 1990), pp. 2–3.
7. Ibid., pp. 4–11.
8. Edward D. Neill, *History of Washington County and the St. Croix Valley* (Minneapolis: North Star Publishing, 1881); and J. Fletcher Williams, *Outlines of the History of Minnesota* (Minneapolis: North Star Publishing, 1881), p. 533.
9. N. A. M. Dudley, "Report of the Superintendent," *Report on the Condition of the State Penitentiary*, Huntsville, 10 Feb. 1870, p. 8, TSA.
10. Ibid., p. 9.
11. A. J. Bennett, *Report of the Superintendent of the State Penitentiary*, 1871, p. 8, TSA.
12. J. K. P. Campbell, "Report of the Inspector," *Reports on the Condition of the State Penitentiary*, 1873–74, p. 4, TSA.
13. A. L. George, *The Texas Convict: Thrilling and Terrible Experience of a Texas Boy* (Austin, Tex.: Ben C. Jones, 1893), pp. 164–67.
14. *The Sweet Smell of Sagebrush: A Prisoner's Diary, 1903–1912; Written Anonymously in Wyoming's Frontier Prison, Rawlins, Wyoming* (Rawlins: Friends of the Old Penitentiary and the Old Penitentiary Joint Powers Board, 1990), p. 79.
15. Ibid., pp. 146–48.
16. Ibid. For community attitudes about vigilantes, see Richard Maxwell Brown, "Violence," in *The Oxford History of the American West*, ed. Clyde A. Milner II, Carol O'Connor, and Martha A. Sandweiss (New York: Oxford University Press, 1994), pp. 395–98.
17. Paul Eduard Knepper, "Imprisonment and Society in Arizona Territory" (Ph.D. dissertation, Arizona State University, 1990), pp. 48–67.
18. See Philip Kent, *History: Montana State Prison*, ed. James R. McDonald (Deer Lodge, Mont.: Powell County Museum and Arts Foundation, 1979), pp. 3–19; and Keith Edgerton, "Power, Punishment, and Poverty: The United States Penitentiary at Deer Lodge City, Montana Territory, 1871–1889," *Western Historical Quarterly* 28 (Summer 1997), 161–84, for an extensive discussion of the early days of Deer Lodge.

19. A. J. Bennett, *Report of the Superintendent of the State Penitentiary,* 1871, p. 11, TSA.

20. Some examples include: Jana Sawicki, *Disciplining Foucault: Feminism, Power and the Body* (New York: Routledge, 1991); David Macey, *The Lives of Michel Foucault: A Biography* (New York: Pantheon, 1993); James Miller, *The Passion of Michel Foucault* (New York: Simon and Schuster, 1993); R. W. Connell, *Masculinities* (Berkeley: University of California Press, 1995); Scott G. McNall, "'It Was a Plot Got Up to Convict Me': The Case of Henrietta Cook versus the State of Kansas, 1876," *Qualitative Sociology* 9 (Spring 1986), 26–47; Laura Engelstein, "Combined Underdevelopment: Discipline and the Law in Imperial and Soviet Russia," Rudy Koshar, "Foucault and Social History: Comments on 'Combined Underdevelopment,'" Jan Goldstein, "Framing Discipline with the Law: Problems and Promises of the Liberal State," and Laura Engelstein, "Reply," all in "An *AHR* Forum," *American Historical Review* 98 (April 1993): 338–81.

21. In the documents I canvassed in my research for this project, I found reference to perhaps four or five Native American women and no Asian women. The preface suggests possible reasons for the absence of representatives from these groups.

1   The Woman Prisoner

All I want is a chance to prove that I am
worthy.
—Jessie Berry Carmon
Colorado State Penitentiary
1913

The woman prisoner may have appeared divorced from the gender dynamics that affected womanhood, but that perception rested on a shallow foundation. The incarcerated female of the nineteenth century bore a double identity—woman and criminal. Conversely, noncriminal women, although they often denied it, shared commonality with the incarcerated woman; if the slender thread of social acceptability—a sometimes frayed and tangled lifeline—snapped, a woman's existence changed in an instant, as Jessie Carmon learned on a Friday evening in a Wyoming boardinghouse.

Jessie Carmon's early life did not portend events that saw her sentenced to the penitentiary for fourteen years. Born to Wilson and Minnie Belle Berry on 5 May 1885, Jessie, one of four children, grew up in rural Nebraska.

Her father, an immigrant from En-

Jessie Berry Carmon, Colorado State Penitentiary.
Courtesy Ruth Georgen Atchison and Kenneth E.
Georgen.

gland, and her mother, a transplanted Illinoisan, raised their three sons and daughter in the Methodist religion and sent Jessie through all twelve grades in the Seward County public schools.

From all accounts, the prosperous Berrys, including daughter Jessie, enjoyed an outstanding reputation in their small community of Beaver Crossing, in eastern Nebraska. Wilson Berry took an active role in civic matters, serving on a number of local boards. Neighbors and friends described the home as a "good Christian" one, in which the atmosphere could only have resulted in "good citizenship" for the Berry children.[1] Matters changed drastically, however, for Jessie, when at age nineteen, she married George H. Carmon, son of a neighbor family, and moved with him to Sheridan, Wyoming.

Within six years, the marriage with Carmon, a fiddle-playing ranch hand rumored to have an affinity for other women, collapsed.[2] Jessie, with her only child, a little girl, returned to her parents' home in Nebraska. Once Jessie reestablished her Nebraska residency, she filed for a divorce from Carmon, who hurried home to Beaver Crossing to protest the proceedings.

Reconciliation did not appeal to Jessie, who continued her legal action. George Carmon then, apparently, turned to harassment of his wife and her family. At one point, Wilson and Minnie Belle Berry found in their mailbox an extortion note, threatening Jessie with death, unless the parents produced a hundred dollars. It seemed unlikely to the Berrys that anyone other than their errant son-in-law had left the warning; they turned the crudely lettered threat over to Jessie's attorney, Harry D. Landis, who reported it to the postal authorities. Nothing further arose in the public record about Carmon's behavior; the divorce was granted.

Free of the unsavory George Carmon, who disappeared from her life, Jessie turned to the matter of earning a living.[3] She left her daughter in the care of her parents and returned to Sheridan. There a local businessman, Jesse G. Newton, hired her to manage his boardinghouse.[4] The Newton House catered to long-term male boarders, many of whom had moved to Sheridan in response to coal discoveries north of town.[5]

Only eight months after taking her job, in April 1910, Jessie Carmon shot and killed an intruder, James McCoy, husband of a woman domestic employed at the Newton House. Violating a restraining order to stay away from his spouse and Jessie Carmon, McCoy, an unemployed miner known for his vicious wife-beating, slipped into the rooming establishment at about nine o'clock in the evening. As he crept up the stairs of the Newton House, McCoy moved toward the last seconds of his life and the end of Jessie Carmon's being as a "respectable" woman.

With the flash of a gun, the exemplary homelife, the good daughter, the wronged wife, the attentive mother, the struggling single parent disap-

peared. In a moment, her existence within the confines of gender acceptability evaporated, and Jessie, educated daughter of nonsmoking, non-
drinking Methodist sensibilities, metamorphosed into someone with a
"weakened sense of moral responsibility" and entered the shadow world of
the woman criminal.[6] By the time the *Sheridan Daily Enterprise,* relishing
the drama of a sensational crime committed outside the vice district, published its screaming headline, "Don't Kill My Husband, I'll Leave: James
McCoy Murdered by Jessie Carmen at Rooming House . . . Victim Visited
House to Bid His Little Baby Girl Good-bye,"[7] the Sheridan community had
transformed the deceased into a loving husband and father, while Jessie
Carmon's identity had taken on the shady hues of a "fallen woman."

Even the young widow, Rose McCoy, given shelter by her late husband's
bartender father and machinist brother, joined in the rapidly developing
images of her former employer as a scheming murderess. Before the shooting, Rose, the battered wife, had frequented the local courts looking for
protection and then as often withdrawn her complaints, reuniting with her
husband until the next round of brutality. When McCoy took to hanging
around the boardinghouse and harassing Rose while she worked, Jessie
Carmon, perhaps mindful of her own difficulties with an abusive spouse,
confronted McCoy, making it clear he was not to bother Rose further. It had
been Jessie, the concerned friend, who asked for the court order and provided Rose with shelter at the rooming house. The very night of the shooting Jessie had changed her sleeping location to intercept McCoy, should he
again attempt to sneak into Rose's second-floor room and attack her.

But immediately after McCoy's bloody demise, Rose shifted from the
persecuted wife to the aggrieved widow. With her tormenter dead, his family enraged, and the threat of criminal implication for herself, Rose publicly
asserted that McCoy "never drank liquor" and "never raised his hand
against her." Within hours of the shooting, Rose declared that Jessie
"looked at me with a terrible expression, . . . like she would kill me."[8]

Building on the theme of Jessie's corrupt character, the newspaper account, in a subsection entitled "Of Unsavory Repute," detailed recent court
charges of illegal cohabitation made against Carmon by Jesse Newton's
estranged wife. That matter remained open on appeal, but after the shooting Mrs. Newton[9] told the paper, "this Carmon woman held some devilish
power over him [Newton] and that she had ruined their previous happy
home."[10] Although circumstances around the shooting made it unclear
whether Jessie Carmon and Jesse Newton shared a common bedroom as
well as a common first name, the terms "alleged paramour," "alleged affinity," and "free love" peppered the newspaper reports. Overnight, Jessie Carmon mutated not only into a murderess but also into the stereotypical
femme fatale.

Her position as a divorced woman in Wyoming contributed to that definition. Prior to the crime, Jessie's marital status had not brought this divorcée public attention or censure in Sheridan. Once she was charged with a crime, however, the divorce became part of Jessie's public biography and added more stigma to her person.[11]

Part of the mystique of the woman prisoner stemmed from a nearly unfaltering refusal to recognize that the issues surrounding her inextricably bonded to all matters of femininity and womanhood in American society. Gender constraints imposed by the social, economic, and political order touched the woman criminal before and after her involvement with illegal activity. Born girl child, she discovered the labels of "woman's role" marked her as any other female. She, regardless of her ethnic heritage or region of domicile, felt the notions a larger society posited about female personal demeanor, sexual conduct, marital standards, and maternal commitment. These concepts, dictated in stiflingly positive terms and closely monitored by watchful communities, enveloped women in the West and across the country. Whether women wished to be wrapped in such a mantle had little impact on the process.

Incarcerated women, drawn from varied ethnic and economic groups, struggled with the ramifications of their lawbreaking, at the same time that society shifted them to the category of "criminal" and rearranged their identity under the rubric of womanhood. The result produced a historical character known as the woman prisoner, a being assigned only a partial place within both womanhood and criminality. The forces that coalesced in the creation of this woman prisoner rippled along a national grid before settling into regional narratives. That larger context helps to illuminate western patterns.

Women who break the law have baffled the American people throughout the nation's history. How to explain them, how to deal with them, how to reconcile what their behaviors say about the larger society—these issues have kept America, ever askew about appropriate policy for its justice system, even more off balance.[12] In part, the dilemma rises out of the blurring of hostile definitions of both "woman" and "criminal."

Obviously, the American judicial system and its agency for punishment, the penitentiary, represent only a fraction of the powerful forces that have defined women's roles and behaviors. Religious, educational, governmental, literary, and economic structures, plus a great wash of cultural practice and public opinion, all shared in the construction of notions of American womanhood prevalent by the second half of the nineteenth century. An energized patriarchal society, armed with a rigid code of feminine values, carved out the parameters of women's lives, attitudes, and conducts.[13] These boundaries complemented America's middle-class dynamic and gained strength until they seemed to assume a life of their own.

Motherhood and domesticity resonated through the nation as goals for women, regardless of ethnic and cultural diversities. Even though a broad range of women, especially from ethnic communities, rejected or ignored these goals, a powerful sentiment championed them as ideal values for emulation. These unilateral standards crystallized into a "madonna" image that froze all women, however unrealistically, into a model of intuitive virtue and maternal instinct.[14]

Within private arenas, women acted out the expectations of various institutional systems. Women who did not directly challenge those confines managed their lives through a variety of personal strategies. White women, especially, could expect in return to be recognized as the "fair sex," "sweet angels," "gentle tamers." Although women used many different venues, especially within a cultural sphere, to exercise agency, they knew how to manipulate gender terminology to their advantage and avoid collision with the public power structures.

Other women brokered their positions less willingly. To do so courted clear risks. The censures and punishments for transgressors who resisted or accidentally broke the yoke of middle-class America and adopted a public posture came swiftly.[15] When those transgressions crossed legal lines, then women like Jessie Carmon careened beyond the sanctity of the woman's private space. A woman who violated the law, sometimes impulsively or unintentionally, appeared to choose personal action and challenged social assumptions of female passivity. The exertion of willfulness that clashed with social structures demanded a formal response from the community.[16] Women who broke the law took on an undeniably public face that both rankled and confused many in society.

The police, courts, newspapers, public discussion, and a healthy dose of local gossip all contributed to advertising that a woman had abandoned the anonymity of her private existence. The publicity generated by a woman's crime—regardless of and sometimes because of her race—thrust her into the spotlight. With her bond to the private world and its standards broken, a criminal woman "enjoyed" a brief notoriety, while the public considered the moral and legal implications of her behavior.

For example, Jessie Carmon's crime dominated the front page of the *Sheridan Daily Enterprise* for three days.[17] Hardly a surprising journalistic response in any era, nonetheless, the reporters of 1910 Sheridan instantly invoked the canons of morality when writing about Jessie Carmon.[18] "The Carman woman was deaf to these appeals. She pulled the trigger and sent a bullet plowing through the brain of the man facing her. . . . The Carman woman is understood to have repeatedly set traps to ensnare the wedded wife of her 'consort' and carried a revolver at all times to shoot Mrs. Newton. . . . in the cab she made a cat-like maneuver to wrest the gun from [deputy sheriff] Thomas."[19] According to Thomas, under a headline that asked "Why Did Jessie Do It," "the murderess seemed cool and collected."[20] On 5 May, the *Daily Enterprise* reported that during the court hearing, "Mrs. Carmen's face adopted a veritable cruel expression evincing a despicable and most treacherous look."[21] For the reading public, the newspapers baptized Jessie Carmon the crafty, vicious Jezebel of Sheridan, Wyoming.[22]

Despite this brief attention from the courts, the press, and the public, women offenders like Jessie Carmon quickly passed into the dark world of the social outcast. By 13 May, when she apparently suffered a nervous breakdown and authorities responded with the questionable medical treatment of solitary confinement, the press buried her story inside the newspaper.[23] Jessie Carmon had begun her descent into the anonymity of the incarcerated woman. By the time of the trial, a year after the incident, the "eye witness" account of Rose McCoy, the dismissal of Jesse Newton as a codefendant, the testimony of a nearly deaf boarder, the questions about Jessie's moral conduct, the miseries of the abandoned wife of Newton, and the flamboyant newspaper reports overpowered McCoy's illegal entry into the house, the darkened condition on the stairway, the struggle for the gun, the matter of self-defense, and Jessie's immediate surrender and confession to the police.

The jury, deadlocked for a time at eleven to one for acquittal, settled for a compromise verdict. It convicted Jessie Carmon, whose lawyer argued she was "insane" because the murder occurred on the first day of a very difficult menses, of manslaughter by reason of accidental shooting. Judge Parmelee sentenced her to serve from four to fourteen years.[24] Jessie Carmon became a woman prisoner in the state penitentiary system.

Perhaps more forcefully than any other institution, the legal system, in concert with the press, defined the legitimacy of an individual. Legal structures, although only one of the forces at play, marked the insiders and outsiders of society with razorlike clarity. Once a woman entered its maze of constraints, the legal institution helped society rearrange the contours of her persona, transforming her from a "respectable female" into a "social deviant."

For all women, this involuntary change, fueled by race and class imperatives, twisted conventional womanly standards into grossly negative definitions. More damning than illegal behavior was the fall from place among the "respectable and virtuous."[25] This demarcation, the loss of membership within the community of respectable women, left a woman convicted of crime outside the concerns of society. Both the language about her and the actions against her, as she moved into the world of the judicial system, helped to codify her new role as a nearly nonhuman.

If, because of the circumstances of her life, society already saw a woman— prostitute, petty thief, vagrant—as deviant, the process quickened and intensified. Society especially gave ethnic and minority women a head start with stigmatization. Native American, Hispanic, Asian, and African American women knew from long experience that Anglos used both formal and informal structures to denigrate and control minority communities. Women of color, with their identities falsely tilted toward sensuality, deviance, and criminality by whites, found a clash with Anglo law further pushed them beyond the dominant society.[26] Having "violated" both intangible social standards and tangible legal rules, neither of which they helped to create, women of color faced added jeopardy within the Anglo judicial system.

Women criminals, banned from a place within the circle of female respectability, entered the penitentiary and lost their high profile as quickly as they had acquired it. Cloaked with a new identity that carried its own set of negative designations, the woman prisoner—now a "moron," a "whore," a "villainess"—no longer demanded public scrutiny. Society easily dismissed women sentenced to the penitentiary because they were "real women" no longer.[27]

These gender difficulties inflated when, near the end of the nineteenth century, society, unable to account for its rising tide of crime, depended on a range of representatives from emerging professional fields to explain the criminal mind.[28] Writers of earlier decades had set the stage for theories of criminality that took shape during the early 1900s. In 1876, one theorist, Ely van de Warker, started matters promisingly by suggesting that female crime had more to do with economics and opportunity than moral stature.[29] His proved a nearly unheard voice, and later criminologists failed to explore his suggestions.

By 1888, the British penal authority Frederick William Robinson wrote about his administrative experiences at the Millbank Penitentiary in *Female Life in Prison*. Robinson collaborated with a matron at Millbank to justify the management of female prisoners, in what amounted to an anti-woman, anti-Irish, and anti-Catholic publication. Together, Robinson and his informant insisted that in the "male prisons there is not one man to match the worst inmates of our female prisons." He contended that male prisoners exhibited "some amount of reason and forethought," but that a woman behaved "more . . . like a madwoman than a rational, reflecting human being." Robinson promoted the idea that women criminals actually surpassed male inmates in ill behavior, because he believed in the inordinate vanity and incorrigible mischievousness of most women.[30]

When the new criminologists, greatly influenced by the growing attention to scientific explanations for social forces, turned their attention exclusively to women, the negative language escalated. Bonding humanistic disciplines with pseudoscientific studies of cranial anthropometry and "pathological anomalies," scholars such as the Italian Cesare Lombroso spoke with new authority about the criminal personality. Lombroso wedded sociology, anthropology, history, literature, psychology, and psychiatry to form a meanspirited theory of criminal biology.

An Italian physician, Lombroso concerned himself with issues of genius, insanity, criminality, and degeneracy from a scientific perspective that lacked precision and investigative controls. Lombroso, who described "normal" females as weakened by a lack of moral fiber and drawn to cunning and revenge, won regard for his forty-year examination of criminality, especially in women.[31] In part, he earned this esteem because he formed his theories under an emerging scientific rubric. Lombroso conducted autopsies on deceased criminals and couched his findings in medical terms, using observations gathered by himself and nearly a dozen fledgling scientists.[32] His ideas meshed with those of the French criminologist Alphonse Bertillon, whose theory that measurement of body parts and physical characteristics scientifically identified the criminal personality gained worldwide currency.

In his earliest writings about the exceptional mind, Lombroso revealed a largely negative regard for females when he concluded, "women have often stood in the way of progressive movements." Later, he introduced his psychological analysis of the female criminal by stating, "women are big children; their evil tendencies are more numerous and more varied than men's, but generally remain latent." Among "normal" women, Lombroso believed their naturally inborn defects were "neutralised by piety, maternity, want of passion, sexual coldness, by weakness, and an undeveloped intelligence."[33] In his view, these "attributes" usually rose to the surface of a woman's demeanor and obscured the grossly corrupt tendencies of the female. Thus, Lombroso retained the popular ideals of purity, piety, and passivity for women, although he defined them as by-products of woman's deep-seated natural baseness.

Lombroso warmed to the subject of women's deficiencies when he moved beyond merely echoing Bertillon's description of the criminal woman's physical measurements, orbital capacity, hairy moles, and cranial asymmetry. Drawing on the opinions of writers before him to provide a foundation for his own analysis, he called on the words of Euripides and Cato, cited the lives of Parysatis and the American West's own Bell-Star [*sic*], and invoked the nasal index and the facial angle to assert that the female criminal "keeps the characteristics of her type even in her aberrations from it." Among his authorities, Lombroso cited a fifteenth-century author, Corrado Celto, who wrote, "No possible punishments can deter a woman from heaping up crime on crime. Their perversity of mind is more fertile in new crimes than the imagination of a judge in new punishments."[34]

In keeping with the tenor of the pseudoscientific explanations of the day, Lombroso laced his writings with a variety of racist conclusions. He associated female criminality with atavism and the virility of "primitive" people. He concluded that criminal women lacked femininity and exuded "savagery." To make his point, he included in his work photo-plates of an African American and a Native American woman, of whom he said, "we have the portraits of [these] Red Indian and Negro beauties, whom it is difficult to recognise for women, so huge are their jaws and cheek-bones, so hard and coarse their features. And the same is often the case in their crania and brains."[35]

Basically, he believed people were born criminal and that membership in the cultures of color meant a closer connection to the "savage, immoral behaviors" of the "primitives." For the criminal woman, regardless of her ethnicity, Lombroso articulated the double jeopardy that shaped societal opinions and responses across time and culture, when he added: "Moreover, the born female criminal is . . . doubly exceptional, as a woman and as a criminal. For criminals are an exception among civilised people, and women are an exception among criminals. . . . As a double exception, the criminal woman is consequently a monster."[36]

Granted, Cesare Lombroso represented only one voice—an extreme and often criticized one at that—in the literature of criminology.[37] Yet he was known as the "father of criminal anthropology"[38] and his work, even as it pulsated with an antiwoman tone, influenced others in the rising field of criminology.

The very fact that he raised interesting new questions about female criminals and drew his answers from apparent scientific studies guaranteed his colleagues would treat his theories with seriousness and grant them a certain credibility. That his answers represented little more than poorly based assumptions predicated on racism and sexism did not seem so obvious in his own day.[39] Other penologists, perhaps with less venom but with matching concepts, supported Lombroso's work in both form and substance. While Lombroso's excessive and absurd language disappeared, its basic sentiment about women's potential for moral depravity permeated theories of female criminology for the next fifty years.[40]

As worldwide interest in penology increased, one writer's ideas added ballast to another's, as all stood under the broad umbrella of "criminologist," and all further devalued women criminals. In 1910, R. F. Quinton, a British physician who managed a woman's prison, concluded that female criminals were "specially dangerous as corrupters of novices."[41] In accord with his medical background, Quinton as a criminologist denounced the filth of prisons and cells. He argued vehemently against the conditions as unfair to the health of guards and matrons, but stopped short of connecting this medical concern to the prisoners for whom he was responsible.

Also writing in 1910, the American Charles Shirley Potts drew on the earlier work of the Italian Enrico Ferri, a colleague of Cesare Lombroso and author of *Criminal Sociology,* to produce a study intended to address crime from a progressive perspective. Ferri had classified criminals as "madmen," "occasional," "habitual," "passionate," or "hereditary." Using this model, Potts declared, "Most habitual criminals seem to be utterly devoid of the quality of moral sensibility." His work stressed the need for penal reform, especially in the selection of prison staff. This reform plea did not overcome the underlying message of his argument that criminals were not "physically normal persons," and that intellectually a criminal was "inferior to the normal man."[42]

Even when women reformers took up the pen to address female criminality, they mainly called for improved treatment within prisons and did not significantly challenge the dominant male theorists. Elizabeth Fry and Mary Carpenter of Great Britain and Maud Ballington Booth and Dorothea Dix of the United States grounded their work in social reform action, rather than the development of theories of criminology. They published—notably Dix's *Remarks on Prisons and Prison Discipline* and Booth's *After Prison, What?*—but these works promoted the activist's desire to address inhumane living conditions and "redeem the fallen."[43]

For example, in 1896 Booth, a founder of the Salvation Army spin-off the Volunteers of America, launched her prison work centered on prayer and conversion. She dismissed notions of criminal heredity and phrenology, for in her perspective "the habitual criminal is made, not born."[44] According to Booth, since sinfulness explained criminality, Christian goodness could eradicate it.

She devoted her energies to holding prayer meetings in prisons across the country and interviewing prospective parolees for residence in Hope Hall, a religion-driven precursor of the halfway house. Prisoners joined her Volunteer Prison League, wherein they swore to pray every morning and night, refrain from the use of profanity, observe the prison rules, and encourage others in "well-doing and right living."[45] Booth delighted in the fact that the prisoners, whom she largely described as sons of the artisan class fallen prey to their own moral weakness, addressed her as "Little Mother," while she called them "my boys." Her success stemmed from her own tireless commitment, the fervor of her religious zeal, and the practical sponsorship she offered prisoners in an era nearly devoid of public social services.[46]

When asked about women prisoners, Booth maintained that her work focused exclusively on state prisons, where females accounted for only a few inmates. For Booth, men prisoners represented the more serious concern by virtue of their numbers and the lack of support available upon their release. Women discharged from prison, she argued, had access to many rescue homes. Although that may have been an optimistic assertion, Booth reflected the general attitude toward women prisoners when she wrote, "because the field is so large . . . time and strength and limited means compel us to draw the line somewhere, and we naturally have chosen . . . where the need is the greatest."[47]

Booth, who traveled widely to prisons in the West, described each woman prisoner as following an "evil life," "yielding to temptation," having a "highly-strung temperament," or entering a "shame-shadowed motherhood."[48] Moral weakness, a rejection of religion, and shallow maternal values explained women's crimes for her. Thus, Maud Booth, for whom the concerns of male inmates superseded those of females, added to ideas that women criminals fell short of womanly virtue and constituted an unimportant segment of the prison population.

In 1900, Frances Kellor, an American sociologist, countered Cesare Lombroso's ideas about women criminals, questioning his methodology and conclusions. She undertook a systematic investigation, using criminal and noncriminal subjects, to argue that social environment more than biology explained criminality in both men and women.[49] Although Kellor directly and specifically challenged Lombroso's notions of the female criminal nature, by the time she emerged as a strong professional voice, forcefully intolerant attitudes about women inmates had thoroughly permeated American penology.

Saddled with a lopsided, highly charged definition of womanhood in general, women criminals, by virtue of their crimes, bore the weight of added burdensome gender labels. Further, criminal women themselves appeared to affirm their evaluators' negative descriptors through illegal behaviors. Whether through attack or compassion, criminologists insisted that female crime stemmed from the natural inferiority of women gone haywire, a situation in which the supposed goodness of woman lost its moral compass and turned to heinous and distorted unwomanly, nonmaternal acts.

Such thinking informed the leaders of the American penal system in the nineteenth century.[50] The notion that women criminals lacked the creative power and originality of mind characteristic of a true human further distanced female offenders from significant consideration as part of the American justice system.[51] Poor preparation on the part of administrators evolved into an institutional refusal to acknowledge a gender component within the prison structure. Women prisoners quickly lost their humanity and, therefore, required neither attention nor civility from anyone. As a result, responses from every level of judicial administration were at their best muddled, at their worst inhumane.

In the nineteenth-century American criminal justice system, hampered by conflicting policies, limited funds, and a bitter dispute over reformation or retribution for prisoners, the woman criminal never assumed a central role.[52] The voices raised for her could hardly be heard above the other strident debates about American prisons. As late as 1911, the reformer Isabel C. Barrows demanded to know why it had taken so many years for legislators to acknowledge the needs of women prisoners, and she called for a national census to calculate the number of women incarcerated in mixed-sex county jails.[53] Prison authorities easily brushed aside such inquiries, as they continued to regard the criminal woman as a deranged female, whose behaviors so violated the patterns of womanhood that her fate demanded no concerned response from society.[54] The criminal woman remained a somewhat curious deviant, whose life meant nothing other than a romantic tale or moral warning for those securely outside the criminal community.

In the American West, where white women's roles appeared to fall neatly into distinct categories such as pioneer wife, schoolteacher, dance hall girl, club member, or suffragist, the national dilemmas over the management of prisons and of women prisoners stumbled over new questions. Why, in the West, playground of somewhat simplistically defined social roles, should there be any women confined to male penitentiaries? How could the West, haven of male dominance, accommodate that rare being, she whose crimes dictated confinement in a major penal institution? Where, in the West, region of great distances, should women convicted of serious crime be housed? When, in the West, zone of ill-formed institutions, should officials recognize the problems that sprang from the incarceration of females with males? What, in the West, arena of mixed and mixing cultures, would convince people that their prisons reflected a microcosm of the racial and gender structures of their communities? In fact, for many years, western communities remained coolly disinterested in these questions and certainly framed no answers to them.

Nothing in the western epic that fascinated the nation after the Civil War allowed for the incarcerated female. In a most superficial manner, the West and the historical memory of its people contented themselves with the occasional flashy outlaw woman.[55] A Belle Starr, a Cattle Kate Watson, a Calamity Jane—these characters breezed through the annals of gunfighters and outlaws, but their relationship to the western penal system played no role in the sensational treatment of their lives.[56] When confronted with the unknown, nonglamorous woman criminal, western communities showed themselves ill prepared to respond with a carefully constructed incarceration program. In the West, prison administrators simply incorporated convicted females into the facilities for male criminals, used an ad hoc approach to individual problems, and ignored the steady growth of criminal women populations after 1865.

In part, a national circumstance helped to create this problem. The West merely replicated the overall national failure to monitor criminal demographics. Across the country, crime statistics remained grossly under-reported prior to 1900. Sporadic and inaccurate record keeping disguised the patterns of crime and the numbers of convicted criminals. It was not until the 1910 census that the federal government demonstrated interest in the criminal component of the nation.[57] By that late date, time had clouded much of the country's criminal history. This was especially true in the West, where romanticism and legend about crime and violence substitut-ed for statistics and documentation.

The immediate outcome in the nineteenth century was that the changing numbers of women prisoners escaped notice and concern. For example, following the Idaho state legislature's 1915 allocation of $1500 to enlarge the women's ward, Governor Moses Alexander captured the long-standing overall regional attitude toward women prisoners when he vetoed the funding. Alexander declared that Idaho would not have any more women prisoners, even though the number had grown in less than a year from three to five—all living in one room, where two suffered from syphilis or tuberculosis.[58]

Governor Alexander's almost amusing dismissal of a penitentiary prob-lem growing before his very eyes was far from unique. The nineteenth-cen-tury conventional wisdom held that women did not and would not repre-sent substantial numbers in prison populations. This position overlooked the reality that although the number of women prisoners remained small, it relentlessly crept upward. Typically, penitentiaries recorded an annual increase of one or two female prisoners per year in the immediate aftermath of the Civil War. As western populations grew, however, and economic el-ements seesawed, women's incarceration rates increased.

The penitentiary rolls at Huntsville, Texas, reflected this growth. In 1865, ten African American women inmates had been confined at Hunts-ville.[59] By 1870, when Colonel N. A. M. Dudley, under orders from the fed-eral government, took control of the prison, the number of women in the filth-infested institution had risen to thirteen.[60] In an 1874 report, military prisoners rescued from Huntsville and sent to the Kansas penitentiary testified that Texas held fourteen women—probably twelve of whom were African American, the other two not identified by race—in confinement.[61] When the state of Texas undertook a major investigation of its prison sys-tem in 1909, the women inmates numbered seventy-one—sixty-seven Af-rican American women, three Anglos, and one Hispanic—all housed at an agricultural camp about twenty-three miles from the Huntsville facility.[62]

Other western states paralleled Texas. From its earliest penal history in 1833, Missouri incarcerated only one or two women a year. In the 1870s, this pattern, influenced by a poor economy, rising crime, and post–Civil War controls placed on African Americans, shifted dramatically, and, by 1874, forty-five women were in the Jefferson City penitentiary.[63] In Louisiana, between 1866 and 1873, approximately sixty-three women entered the state penal system. But between 1875 and 1880, about seventy-nine women were admitted and between 1895 to 1903, the number increased to at least 110 new women prisoners.[64] In Nebraska, during the decade between 1875 and 1885, ten women or a raw average of one per year, entered the penitentiary. Between 1890 and 1900, thirty women or a raw average of three per year arrived at the Lincoln prison.[65]

Other states, such as Nevada, Arizona, and New Mexico, embraced such small general populations that women prisoners seemed barely noticeable in a crime census. Prior to the construction of a local facility, some of these states and territories with limited populations shipped their prisoners to a neighbor. Wyoming sent women, Jessie Carmon among them, to Colorado and Oklahoma sent women to Kansas. These practices helped to perpetuate a false sense that women did not represent a rising prisoner constituency with permanent needs and a place within the penitentiary. In the West, the scant prison statistics for individual states obscured the larger picture of women and incarceration within the region.[66]

Small numbers and great distances melded with social standards and crippling imprisonment to guarantee that the western woman prisoner disappeared from society's stage. Yet the women did not disappear. They lived in the penitentiary until freed either by death or release. Of the former, society said that a woman "died as a prisoner," often sending her, with her permanent criminal identity, to a pauper's grave in the penitentiary cemetery.[67]

But what of the woman prisoner released by the authorities? How did her female identity lose its prisoner designation and return to its basic womanly definition? The answer, of course, is that it did not. Once labeled "convicted criminal and prisoner," a woman found it nearly impossible to extricate herself from the tentacles of the social and legal constraints that kept her tied to her prison record.

This proved another of the lessons learned by Jessie Carmon, just as she had come to understand the elusive quality of her legitimate place in Sheridan society. By 1912, Jessie's parents, grieving over the outcome of the murder trial, had engaged lawyers to advance their daughter's application for a pardon. Shortly, Jessie Carmon's legal entanglements spread across three western states, diluting her case in any one locale. Metz and Sackett, the Berrys' Wyoming attorneys, submitted a number of favorable parole petitions, a clemency recommendation from the warden of the Colorado penitentiary that housed Jessie, and a request from Harry D. Landis, Jessie's Nebraska divorce lawyer, to appear on her behalf before the pardon board.[68] Leaving nothing to chance, someone among Jessie's advocates prompted her daughter to send a pre-Christmas appeal to Governor Carey. In her child's hand, seven-year-old Grace Leone Carmon pleaded: "Won't you please let my Mama Jessie Carmon come home I want to see her so bad. I am a little girl 7 years old and go to school. I hope you have a little girl, and if you have you will know how bad she would feel to have her Mama a way [*sic*] and how happy she would feel to see her a gain [*sic*] so won't you please let my Mama come home please. Please let her be my Christmas present. I will send you my picture and wish you a Merry Christmas."[69]

Despite Leone's Oliver Twistian letter, Governor Carey remained untouched, avoiding a potential political charge of insensitivity to children by replying, "I am interested in little girls and would do almost anything I could for them, but it is beyond my power to send your mama home."[70] Carey's claimed inability to act was at the least disingenuous, but his message was clear—Jessie would not be home for Christmas. Grace Leone, an innocent in a move to use childhood and the Christmas season to influence men in authority, was no match for those in power.

No amount of seasonal pleading from a child swayed the governor from his conviction that Wyoming should continue to punish Jessie Carmon. Family and state had given the small girl her baptism into the strategies and limitations of gender manipulation. Thus, Jessie's daughter, at a mere seven years of age, came face to face with the rigid structures of society and the law, as played out through the mutual exploitation between the strong and the weak, forces certain to dominate the remainder of her life.

The holiday season passed and, in February 1913, an anxious Jessie herself wrote to the governor and the board of pardons. Her letter, a model of good grammar, correct spelling, and graceful penmanship, reflected the schooling of her earlier life. She framed her words carefully, conveying the appropriate tone of deference expected by the board. Her sense of injustice at the events that had controlled her life for the past three years surfaced briefly in her assertion that she was "entitled to a pardon," but she immediately retreated from any appearance of personal spirit with a humble entreaty for a parole. She rejoiced at a recent report from her attorney that she should be released within thirty days and told the authorities, "This is news I have long been looking for. I want to say . . . if you will grant me a parole I will earn a pardon. . . . I have worked hard for a chance to prove to the world that I am not a criminal."[71] If society viewed Jessie Carmon as one who had transgressed the boundaries of womanhood, she clearly did not. With some courage, she pointed to the accidental circumstances of her crime and her superb behavior in confinement as reasons she should have a chance to return home to care for her daughter and ailing mother.

About the time that Jessie Carmon composed her letter to the state board, C. H. Parmelee, judge at the 1911 Sheridan trial, was drafting his own ideas on Jessie's situation. Judge Parmelee set aside his usual practice of noninterference with parole board decisions to oppose a pardon for Jessie Carmon. Astonishingly, he attributed his opposition and intervention to information he received that the responsible party in the crime had been the slippery Jesse Newton. Thus, the judge took the illogical position that Jessie Carmon should not be pardoned because another person bore the main guilt for the murder.

Parmelee referred to the commonly known fact that Newton had been telephoning the police at the actual moment of the shooting. Asserting that the confidences from his anonymous informant came after the trial, the judge added that as "the man who dominated her life" left the room he said to Jessie, "If he stirs, pop it to him."[72] Judge Parmelee conceded it "unfortunate that Newton, who, in the eyes of many, was in a far greater degree blameworthy than the woman, could not have been brought to account for his misdeeds." Parmelee dismissed the apparent miscarriage of justice because Jessie was "not an entirely normal person," and "[was] easily led and influenced by others." He declared that her parents, Wilson and Minnie Belle Berry, deserved full credit for Jessie's excellent reputation in her youth and that away from them, "she very naturally fell into a corrupt life."

Thus, he argued for a parole that would place Jessie under the control of her parents, warning that, "if they should lose influence over her she would doubtless, by the natural tendency of her nature and habits, gravitate into a disreputable life."[73] He endorsed the petitions for parole only because Jessie's parents were "good" people, for whom he had personal esteem. In Judge Parmelee's view, Jessie Carmon's twenty-four years of "respectability" had no connection to the woman herself and, in fact, belonged to her father and mother.

Indeed, Judge Parmelee dismissed everything about Jessie's "good" conduct, in essence suggesting there was nothing that she had done in the past or could do in the future that would make her eligible for a parole. From the judge's Lombrosian perspective, Jessie's essentially flawed womanly nature explained the danger she posed as a criminal. Brushing aside matters of fairness at trial, prison time served, or a "paid debt to society," Judge Parmelee urged that Jessie be kept under some watchful authority, because of her "abnormal" womanly character. The need to restrain the weaknesses in her moral fiber concerned him more than the possible irregularities of her treatment within the judicial system. Her conviction, despite the freeing of a man the judge acknowledged equally responsible, wiped out

Jessie Carmon's earlier life, her exemplary conduct as a prisoner, and her future as a woman and a citizen. For Judge Parmelee, Jessie's crime had little to do with the circumstances that left James McCoy dead on the floor and everything to do with the woman's inherently debased self.

Judge Parmelee's opinions aside, in March 1913 the Wyoming board paroled Jessie into the custody of her divorce attorney, Harry D. Landis. A grateful Jessie reported to Governor Carey that she had arrived home in Friend, Nebraska, by 21 March and she promised to "be true to my parole."[74] Her effort to abide by that promise led Jessie Carmon into another phase of the life of the woman prisoner, one that underscored the futility of trying to elude the censures and labels generated by incarceration. Jessie's new difficulties stemmed from her desire to marry.

In May 1913, John W. Neal, owner of a livery business in Buffalo, Wyoming, and suitor for Jessie's hand, visited the Berry home in Nebraska. Neal, a widower with two small sons, had come to know Jessie while she languished in the Sheridan jail, awaiting trial. During that year, Jessie had fallen into poor health and Jack Neal, as sheriff, had been responsible for her care. How he may have figured in the decision to place her in solitary confinement after her first nervous collapse remained a moot point in the marriage negotiations.

Nevertheless, he had continued his attentions to Jessie all through her imprisonment in the penitentiary. After Jessie's release, Neal pursued the traditional ritual of seeking permission to marry a daughter of the house. That would seem one more indicator that Neal, Jessie, and her parents, unlike the authorities, considered her descent into criminality a temporary disruption to the usual conduct of her womanly life.

All the parties acquainted with Jessie's troubles rose quickly to testify to the merits of Neal's character. The long-supportive divorce attorney petitioned for the couple, pointing to Neal's good reputation.[75] Wilson Berry not only wrote of his good impression of his prospective son-in-law, who "impresses us as an honest man and sincerely desirous of making a good home for Jessie," but included a warm assessment of Jessie's routines since her return to the family.[76]

It was, however, C. L. Sackett of the appeals attorneys who provided the longest personal history of Neal, explaining he had known the former sheriff for over eighteen years. Sackett described Neal as "thoroughly honest and honorable, trustworthy and loyal." As a young cowboy, Neal had worked "with those men in the western towns where the moral surroundings were not always the best . . . though . . . I have never known him to associate with women of bad character morally." Thus, Sackett apparently wanted to deflect any suspicion that Jessie had snared Neal with a siren's song made sweet and intimate through a year's stay in the Sheridan jail.

Sackett's letter described a happy and decent man, one known for his considerate and affectionate demeanor toward his first wife and loving relationship with his children. The solid, likeable qualities of Jack Neal resonated through the recommendation and were summed up in Sackett's rather poetic remark, "he will remain in his loyalty and fidelity to her [Jessie] as steadfast as the stars."[77]

Amidst these various tributes to Neal, Jessie's voice captured the promise she too saw in this union, calling the former sheriff's character and reputation "splendid," and citing her poignant desire to "go back there [Buffalo, Wyoming] and make a good clean record for myself." After years of travail, Jessie certainly spoke from her heart when she told the governor, "I want to begin my life all over again." She assured Governor Carey that Neal knew everything about her legal record and that "All the long months I was at Canon City he was loyal to me," and he "stands ready to marry me. ... We have waited long for this."[78]

In an unusual turn of events for a criminal woman, Jessie Carmon stood poised on the threshold of "respectability," ready to resume her role as wife and mother with a marriage partner apparently far different from her first unreliable, abusive spouse. Jack Neal represented more than any parole board could have imagined—a settled, slightly older man with a solid business, regular income, and impeccable family reputation wished to marry a convicted murderess who had been labeled someone "[with] something lacking," and a "natural tendency ... [to] gravitate into a disreputable life."[79] It would have seemed that even Judge Parmelee would approve of this arrangement, in which Jessie would live under the watchful care of a well-respected husband. Alas, the happy couple had not counted on Governor Joseph Carey who, like Judge Parmelee, believed Jessie needed constant monitoring from authorities better equipped to make her decisions.[80]

Throughout July and August of 1913, a flurry of letters kept Carmon and Neal confused about their future. Because of a miscommunication from the secretary of the parole board, Jessie believed that she had been given permission to set a wedding date and that immediately prior to that day a pardon, without which she could not marry, would be forthcoming.[81] In her delight, Jessie wrote to the governor, outlining her plans to move to Buffalo and get the children settled for school; she thanked all concerned for "giving me a chance to be a useful, happy woman."[82] Governor Carey was not so ready to release Jessie Carmon from her linkage to the state, and he still considered himself the appropriate person to make decisions about her life. Uncertain that it was the "best thing" for Jessie and Jack to marry, the governor vetoed the planned wedding date, declaring "I am afraid the whole thing would prove a failure."[83]

Instead, the governor wrote to Jack Neal and directed him to travel to

Cheyenne for a personal interview.[84] As for Jessie, the governor fired off a short note, chiding her that plans to be married on 25 August were a "little premature." Without explanation Carey told Jessie, "I think it would be an exceedingly dangerous thing for you to go back to Buffalo and live. It will bring up all the old trouble, and what you want . . . is to have a sealed book."[85] Governor Carey's intense personal involvement in Jessie's future life not only captured the state's primitive mechanics for treatment of parolees, but the special precautions used with released women prisoners.[86]

Jessie Carmon's long experience with the prison bureaucracy surfaced instantly, as she recognized that she had overstepped in the eyes of the governor. With all at risk, she quickly drew on her knowledge of the system and crafted a letter of length and tone designed to secure the necessary pardon. She began with an abject apology for her hasty plans, explaining that she had made them only because of the communication she received from the parole board. Then, in a daring move in which she realistically assessed her position in society, she countered Carey's objections to her move to Buffalo. With the common sense of a woman who knew it unlikely she would be free of the criminal shadow that had fallen on her, she told the governor: "I am living conscientiously, and will continue to live so till the end. I feel sure that I can be as good wife and mother by going back to Buffalo to live as I could by going anywhere else. I could never go anywhere but there would be someone that would know my past record—they would think I was running away from it and trying to cover it up—they would tell it and talk about it and I would excite more curiosity than I would by going back to where it has been threshed out and talked over."[87]

Moreover, she demonstrated her concern for Jack Neal, pointing to his long roots in the Buffalo community and the hardship a move could prove for him. Should he, she said, "get along less successfully, either in health or in business, I would always regret it."[88] Nothing in her letter to the governor suggested the words came from the mind of a woman who lacked moral sensibility or human decency. Nothing suggested this woman, who said "I care nothing at all for society," was of such low intelligence that she would—for good or ill—heedlessly follow those around her.

In fact, the quiet courage of her letter affirmed that Jessie Carmon still retained the fiber to respond to many adversities. While only a young woman, she refused to accept the abuse and insecurity of an unstable marriage and sought a divorce, even in the face of mortal threats from her spouse. As a single mother, she left the economically uninviting farm life of Nebraska and found urban employment to support her daughter. In Sheridan, she managed the business complexities of Jesse Newton's rooming house, large enough that she needed additional domestic help to complete the cooking and cleaning chores. She weathered an estranged wife's public assault on her moral character, charges perhaps fueled more by anger than reality. She dared to become the advocate for the battered Rose McCoy and she balked at the threats and abuse of James McCoy. She alone stood in a darkened hallway, protecting Rose McCoy from yet another beating. Finally, she returned violence with violence and, abandoned by her associates, began her painful experiences with the western legal system.

In an ironic twist, even the governor seemed to recognize the many constraints that had enveloped Jessie Carmon. In asking that Neal leave his business and travel to Cheyenne for the meeting, Carey declared that his only desire was for the "best interests of Mrs. Carmon." The governor regretted that "she had to suffer punishment for the disreputable man with whom she was associating. . . . the man should have borne an equal punishment to herself." Carey then elevated his regret to a cosmic level, noting "the woman gets the worst side, for man and woman kind will not recognize . . . that the woman has just as much right to do a certain kind of wrong as a man has."[89]

On 16 August 1913, Governor Joseph Carey handed Jack Neal a pardon, to be presented to Jessie Carmon before the marriage ceremony.[90] On 22 August, Harry D. Landis wrote to Governor Carey that Jessie Carmon and Jack Neal had been married in Lincoln, Nebraska. Landis added, "By issuing a pardon you have made right a wrong. . . . Jessie Carmon did not murder McCoy, it was an accidental shooting without blame on her part, but her life had not been ideal and that was the sole reason of her conviction."[91]

Jessie Carmon's experiences as a woman charged with crime and her life after her release from the penitentiary encompass much of the aura of the woman criminal. The public destruction of her womanly reputation, the assumption of her deep-seated immoral nature, the inflexibility of the courts, and the patronizing policing of her life after prison—these proved usual for women prisoners. Although these elements formed part of the lives of all criminals and prisoners, the aspect of gender, as codified by written word, legal structure, and common practice, significantly altered the experience for women.

Furthermore, a western society that lacked a careful construction of its institutions further intensified these dynamics. As western communities jockeyed for civic order, they showed themselves unwilling to define a generous place for those who appeared to make the struggle for social conformity and "mainstream" morality more difficult. Instead, they relied on the thought current among eastern and European criminologists and penologists and imposed those notions onto western circumstances. From those published in the *Sheridan Daily Enterprise* to those expressed by Governor Joseph Carey, most public attitudes about Jessie Carmon matched neatly with the overarching views about women prisoners that had developed throughout the nineteenth century.

In other ways, Jessie Carmon's battle to regain control of her life did not mirror the experience of most women criminals and prisoners in the West. These women, lacking the comfortable family to back appeals and lend emotional support or hampered by race and class constraints, did not shed the label of "woman prisoner" and reach such an apparent pleasant outcome after the penitentiary. The constant family attention, the availability of funding for lawyers and appeals, the constancy of Jack Neal, and an opportunity to reengage the middle-class society of her childhood through a new marriage set Jessie Carmon apart from many women prisoners. Most encountered attitudes like those of one warden who commented, "I am dubious to the complete reformation of any woman after she has once served a prison sentence."[92] For them, the experience to and from the penitentiary took less happy roads and much of what shaped their lives took place inside the prison environment, an unexplored world in Jessie Carmon's story. Yet, Jessie Carmon caught the mournful sound of her sisters in penitentiaries across the West when she said, "I have done things wrong and I have suffered."[93]

Notes

1. J. J. Thomas to the Governor of the State of Wyoming, 5 Feb. 1913, Jessie Carmon File, State of Wyoming, Petitions for Pardon, Governor Joseph M. Carey, WSAHD. Hereafter, Petitions for Pardon, WSAHD.

2. Cynde Georgen, Site Superintendent, Trail End State Historic Site, Sheridan, Wyo., to author, 14 Jan. 1996. I wish to thank Cynde Georgen, great-granddaughter of Jessie Carmon, for the many family details she provided.

3. Jessie Carmon's prison records did not indicate whether she received alimony or child support from Carmon. He was not a presence at the time of Jessie's legal troubles; his whereabouts seemed to be unknown. Given the history of their relationship, she probably would have had trouble collecting the money, even if it had been awarded. At some point, George Carmon did establish a correspondence with his daughter Grace Leone Georgen, presumably after she was an adult (Cynde Georgen to author, 14 Jan. 1996). For a discussion of the problems nineteenth-century divorced women had with alimony and/or child support, see Glenda Riley, *Divorce: An American Tradition* (New York: Oxford University Press, 1991), pp. 82–83.

4. H. D. Landis to P. O. Inspector in Charge, Kansas City, Mo., 11 Aug. 1909; Biographical Sketch of Prisoner Eligible to Parole . . . Wyoming State Penitentiary, Registered Number 8223, Jessie Carmon File, Petitions for Pardon, WSAHD.

5. Cynde Georgen, letter to author, 7 Nov. 1995.

6. Judge C. H. Parmelee to Mae Woodriff, Clerk, State Board of Charities and Reform, 12 Feb. 1913, Jessie Carmon File, Petitions for Pardon, WSAHD.

7. Jessie Carmon's name appears in the documents with a variety of spellings— "Carmon," "Carmen," "Carman." In a letter to Governor Joseph M. Carey, she signed

her name "Jessie Carmon" (Jessie Carmon to Hon. Joseph M. Carey, 21 June 1913, Jessie Carmon File, Petitions for Pardon, WSAHD). Other spellings indicate "as is" usage in the documents. The family considered "Carmon" the correct spelling (Cynde Georgen to author, 14 Jan. 1996).

8. *Sheridan Daily Enterprise*, 2 May 1910.

9. In this text, the use of a marital title for a woman indicates that no other name information was available in the record. After the initial designation using the marital title, the woman is mentioned by last name only.

10. *Sheridan Daily Enterprise*, 30 Apr. 1910. Because of her status as a divorced woman, Jessie Carmon may not have ranked among the elite in Sheridan society. She certainly did not rate the same gentle treatment as another woman, who apparently wounded her husband in a domestic dispute. The newspaper discreetly reported, "The matter was supposed to be accidental and for other obvious reasons the *Daily Enterprise* was requested not to mention names of the participants" (18 Apr. 1910).

11. Erving Goffman, *Stigma: Notes on the Management of Spoiled Identity* (Englewood Cliffs: Prentice-Hall, 1963), pp. 53, 70–72.

12. Blake McKelvey, *American Prisons: A Study in American Social History prior to 1915*, Patterson Smith Reprint Series in Criminology, Law Enforcement and Social Problems 17 (1936; reprint, Montclair, N.J.: Patterson Smith, 1968), pp. ix–x, 6; Orlando F. Lewis, *The Development of American Prisons and Prison Customs, 1776–1845*, Patterson Smith Reprint Series in Criminology, Law Enforcement and Social Problems 1 (1922; reprint, Montclair, N.J.: Patterson Smith, 1967).

13. For discussions of this point see, for example, John D'Emilio and Estelle B. Freedman, *Intimate Matters: A History of Sexuality in America* (New York: Harper and Row, 1988), esp. parts 2 and 3; Cynthia Fuchs Epstein, *Deceptive Distinctions: Sex, Gender, and the Social Order* (New Haven: Yale University Press, and New York: Russell Sage Foundation, 1988); Carroll Smith-Rosenberg, *Disorderly Conduct: Visions of Gender in Victorian America* (New York: Alfred A. Knopf, 1985); and Carl N. Degler, "What Ought to Be and What Was: Women's Sexuality in the Nineteenth Century," *American Historical Review* 79 (Dec. 1974): 1467–90.

14. The power of the madonna image can be seen in a variety of popular literary forms, and much of it spilled over into the twentieth century. For example, a 1918 publication that went to the fourth reprint of its eighteenth edition by 1927 said "there is no joy and pride greater than that of a woman who is bearing the developing child of a man she adores" (Marie Carmichael Stopes, *Married Love: A New Contribution to the Solution of Sex Difficulties*, 18th ed. [London: G. P. Putnam's Sons, 1927], p. 114). Forty years later, these notions continued to be prevalent as demonstrated by such comments as "deep within a woman's nature, embedded in her physical being, lies the potency of maternal love" (Wilmon H. Sheldon, *Woman's Mission to Humanity* [Boston: Christopher, 1968], p. 15). The historical implications of this concept are addressed by Joyce Antler in "Was She A Good Mother: Some Thoughts on a New Issue for Feminist Biography," in *Women and the Structure of Society*, ed. Barbara J. Harris and Jo Ann K. McNamara (Durham, N.C.: Duke University Press, 1984), pp. 53–66.

15. Meda Chesney-Lind states: "Once a female offender is apprehended, her behavior is scrutinized for evidence that she is beyond the control of the patriarchy, and, if this can be found, she is harshly punished" ("Women and Crime: The Female Offender," *Signs* 12 [Autumn 1986]: 96). For a discussion of women's response to the double standard in society, see Smith-Rosenberg, *Disorderly Conduct*, pp. 109–28. Also see Epstein, *Deceptive Distinctions*, pp. 120–21.

16. The right of the state to punish was a frequent topic of discussion among

criminologists and prison administrators. In such a debate, one writer specifically called for the state's responsibility to both stop the illegal action and control the will that had been manifested in the criminal, declaring, "Crime establishes a condition of war between the individual and society" (Harold Höffding, "The State's Authority to Punish Crime," trans. Samuel C. Eastman, *Journal of the American Institute of Criminal Law and Criminology* 2 [Jan. 1912]: 694, 698).

17. See *Sheridan Daily Enterprise*, 30 Apr., 2 May, 5 May 1910.

18. For a discussion of this dynamic see Robert D. Highfill, "The Effects of News of Crime and Scandal upon Public Opinion," *Journal of the American Institute of Criminal Law and Criminology* 17 (May 1926–Feb. 1927): 40–103, esp. pp. 67–71, 81, 83–84.

19. *Sheridan Daily Enterprise*, 30 Apr. 1910.

20. Ibid., 2 May 1910.

21. Ibid., 5 May 1910.

22. Jesse Newton, owner of the Sheridan Automobile and Garage Company, received only passing attention in the newspapers for his role in the dramatic events. The county attorney reluctantly dropped the charges against Newton (ibid.).

23. Ibid., 13 May 1910.

24. Biographical Sketch of Prisoner Eligible to Parole . . . Registered Number 8223, Jessie Carmon File, Petitions for Pardon, WSAHD.

25. Some criminologists did argue that the true purpose of the criminal law was not to punish moral guilt but rather to protect the well-being and safety of society. They, however, were generally discussing male criminals, as only a few writers concerned themselves with women. See W. W. Willoughby, "Anglo-American Philosophies of Penal Law II: Punitive Justice," *Journal of the American Institute of Criminal Law and Criminology* 1 (Sept. 1910): 354–77.

26. For how bias touched women from cultures of color, see Rayna Green, "The Pocohontas Perplex: The Image of Indian Women in American Culture," in *Unequal Sisters: A Multi-Cultural Reader in U.S. Women's History,* ed. Ellen Carol DuBois and Vicki L. Ruiz (New York: Routledge, 1990), pp. 15–21; in the same volume, Deborah Gray White, "Female Slaves: Sex Roles and Status in the Antebellum Plantation South," pp. 22–31, and Darlene Clark Hine, "Rape and the Inner Lives of Black Women in the Middle West: Preliminary Thoughts on the Culture of Dissemblance," pp. 292–97; Sherry L. Smith, "Beyond Princess and Squaw: Army Officers' Perceptions of Indian Women," in *The Women's West,* ed. Susan Armitage and Elizabeth Jameson (Norman: University of Oklahoma Press, 1987), pp. 63–75; Shirley Hill Witt, "Native American Women Today: Sexism and the Native American Woman," *Civil Rights Digest* 6 (Spring 1974): 29–35; Sylvia Van Kirk, *Many Tender Ties: Women in Fur Trade Society, 1670–1870* (Norman: University of Oklahoma Press, 1980), pp. 159–60, 170, 240; Alfredo Mirandé and Evangelina Enríquez, *La Chicana: The Mexican-American Woman* (Chicago: University of Chicago Press), pp. 60, 68–71, 75–78; Arnoldo De León, *They Called them Greasers: Anglo Attitudes toward Mexicans in Texas, 1821–1900* (Austin: University of Texas Press, 1983), pp. 36–48; Robert B. Yoshioka, "Asian American Women: Stereotyping Asian Women," *Civil Rights Digest* 6 (Spring 1974): 44–45; and Lucie Cheng Hirata, "Chinese Immigrant Women in Nineteenth Century America," in *Women of America: A History,* ed. Carol Berk and Mary Beth Norton (Boston: Houghton Mifflin, 1979), pp. 224–44.

27. Goffman, *Stigma,* p. 5, 19.

28. By 1870, almost 33,000 persons were incarcerated in the United States. After 1900, the numbers increased so dramatically that between 1904 and 1935 the prison population in the United States jumped by 140 percent. See Michael A. Kroll, "The Prison Experiment: A Circular History," *Southern Exposure* 4 (1978): 9.

29. Eileen B. Leonard, *Women, Crime, and Society: A Critique of Criminology Theory* (New York: Longman, 1982), pp. 1–2. For an examination of the ideology that guided ideas of criminals and punishment before the late nineteenth century, see Michel Foucault, *Discipline and Punish: The Birth of the Prison,* trans. Alan Sheridan (New York: Pantheon Books, 1977), pp. 3–131, 231–56; and Michael Ignatieff, *A Just Measure of Pain: The Penitentiary in the Industrial Revolution* (New York: Columbia University Press, 1978); and for the impact of those ideas on prison growth in the United States, Sullivan, *Prison Reform Movement,* pp. 4–16. These works demonstrate the efforts of Western societies to organize penal theories that translated into formal policy. The early efforts, especially those grounded in the human sciences, provided the foundation on which the "new" thinkers of the late nineteenth and early twentieth century built their modern assessments of the criminal. Since that foundation was so dominantly negative, it would have required a Herculean intellectual effort to excise the powerful notions of the morality of punishment that had already taken shape by 1865.

30. Frederick William Robinson, *Female Life in Prison,* 4th ed., rev. (London: Spencer Ballantyne Press, [1888?]), pp. 43, 46.

31. After Lombroso died on 19 Oct. 1909, Adalbert Albrecht, a criminologist from Massachusetts, stated in a tribute to him that Lombroso's work on the connection between prostitution and all other kinds of crime would always remain a masterpiece ("Cesare Lombroso: A Glance at His Life Work," *Journal of the American Institute of Criminal Law and Criminology* 1 [July 1910]: 71–83). The suppression of women and a negative judgment about their capabilities was not the singular province of Cesare Lombroso; he, however, made a striking impact because he cast his opinions within a "scientific" framework.

32. Cesare Lombroso and William Ferrero, *The Female Offender* (1900; reprint, New York: Philosophical Library, 1958), pp. 45–47.

33. Cesare Lombroso, *The Man of Genius* (New York: Charles Scribner's Sons, 1896), pp. 138–39, 151.

34. Lombroso and Ferrero, *Female Offender,* pp. 112, 147.

35. Ibid., p. 112.

36. Ibid., pp. 151–52. Lombroso's work, despite its excessive language, retained favor with some, as noted by the introduction to the 1958 reprint edition, which stated, "The present study in criminal biology . . . (although [written] almost a hundred years ago) should be particularly welcome to counterbalance the mainly analytical and psychologically dynamic hypotheses of today" (Frank J. Pirone, M.D., introduction to Lombroso and Ferrero, *Female Offender,* n.p.).

37. Criticisms of both his theories and his methods did arise quickly. His attempts, however, at scientific study and the notions he postulated energized other criminologists for decades. For a discussion of responses to Lombroso's work see Christopher Hibbert, *The Roots of Evil: A Social History of Crime and Punishment* (Boston: Little Brown, 1963), pp. 185–96.

38. Epstein, *Deceptive Distinctions,* p. 7.

39. Lombroso also argued that the press was one of the primary causes of crime because depraved criminals sought to imitate the exciting tales of mayhem they read about in newspapers. This seems to conflict with his other view of criminals as illiterate persons of low intelligence, not interested in or capable of intellectual study (Highfill, "Effects of News of Crime and Scandal upon Public Opinion," pp. 42–44).

40. The sexual theories of Sigmund Freud also added significantly to notions of female criminality. See Rita James Simon, "Women and Crime," in *Encyclopedia of Crime and Justice,* ed. Sanford H. Kadish (New York: Macmillan, Free Press, 1983), vol.

4, p. 1665; Lee H. Bowker, ed., *Women and Crime in America* (New York: Macmillan, 1981), p. 2. For a discussion of the lingering impact of Lombroso's theories, see Carol Smart, "Criminological Theory: Its Ideology and Implications concerning Women," in Bowker, pp. 6–16.

41. Charles Richmond Henderson, "The Cell: A Problem of Prison Science," *Journal of American Institute of Criminal Law and Criminology* 2 (May 1911): 60.

42. Charles Shirley Potts, *Crime and the Treatment of the Criminal*, Bulletin of the University of Texas 146 (Austin: n.p., 1910), pp. 9, 13–14.

43. In America, women turned to prison reform as volunteers, hoping to uplift female prisoners through religion and good works. After 1860, women expanded the range of their activism, seeking positions on decision-making state charity boards and prison commissions. For a thorough discussion of the thought and action of women reformers see Estelle B. Freedman, *Their Sisters' Keepers: Women's Prison Reform in America, 1830–1930* (Ann Arbor: University of Michigan Press, 1981).

44. Maud Ballington Booth, *After Prison—What?* (New York: Fleming H. Revell, 1903), p. 121.

45. Ibid., p. 55.

46. Ibid., pp. 11–47, 190–92.

47. Ibid., pp. 281–82.

48. Ibid., pp. 282–87.

49. A summary of the contrast between Lombroso and Kellor is found in Freedman, *Their Sisters' Keepers*, pp. 111–15.

50. Although it may seem that the wardens and managers of western penitentiaries were far removed from the scholarly debates about female criminality, the notions in vogue were widely advertised through such events as the annual meeting of the National Prison Congress and the publication of the *Journal of the American Institute of Criminal Law and Criminology*. In 1874, Colonel A. J. Ward, a particularly indifferent manager of the Huntsville, Texas, penitentiary, answered charges of prison abuse at the National Prison Congress (Ward, Dewey, and Company, Lessees, "The Texas State Penitentiary," from "Transactions of the Prison Congress, 1874"; reprinted in Board of Commissioners of Public Institutions, *Second Annual Report*, 1874, p. 339, UKKC). In 1911, the proposals for reform from the governors of Idaho, Iowa, Utah, Arkansas, Kansas, South Dakota, Colorado, Minnesota, and Wyoming reported in the "Notes on Current and Recent Events" column of the *Journal of the American Institute of Criminal Law and Criminology* showed that state executives were well informed about prison conditions. In the same issue, a Texas judge complained that confessions were not being used in court procedures (2 [Sept. 1911]: 319, 429–30).

51. Albrecht, "Cesare Lombroso," p. 79.

52. McKelvey, *American Prisons*, pp. x, 77, 78, 141. In 1911, the president of the English Prison Commission and International Prison Committee, Sir Evelyn Ruggles-Brise, wrote about the diversity of penal practices in the United States, "The whole continent abounds in new ideas and experiments." He especially urged reform for women in the United States, asserting that in New York alone more than 26,000 women went to jail each year ("An English View of the American Penal System," *Journal of the American Institute of Criminal Law and Criminology* 2 [Sept. 1911]: 356, 367–69).

53. Isabel C. Barrows, "Notes on Current and Recent Events," *Journal of the American Institute of Criminal Law and Criminology* 2 (May 1911): 126–27.

54. Marilyn G. Haft, "Women in Prison: Discriminatory Practices and Some Legal Solutions," in *Women, Crime and Justice*, ed. Susan K. Datesman and Frank R. Scarpitti (New York: Oxford University Press, 1980), pp. 320–21; Clarice Feinman,

"Sex-Role Stereotypes and Justice for Women," in *Women and Crime in America,* ed. Bowker, pp. 383–84. Estelle B. Freedman offers a balanced assessment of the successes and failures that came from the establishment of separate facilities for women prisoners in *Their Sisters' Keepers,* pp. 143–57.

55. A slight literature focuses, usually with little analysis, on women outlaws. For example, see Harry Sinclair Drago, *Wild, Woolly and Wicked* (New York: Clarkson N. Potter, 1960), and Grace Ernestine Ray, *Wily Women of the West* (San Antonio: Naylor, 1972). Bill O'Neal, *Encyclopedia of Western Gunfighters* (Norman: University of Oklahoma Press, 1979), contains no mention of women.

56. Glenn Shirley treats the varied forms of popular attention given to Belle Starr in *Belle Starr and Her Times: The Literature, The Facts, and the Legends* (Norman: University of Oklahoma Press, 1982).

57. Ruggles-Brise, "English View of the American Penal System," pp. 362–63.

58. *Idaho Daily Statesman,* 19 Feb. 1916, p. 10.

59. Herman Lee Crow, "A Political History of the Texas Penal System, 1829–1951" (Ph.D. dissertation, University of Texas, Austin, 1964), p. 85.

60. N. A. M. Dudley, "Report of the Superintendent," *Report on the Condition of the State Penitentiary,* Huntsville, February 10, 1870, Exhibit H, n.p., TSA.

61. Board of Commissioners of Public Institutions, *Second Annual Report,* 1874, p. 346, UKKC.

62. *Report of the Penitentiary Investigating Committee, Including All Exhibits and Testimony Taken by the Committee,* 1910, p. 14, TSA. Hereafter *Report of the Penitentiary Investigating Committee,* TSA.

63. Gary R. Kremer, "Strangers to Domestic Virtues: Nineteenth-Century Women in the Missouri Prison," *Missouri Historical Review* 84 (Apr. 1990): 293–302.

64. Louisiana State Penitentiary, Register of Convicts Received, 13 Feb. 1866–29 Dec. 1889, Prisoners nos. 1–9093, Office of the Warden, LSP. Hereafter, Register of Convicts Received, LSP.

65. Despite these increases, Nebraska did not construct a separate facility for women until 1920. Information provided by Mary Norquest, Records Manager, Department of Correctional Services, Nebraska Center for Women, York, Nebr., 13 July 1987.

66. Even within the modern era, when compilation of prisoner statistics took on more systematic form, record keeping has been haphazard and accurate tabulations illusive. See figures for prisoners in state and federal institutions from 1925 to 1992 and sentenced prisoners by region, 1972–92, in U.S. Department of Justice, Bureau of Justice Statistics, *Bureau of Justice Statistics Sourcebook of Criminal Justice Statistics, 1993,* ed. Kathleen Maguire and Ann L. Pastore (Washington: G.P.O., 1994), pp. 600–601.

67. Prisoner no. 1270, Nebraska State Penitentiary, Descriptive Records of Prisoners, vols. 1 and 2, roll 1, RG 86, NSA. Hereafter, Descriptive Records, NSA. In 1912, one member of the penitentiary investigating committee in Texas recommended that, as one means for reducing financial losses at the prison, a new law that provided for the shipment of corpses of deceased prisoners be repealed (*Record of Evidence and Statements before the Penitentiary Investigating Committee,* 1911–12, p. 39, TSA).

68. W. S. Metz to Governor Joseph M. Carey, 18 Dec. 1912, Jessie Carmon File, Petitions for Pardon, WSAHD. By 1910, thirty-seven states were experimenting with various forms of parole and probation, although the procedures came more slowly to the far West than other regions of the country (Wilfred Bolster, "Adult Probation, Parole, and Suspended Sentence: Report of Committee C of the American Institute

of Criminal Law and Criminology," *Journal of the American Institute of Criminal Law and Criminology* 1 [Sept. 1910]: 438).

69. Leone Carmon to Dear Governor Carey, 15 Dec. 1912, Jessie Carmon File, Petitions for Pardon, WSAHD. Throughout this work the indicator [*sic*] is used for many misspellings, especially those that appeared in the writing of the various women prisoners. The usage implies no educational censure of the subjects. Rather it is intended to highlight the difficulty with which many women, often schooled mainly in an oral tradition or the languages of non-Anglo cultures, struggled to communicate with a bureaucracy predicated on a command of written English.

70. Governor Joseph Carey to Leone Carmon, 20 Dec. 1912, ibid.

71. Jessie Carmon to the Honorable Governor and State Board of Pardons, 10 Feb. 1913, ibid.

72. C. H. Parmelee to Mae Woodriff, 12 Feb. 1913, ibid. Accounts in the *Sheridan Daily Enterprise* placed Newton in the dining room, making the call to the police, when the shot rang out, a point verified by the "hello girl" in the central office, who testified that she heard the gun fired (30 Apr., 2 May 1910).

73. C. H. Parmelee to Miss Mae Woodriff, 12 Feb. 1912, Jessie Carmon File, Petitions for Pardon, WSAHD.

74. Jessie Carmon to Governor J. M. Carey, 21 Mar. 1913, ibid.

75. H. D. Landis to Governor Joseph M. Carey, 20 June 1913, ibid.

76. Wilson Berry to Governor Joseph M. Carey, 21 June 1913, ibid.

77. C. L. Sackett to Governor J. M. Carey, 27 June 1913, ibid.

78. Jessie Carmon to Governor Joseph M. Carey, 21 June 1913, ibid.

79. C. H. Parmelee to Miss Mae Woodriff, 12 Feb. 1913, ibid.

80. In this, both men followed current thinking about the importance of "supervision and control . . . close and friendly" in parole or probation procedures (Warren F. Spalding, "The Cost of Crime," *Journal of the American Institute of Criminal Law and Criminology* 1 [May 1910]: 100).

81. State Board of Pardons to Harry D. Landis, 14 July 1913; Jessie Carmon to Governor Joseph M. Carey, 28 July 1913; Governor Joseph M. Carey to Harry D. Landis, 31 July 1913, Jessie Carmon File, Petitions for Pardon, WSAHD.

82. Jessie Carmon to Governor Joseph M. Carey, 28 July 1913, ibid.

83. Governor Joseph M. Carey to Harry D. Landis, 31 July 1913, ibid. In fact, the couple lived successfully in Buffalo for twenty years before moving to Idaho. Jessie and Jack had two children of their own, bringing to five the number they raised. When they moved from Wyoming, the *Buffalo Bulletin* noted a "favorite" family was leaving and would be missed. Jack Neal died in Buhl, Idaho, in 1948. Jessie Carmon Neal died in Twin Falls, Idaho, in 1953 (Cynde Georgen to author, 7 Nov. 1995, 14 Jan. 1996).

84. Governor Joseph M. Carey to J. W. Neal, 24 July 1913, Jessie Carmon File, Petitions for Pardon, WSAHD.

85. Joseph M. Carey to Mrs. Jessie Carmon, 1 Aug. 1913, ibid.

86. Symposium on Adult Probation, proceedings reported in Bolster, "Adult Probation, Parole, and Suspended Sentence," p. 461. Administrators seemed to make up the rules for parole as the system evolved. For example, between 1907 and 1913, New Mexico paroled three different women convicted of murder. The first, Dolores Nolan, no. 1668, reported her whereabouts for six and one-half years. The second, Susanna Ford, no. 1864, sent monthly work reports from 1909 until 1913, when officials ordered her to stop. The third, Irene Kent, no. 2754, quickly got permission to leave New Mexico for El Paso, Texas, where her parole time expired in less than a year (New Mexico Penitentiary Records, Parole Book, NMSA [hereafter, Parole Book, NMSA]).

87. Jessie Carmon to Governor Joseph M. Carey, 6 Aug. 1913, Jessie Carmon File, Petitions for Pardon, WSAHD.

88. Ibid.

89. Governor Joseph M. Carey to J. W. Neal, 7 Aug. 1913, ibid.

90. Governor Joseph M. Carey to J. W. Neal, 16 Aug. 1913, ibid.

91. Harry D. Landis to Governor Joseph M. Carey, 22 Aug. 1913, ibid. In the public record, Landis's comment is the single reference to any "unacceptable" conduct on Jessie Carmon's part before the shooting. The newspapers made no particular slur against her for her divorce or for her work as manager of the Newton Boarding House. Although "boarding houses" were often brothels, it is highly unlikely that Jessie Carmon had any connection to prostitution. The Newton Boarding House was at least five blocks from the Sheridan red light district, separated from it by the central business district (City of Sheridan Map by C. E. Worthington and J. H. Helvey, personal possession of Cynde Georgen). Among the boarders at the Newton house were Mr. and Mrs. William Kimmel. He owned the Kirby Opera House in Sheridan, and she purchased the house from Jesse Newton and ran it as the Kimmel Boarding House (Cynde Georgen to author, 5 Nov. 1995, 14 Jan. 1996).

92. Statement of Warden, Parole Application, 26 Sept. 1913, Ludy Lee File 8577, Wyoming Penitentiary Records, Female Inmates File, WSAHD (hereafter Female Inmates File, WSAHD).

93. Jessie Carmon to Governor Joseph M. Carey, 6 Aug. 1913, Jessie Carmon File, Petitions for Pardon, WSAHD.

Photographed around 1890, this scene at the Arizona Territorial Prison at Yuma shows the fence (right foreground) that separated the women's quarters (right rear) from the main prison yard for men. Courtesy of the Arizona Historical Society, Tucson, Ariz.

Pearl Hart in attire she apparently rarely wore. Courtesy of the Arizona Historical Society, Tucson, Ariz.

The photographer captured the notion of "Hart and her heart" in this prison image. Courtesy of the Arizona Historical Society, Tucson, Ariz.

Although intended to reinforce Hart's reputation as a bandit, this posed photo actually depicted her preferred style of dress. Courtesy of the Arizona Historical Society, Tucson, Ariz.

These four diverse renderings, all taken inside the territorial prison, suggest that someone wanted to capitalize on Pearl Hart's notoriety as an Arizona inmate by producing marketable souvenir photos. Courtesy of the Arizona Historical Society, Tucson, Ariz.

Mattie Lemmon, an illiterate Denver prostitute, as she appeared before her conviction in the death of a customer in Bell Warden's brothel. Courtesy of the Colorado Historical Society, Denver, Colo.

Mattie Lemmon died in the Colorado penitentiary less than three years after she began a decade-long sentence for murder. Courtesy of the Division of State Archives and Public Records, Denver, Colo.

Bell Warden, a Denver madam and hairdresser, in a studio portrait before she entered the Colorado penitentiary with Mattie Lemmon, one of her brothel employees. Courtesy of the Colorado Historical Society, Denver, Colo.

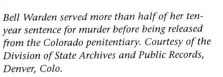

Bell Warden served more than half of her ten-year sentence for murder before being released from the Colorado penitentiary. Courtesy of the Division of State Archives and Public Records, Denver, Colo.

Jessie Berry Carmon in a family photograph many years after she left prison and built a successful marriage and family with Jack Neal. Courtesy of Ruth Georgen Atchison and Kenneth E. Georgen.

2 The Male Prison World

There was a sickening sense of loneliness
seemed to come over me when the great
iron bar was drawn and bolted.
    —Belle Harris
    Utah Territorial Penitentiary
    1883

In 1883 Belle Harris, a member of the Church of Jesus Christ of Latter-day Saints, refused to testify against her former husband, Clarence Merrill, in a polygamy trial; an unhappy federal judge sent Belle to prison until she complied with the court subpoena.[1] Driven not by loyalty to the man who had abandoned her and two small children but by her distaste for government coercion, Belle entered the Utah penitentiary as its first woman prisoner. Territorial Utah, locked in a religious and civil struggle with its Mormon constituency, gingerly faced the incarceration of a woman, along with her infant son.[2] Although Belle suffered both physically and emotionally during her confinement, many aspects of her imprisonment differed radically from the usual routines of women prisoners.

On Belle's first day in prison, Emmeline B. Wells, Isabelle Horne, Ellen C.

Louisa C. Gifford, Colorado State Penitentiary.
Courtesy Division of State Archives and Public
Records, Denver, Colo.

49

Clawson, and Presondre L. Kimball, among the most prominent women in Mormondom, came to visit and offer sympathetic encouragement. On that occasion, they brought Belle a selection of delicacies, and thereafter a steady stream of visitors kept her carpeted room stocked with canned tomatoes, cherries, pears, blackberry jam, oysters, sardines, butter, lemon candy, nuts, crackers, and cakes.[3] One man, perhaps the grateful ex-husband, sent her a Moroccan leather–bound case lined with rose satin, in which she found a mirror, hair brush, combs, toothbrush, glass, buttonhook, and glove stretcher; two others took her infant son for a ride outside the penitentiary walls.[4]

Because she symbolized an injustice imposed on her community, Belle Harris enjoyed public support and sympathy uncommon to the woman prisoner. The friendship and sense of cause sustained her, as she steadfastly maintained her resistance to forced testimony. Unlike the censure that Jessie Carmon's law breaking heaped on her, Belle Harris's "criminality" brought her accolades. By the time she left the penitentiary in the fall of 1884, Belle Harris had gone from obscurity as an abandoned wife in rural Utah to celebrity as one of the most admired women in the territory.[5]

Perhaps because she entered a somewhat new penal system, perhaps because she could maintain direct contact with her church and her culture, perhaps because some of her own mingled among the guards, perhaps because of her high public profile, Belle Harris left the penitentiary without knowing what it meant to have the full press of a prison environment descend upon her. In spite of that, her confinement nearly overwhelmed her. Belle endured ill health, personal humiliation, and stifling boredom before her release.[6] Her case demonstrated that even in the best of circumstances, women found the male penitentiary debilitating.

Four elements produced the environment inside a penitentiary: widespread fiscal corruption, conditions inappropriate for human habitation, institutionalized violence, and masculine community. The boundaries of the four often overlapped, compounding the impact of each single ingredient. Each contributed to shaping a world designed to be hostile to its main constituent—the prisoner; each helped to intensify that hostility when the constituent happened to be a woman.

Western prison organization, construction, and management fell within the province of men. That province ranged far outside the prison itself and began with the governors and legislators who authorized state expenditures. It spread to the contractors, architects, and builders who supervised the construction. Ultimately, it embraced the population inside the walls—the wardens, employees, guards, and male prisoners of any one penitentiary. Masculinity, in its social, economic, and political organization, controlled western prisons.

Women, closed out from voice and place inside the offices of govern-ment, assumed no overt role in decisions about early prison building or oversight of penitentiary routines. In the young communities of the West, public institutional management did not constitute one of the areas of fe-male influence in the 1860s. Even had their opinions been queried, wom-en in the post–Civil War West certainly would not have endorsed the min-gling of men and women that occurred in penitentiaries.[7]

As the nineteenth century rolled on, women broke a series of public barriers and began to sit on many kinds of welfare commissions and boards. Their new public stature did not mean that they could or even wanted to undo the masculine organization of the penal system. Rather than trans-forming the state penitentiary, women focused on demanding new correc-tion facilities for females, such as industrial farms and reform schools. With such institutions, they strove to remove women, literally, from the reach of male administrators, wardens, guards, and prisoners and substitute an entirely different concept of penal care. They directed their outreach to the youthful offender, believing that an all-woman correctional environment promised to reduce criminal recidivism and "save the fallen."[8]

These activists, women working for women, did not find themselves totally welcome in the male power structure, even after ten or twenty years of public service. At least Julia Perry, director of the Girls Industrial School at Beloit, Kansas, held that opinion. In 1913, on the occasion of her resig-nation, following a political controversy that pitted Perry against reform-er Lucy B. Johnston, the deposed director wrote a bitter letter to her former ardent supporter. Among her comments to Johnston about the male lead-ership in the state, Perry remarked, "there is not *one* there that appreciates women—they tolerate them but would down them any minute if they could."[9]

By the time women like Lucy Johnston and Julia Perry, in spite of the resistance of male politicians, built reputations as influential public figures, the boundaries of the penitentiary world had been drawn. Men built pen-itentiaries for men. It would not be until after the fact that male politicians and prison administrators, prodded by women reformers, acknowledged that new facilities had to be constructed, or, at a minimum, standing pris-ons adapted to accommodate women. In the meantime, women prisoners across the West lacked a gendered space within the penitentiary.

The first element that defined the atmosphere of the western peniten-tiary—widespread fiscal corruption—began with the political decision to build a prison and spread until it assumed a life of its own in the history of any one penitentiary. It derived its power from the fundamental in-efficiency that encumbered the entire penal system. The legacy of indeci-sion, slight legislative attention, and conflicting authorities that marked the emergence of western penitentiaries after 1865 took shape in a general regional confusion about prison management. That confusion aided and disguised unlimited graft and misuse of public office. These abuses swept through a penitentiary at its planning stage and took on more aggressive hues with each passing year, always moving the institution further and further from concerns for ethical public service.

By the end of the Civil War, well-established patterns of corruption strangled western penal systems. Their roots reached back into the formative days of local governments, even though the law sought to check abuses. Texas, for example, attempted through legislation to derail political self-interest in penitentiary matters, but failed to intervene at the first deviation from publicized guidelines.[10]

In 1848, the prison commissioners, state-selected agents for the business transactions of the penal system, yielded to the Walker County interests of committee member William Palmer and selected Huntsville as the site for the new penitentiary. In turn, the Texas legislature agreed to build on the land owned by Huntsville organizer and businessman Robert Smithers, a family name connected to the penitentiary for the next several generations. At the very least, the politicians and businessmen arranging the prison deal ignored a legislative charge to select a location with easy access to existing transportation. With Houston well over sixty miles away and nearby water transportation unreliable at best, the Huntsville penitentiary lurched off to a start that countermanded government intent.[11]

The problems of poor planning surfaced immediately, when prison construction slowed to a near standstill. The inaccessibility of good building materials, the scarcity of free artisans for skilled labor, and an unsatisfactory remuneration system for workers pointed to the careless and/or venal decisions that brought the prison to Huntsville. Fiscal irregularities plagued the project from the start, but several years passed before the legislature hired a financial officer to monitor all prison transactions.

The new position of penitentiary agent only compounded the illegal snarl. Politicians in Austin invested the prison superintendent and the financial agent at far distant Huntsville with wide powers and few counterchecks. The arrangement led to complaints and accusations against these officials from one governmental administration to the next. Questionable expenditures, shoddy bookkeeping, and yearly requests for increased appropriations emerged as the modus operandi of the Texas penitentiary.[12] Texans witnessed a series of scandals and investigating committees that characterized the state's penitentiary history.[13]

Small wonder that those outside the circle of prison administration had trouble keeping up with the fluid financial record keeping. In 1871, a special investigating committee reported that in its opinion former financial agents "had almost, if not entirely, ignored the debits . . . thereby injuring very seriously, the credit of the institution."[14] The penitentiary books, a haphazard tangle, made it impossible to give more than an estimate for the final audit figures. Part of the bookkeeping disorder the committee attributed to its inability to sort out the excessive charges made by county sheriffs for transporting prisoners to Huntsville. It cited such typical cases as one where a sheriff charged six hundred dollars for nine guards to escort six prisoners, and another where a trip of only eighty miles cost $240 for ten guards to convey ten prisoners.[15]

The financial trail proved just as difficult to follow within the regular annual penitentiary reports. For example, in 1874, the prison inspector commented on the overwhelming illiteracy among the 675 inmates, of whom he asserted no more than ten had attended school. Of the others, he thought possibly three-fourths could read and write slightly, while he doubted that the remainder knew the alphabet.[16] Further, he mentioned that the law allowed well-behaved convicts to write a letter once a week and he claimed the weekly mailings came to about two hundred letters. He then requested the prison lessees be reimbursed $1,000 for postage and stationery provided to inmates and an annual allocation of $500 be allowed to support the stationery budget of the inspector's office, including the convicts' paper and postage needs.[17]

Granted, some illiterates might have prevailed on more educated prisoners to write for them, thus accounting for the weekly postings from an institution with only ten truly literate inmates. This depended on a continuous stream of willing inmate amanuenses. Given the poor treatment of prisoners under the Ward and Dewey lessees, it remains difficult to understand how the few literate inmates, their generosity aside, could have produced two hundred letters a week and used $1,000 in stationery expenditures.[18]

Sometimes the stakes ran much higher than just stationery expenses. In 1880, the superintendent's report indicated that the lessees earned a credit of almost $200,000 for their improvements and additions to Huntsville and a second facility at Rusk. Given work completed and to be completed, Superintendent Thomas J. Goree estimated that currently the state owed lessees Cunningham and Ellis $37,420.14.

Elsewhere in the report Goree stated that the Huntsville prison had 282 unheated cells with limited ventilation for 600 prisoners. Wooden cell buildings stood against machine shop areas; the danger of a devastating fire kept guards and prisoners uneasy. But the lessees charged at least $1,967 for improvement in the cell area, $3,789 for additions to the dining room and chapel, and another $5,309 to the superintendent's residence.[19] If Texas citizens had stayed even slightly attuned to penitentiary business, they reasonably might have questioned how exactly the lessees spent state funds at the Huntsville location.

If the improvements seemed dubious, even more so was a charge of $10,659.85 for clothing and transportation expenses given to discharged prisoners. With 742 prisoners receiving discharges that year, the prison claimed that it invested an average of $14.36 (a new suit of clothing, plus five dollars for transportation) in each departure.[20] Yet one of the most common complaints of former prisoners concerned the refusal of wardens and guards to comply with these provisions.[21]

Few prisoners, with the gates of the pen swinging open, wanted to linger to dispute clothing with the discharge officer. Many prisoners stepped out into the world wearing an old suit removed from some other inmate during the in-take process. Officials simply recycled the personal clothing of those still in stripes and charged the state for the nonexistent new suits.[22] It required only a slight bookkeeping maneuver to bury thousands of dollars in stolen funds in a legitimate category in the annual report to the governor.

By 1911, the legion of administrators who siphoned off large chunks of prison-allocated funds for personal profit had not lessened. Further, some had even devised ways to expand their moneymaking schemes beyond the prison's state finances. One assistant manager at a Texas farm testified in a prison investigation that two white bookkeepers, one a citizen and one an inmate trusty, used their information about pending discharges to coerce black convicts into debt that would leave them penniless upon release.[23]

As a convict's term neared completion, the bookkeepers approached the inmate and offered to lend him money, since he was a "good Negro." The convict expected to use his overtime pay or ten cents per diem earnings to pay back the loan, but instead the debt, with its hefty interest rate, rumored to be 300 percent, just kept increasing. On the day of discharge, the two bookkeepers isolated the convict, assaulted him, and took any money due him at release. Anxious to leave the penitentiary alive, stung from a fresh beating, and aware of how tenuous freedom could be for black ex-convicts in Texas, the inmate usually signed a receipt for personal property received and left the prison empty-handed.[24]

Some of these fiscal problems stemmed from the state's failure to audit the prison system until 1909, more than fifty years after its organization. By that time, hundreds of thousands of dollars had lined the pockets of a collection of politicians, entrepreneurs, and prison officials. A 1911–12 committee investigating the Texas prisons was staggered by the penal system's indebtedness, which amounted to well over one million dollars, and protested vehemently a whole series of "unjustifiable expenditures." In an unusually forceful committee statement, members identified the central

cause of the corruption as "the idea, almost universal in penitentiary cir-
cles, that the penal system is a law unto itself." According to the committee, the blame for such a notion lay not only with prison officials but with
all citizens for treating the penitentiary as an "outlying province, responsible to no one but itself."[25]

In specific terms, the committee focused on fourteen hundred acres of
cultivated land, known as the Ransome Tract. Texas had poured almost
twenty thousand dollars, or three-fourths of the total cost, into Ransome
improvements—prison building, repairs to residences, construction of
ditches, building of roads—for what remained private property. Although
the arrangement allowed for state purchase of the property, nowhere did
the contract provide reimbursement to the state, should it decide not to
settle on the Ransome Tract. Further, a third party, rather than the property owner, had arranged the Ransome transaction with government officials, a point the committee found particularly sticking.[26]

The committee judged the organization, management, and finances of
the penitentiary to be in shambles, due to long years of malfeasance. It
complained about the general lack of efficiency throughout the system and
identified a major problem, despite the quick business acumen of Walker
County businessmen of an earlier day, as the "unfortunate locations" of
both the Huntsville and Rusk facilities. The committee declared neither
prison to be positioned in a useful or well-chosen site. Regardless of the
$120,000 poured into the 1880 improvements, this committee bemoaned
the "tremendous losses sustained . . . at Rusk since its establishment" and
declared the "property of comparatively little value."[27]

The tangled political administration of the Texas penitentiary by those
charged with its oversight was not singular. Through the West, neighbors
near and far accumulated similar records. In 1875, Arkansas overran its
$100,000 penitentiary improvement appropriation by at least $49,000, but
the institution reflected little of the investment and remained in disrepair.
The single new building began to show its shoddy construction quickly, as
the contractor's failure to seal the roof, concrete the floors, or install ven-
tilating flues became apparent.[28] The buildings continued to deteriorate
and in 1899, after a series of inadequate efforts to refurbish the facility,
Arkansas moved its penitentiary to another Little Rock location. In an ironic twist, Arkansas constructed the state capitol—symbol of the just processes of a democratic government—on the original prison grounds.

Also in 1875, selection of a site for the Arizona territorial prison replicated some of the local political maneuvering evident in Texas almost thirty years earlier. Two Yuma County members of the legislature removed the
word "Phoenix" from the authorizing resolution and substituted their own
locale. One of them, José María Redondo,[29] owned vast lands in Yuma

County and along with his colleague hoped to energize the area's economic development through the prison. Subsequently, Redondo gained direct access to all the purchasing contracts made for supplies to the penitentiary by serving on the board of prison commissioners.[30]

There followed the usual cycle of shortfall appropriations and shifting centers of authority. Arizona tried, without success, to streamline its business procedures and curtail expenses. In 1882, 1891, and 1893, gross financial irregularities prompted penitentiary investigations, all of which revealed that those in authority could not account for thousands of dollars in money and materials.[31]

The constant turnover in the political appointees who served on boards of commissioners and as wardens helped to generate the atmosphere of corruption that enveloped penitentiary matters. Even after years of building penal institutions, western states continued to grapple with the problems that stemmed from this rapid change in personnel. In 1892, when the Colorado State Board of Charities delivered its report at the National Conference of Charities and Correction, it primarily recommended that in the future political appointees be denied access to penitentiary positions.[32]

The next year, however, this same board gave only the mildest reprimand to F. A. Raynolds for holding, without paying interest, thousands of penitentiary dollars in his own bank, contracting with his own mill for penitentiary flour, leasing his own lands for penitentiary gardens, and using state funds to improve the sidewalk of his residence. Conceding that future contracts might better protect the interests of the state, the board, nonetheless, strongly urged that the governor make no change in the prison management.[33]

In 1896 and again in 1899, the same board noted familiar stories—the political "spoils" system, with its constant new patronage appointees, ruined the chances for progressive penitentiary management, somehow past appropriations had not resulted in authorized improvements, and the penitentiary teetered along in an unsafe condition.[34] Over the preceding thirty years, those involved in Colorado's penitentiary business had joined their peers in other western states in blazing a trail of embezzlement and thievery.

In beleaguered Colorado, yet another investigation in 1910 uncovered a felonious practice, facilitated by the exclusion of inmates from management of their own affairs. The attorney general, John T. Barnett, charged that the warden deposited the personal money of prisoners, as well as their convict earnings, into his own account with his private funds. With all these monies conveniently mingled, the warden used the account for his personal expenditures.

Further, the warden had access to the state's prison funds and had drawn regularly on them for his own business affairs; when that account ran to overdrafts, the unwitting state paid the resulting interest charges.[35] Along with the warden, the prison commissioners had participated in the misuse of funds, purchasing huge quantities of coal and lumber, none of which they had delivered to the penitentiary. At the prison, accountants kept no records to show delivery of goods and submitted no vouchers to the state auditor. In the face of this information, the local district attorney still refused to prosecute the offenders.[36]

Barnett, understandably frustrated, hoped to have better success in the civil and criminal courts, with charges against a former secretary of the board of pardons. This state employee solicited money in return for scheduling a pardon or parole hearing. The ousted secretary apparently traveled about Colorado and aggressively sought out the families and friends of those incarcerated. He indicated that only a bribe of several hundred dollars guaranteed the imprisoned loved one a chance of early release.[37] Despite Barnett's optimism about the prosecution, the case had been thrown out of court twice, as local authorities showed themselves reluctant to bring an indictment.

The pervasive graft and corruption did not limit itself to business and political transactions outside the penitentiary. The easy opportunities for politicians and political appointees to profit from penitentiary service and the few repercussions for this behavior colored the atmosphere inside the walls as well. Wardens and guards each day witnessed the tangible results of the malfeasance and seized their own opportunities to skim off profits. Few resisted the chance to bilk the state.[38] The corruption created a spirit among public servants that money allocated for the penitentiary could and should be used for personal gain. Through the nineteenth and into the twentieth century, an aura of the acceptability and inevitability of material corruption encompassed the western penitentiary.

The widespread use of political position to divert public funds led directly to the second element in the prison environment—conditions inappropriate for human habitation. With the unceasing illicit drain on the limited funds designated for construction and maintenance, prison facilities never rose above inadequacy or obsolescence. That reality clashed with the growing prison populations of the nineteenth century. As the West continued to draw more residents, as contractors wanted larger labor pools for state-run industries, and as states used the penitentiary to retain social control over persons of color, prison registers began to fill.[39] The facilities needed to shelter the growing numbers, in even a modicum of decency, did not mushroom in parallel fashion.

Almost before a prison opened, officials declared it would not meet growing demands for prisoner housing. The shortage of cells was only one indicator of inferior prison structures from Nevada to Iowa to Missouri to Arkansas. It played, however, a major role in the deterioration of prisoner well-being, both physically and mentally. Few prisoners would not have agreed that living arrangements inside a penitentiary violated the domestic custom of any of their cultures.

For example, Wyoming opened its territorial prison, built with single bunk cells for forty-two inmates, in 1873, but only four years later almost eighty prisoners packed the crowded facility.[40] As early as 1872, the outgoing inspector of the Texas penitentiary warned of overcrowding at the prison and urged the completion of at least one new facility for the state.[41] In Arkansas, inmate numbers ballooned during the same period, increasing from 117 in April of 1869 to 199 by the end of 1870.[42] In 1878, a visiting committee at the Anamosa prison, in Iowa, declared the convicts to be in good health, although 177 prisoners lived in ninety-three small cells designed for single occupancy.[43] Colorado opened its territorial prison in 1871 with "forty-two cells, entirely inadequate under the frontier conditions of that period," improved it every year, and in 1903 again declared the three cell houses "entirely inadequate."[44] In Missouri, the cell house roof leaked to the point of collapse, prisoners shivered during bitterly cold winter nights without heat, and sweltered during the summer with six prisoners confined to one room.[45] In Minnesota, nothing seemed to rid the cells of bedbugs, despite an official boast that inmates kept the facility remarkably clean.[46]

Coupled with the overcrowding and inferior facilities, insufficient drinking water and primitive sewage systems further outlined the prison landscape. Located on the least desirable acreage and hampered by the vicissitudes of local geology, poor drainage, and inferior sewer construction, penitentiaries did little to promote basic sanitation and personal hygiene. Even in a nineteenth-century world of outhouses and chamber pots, prisons surpassed the rest of society in creating a squalid horizon.

Prison sewage removal, often connected to the system of the nearest town, added to a general growing crisis in western urban disposal and significantly lowered the quality of life inside the walls. These issues concerned Minnesota professor William W. Folwell, who, in 1888, addressed the state historical society meeting on matters relevant to western cities and their neighbors at the penitentiary. On that occasion, Folwell identified four factors critical to sanitary maintenance. These included: a well drained terrain, an abundant supply of pure water, the uninterrupted access to fresh air for all passages and enclosures, and the removal of filth and rubbish of every kind.[47] Western prisons generally violated each of the criteria Folwell called essential for basic sanitation.

Devoting most of his talk to proper methods for removing human excreta, Folwell did not paint a very favorable picture of western sanitation practices. He condemned any system that allowed raw sewage to run into closed underground drains, from which deadly gases could seep into human living areas. Folwell also disliked the "water-carriage" system, wherein all fecal matter ran into a "common sewer to float off to the point of discharge." He ruefully acknowledged the latter process was so cheap, it would probably be retained by city governments for years.[48]

Basically, the two systems of sewage removal Folwell criticized most severely dominated western prisons for over fifty years. For example, the Missouri prison operated for almost twenty years before it did away with its common privy in 1866. The privy, little more than a crude open trough, gave way to a few water closets installed in the shop buildings. No water closets graced the cell area, where slop buckets remained in use for lockdown hours. The warden hoped for a "complete system of sewerage" and "an abundant supply of water" that would "pay ten fold [their] cost in the healthful cleanliness of the institution."[49]

With these systemic drawbacks at the prison, personal hygiene barely improved for the three hundred convicts with the completion of a small bathroom. This addition, equipped with one or two tubs for the whole prison, prompted the warden to require each prisoner to "bathe" once a week. The bathroom, little more than a shed, also served as the in-take location for inmates to strip naked, give up their clothing, submit to a physical, and have a mandatory haircut, shave, and bath upon arrival at the prison.[50] After that day, prisoners seldom had as much organized attention given to their personal hygiene.

Iowa, also concerned about its rapidly growing prison population, looked for a number of solutions to its sanitation difficulties at Anamosa, which opened in 1872. Recognizing that a sealed off penitentiary, where inmate numbers steadily rose, led to inevitable health problems, the prison committee in 1878 insisted that a sewer be built "to drain the constant production of filth." The committee included in its recommendation that the sewer system empty below the point at which the water works secured its supply—an obvious suggestion but not for a prison beset by a history of mismanagement.[51]

In Arkansas in the 1860s, prisoner cells had neither ventilation nor light. Prisoners shared dark, bug-infested cells, using common waste buckets.[52] The stench-filled stagnant air reeked of noxious gases, widely recognized as highly toxic to the human respiratory system. A new cell building constructed in 1885 lacked flues for ventilation and, in 1891, the Arkansas penitentiary still needed a sewer system. Warnings from such experts as William Folwell aside, the state ultimately contracted for a sewer to drain directly into the Arkansas River.[53]

Proximity to a river compounded, rather than alleviated, sewer and water supply problems for some facilities. The closeness of the Gila and Colorado Rivers to the Yuma territorial prison exacerbated sanitation difficulties at the outpost penitentiary. The original system, installed under Superintendent John Behan, gave off the fetid gases so conducive to illness. The drinking water, thick with mud and laced with minerals, was more than just unpalatable, adding to the unhealthy environment. Into the twentieth century, the need for fresh water and a decent sewage system heightened the disorder at the Yuma location.[54]

In the early 1900s, Louisiana introduced a series of sanitation reforms, including an improved diet, intended to reduce prisoner mortality. The lack of a sewer system in the hot humid swamps, where men urinated and defecated into the ground, remained a major obstacle to good health. At the steamy prison, diarrhea and dysentery ran rampant, keeping mortality figures high.

Authorities, convinced that the area's sandy loam soil trapped the effluvia only to release it in more poisonous form, considered constructing cement ditches to carry off the human waste from the earthen urinals.[55] Despite this official interest in possible ways to reduce filth, only three years later the monthly expenses for the Louisiana penitentiary at Angola included the almost stunning notation, "$6.50 for toilet paper (for free personnel)."[56] As one more element in their mechanisms, prison officials, while acknowledging that poor sanitation contributed to high death rates, continued to deny inmates even the most basic materials for personal body care.

The conditions at Angola were not simply an unavoidable by-product of local geography. Other prisons in other regions also could not or would not solve water and sanitation difficulties. As late as 1904, Idaho had not resolved its historic problem with an irregular water supply. Although spring runoff from the nearby foothills threatened to inundate the penitentiary buildings with an unwanted rush of water, a clean supply for drinking remained elusive. From 1890 until 1903, authorities insisted they had no reliable source of drinking water.

In 1903, the warden reported that a nearby spring had dried to such a low level it could no longer supply the daily water.[57] Also, an artesian well that once gave off hot mineral water for bathing appeared to have nearly evaporated. In response to the ever growing water crisis at the prison, the 1903 legislature appropriated $20,000 for construction of a water works.

A political dispute over the location of the new water supply left the matter at a standstill, and the prisoners without access to a fundamental human need. Two years later, the lack of a proper water supply continued to torment the Idaho penitentiary. Efforts in 1905 to link a tunnel to a good water source ended in failure, and by 1907 only about five and one-half miles of a seven-and-a-half-mile irrigation ditch to the prison had been completed.[58]

As the water crisis dragged on, the shoddy provisions for sewage disposal at the prison added to the sanitation problems. Eventually, the warden installed a main sewer pipe, as well as some smaller connecting pipes from various buildings. As Idaho tried to push its sewer system into a more modern mode, it did so by emptying the prison sewage directly into the Boise River.[59] Not until 1907 did the penitentiary alleviate some of these difficulties by connecting its sewer system to that of Boise City.[60]

The inferior water supply and sewerage systems for penitentiaries produced filthy, vermin-filled facilities. Housing accommodations from state to state rivaled each other for crudeness and overcrowding. This failure to deliver the most basic human amenities was not confined to any one institution or penitentiary administration. Throughout the West, the prison environment spread disease, sickened inmates, and reduced the chances that a prisoner would survive incarceration.

That image fits well with nineteenth-century prison history, with its great need for reform. In fact, inmates of the twentieth century—regardless of how many investigative reports had appeared—did not find life inside a prison very different from that of fifty years earlier.[61] In 1910, dripping wet inmates at the Texas farm camps left their mud-soaked clothing on a post to dry in a crowded bunkhouse, infested with lice and cockroaches. Naked men—sorting themselves out by race—bunked together on common three-tiered beds made of corn cobs stuffed into rough sacks. Their one shower a week was a community affair; inmates grouped by tens stood in an open pit inside the bunkhouse to be hosed off with cold water. Lye soap, bath towels, underclothing, socks—these luxuries existed only for those inmates with the money to purchase them.[62]

But beyond the obvious day-to-day squalor of the prison environment, this universal disregard for the rudiments of human maintenance underscored the way in which penitentiary managers, all agents of the state, inflated political control to encompass fundamental matters of biology. Satisfied to make halfhearted improvements at best, states allowed housing conditions and sanitation ills to go unchecked for decades, always asserting to prisoners the worthlessness of their own bodies. In an atmosphere charged with power differences, denial of basic human cleanliness became one more twist in spiraling prisoner indignity.

No male prisoners, drawn largely from Euro American, African American, and Mexican American communities, came from a cultural background compatible with the housing and hygiene of the prison. Even among those from the most rural or unsophisticated homes, cultural standards ordered living arrangements and hygienic practices. Penitentiary life denied that those standards existed and isolated prisoners from the rituals of their own upbringing. Disgusting filth, with its debilitating mental malaise and physical ills, promoted loss of human dignity and early death. Given this aura of disorder, it is not surprising that violence rushed to fill the vacuum created when society removed individuals from their own cultures and drummed into them each day the cheapness of human life. In the prison world, violence, an unpredictable but ever-present ingredient, energized the daily routines. This third element in the construction of the prison environment—institutionalized violence—organized around a layered hierarchy that flowed from officers to prisoners and back again. In this exchange, race and class often determined, not just privilege, but avoidance of the most terrifying punishments and an ugly death.

The first layer of violence rested with the government. Under the guise of discipline and "corrective" measures, state-sanctioned punishment not only took on a violent character but transmuted into every sort of torture.[63] The ultimate goal, to impress convicts with the undisputed power of the state, bonded in the West with unchallenged personal brutality.

In 1874, the Kansas board of commissioners endorsed the system of punishment used at the penitentiary and insisted that corrections not be inflicted in an indiscriminate manner. It listed as its mild punishments: use of the ball and chain, confinement on limited food and water, deprivation of light in the cell, removal of articles of bedding or reading and writing materials.[64] Further, the board pontificated, "Nothing can be accomplished for good by humiliating and paining a man who is powerless."[65]

Despite these assurances, in 1890 former Kansas prisoner John N. Reynolds charged that officials used a ten-day sentence to the dungeon, where temperatures dropped in winter below zero and in summer rose to over 100 degrees, as the common punishment for any infraction. If especially recalcitrant, an inmate was stripped, tied to a post, and a cold hose "turned upon his naked body."[66] Despite legislation that prohibited the use of the strap and the whip, as late as 1910 the Kansas penitentiary used punishments that violated both the spirit and the letter of the law.[67]

Punishment, state prison boards insisted, should be guided by precise regulation, a principle intended to measure discipline and standardize it. In Texas, the law required guards to secure a written whipping order from a supervisor, limit the number of lashes to thirty-nine, and confine the beating to the area below the waist. These rules, observed more in the breech than the practice, meant little to guards who assaulted prisoners far beyond the heinous boundaries allowed. Over many years, Texas convicts knew about the "hide house," where guards lashed naked prisoners to an iron post and flogged them from head to toe.[68]

One former inmate, Henry Tomlin, dismissed state laws as ineffective and ridiculed the idea that officials kept accurate records about disciplinary procedures. Only the legal limit of thirty-nine lashes appeared in punishment registers, although Tomlin insisted that guards routinely gave one hundred strokes, poured iodine into the wounds, and left the inmate to recover on the concrete floor of solitary.[69] Without admitting their legal violations, guards still recorded staggering procedures in punishment registers. Routinely prisoners went to the dark cell for twelve hours to several weeks, were handcuffed to the cell door, strung up by their heels, and lashed.[70]

Although prisoners knew these punishments came swiftly and often, they felt that such torments should have limitations. When an administration exceeded those boundaries for an extended period of time, some prisoners risked voicing their complaints. In 1907, five inmates wrote to Acting Governor J. W. Raynolds, reporting the "inhumane punishment for petty offense, and colossal brutality for ordinary ones" of Arthur Trelford, superintendent of the New Mexico penitentiary. They compared Trelford to the previous superintendent under whom "Order was kept without resorting to cruelty" and begged for an official investigation.[71] The request granted, their bold move had met with a success not expected by other inmates who refused to sign the letter for fear of the reprisals.

In 1910, several Texas prisoners showed themselves also ready to testify against overly zealous guards, even though to do so chanced life and limb. John Lenz, with five years in the system, indicated he had seen every possible horror inside the camps. He told of a white inmate who tried to escape after a whipping. Once the guards had apprehended the prisoner by shooting him in the neck, they allowed him to recover from the wound and then whipped him again.[72]

Not only did guards administer punishment but they forced inmates to participate in the ritual as well. By so doing, guards brought inmates into the punishment process and underscored convict vulnerability. H. W. Johnson, whipped at least three different times, described how four other prisoners held him, while a sergeant administered the flogging. Johnson reported he had seen as many as fifteen whippings in a day, none authorized by the mandatory written order. He told of a guard who tied a prisoner by the neck, hitched the rope over the saddle of a horse, started off at a trot, and dragged the convict beside, as another guard administered a beating. The committee heard from Johnson the chilling story of a twelve-year-old boy caught with matches in his pocket and whipped "unmercifully." He talked of a guard who made an inmate from a burial detail dance on the coffin of the deceased and on another day forced a convict to eat his own excrement.[73]

The unsparing savagery that permeated the system, the regularity of its occurrence, the indifference it generated, and the laws that perpetuated it guaranteed prisoners would see violence as one of the ordinary elements in their prison time.[74] In response, prisoners devised their own violent strategies. Sometimes they exercised these in open contests with guards, even though the outcome meant more physical abuse for themselves.

In Wyoming, a prisoner heaved a hot contraband pie into the face of a guard.[75] Others deliberately started fights with each other to test the quickness of the guards and to inflict as much damage on their jailers as possible before a relief team intervened. Escape attempts and prison mutinies pitted inmates and guards against each other like warring armies. Some eschewed physical confrontation and entered into a contest of wills with guards, as did Henry Tomlin in Texas. Tomlin viewed his challenge to one guard as a match of intellects, in which he triumphed because "I met his cunning with cunning and mystery."[76]

Others entered into the violence of the prison world by bonding with the administration and in both subtle and overt ways adding to the malevolence. The inmate trusty system gave structure and legitimacy to prisoner violence. Devised as a way to reduce the number of guards and, thus, cut the state payroll, the trusty plan quickly changed from inmate reward to inmate elitism. Certain inmates rose above others who lacked the favor of the guards or the money to buy it. Designation as a trusty brought with it multiple rewards that literally made it possible for an inmate to survive incarceration.

In Texas, by the early twentieth century, the trusty system reigned as a regular feature at the prison camps. Prisoners understood that the range of privileges for "pet convicts" included a separate diet enjoyed in a private dining room, better quality clothing available upon request, sleeping quarters outside the bug-infested bunkhouses, and free Sundays to roam the prison yard.[77]

Trusties also enjoyed regular access to the outside community. It was not uncommon for an unescorted trusty to pick up freight or meet incoming officials at the train depot.[78] In Montana, in the 1890s, trusties worked on a variety of building projects in the Deer Lodge area, cooked in private homes, and went on a two-day fishing trip.[79]

Texas guards also used a complex reward system for trusties, both white and black, who routinely ran errands or hauled supplies through the community. On Sundays trusties attended picnics and fishing expeditions with guards and their families. At the Clemens Farm, favored trusties were permitted to have wives spend the weekend.[80]

In addition, guards often took African American trusties into Brazoria, a town close to the camp. There the trusties served as lookouts while the white guards visited black brothels, drank, and gambled. These occasions offered prisoners a chance to acquire tobacco and whiskey and have a sexual encounter; the trips only required they watch for the superintendent, carry inebriated guards back to the prison camp, and maintain complete silence if questioned by officials.[81]

But more than just hoarding personal privilege, trusties also participated in the overall oppression of other convicts. Trusties confiscated the few material goods distributed to the prisoners, reported on other inmates, and took part in the violence against them. The trusty system gave some convicts, usually whites with office skills or education, an opportunity to better their penitentiary position at the expense of other prisoners.[82]

The trusty plan appeared to offer good-conduct incentives to convicts while easing the cost of prison maintenance for the state. In truth, it was a program that encouraged corruption and furthered both passive and active violence. Trusties found their own chances for exploiting the graft opportunities they saw among those who ran the penitentiary for the state.[83] The system enhanced race and class divisions among inmates and it brought trusties into an alliance with officials against other prisoners.[84] Together guards and prisoners embraced the violence of the penitentiary, recognizing it as an operative in the daily routines. In all prisons, some inmates bargained their way into more personally agreeable situations. In so doing, they took action in an institution that allowed them little, but they also entered into and expanded the general corruption and violence of the prison.

The fourth element in the prison environment—masculine community—forged itself out of the reality of hundreds of men living in a confined space defined as the province of one gender. Male prisoners, wrapped in nineteenth-century definitions of masculinity, juggled the corruption and violence within a community of their own gender and devised responses to survive life in an inhumane setting. In very practical terms they did this in a world designed to have a male focus.

For example, the Wyoming territorial penitentiary opened in January 1873, but had no cells or toilet facilities for women until 1889.[85] In the 1860s, men and women prisoners in Arkansas shared cells and common waste buckets.[86] Nevada's prison operation got under way with just a few cells in 1862. Five years later, the primitive site did not have a water supply for bathing or a substantial wall around the property.[87] In a facility that limped along with a small well operated by hand pumps and did not construct a water works until 1879, women's accommodations did not generate much concern.[88] Arizona's territorial prison, little more than an adobe building and two stone cells, accepted its first fifteen convicts in 1876 but did not provide even the semblance of a female ward until 1897.[89]

More populous western states, with longer penal histories, planned, or failed to plan, prisons accordingly. Missouri had no intention of incarcerating women in the men's penitentiary and did not include female quarters in the building. An area designated the "female department" was so inadequate wardens pushed to have it abolished. The awkwardness caused by these inferior arrangements early on brought wardens to governors, seeking pardons for females.[90] By the time Governor Thomas C. Fletcher assumed office in January 1865, Missouri wardens had a long history of asking that women be released, requests that often bogged down in the slow-moving bureaucratic process. Fletcher showed himself generally receptive to these appeals, and, within two weeks of his ascent to the executive office, he pardoned Louise Emmerly, who had already served almost fourteen months at the male penitentiary.[91]

In neighboring Kansas, authorities intended to reserve penal institutions for male criminals as well. That intention fell by the wayside, as Kansas, with no state female facility, incarcerated women convicts at the penitentiary.[92] By 1883, Kansas had codified rules and regulations for the management of female prisoners, but the women remained inside the male facility.[93]

Finally, in 1916, Kansas moved to redo its prison arrangements for women. Spurred by the decision of the federal government to remove its twenty-six women prisoners to other institutions, Kansas sought new accommodations for the remaining sixteen state inmates. Bowing to mounting pressure for reform, authorities transferred the female inmates to an old house about one mile from the main penitentiary. The women, still under the supervision of the male facility, stayed in these rundown quarters until the female industrial farm opened the following year.[94]

Women simply did not fit into the housing plans of any prison, and in every location they were outnumbered by male inmates. Inmate registers attested to the raw numerical force of men versus women in all of the western prisons. For example, immediately after the Civil War, Texas held approximately 200 male prisoners and ten women. Within a year, more than 260 new prisoners, of whom only two or three were women, came to the Texas penal system. In the new prisoner group, a few white men mingled among the black male prisoners, but the women inmates included only African Americans.[95]

By 1870, the Texas prison population had climbed to 489 inmates and only four years later stood at 1,453.[96] In 1880, the superintendent for prisons reported an all-time high of 2,157 inmates, of whom the number of whites hovered around 2 percent.[97] The total number included thirty-six women, up from the dozen or so of the 1860s. Assigned to the main Huntsville prison, where 342 inmates worked, the women represented approximately 10 percent of those inside the walls.[98]

By 1912, Texas counted almost 3,500 prisoners in its state system. Most of these, blacks or Mexican Americans, worked under grueling conditions, farming cotton, sugar cane, and potatoes. Convinced of the "limited capacities of these races," the penitentiary board, displeased by the lack of complete racial segregation in the prison, recommended a formal policy reserving the farm camps for persons of color.[99] The board, relying on both intellectual and institutional racism, argued that nonwhites, who comprised about 70 percent of the prisoner population, could not "acquire technical knowledge," and if they did, could not "make use of such knowledge after release."[100]

The steady rise in convicts in Texas occurred, at least partially, because of the board's determination that the state needed a "considerable increase in the number of colored convicts" to ensure future profits for the agricultural camps.[101] Compliant counties around the state continued to run hundreds of African Americans through bogus court proceedings and ship them off to the penitentiary.[102]

To expedite the transfer of inmates from local jails to work farms and to reduce processing costs, the penitentiary board suggested a central railroad station be constructed for black and Mexican American prisoners. From this location, incoming nonwhite prisoners moved to their work sites, and those who managed to survive the camps could be released from the same depot. Criminal whites, otherwise repugnant to and rejected by their cultural counterparts, were "spared" contact with blacks. The manufacturing operations at Huntsville, "offering better opportunities for reformation work, providing useful technical knowledge after release and assuring greater intelligence and skill in workmanship," remained largely reserved for white prisoners.[103] In this manner, the state, with an aggressive policy of organized racism, furthered racial segregation, even to the extent of "protecting" its least acceptable white citizenry.

Committed to racial practices that kept blacks and Mexican Americans removed from white convicts as much as possible, officials bent the segregation rule slightly at the women's camp. At Eastham Camp, located twenty-three miles from the main prison, sixty-seven black women bunked in one house and three white women and one Mexican American woman shared quarters.[104] The black women, much as their foremothers had in slavery, performed all the heavy field labor for the production of corn and cotton. Although the seventy-one women inmates no longer had random daily contact with all the male prisoners, men continued to supervise the camp and trusties worked there. The benefit of separating the male and female prisoners, after years of scandal within the Huntsville walls, eluded the board, which complained about the additional costs for guards, physician, and chaplain at Eastham.[105]

To the west of Texas, Arizona's territorial prison also made the case for women's slight numbers in the male prison world. According to Paul E. Knepper, who has written extensively on the Arizona territorial prison system, between 1876 and 1909 only twenty-eight women passed through the gates at Yuma, while 3,000 men did so.[106] Over that stretch of time, wardens, guards, and prisoners came and went with no inkling of what it meant to have women present in the prison compound. Such a few women, less than 1 percent of the prison's population in a thirty-three-year period, guaranteed that the institution never had to consider its long-range response to dual gender needs.

When Warden James E. Gregg accepted charge of the New Mexico penitentiary on 20 August 1885, he had neither a large inmate population nor any women prisoners. Only sixty-two inmates had been incarcerated over the previous nine months, since early November 1884. Two Mexican American women had already been discharged and only forty-six of the men remained for Gregg's attention. Of the total group, the males came from among four cultural groups: one African American, twenty-four Anglos, one European, and thirty-five Mexican Americans.

Despite differences in cultural background, most of the personal characteristics of the prisoners fell into similar patterns. Their occupations included miner, butcher, tailor, barber, molder, carpenter, and a hefty collection of common laborers. Drawn from a region of limited economic diversity, none followed occupations that would have required advanced education nor classified them as "professionals."[107]

They ranged in age from seventeen to forty-eight, with at least forty-six men no older than thirty-five years. The youthfulness of the male prisoner population was not singular to New Mexico. In 1904, Idaho reported that of 167 prisoners, 115 fell between the ages of sixteen and thirty-five and in 1908, of 213 prisoners, 147 were between fifteen and thirty-five.[108]

Louisiana and Texas set their own particular records concerning the ages of male inmates. In the former state, where male inmates ranged in age from twelve and thirteen to the late twenties, one nine-year-old child did six months in the penitentiary before he was pardoned in 1874. During the same year in Texas, thirteen children under the age of fourteen, including one seven-year-old boy, served among adult prisoners, one-third of whom were under the age of twenty-one.[109]

In New Mexico, during the in-take process, some convicts volunteered the time at which they had moved out from the economic protection of their family. Fifty-one prisoners were able to pinpoint the time in life they saw themselves as self-supporting. Twenty-one said their self-reliance began before sixteen, ten of them at ten years old or younger. The ages for this youthful independence, which may not have included social separation from a family, crossed ethnic lines. It showed that, whether for economic need, cultural practice, or personal choice, by the time young men went to the penitentiary, most had acquired several years' experience negotiating the path of life, finding their own strategies for survival.[110]

The prisoners also shared common reasons for their crimes, explanations which reflected the stringent economy of the area. By far the most usual explanation given for law-breaking was drunkenness, although bad company and fighting ranked high as well. Others claimed hunger and at least three killed a steer for food. One got into a dispute about his wages, and one objected because another party used his name. In the crimes committed, the differences of the men narrowed even more. Convictions for some form of thievery sent thirty-two to the penitentiary; another twenty-two went for violent crimes, typically murder and manslaughter.[111]

This small collection of New Mexico prisoners pointed to the composition of male populations in western penitentiaries.[112] Overwhelmingly, occupants of western prisons were young men, accustomed to independence, in the fullness of their adult sexuality. Usually from the poorer classes of a community, convicts appeared to commit crimes based on the economy of their environments. Their occupations as laborers and artisans meant they knew how to work with their hands, but the formalities of education eluded many.[113]

As a group, male prisoners brought far more than masculine numbers to the penitentiary. Their manhood defined the cast and tone of the prison yard. Although wardens, contractors, and guards joined in an adversarial relationship with prisoners, all parties understood a common sense of gender and the stress of sexual deprivation. The presence of true homosexuals, not same-sex opportunists, may have meant some men did not share an identical view of gender, but each nonetheless knew of the ritual and expectations of masculinity.[114]

This meant that woven into the brutality of the prison was a shared understanding of its dynamic for men. Even in the unattractive conditions of the prison, male inmates found humor, using masculine standards of a joke. In 1910, Sam Tubbs, a Texas trusty inmate, refused to criticize the prison sanitation, even when asked about the condition of the night waste bucket. He suggested the unscrubbed wooden bucket represented no great offensive hardship, as prisoners trained themselves not to use it during night hours. Then he explained, almost with good cheer, the male humor of the circumstance: "The boys perfume the room more without using the bucket than they do with it; seem to enjoy that part of it; that is part of the prison."[115]

The exchanges between prisoners and guards involved more than watched and watcher. The possibility always existed that each could step aside from his prison role and construct interactions based on masculine terms. When it occurred, the camaraderie between prisoners and guards surfaced unexpectedly, but needed no explanation.

A Wyoming convict, for whom suspicion and dislike characterized his relationships with law enforcement officers, reluctantly conceded this masculine point. On two different occasions, during transfer to the penitentiary, the escort surprised the convict with a gift of cigars. One episode actually took on the show of male dining, despite that the guard kept the prisoner chained around waist, ankles, and hands.

After a day of excruciating travel, the sheriff took the convict to a local restaurant for supper. Following the meal shared at table together, the pair returned to the depot to wait for the connecting train to Rawlins. Without comment, the guard lit a cigar, freed the prisoner's hand, and retired to the other side of the waiting room, leaving the convict to enjoy the decidedly masculine after-dinner treat.[116]

Everyone understood the ephemeral nature of such indulgences, but they eased the otherwise taxing existence. If prisoners could win the approval of administrators, the prison activities might take on almost normal hues. When Warden Felix Alston of Wyoming decided he liked the inmate baseball team, he endorsed it beyond the prisoners' expectations.

Within a short time, the warden had the team outfitted in excellent uniforms and supplied with the best equipment. Proud of their progress, the warden took the prisoners to town for a game with local citizens. Their victories and the enjoyment of organized sporting activity dissipated when Alston received orders to hang the star catcher, who until one month before his execution mingled with the prison population and dazzled the town with his baseball skills. The catcher went to the gallows, officials transferred the captain of the team to a work detail, and baseball at the Wyoming penitentiary collapsed.[117]

As Warden Alston demonstrated, the masculine bonding of prisoners and guards had its limitations. Still, it provided a common basis for understanding the procedures, latitudes, and constraints of the prison community. As the nineteenth century shaped some western men into legends and heroes, the criminal behind bars was not left out of the manliness of the West. Masculine community gave male prisoners a standard, one that had emerging regional hues, from which to negotiate their place within the system.

Whatever their individual sense of masculine demeanor, both the prisoners and guards also brought with them, along with personal cultural identities, their world experiences of work, poverty, class discrimination, and violence. Embedded in these life forces were their gender definitions, commitments, perceptions, and biases, in reference to themselves and to women. While men and women in all societies constructed strategies for dealing with each other, male inmates found that prison suspended those practices. Many at the height of their male potency entered a prison cell never expecting to have sexual or social contact with women during the length of their incarceration. They had no reason to anticipate that the gender interactions of any culture would be an ingredient in their imprisonment.

Thus, the gender attitudes of male prisoners froze into the ideas they held about women as teenagers and young men. The penitentiary inhibited the maturing of inmates' male and sexual conduct and removed young men from the gender training grounds of their own cultures. If male prisoners clung to personal memories, values, hopes for future relationships, the prison environment quickly disabused them of any lingering notions of civility. The monotony of prison, real and imagined injustices, and racial antagonisms added to the reality of sexual deprivation for which prisoners had no preparation. Divorced from the outside society, young men entered into a state of limited sexual opportunity. Their new sexual lives depended on masturbation, same sex encounters with other inmates and guards, fanciful discussions, or the occasional female partner—wife, woman friend, or prostitute—arranged through bribing a jailer.[118]

Overall, the pervasive fiscal corruption, the unsuitable and inhumane conditions in prisons, the institutionalized nature of violence, and the force of masculine community created a powerful but destructive prison world. When these forces coalesced suddenly, they had the potential to unleash a fury of race, class, and gender. Anything could and did happen, usually to the most vulnerable inside the walls. When Wyoming inmates, ranchers incarcerated for vigilante activity, organized and carried out the lynching of an unpopular black inmate, administrators and politicians drew a curtain of silence around the incident. In a prison where inmates did ten days in the hole for the slightest infraction, this grotesque murder resulted in no investigation or punishments.[119]

Regardless of what triggered the explosions, the results made the penitentiary a world of excesses. Male prisoners, especially those of color, faced a range of hardships and abuses. Their health broke. Their mortality rates soared. To endure and survive, they anchored themselves in the masculine world, as they understood it.

In this environment grounded in intense distrust, suspicion, and hatred, hostility toward women resonated without obstruction. The women, just a few at a time, who entered this world confronted a society polarized in its race, class, and gender relationships. Corruption moved easily from abuse of material goods to abuse of humans, unfit housing took on extraordinary meaning for women, the nature of the masculine community closed them out, and the violence engulfed them.

In the prison, human biology assumed new importance as a powerful weapon in control of all prisoners. For a woman prisoner, whose very definition society grounded in biology, this only further delineated her tenuous position within the male-driven penitentiaries. A complete lack of privacy for toilet and bathing, the onset of a monthly period, the prospects of pregnancy, and the stresses of childbirth—all these created female needs for which the male prison world had no accommodation.

Further, the absence of a diverse community of women, such as could be found in free society, intensified the difficulties faced by women inmates. In a town or city, the presence of many different kinds and groups of women diluted the impact of the male hierarchy, in its many forms. In private, women exercised familial and cultural power. In public, they gave visual witness to the ritual and tradition of gender interactions in all cultures. Even if the women who entered the penitentiary had little or no contact with those of other cultural groups and class standing, all together defined femaleness to the open society that a prison lacked. Within the penitentiary world, neither by sight nor sound did men observe and learn to adjust to the changing womanhood of the nineteenth and early twentieth centuries.

When Lottie Franklin, alias Alice Foster, alias Eliza Sánchez, shot and killed a vagrant with whom she shared a house, Montana newspapers went beyond declaring her guilty before her trial. One editor commented, "she is very depraved and will probably be better off in the penitentiary than anywhere else."[120] Within three weeks of the killing, Lottie, under the name Felicita Sánchez, entered the Montana penitentiary as its first female inmate.[121]

Small wonder that the guards at the Montana penitentiary greeted their first woman inmate with sniggering jokes and job resignations. In the prison world, with its corruption, filth, violence, and single gender perspective, men really had no preparation for bonding the definitions of woman and prisoner. For women, the prison world offered an unshaded landscape of masculinity.

Notes

1. Albert Silas Harris, "Life of Belle Harris Nelson: 1861–1938," photocopy of typescript, pp. 14–20, MS. 1818, folder 1, CLDS.

2. In 1882, a judge ordered Annie Gallifant to the penitentiary for refusing to answer questions about her polygamous husband. Gallifant, who was pregnant at the time, was held for a few hours and released (*Ogden (Utah) Daily Herald,* 19, 20 Nov. 1882, clippings in *Journal History,* CLDS). Mormon men were the primary targets during the period of federal arrests for polygamy, although both husbands and wives went underground to avoid prosecution. Sometimes authorities arrested a wife to flush out a husband, as in the case of Joseph Perry, who surrendered so that his wives

would not be required to testify. Once the husband was in custody, charges against the women were dropped. Perry subsequently served six months in the penitentiary, which he dubbed "the great reformatory schooll [*sic*] of Uncle Sam" (Joseph Perry, Autobiography, 1908, typescript, pp. 30, 57, MS. 5709, Access. 21274, CLDS).

3. Albert Silas Harris, "Life of Belle Harris Nelson," pp. 43, 45, 61, 62.

4. Ibid., pp. 53, 62.

5. Known later in life as Belle Harris Nelson, this woman seemed to find her defining life moments in her incarceration. Prison brought her power and attention. After her release a promising new marriage ended badly, as she grew stifled by the demands of child rearing and her absence from the field of public action (ibid., pp. 84, 96–98).

6. Extensive coverage of Belle Harris's unusual story is found in the *Deseret Evening News*, 17 May 1883–1 Sept. 1884. Most detailed articles appeared during the summer of 1883.

7. Estelle B. Freedman discusses the stages through which American women moved as reformers, developing their insistence on separate facilities in *Their Sisters' Keepers*, esp. pp. 46–58. In the West, women began to take their places on state boards of charity and reform by the 1890s. For example, Dr. Minnie T. C. Love served in Colorado in 1893, and Kate Barnard created a reform stir in Oklahoma and Kansas in the early twentieth century (*Third Biennial Report of the State Board of Charities and Corrections*, p. 7, CSA; and Harvey Hougen, "Kate Barnard and the Kansas Penitentiary Scandal, 1908–1909," *Journal of the West* 17 [1978]: 9–18).

8. Freedman, *Their Sisters' Keepers*, pp. 50–58.

9. Julia Perry to Lucy B. Johnston, 4 July 1913, Lucy B. Johnston Papers, General Correspondence, collection 61, box 16, KSHS.

10. For a complete history of the Texas prison, see Donald R. Walker, *Penology for Profit: A History of the Texas Prison System, 1867–1912* (College Station: Texas A&M University Press, 1988).

11. Crow, "Political History of the Texas Penal System," pp. 35–38.

12. Ibid., pp. 40–41, 43–44.

13. Ibid., pp. 48, 52, 63–65, 71. See also "we should inquire into the financial affairs and general management of the institution . . . for the reason that various committees have been sent . . . for similar purposes under other administrations" (*Report of Special Committee on Penitentiary*, 1871, p. 1, TSA); also "From time to time the people of Texas have been officially advised of these conditions" (*Report of the Penitentiary Investigating Committee*, p. 19, TSA; *Record of Evidence and Statements before the Penitentiary Investigating Committee*, 1911–12, TSA).

14. *Report of Special Committee on Penitentiary*, 1871, p. 1, TSA.

15. Ibid., pp. 8–9.

16. *Reports on the Condition of the State Penitentiary*, 1873–74, p. 11, TSA.

17. Ibid., p. 12.

18. In 1874, penitentiary officials in Kansas, after receiving starving military prisoners from Texas, castigated Ward and Dewey for the conditions under their lease system (Board of Commissioners of Public Institutions, *Second Annual Report*, 1874, pp. 338–53, UKKC). For a complete and balanced assessment of the Ward-Dewey lease, see Walker, *Penology for Profit*, pp. 29–45.

19. *Biennial Report of the Directors and Superintendent of the Texas State Penitentiary*, 1880, pp. 11, 22–24, 37, TSA.

20. Ibid., p. 56. The amount allowed for discharge seems high given that the state did not even accept responsibility for feeding prisoners until 1898, at a rate of $4.50 per convict per month or a daily food allowance of fifteen cents per person

(*Record of Evidence and Statements before the Penitentiary Investigating Committee,* 1911–12, p. 3, TSA).

21. Ibid., p. 11; the *Fourth Biennial Report of the State Board of Charities and Corrections* reported, "In most penitentiaries, . . . he [the prisoner] is furnished with a suit of clothes and enough money to pay his fare to the city or county seat where he had formerly been convicted" (p. 129, CSA).

22. On leaving the Wyoming prison, one convict wrote, "I was handed a suit of clothes, underwear, hat, shirt and shoes. . . . the clothes would hardly hold together long enough to get them on" (*Sweet Smell of Sagebrush,* p. 17).

23. *Record of Evidence and Statements before the Penitentiary Investigating Committee,* 1913, pp. 254–55, TSA.

24. The bookkeepers, several guards, and black inmates testifying before the same committee denied the loan-sharking scheme existed at the farm (ibid., pp. 345–76). As for attitudes of black inmates toward these practices, the historian Donald R. Walker has said that "black Texans existed essentially outside the protections of the law," a circumstance that certainly made inmates wary of worsening their situation (*Penology for Profit,* p. 115).

25. *Record of Evidence and Statements before the Penitentiary Investigating Committee,* 1913, p. 16, TSA.

26. Ibid., pp. 18–19.

27. Ibid., p. 27.

28. Hiram U. Ford, "A History of the Arkansas Penitentiary to 1900" (M.A. thesis, University of Arkansas, 1936), pp. 79–82.

29. In the documents used for this study no diacritical marks appeared for the names of any of the persons identified as "Mexican." The inclusion of these marks represents an attempt to conform to present-day usage, recognizing that this alters the historical documents. In addition, in the records all persons with Spanish surnames were labeled "Mexicans," though some were born in Mexico and others in U.S. territory. Some common Spanish surnames may appear to be presented incorrectly. Since the names were recorded under less than ideal circumstances (by a court stenographer or an inmate secretary of records), it is entirely possible that misspellings occurred. Some names may represent older forms that have been discontinued. I have used the terms "Spanish-speaking," "Hispanic," and "Mexican Americans" to refer to those with Spanish surnames. These terms do not reflect all trends in current usage, nor do they necessarily capture the terms of self-reference common to the Spanish-speaking people of the era considered. They do fit with the tone of the historical documents and serve to encompass persons whose birth location (in the United States or in Mexico) could not be determined with certainty. In quotations, I have retained racial slurs against all cultures that appeared in the historical record, as they serve to document the less visible but widespread forms of racism that touched women prisoners' lives.

30. Knepper, "Imprisonment and Society in Arizona Territory," pp. 80–81.

31. Ibid., pp. 221–24.

32. William P. Letchworth, *State Boards of Charities* (Boston: Geo. H. Ellis, 1892), pp. 19–20.

33. *Second Biennial Report of the State Board of Charities and Corrections,* 1894, pp. 13–16, CSA.

34. *Third Biennial Report of the State Board of Charities and Corrections,* 1897, p. 6; *Fourth Biennial Report of the State Board of Charities and Corrections,* 1899, p. 29, CSA.

35. *Biennial Report of the Attorney General of the State of Colorado,* 1909–10, pp. 11–13, CSA.

36. Ibid.

37. Ibid., pp. 10–11.

38. For examples, see activities of Warden Thomas P. Gable in Report of the Special Committee to Investigate the Penitentiary, 29th Legislative Assembly, Dec. 1890–Feb. 1891, Territorial Records, reel 9, frames 431–78, NMSA; and Superintendent Arthur Trelford in "Removal of Arthur Trelford, Superintendent of the Penitentiary, 1907," Governor's Papers, George Curry, 1907-10, special issues, reel 178, frames 177–291, NMSA; concerning Warden Seth Chase of Kansas, see Amos B. Ferguson to Governor Edmund N. Morrill, 11 Apr., 5, 11, 12 May 1895, Governor Edmund N. Morrill Papers, State Agencies Files, box 3, folder 1, KSHS; for Warden Martin Heisey of Iowa, see "Investigation into the Taking of Supplies—Coal, Lard, Wheelbarrows, Etc., May 1876," in Governor's Office, series 8, Reports: Penitentiaries, Anamosa, box 11, ISA; Investigation of Warden Seth Craig, 1880, Transcript of Testimony, Governor's Office, series 8, Reports: Special Commission Investigations, boxes 16 and 17, ISA.

39. In 1866, the warden of the Missouri penitentiary stated in his annual report, "The increase in the number of convicts in the future can be estimated . . . with sufficient accuracy . . . that we shall have . . . a number of able-bodied laborers sufficient to keep our contracts full at all times" ("Warden's Report," *Biennial Report of the State Penitentiary, Journal of the House of Representatives of the State of Missouri: Appendix,* p. 550, MSA [Missouri penitentiary reports are located in the appendices of the House and Senate journals of the state legislature]).

40. Banner Associates, "Wyoming Territorial Penitentiary: Historic Structure Report, Penitentiary Structure," in author's possession, pp. 4, 6, 11.

41. Ed T. Randle, "Report of Inspector," *Report on the Condition of the State Penitentiary,* 1871-72, p. 6, TSA.

42. Ford, "History of the Arkansas Penitentiary to 1900," p. 75.

43. Report of the Visiting Committee of the Additional Penitentiary at Anamosa [undated, marked "1878"], Governor's Office, series 8, Reports: 1877, box 13, ISA.

44. Wilbur Fisk Stone, ed., *History of Colorado,* vol. 1 (Chicago: S. J. Clarke Publishing, 1918), pp. 817-18.

45. "Warden's Report," *Biennial Report of the State Penitentiary,* p. 551, MSA; Mary Williams File, 23 May 1864, box 17, folder 43; Margaret Doyle, Jane O'Brien, Mary Clarey, Kate Fay, Rosa McMahan, Sarah Skelton File, 31 July 1866, both in box 21, folder 48, Missouri, Secretary of State, Pardon Papers, 1844-72, RG 5, MSA. Hereafter, Pardon Papers, RG 5, MSA.

46. W. C. Heilbron, *Convict Life at the Minnesota State Prison, Stillwater, Minnesota,* 2d ed. (St. Paul: Heilbron, 1909), p. 54.

47. William W. Folwell, "The Disposal of City Cleanings, a Presentation to the Eleventh Annual Session of the State Historical Society Meeting," in *Executive Documents of the State of Minnesota,* 1887-88, vol. 2, p. 335, MnHS.

48. Ibid., pp. 337, 344-45. Folwell denounced all current methods of waste removal and endorsed the early experiments with mechanical filtration.

49. "Warden's Report," *Biennial Report of the State Penitentiary,* p. 551, MSA. Neighboring Kansas had no regular culinary water either and used a wind pump to draw its daily supply from a nearby creek. This unreliable system was of no use on windless days, when gangs of convicts had to pump the water by hand, while others hauled the minimum required seventy-five barrels full to the prison yard (Board of Commissioners of Public Institutions, *Second Annual Report,* 1874, pp. 301-2, UKKC).

50. Henry Tomlin, *Henry Tomlin, the Man Who Fought the Brutality and Oppression of the Ring in the State of Texas for Eighteen Years and Won. The Story of How Men*

Traffic in the Liberties and Lives of Their Fellow Man (Ennis, Tex.: n.p., 1906), p. 16; *Sweet Smell of Sagebrush*, p. 9.

51. Report of the Visiting Committee of the Additional Penitentiary at Anamosa [undated, marked "1878"], p. 3; and Warden Heisey, Warden Investigation, 1877, Governor's Office, series 8, Reports: Special Commission Investigations, ISA.

52. Ford, "History of the Arkansas Penitentiary to 1900," pp. 75–76.

53. Ibid., pp. 82, 84. Just a few years later, the Colorado penitentiary had problems with water for the prisoners. When citizen water consumption fell off on Sundays, inmates were sent to work an irrigation ditch along the Arkansas River to shore up the supply for the prison (Board of Penitentiary Commissioners to Governor Charles S. Thomas, 13 Dec. 1899, Colorado Penitentiary Records, Miscellaneous Publications, Reports, Studies, CSA).

54. John Mason Jeffrey, *Adobe and Iron: The Story of the Arizona Territorial Prison* (La Jolla, Calif.: Prospect Avenue Press, 1969), pp. 39–43.

55. Roger S. Thomas, Asst. Warden, to Frank C. Blackburn, Warden, "History of Angola," 10 Apr. 1986, p. 4, LSP; one in a series of internal, unpublished historical reports circulated among various administrators at the Louisiana State Penitentiary and filed in the office of the assistant warden.

56. Ibid., 12 Mar. 1986, p. 4, LSP.

57. William E. Tydeman, "The Landscape of Incarceration: Idaho's Old Penitentiary," *Idaho Yesterdays* 38 (Summer 1994): 10–11.

58. "Report of the Warden," *Biennial Report of the Idaho State Penitentiary, 1907–8*, p. 4, ISL.

59. Ibid., 1903–4, pp. 9–11, ISL.

60. Ibid., 1905–6, p. 5; ibid., 1907–8, pp. 4–5, ISL.

61. The constancy of penitentiary conditions affirms the argument of Michel Foucault that a society has the prisons it desires and that reformation initiatives are not intended to alter the fundamentals of punishment (Foucault, *Discipline and Punish*, pp. 23–24, 49, 55–57, 80–82).

62. *Report of the Penitentiary Investigating Committee*, pp. 228–30, 237–38, 255, 262–64, TSA.

63. Foucault, *Discipline and Punish*, p. 8–10.

64. Board of Commissioners of Public Institutions, *Second Annual Report*, 1874, p. 305, UKKC.

65. Ibid., p. 314.

66. John N. Reynolds, *The Twin Hells: A Thrilling Narrative of Life in the Kansas and Missouri Penitentiaries* (Atchison, Kans.: Bee Publishing, 1890), pp. 90–97.

67. Governor George Hodges Papers, Correspondence, 1913–15, Board of Corrections: Investigations of Punishments, box 33, KSHS.

68. George, *Texas Convict*, pp. 157–61. According to former inmates who testified to the legislature, the use of the bat and whip were routine punishments in the 1920s (*It's Hell in a Texas Pen: The Barbarous Conditions as Told by the Ex-Convicts and Unearthed by the Legislature* ([Dallas?]: n.p., 1925).

69. Tomlin, *Henry Tomlin*, pp. 20–23.

70. See New Mexico Penitentiary Records, Punishment Record Book, 1885–1917, esp. pp. 20, 46, 95, 134, NMSA (hereafter, Punishment Record Book, NMSA); Punishment Register, Missouri State Penitentiary, 24 Mar. 1871–21 June 1881, 3 Jan. 1881–31 Dec. 1896, RG 213, MSA (hereafter, Punishment Register, MSA).

71. W. Mears, Claud Doane, J. S. Baca, A. March, and David Thomas to Acting Governor A. J. Raynolds, 15 June 1907, "Removal of Arthur Trelford, Superintendent

of the Penitentiary, 1907," Governor's Papers, George Curry, 1907–10, special issues, reel 178, frames 177–291, NMSA.

72. Testimony of Inmate John Lenz to the Investigating Committee, "Stenographer's Report of Evidence Adduced before the Penitentiary Investigating Committee," in *Report of the Penitentiary Investigating Committee,* p. 227, TSA.

73. Testimony of Inmate H. W. Johnson to the Investigating Committee, ibid., pp. 245, 247, 254–56, TSA.

74. For a full treatment of the experiences of male prisoners in Texas prisons, see Walker, *Penology for Profit,* esp. chap. 5.

75. *Sweet Smell of Sagebrush,* p. 87.

76. Tomlin, *Henry Tomlin,* p. 32.

77. Testimony of Inmates John Lenz, William Ogle, J. L. Price, Will Smith, H. H. Bullock, W. J. Dent to the Investigating Committee, "Stenographer's Report," in *Report of the Penitentiary Investigating Committee,* pp. 222–23, 233, 237, 242, 262, 284, 291, TSA.

78. Testimony of Inmates Bill Henderson, Sam Stiles, and Al Woods to the Investigating Committee, ibid., pp. 360–66.

79. Keith Edgerton, "Power, Punishment, and Work: The Montana Prison, 1889–1921," paper delivered at the Western History Association, Denver, Colo., 12 Oct. 1995.

80. Testimony of Inmates Bill Henderson, Sam Stiles, and Al Wood to the Investigating Committee, "Stenographer's Report," in *Report of the Penitentiary Investigating Committee,* pp. 360–66, TSA.

81. Testimony of Steward D. Mason, Captain E. B. Mills, Inmates Bill Henderson, Sam Stiles, and Al Woods to the Investigating Committee, ibid., pp. 346, 351, 360–66, TSA.

82. One former inmate of the Rusk prison in Texas declared that only those with "pull" or the "long green" secured trusty positions. These inmates, he said, would never give an honest account of the prison because they "have no kick coming." Denouncing a trusty as a "flunky," this inmate refused to work for the guards. Of the guards, he wrote, "I intended to devote a chapter to the . . . guards, but . . . I decided I would not defile a clean sheet of paper in any such way" (Charles C. Campbell, *Hell Exploded: An Exposition of Barbarous Cruelty and Prison Horrors* [Austin, Tex.: n.p., 1900], p. 30, UTBC).

83. In the 1890s, C. C. Leech, a former county treasurer imprisoned for embezzlement, managed the books at Huntsville and supervised the incoming prisoner mail, from which he pilfered the little money he found there (George, *Texas Convict,* pp. 208–9).

84. In Arizona, Anglo prisoners were assigned to be foremen over Mexican American work gangs, never the reverse (Knepper, "Imprisonment and Society in Arizona Territory," pp. 130–41, 301–20). Years after his release from the Texas system, Henry Tomlin complained bitterly about those occasions when African American trusties supervised white inmates (*Henry Tomlin,* p. 21).

85. Banner Associates, "Wyoming Territorial Penitentiary," pp. 9, 15.

86. Ford, "History of the Arkansas Penitentiary to 1900," pp. 75–76.

87. *Journal of the Senate during the Third Session of the Legislature of the State of Nevada,* 1867, p. 329, NSL.

88. First Biennial Message of His Excellency, Governor John H. Kinkead to the Legislature of the State of Nevada, 10th Session, 1881, p. 4, NSL.

89. Knepper, "Imprisonment and Society in Arizona Territory," pp. 82, 160; Jeffrey, *Adobe and Iron,* p. 25.

90. The first woman convict entered the Missouri penitentiary in 1842 (*Jefferson City Republican*, 28 May 1842). As early as 1844, a citizens' petition asked for the release of Martha Castro, who had just given birth in the prison. With winter approaching, no separate women's wing available, and the men's cells unheated, a pardon from Castro's five-year sentence seemed the only reasonable solution (Citizens' Petition to Governor John Edwards, 24 Nov. 1844, Martha Castro, Pardon Papers, box 2, folder 19, RG 5, MSA).

For other women dismissed because of inadequate facilities, in the same record group see also Ann Drumple, no. 1844, box 2, folder 20; Mary Green and Mary Hurley, 2 Mar. 1849, box 4 folder 36; Agnes Roach, 25 Oct. 1855, box 8, folder 16; Emily Morland, 1 Dec. 1855, box 8, folder 28; Sophia Ware, 28 July 1856, box 9, folder 20; Emily Moreland, Margaret Travers, Sarah Haycroft, and Eliza Sly ("pardoned on condition that they leave the state and not return during their natural lives"), 27 Feb. 1858, box 10, folder 6; Louise Flagg, 9 Dec. 1859, box 12, folder 3; Ellen Burns, Ellen Dwyer, Rose Madden, Henrietta Fitzgerald, 4 June 1861, box 15, folder 25; Mary Williams, 23 May 1864, box 17 folder 43.

91. Louise Emmerly, Pardon Papers, box 18, folder 39, RG 5, MSA. Governor Thomas Fletcher, dealing with post–Civil War conditions in Missouri, pardoned women on a fairly regular basis. For examples, in RG 5 see Sarah Fleming, Joana Smith, Elizabeth Woolman, 24 Feb. 1865, box 19, folder 8; Sarah King, 25 Feb. 1865, box 19, folder 9; Elizabeth Butler, 10 Mar. 1865, box 19, folder 20; Ann Stranger, 12 May 1865, box 19, folder 43; Mary J. Fields, Sarah Rhodes, Elizabeth White, Lauda Bowden, Lucinda Young, Alice Shaw, 19 Feb. 1866, box 21, folder 11; Margaret Johnson, Amanda Jackson, 28 May 1866, box 21, folder 29; Mary Cavanagh, 1 Oct. 1866, box 22, folder 11; Ann Divine, 7 Oct. 1868, box 27, folder 24, MSA.

92. For early woman inmates, see Prisoners nos. 3203 (1865), 2320, 2948, 3082 (1868), Kansas State Penitentiary, Statement of Convicts, Prisoner Ledger A, 1864–85, KSHS. Hereafter, Statement of Convicts, Prisoner Ledger A, KSHS.

93. *General Rules and Regulations of the State Penitentiary, Kansas*, p. 19, UKKC.

94. *First Biennial Report of the Board of Administration*, pp. 4, 43, in *Biennial Report of the Women's Industrial Farm at Lansing*, 1916, UKKC.

95. William H. Sinclair to Lt. J. F. Kirkman, 26 Feb. 1867, Records of the Bureau of Refugees, Freedmen, and Abandoned Lands, Texas, Assistant Commissioner, Letters Received Register, vol. 1, 1866–67, box 4, N-S, RG 105, NA (the author thanks Barry A. Crouch for this research material); Crow, "Political History of the Texas Penal System," pp. 85–86.

96. *Report on the Condition of the State Penitentiary*, 1870, p. 6; *Reports on the Condition of the State Penitentiary*, 1873–74, p. 5, TSA.

97. *Biennial Report of the Directors and Superintendent of the Texas State Penitentiary*, 1880, pp. 39–40, TSA.

98. Ibid., pp. 12, 40.

99. The board wanted to codify more rigidly the general segregation policy that had been in place since the Civil War. See *Record of Evidence and Statements before the Penitentiary Investigating Committee*, 1913, p. 24, TSA.

100. Ibid., pp. 22–23.

101. Ibid., pp. 22, 23, 25, 26, 36.

102. For the 225 African American men in the Huntsville penitentiary in 1866, the reasons for their incarceration often involved little criminal evidence against them or activities that could hardly be considered criminal. For example: one man jokingly held the pocketbook of another servant for about three minutes (two years); a servant was sent to prison because another servant sold the master's horse (ten

years); two men bought goods in Houston and denied the right to their witnesses (two years); one man was charged with stealing twenty-one bushels of corn, which he was hauling for his employer (three years); a man was charged with assisting in a jailbreak, although the accused was twelve miles from the scene and denied the right to his own witnesses (two years); one man fired on a dog set on him by a white man (seven years); a boy gave a torch to a stranger, who used it for arson (four years); a man was arrested on suspicion of burglary (twelve years); a runaway servant refused to "contract" again and stabbed the white employer who cornered him with a rifle (ten years); an elderly man on crutches who was accused of "stealing" seven pigs' feet, after the white employer forced his cook to testify the old man had never been given permission to take food (two years) (William Sinclair to J. F. Kirkman, 26 Feb. 1867, Records of the Bureau of Refugees, Freedmen, and Abandoned Lands, RG 105, NA). In Louisiana in 1868, thirty-one black laborers were sentenced to one year in the penitentiary on the single charge of "riot"; in 1875, three blacks were sentenced to two years with the notation, "no crime specified" (Roger S. Thomas, Assistant Warden, to Peggy Gresham, Assistant Warden, "Interesting Facts about the Department of Corrections," 10 Sept. 1984, p. 3, Warden's Office, LSP).

103. *Record of Evidence and Statements before the Penitentiary Investigating Committee*, 1913, p. 23, TSA.

104. *Report of the Penitentiary Investigating Committee*, p. 14, TSA.

105. Ibid, p. 13.

106. Paul Eduard Knepper, "The Women of Yuma: Gender, Ethnicity, and Imprisonment in Frontier Arizona, 1876–1909," *Criminal Justice Review* 17 (Autumn 1992): 236, n. 2.

107. Even in those registers that listed some emerging professional occupations for prisoners, such individuals were a small number in comparison to the whole prison population. In 1880, for example, Texas records showed twenty inmates had been doctors, lawyers, engineers, or dentists. Among the same group, along with the factorymen, servants, and brick masons, were 1,753 common laborers (*Biennial Report of the Directors and Superintendent of the Texas State Penitentiary*, 1880, p. 48, TSA).

108. *Biennial Report of the Idaho State Penitentiary*, 1905-6, p. 49, and *Biennial Report of the Idaho State Penitentiary*, 1907-8, p. 53, ISL.

109. Roger S. Thomas, Assistant Warden, to Peggy Gresham, Assistant Warden, "Interesting Facts about the Department of Corrections," 10 Sept. 1984, p. 2, LSP; *Reports on the Condition of the State Penitentiary*, 1873–74, p. 5, TSA.

110. According to the historian Elliott West, children ran away fairly commonly in the West. See *Growing Up with the Country* (Lincoln: University of Nebraska Press, 1989), pp. 154–55. One inmate diarist indicated he ran away from an abusive father several times and finally just kept going (*Sweet Smell of Sagebrush*, p. 5).

111. All material drawn from Prisoners nos. 1–62, New Mexico Penitentiary Records, Convict Record Book, 2 Nov. 1884–20 Apr. 1904, microcopy roll 1, NMSA (hereafter, Convict Record Book, NMSA). In the same era, Texas reported that only 23.52 percent of the convictions had been for crimes against persons (*Biennial Report of the Directors and Superintendent of the Texas State Penitentiary*, 1880, p. 45, TSA). Idaho in 1904, with 225 prisoners and 1908 with 213, reported that about 34 percent of the prisoners had been convicted of violent crimes (*Biennial Report of the Idaho State Penitentiary*, 1903-4, p. 30; *Biennial Report of the Idaho State Penitentiary*, 1907–8, p. 53, ISL).

112. A random sample of sixty-two prisoners in 1895 and 1905 demonstrated that in all categories, male prisoners reflected almost the same characteristics breakdown as the 1884 group. Social and economic factors that underlay western crime

had not altered significantly at the penitentiary (Convict Record Book, microcopy roll 1, pp. 53–57, and Prisoners nos. 1844–1906, NMSA).

113. Among the Texas prisoners in 1880, only 396 of 2,157 claimed a common school or better education. Of the remaining, 768 were completely illiterate (*Biennial Report of the Directors and Superintendent of the Texas State Penitentiary*, 1880, p. 49, TSA).

114. For a discussion of the erroneous notion that homosexual men lack masculinity or knowledge of masculine social mores, see Connell, *Masculinities*, pp. 141–47.

115. Testimony of Inmate Sam Tubbs to the Investigating Committee, *Report of the Penitentiary Investigating Committee*, p. 276, TSA.

116. *Sweet Smell of Sagebrush*, pp. 66, 89.

117. Ibid., pp. 130, 141.

118. Joseph F. Fishman, *Sex in Prison: Revealing Sex Conditions in American Prisons* ([New York]: National Library Press, 1934), p. 21.

119. *Sweet Smell of Sagebrush*, pp. 145–48.

120. *New North-West* (Deer Lodge, Mont.), 22 Nov. 1878.

121. Ibid., 6 Dec. 1878. Sánchez served less than two years of a three-year sentence and was pardoned in September 1880 (State of Montana, Descriptive List of Prisoners Received, 1 July 1871–1 Oct. 1885, p. 57, MtHS).

3 *Women of the Prison World*

> I am weary of this dreary imprisonment . . .
> my health is failing . . . and [I] feel that I
> could not live long to indure [*sic*] what a
> prisoner must undergo.
> —Mollie Forsha
> Nevada State Penitentiary
> 1874

The generic term "the woman prisoner" does little to illuminate a clear definition of the western women who went to the penitentiary. No single western woman typified the female inmate. They shared characteristics, but women prisoners also reflected diversity. Overarching issues of race, class, and gender helped to etch a basic prisoner profile, but perhaps the most universal marker of these women sprang from the perverse legal treatment they encountered in the courts.

Life in the prison world brought its own set of assaults, but the constraints that women prisoners faced began outside the penitentiary. Women, regardless of whether they were "respectable" or "fallen," the majority or the minority, shared a common gender designation that placed them at jeopardy. Minority and ethnic women in the West

Ida Jones, Colorado State Penitentiary. Courtesy Division of State Archives and Public Records, Denver, Colo.

struggled with one set of risks, those of the emerging white middle class with another.

If a woman accumulated a record of minor offenses or earned an unsavory name with the local police, these weighed heavily against her when she was charged with major felonies. A woman with a public identity had already challenged the existing social structure and required firmer chastisement. A string of arrests, county jail time, negative newspaper reports—all these made women—regardless of race or ethnicity—from the so-called vice community easy targets for conviction and imprisonment in the penitentiary.

Ida Jones, an African American prostitute in Denver, Colorado, had attracted just such unfavorable public notice by the time she faced a murder charge in August 1890. Her earlier skirmishes, which stemmed from an ongoing feud within the Market and Blake Streets vice community, brought her to the attention of the Denver authorities.[1] Apparently angered by her neighbors' part in a fall 1889 arrest for maintaining a house for "lewd women and common prostitutes and wicked, deluded, lascivious men,"[2] Ida Jones struck back. Once released from jail, Jones made a destructive sweep through her accusers' home. Not only did the owner, Lizzie Ames, claim that Jones broke all the windows but Ames listed in detail the fourteen dollars and ten cents worth of destroyed possessions—five plates, six meat platters, three cups, four saucers, one bed, one washstand, and two yards of wallpaper.[3] Ida Jones made her fury known in the neighborhood.

Within two weeks, Jones again faced charges of "keeping a lewd house and place for the practice of fornication." On this occasion, eight area residents, including Lizzie Ames, her husband, and two others from the recently besieged Blake Street address, appeared as witnesses for the state.[4] Among the other men and women of the vice district, Ida Jones had crossed a line into unacceptable behavior. She had not only offended noncriminal Denverites but had discredited herself among members of her own community, a dangerous circumstance for one who lived within society's marginal groups. An outcast from both the "respectable" and the "nonrespectable" of Denver, Jones floundered along with virtually no public backing as her legal troubles escalated.

By the time Ida Jones came to criminal court in 1890 charged with murder, her problems mushroomed beyond her black neighbors and drew in one of the best-known white families in the Denver vice neighborhood. The Ryan/Wallace family, prominent brothel and saloon owners, testified for the state against Ida in the murder of Stephen Zemmer.[5] The mother of the family, Jane Elizabeth Wallace Ryan, her daughters, Julia Wallace and Annie Ryan, along with the youngest child, Buddy Ryan, joined a long list of witnesses from the Market/Blake Streets area.

The cluster of subpoena addresses issued for Ida's various arrests showed her troubles centered in her neighborhood, close to the property of the Wallace family.[6] Most state witnesses lived within a four block range of the Wallace Saloon at 1937 Blake Street, where John "Buddy" Ryan received his summons, while officials delivered Laura Reed's to her residence "up the alley."[7] Laura's alley address meant her prostitute's crib, rented from the Wallaces, who kept a number of these shacks behind their saloons. Laura Reed, working outside the safety of a well-managed house of prostitution and among the lower strata of western prostitutes, made a wise choice to cooperate with the powerful Jane Wallace Ryan. Ryan, a former owner of brothels and cribs in Cripple Creek, Colorado, had moved her family business to Denver, where, with her three daughters and son, she expanded her vice operations.

 With one of the most influential white families in the vice district aligned against Jones, the issue of race increased her precarious position with Denver authorities. A black prostitute could not hope for the same considerations her white counterparts often negotiated. After all, in the late 1800s, Annie Ryan, daughter of Jane Elizabeth Wallace Ryan, shot the bartender, her paramour, in her saloon but did not go to the penitentiary. And early in the twentieth century, Rosie O'Grady, a white prostitute and drinking friend of at least one city detective, killed Clarence Sears, her African American lover and was acquitted.[8] Authorities often exhibited contradictory attitudes toward the white vice community, indulging it on one hand, punishing it on the other.[9]

African Americans in the vice districts confronted a less flexible and forgiving power structure. This, even though minority people in the late nineteenth and early twentieth centuries, strapped for economic options, responded to the encouragement of white male patrons to operate small vice establishments.[10] Regardless, no privileged outcome awaited Ida Jones. In her case, the attitude of the police toward blacks in Denver brothels and saloons crept into the paper work drawn up for the fifteen witnesses, with two notations for state's witness W. L. Swoap, identified as a "Good Black."[11] As usual, authorities willingly called on members of a red light district for testimony that would aid the prosecution, but held dear the negative racial and cultural biases that kept certain groups at the edges of citizenry.[12]

A Kentuckian transplanted to Denver, Ida Jones, who could neither read nor write and counted no allies among the many witnesses, was lost before she entered the court. Her attorney's attempt to have four other women charged with premeditated murder failed, and Ida faced a jury of twelve white men. By the time the judge delivered his jury instructions, which included the suggestive remarks that jurors should "not allow the fact that the prisoner has been in the habit of practicing fornication," or "the prevalence . . . of crime in the community . . . prejudice your mind against the prisoner,"[13] the court had sealed the fate of Ida Jones. Her public identity melded with her crime to send the young woman to the Colorado State Penitentiary for a term of fifteen years.

In keeping with the dynamic for incarcerated women, Jones disappeared from the minds of Denver residents for the next nine years. Denverites did not worry about Ida Jones again until she returned to their community. Discharged from prison on 13 August 1899, Ida Jones surfaced again in the city court records in October 1901. Referred to as "Black Ida," Jones had returned to the old neighborhood of Market Street, where one Charles Peterson accused her of stealing two hundred dollars. This case dragged out over the next ten months; Ida, convicted in March 1902, apparently felt she knew enough about local justice and by August police listed her as a fugitive. Reporting the event the newspaper described Ida Jones, now only about thirty-seven years old, as "the most dangerous and vicious woman in Denver."[14]

"Dangerous and vicious" women such as Ida Jones stirred up public censure, but those very qualities empowered Jones to withstand the environment she found inside the Colorado penitentiary. Her experiences with customers, neighbors, and competitors gave her some preparation for the world behind bars. It seems unlikely that the penitentiary, with its many abuses, surprised Ida Jones and when it did, she possessed a reservoir of knowledge about life for marginal women to sustain her. If anything helped her to survive nine years of confinement, a near record among imprisoned women, it must have been the "dangerous and vicious" qualities that infused her spirit.

Other women entered the prison world without as much of this critical grit. These women, accustomed to a private existence, lacked the personal advantage of physical and mental combat with male public authority before imprisonment. They collided unexpectedly with the law and fell from the good graces of their own communities. These women lacked the insight about the realities of an unrestrained male hierarchy that might have helped them to adjust quickly. Ill-prepared for the masculine community around them, some faltered both in spirit and health, stunned by a world they had never imagined to inhabit.

On 3 June 1888, Prisoner no. 1270, a forty-four-year-old houseworker from Illinois, concluded that the first nine months of her twenty-five-year sentence to the Nebraska State Penitentiary had been more than enough. At 6:30 in the morning, she, a woman of "temperate habits" and no previous convictions, committed suicide by cutting her throat. She left little personal record of herself, only that she had lived in Nebraska since the age of fourteen, had a "poor" education and a Methodist background, and had pleaded "not guilty" to a charge of murder. She listed her politics as "none," and her family as "nobody."[15] Beyond these dreary, brief notations in the convict register, Prisoner no. 1270 left no indication of the circumstances that prompted her to slit her own throat as the early daylight touched her cell.

Unlike this prisoner, others managed to live out their terms, but often they faced a shorter sentence or drew strength from the knowledge that family members continued to pursue legal options that might lead to freedom. Still, for some women the events that led to imprisonment grew out of the utterly improbable. Such appeared to be so in the case of a mother and daughter from Wyoming.

In 1904, Viola Biggs, a stenographer, and her mother, Anna E. Trout, a forty-two-year-old dressmaker, entered the penitentiary at Rawlins, Wyoming, convicted on charges of kidnapping. During the previous year and a half, Viola Biggs had struggled with a mounting domestic crisis, but nothing that foreshadowed a criminal trial, conviction, and penitentiary time for the young wife. The same could be said of her mother, the law-abiding Anna Trout, caught up in the collapse of her daughter's marriage.

In May of 1903, John Biggs, Viola's husband of six months, abandoned his pregnant wife. Biggs immediately notified the family physician that he would not cover any medical expenses for the coming birth and also conveyed the same message to local merchants about bills for Viola and the child.[16] On 16 August, twenty-year-old Viola gave birth to a son; she named him Leonard. John Biggs did not attend the birth, never came to see the infant, and, as he had declared, paid nothing in support. In early September, Viola, deserted by her husband and without economic means, directed her mother, Anna Trout, to take three-week-old Leonard to Denver and place him for adoption.

At the train depot, Anna Trout chanced to encounter none other than the errant father, who knew the purpose of his mother-in-law's Denver trip but neither protested nor tried to prevent her departure. Shortly, in what appears to have been an impulsive gesture, perhaps symptomatic of most of his life decisions, John Biggs filed kidnapping charges against his wife and her mother. Basing his claim on a statute that gave fathers the right of guardianship of a minor child in preference to the mother, Biggs found the Casper, Wyoming, district attorney receptive to the case.[17] In short order, Viola Biggs and Anna Trout came to trial before a judge who disallowed the substantial testimony of various Casper residents, ready to document John Biggs's refusal to support a son he openly acknowledged as his own.

Viola Biggs's troubles began with a husband who abandoned her almost immediately after their marriage. They mounted as the summer of 1903 moved forward and Viola had neither emotional nor economic support. These difficulties paled in comparison to the results produced by a court that permitted only the father's voice and penalized the mother's action on behalf of the infant.

Although the appellate court reversed the decision, the wheels of corrective justice ground slowly. Mother and daughter entered the penitentiary in February of 1904. The higher court rendered its opinion in April, but the two women remained in the Rawlins prison until the end of August.[18] In the meantime, the men of this episode—the father, the district attorney, and the judge—lived on in Casper, while it remained unclear who cared for baby Leonard Biggs. It was not his mother and grandmother, serving penitentiary time for trying to guarantee his upbringing within a family environment of Viola's choosing.[19]

Well into the twentieth century, middle-class white women continued to feel the impact of a legal system that could take on decidedly western hues. This could occur especially in those cases when a woman ignored the pressures to conform to male expectations. Such forces apparently fueled the criminal conviction of Ella Smith, a stock raiser and freighter from Wyoming.

In May 1908, Ella went on trial in Big Horn County, Wyoming. State's witnesses agreed they had known Smith, a Texas transplant, for about seven years as an independent business owner in their Wyoming community. She established a solid reputation as a hard worker, who handled all the heavy outdoor labor required of one raising horses and running a freighting business.[20] Apparently, however, she offended the powerful stockmen, whose association in nearby Johnson County had a few years earlier conducted an infamous western range war. Ella Smith, who had resisted mounting pressures from the stockmen to abandon her business, found herself charged with misbranding stock.[21]

At her trial, Ella Smith admitted rounding up two colts off the open range and branding them, but explained why she had good reason to believe the animals belonged to her. Smith pointed out that the animals had been ranging in a common stock area, and that she did not hide the colts from anyone. In broad daylight, she drove them over a public road through town to a barn, where she finished the branding.

She also detailed her efforts to compensate rancher John M. Baldwin, after she learned he was accusing her of the theft.[22] Surely, Ella Smith heard whispers from the stockmen's association in the charges, as she hurried to deflect further trouble by offering Baldwin the colts, other horses, or money. She must have recognized the seriousness of her situation when Baldwin told her he would settle if he could, but the stockmen would not allow it.[23]

On the witness stand, the neighbor, John Baldwin, readily agreed that Ella Smith tried to end the dispute in advance of any criminal charges, coming to see him before he swore out a warrant. Baldwin testified that Smith acknowledged the branding and told him she thought she owned those particular colts. If he felt otherwise, she offered to make monetary restitution or give him horses from her herd. Baldwin admitted he told Smith the matter had gone too far to be resolved, but hedged on what he might have revealed about the role of the stockmen's association in her troubles.[24]

Smith's attorney offered a spirited defense, pointing to his client's long record in the community, the openness of her actions, the lack of criminal intent, and the vagueness of the lease lines in the area where the horses of several people ranged. In an unfriendly court, attorney Ridgley protested repeatedly as the judge allowed wide conjecture and hearsay evidence from the state's witnesses. Of thirty-one times that the defense attorney objected or moved for dismissal, the judge overruled Ridgley twenty-eight times, while the district attorney was overruled on three of five objections.[25]

Despite the vigor of her attorney, Ella Smith went to the penitentiary at Rawlins for misbranding stock. If her attorney had planned through his many objections to pave the way for a reversal from the appeals court, such did not happen. Smith served her full sentence of eighteen months, perhaps, as a single parent, determined to do so for the young daughter who awaited her return.[26] Ella Smith, who had ridden the range for weeks at a time, singlehandedly thrown colts to the ground for branding, and managed a freighting business, had crossed gender and economic lines, an offense to her neighboring stockmen.

They softened their response more than Wyoming stockmen of an earlier era who lynched their female competition, Ella "Cattle Kate" Watson, during the 1888 Johnson County War. Perhaps hesitant to repeat a nineteenth-century vigilante action, local cattle barons still devised ways to retain control of the stock industry. Whether by death or imprisonment, women received clear signals about the limits of gender in western enterprise. In the nineteenth century, economic opposition from the local stockmen meant death for "Cattle Kate" Watson. In the twentieth century, it meant penitentiary time for Ella Smith.

Like Ida Jones, Viola Biggs, Anna Trout, Ella Smith, and perhaps Prisoner no. 1270, many women went to a penitentiary under questionable circumstances, convicted on circumstantial or manipulated evidence.[27] Because the women came largely from groups with limited political and economic status, prosecuting attorneys, judges, and juries, usually white males, acted with a free hand to bring about convictions. Local jurisdictions moved quickly, often denying poorly informed defendants a chance to organize a case or locate witnesses. Families and friends saw women tried and convicted before legal assistance could be mobilized. The power of those orchestrating the procedures swept over the women with such force that the accused had neither time nor means to question or affect the outcome.[28] Whether truly guilty or truly innocent of the charges, women barely caught a glimpse of due process.

A weak understanding of the legal system and the language used there further hurt the women. Their grasp of the formal statutes was often sketchy or incorrect, their understanding of the courtroom events even more fragmented. Many did not read or write, few had more than a rudimentary education—situations that kept them confused during court proceedings.[29] In 1888, Lizzie Gibson, an African American woman, incriminated herself, admitting she stole $1.50. But since she took the money by pushing a door open and reaching into a house, Lizzie thought she had not been breaking and entering; Lizzie went to the Texas penitentiary for two years, although within three days of her trial local citizens began petitions on her behalf.[30]

Other women, even if not schooled in the refinements of the law, fully realized the dangers for black persons who faced the nineteenth-century court system. Susan Wallace, whose "agony . . . suffered . . . in jail . . . almost bereft her of her reason," knew not only that harsh time awaited in the Texas penitentiary but that her six small children faced an uncertain future with their mother imprisoned. Wallace, the only support of her youngsters, had taken a silver plate, a shawl, and a hat from the white family for whom she worked. She defended her actions by reason of her long service to the white woman, who over a period of three months paid the servant a total of twenty-five cents. The jury convicted the black woman of the theft, then asked for a pardon before she could be transported to the penitentiary.[31]

In support of the state, juries tended to uphold arrest and trial procedures of court officers; they feared acquittals undercut the decisions of their elected officials. To distance themselves from responsibility in a blatantly unfair or questionable case, juries often used the "instant" citizens' petition as a way to undo their own actions.

For example, jurors in Reno, Nevada, asserted in their 1877 petition for Maggie Hart that they had convicted her based on the promise of the district attorney that the woman would be immediately pardoned. In his summation, the prosecutor demanded a guilty verdict, not because of evidence against Maggie Hart in an arson case, but to disprove public rumor that Washoe County could not get a conviction. Jurors claimed that the "declaration and promise of the district attorney . . . was taken into consideration while . . . rendering their verdict, and that verdict . . . was . . . with the distinct understanding that a petition for her pardon . . . be at once circulated."[32] While the jury, comfortable within the confines of home and community, may have agonized over the turn of events, in October 1877 it was Maggie Hart who went to the state penitentiary for a one-year sentence.

Whether juries such as this one wanted to acknowledge their role or not, such trials for women increased the immediate local power of state officers and agencies. While pardon and parole boards then mulled over the particulars at their leisure, women served long months and years inside male penitentiaries. In the cases of Susan Wallace and Maggie Hart, state authorities showed little interest in jury reversals of sentiment; Susan Wallace went to the penitentiary for two years and Maggie Hart still had no action on her pardon application by June 1878.[33]

In some cases, local politics, rather than issues of justice, influenced both the convictions and the pardons. For example, in the case of Essie Sara, her attorney, J. S. Hill, charged that the trial judge made public statements of his determination to convict the defendant and used incorrect courtroom procedures. From the firm of Fly and Davidson, another attorney wrote that although he did not know the woman or the case, he believed the governor could rely on certain local citizens, including a former member of the legislature, in the request "to undo what has been done by *our* county court."[34]

Local political rivalries explained some of the actions taken by whites on behalf of black women. In 1892 when Sarah Thomas, a chambermaid at a hotel in Belton, Texas, went to the penitentiary for receiving stolen goods, almost one hundred citizens signed a clemency petition for her. George Pendleton, her white attorney, introducing the black citizen who carried the petition to the governor, asserted that Sarah was "poorly defended and probably innocent."[35] A second lawyer from the Pendleton firm demonstrated that politicians saw executive clemency less as an issue of justice, and more as political opportunity. D. R. Pendleton recommended Sarah's pardon because he told the Texas governor, James Hogg: "if you can possibly take up this case . . . it will help your cause here wonderfully with the Negroes. We have some few in line already, some on the fence and some for Clark. However, Curry will be here soon and I am afraid of his influence with them."[36]

Whether the convictions were against black women or poor white women, whether they oozed with the tensions of local political competition or court corruption, each involved keeping the woman in the local jail for a lengthy period, assessing her with a heavy fine, and threatening her with or committing her to the penitentiary. Regardless of the jockeying between court official and local politicos, the result for women meant public censure and questionable justice; for the community it meant greater awareness of just who retained political and social control. At least that appeared to be the thinking of Texas attorney G. I. Turnley, who endorsed a pardon from fines for a young black couple convicted of unlawful fornication. Turnley asked for relief for the local pair, who scraped by raising corn and cotton, because he believed the executive action, "would have a good effect upon other uninformed and ignorant negroes."[37]

Juries, instruments of the judiciary, reinforced a double-edged system of punishment and "sympathy" that further intensified the hold courts maintained over women and a white system held over black citizens. Knowledge of such matters circulated widely in poor communities, where residents enjoyed, at best, an uneasy truce with the law. The possible punitive outcome of a clash with the law guided the choices of some, when confronted with the force of the legal authorities.

In 1888, African American Minnie Mitchell, mother of three small children, went to the Texas penitentiary for two years, charged with concealing stolen property. A year later, she received a pardon when the trial judge and prosecuting attorney filed on behalf of the "honest and hard working girl," because of "new evidence" that revealed Minnie had been protecting her eleven-year-old sister, who had taken a ring.[38] Minnie understood about the Susan Wallaces of her world and knew it possible for her sister to join other black youngsters incarcerated at the Huntsville prison. Mitchell, aware that under the ordinary mechanisms of punishment a black child could and would go to the penitentiary, chose defense of her family over personal security and risked the dangers of imprisonment.

Not every woman had the opportunity to make such well-thought-out choices. Texan Amanda Roads, a former slave said to be "old and feeble," served two years for "not returning money she had found."[39] Roads, convicted of what appeared to have been no true crime, received a pardon in 1883. Close to the same date, another Texas inmate, Lena Gayhart, "a young German girl, not knowing English," was also pardoned. Charged with a grand larceny offense of stealing over twenty dollars, Gayhart served a year in the penitentiary before officials acknowledged the prisoner could not understand the proceedings and had no chance to secure witnesses for her defense. On the day of the conviction, jury members signed a petition for Gayhart's pardon because they "doubted the justice of their verdict."[40]

Four years later, questionable trial practices in Texas continued to haunt women, especially African Americans. On 19 November 1887, authorities arrested Ellen Smith, "an ignorant but honest and industrious colored woman," and took her immediately to the courtroom. She had no "opportunity to obtain advice or know her rights," and was convicted on her own testimony of maiming a hog. Smith's "confession" consisted of explaining how one dog (not necessarily hers) attacked the swine, but a second, which Smith had tied up, broke loose and did the damage.[41] On this evidence and without understanding self-incrimination or how such a civil case might be resolved, Smith was convicted.[42]

Regardless of the western location or the trial procedures, the process of arrest and conviction threw women off balance. They exercised limited control in the legal negotiations, as they received their first lessons in the power of the courts. Town and county officials moved swiftly for arrest and conviction. Although court officers often willingly threw themselves into the appeals process for a woman convict, they initiated such action only after women had been detained for long periods in some type of custodial care. Thus, at the local level, women experienced the first phase of transformation into a female prisoner. They then faced a new world of power, one fueled by race, class, and gender imperatives, inside the penitentiary.

Race, the first of these forces, shaded prisons with the many hues of women of color. At the Kansas penitentiary, at least 150 of 200 women received between 1865 and 1906 were black.[43] In Missouri between 1865 and 1871, of approximately 110 women who went to the penitentiary, thirty-seven were clearly black, while the racial designation of twenty-six could not be determined.[44] Depending on the race of individuals in the latter group, between 34 percent and 57 percent of the Missouri women prisoners were black. Between 1866 and 1872, sixty-seven women, sixty-four of whom were African American, entered the Louisiana state prison system.[45] Of 107 women prisoners in the Iowa prison at Anamosa between 1883 and 1907, eighteen, or almost 20 percent, were black, but the racial heritage of another thirty-four, or 23 percent, could not be determined with certainty.[46] In Montana, of sixty identified women who entered prison between 1890 and 1910, twenty-nine were African Americans.[47] Even Idaho, with its small number of women prisoners across time, reported that between 1903 and 1904, of its three female inmates, two were African Americans.[48] Of Arizona's twenty-eight women held at the Yuma prison, fourteen, or 50 percent, were Mexican American and six, or approximately 21 percent, were African American.[49] None of these states included any Asian women in the registers. Regardless of western location, African American women, against whom the state often used slight criminal evidence, went to state penitentiaries in proportionately greater numbers than females of other groups.

These figures, though they might not be precise, aligned with one of the first surveys about criminal statistics in the United States. According to findings from the 1910 census, African Americans equaled 10.7 percent of the total national population, but 21.9 percent of all committed prisoners in the country. In addition, the ratio for incarcerated black women (418.3 per 100,000) soared almost six times above the corresponding ratio for white women (70 per 100,000). Overall, in proportion to total population figures, eleven times as many African American women as Caucasian women were committed for larceny and about thirty-three times as many for crimes of assault. In crimes designated as "moral offenses," black women went to prison about five times more frequently than white women. Although sectional differences might be thought to skew the survey results, in every geographic region, including the West, the percentage of African American women incarcerated, relative to the area's demography, surpassed that of any other group, including black males.[50] Arrest and conviction practices that favored some white women tipped prisoner statistics against black women and thus artificially inflated their appearance of criminality.[51]

More than just the greater likelihood for imprisonment, other factors influenced the time served for nonwhite women. In Nebraska, between 1869 and 1910, of ninety females sentenced to the penitentiary, fifty-one were African American women, nine white, one Native American, one Hispanic, and the racial identity of twenty-eight women could not be ascertained with certainty.[52] Of the nine white women, four were released early through good time credit, one spent her sentence in and out of the insane asylum, one died in prison, and three received pardons, two of these from murder and manslaughter convictions.[53] A dressmaker sentenced to life was pardoned after two years, and a prisoner serving a year for manslaughter received not parole but a pardon after nine months.[54] Of the fifty-two black women, none saw the penitentiary gates swing open before the expiration of their sentences through a good time allowance and none received pardons. Of the twelve incarcerated for crimes of violence, only one served less than one-half to three-quarters of the full sentence.[55]

In Arkansas, these racial distinctions in time served also prevailed. A sampling of 270 women prisoners, from among those imprisoned at some time between 1881 and 1915, showed that eighteen whites had been sentenced to the penitentiary, in contrast to 252 African American women.[56] Among these, prisoner files could be identified for sixty-eight women, six whites and sixty-two blacks.[57]

Of the white inmates, one, Sarah Weidner, a fifty-eight-year-old woman, served twenty months of a five-year term for murder and died in the prison hospital of heart failure.[58] Two young white women were transferred to a correctional home for girls, one the day after arrival at the penitentiary. One white woman was pardoned after serving two and a half years of a four-year sentence, one after serving five months of a twelve-month term, and one was pardoned after three weeks.[59]

African American women did not experience so lenient a release and pardon system.[60] Of the sixty-two black women, fifty-two served at least until expiration of term through good time, one died in prison, and nine received pardons. Unlike the white women, whose pardons arrived promptly, only two blacks served less than half the full sentence. Four of the African American women secured pardons after imprisonment of several years—thirteen out of a fifteen-year sentence, six out of seven years, eight out of ten.[61]

In 1910, all thirty-seven Arkansas women prisoners were African American. This prompted one citizen to protest the figures, noting the high incarceration numbers conflicted with the fact that "the negroes are far in the minority in population." He complained about this imbalance and felt sure that "statisticians" would use the biennial report of the penitentiary superintendent to "'prove' the depravity and criminality of the negro." He asserted that it was "well known . . . that white women are convicted for every crime, . . . receive penitentiary sentences, but are pardoned forthwith." Further, he claimed the governor boasted that no white woman would be within the walls during his administration. White women received gubernatorial pardons with such "frequency as to excite the disgust of even the white daily papers and the court itself."[62]

Black women not only faced incarceration more often and served hefty portions of their sentences but their punishment had community application as well. For example, at the age of seventeen, Caroline Williams, an African American woman from Lamar County, Texas, entered the penitentiary on a life sentence for murder. Nearly sixteen years later, the supervising sergeant endorsed her application for a pardon, acknowledging Williams's generally satisfactory conduct. His main argument, however, concerned the impact her release would have on the other convicts at the camp. He stressed that the "long time ones" looked "with eagerness" to marking fifteen years in the penitentiary, as they anticipated that anniversary would automatically bring them freedom. The sergeant did not fear that "criminals" who had "paid their debt to society" would be wronged by unduly severe terms or that a crime might not be adequately punished. Rather, he worried that disappointing those prisoners with lengthy sentences would endanger discipline.[63] Caroline Williams received her pardon, and Texas conveyed a message about its power to black communities, both free and imprisoned.

Race guaranteed that African American women faced a daunting set of legal procedures. Under a rubric that defined all female criminals as "unfit," the nonwhite became more unfit, until a whole set of racial imperatives underscored the practices inside the prisons.[64] The penitentiary served as one more societal location where black women found that race propelled a wide spectrum of policies reinforcing social, economic, and political control over minority groups.

At the same time, the punishment of women functioned as a way to weave folk controls through ethnic families. Using the powerful oral network of the black and Hispanic communities, mothers, aunts, grandmothers, and sisters imposed familial restrictions on children before youngsters stumbled across inflexible racial rules.[65] Drawing on the bitter experiences of their communities, these women of color tried to blunt the racism of the dominant culture as they sought to protect their own families. This was exactly the desired outcome in the perspective of the dominant culture, with its many-faceted strategies for racial control.

Along with race, the infrastructure of punishment also incorporated class assessment into the treatment of women prisoners. Class designations, however, slipped across a slick surface, shifting as convenient for officials. Judgments appeared based on impression and circumstance, as much as on rigid definition. In St. Louis several missionaries petitioned for the release of Mary Godfrey because the inmate had "proved by her general conduct that she is not of the class of females usually found in such places."[66] What they meant by this assertion, they did not feel compelled to explain. In the New Mexico penitentiary, Mexican American women dominated in numbers, but received fewer privileges than Anglo women.[67] But in nearby Texas, authorities segregated Spanish-speaking women with white inmates, giving both significantly better living accommodations and work assignments than the larger group of black females.[68] Also in Texas a petitioner argued that Mrs. W. J. Stewart, a white woman, deserved a pardon because her father was, "a *gallant Confederate Soldier* and served the entire war."[69] Local determinations within western regions and the personnel managing the women prisoners apparently influenced class designations.

In Utah, Belle Harris despised the humiliation she felt when the warden's wife brought women visitors to stare at the "polygamous prisoner." At the same time, Belle failed to see the irony in herself when she protested vehemently that she had to share her small quarters and "eat at the same table" with a "common prostitute." Belle complained in her journal, "She is one of the lowest classes though she acts very well so far." Loneliness and motherhood quickly showed the two outcasts they had more in common than they thought, and Belle grieved when her new friend departed through an early release.[70]

The social thinker Kate Richards O'Hare saw more precisely that class distinctions inside the prison reflected those of the outside world. Among the women at the Missouri penitentiary, federal and political prisoners respectively ranked as the "upper class" and the "aristocracy," while third place went to those who "disposed of undesirable husbands." O'Hare, herself a political prisoner, referred to the African American inmates as "colored girls" and somewhat regally reported that one said it a shame that women like "Miss Emma [Goldman] and Miss Kate" had to be in a penitentiary.[71] Nonetheless, an appreciation for the common suffering marked

O'Hare's interaction with all the women prisoners, and she actively cultivated relationships throughout the cell block.[72]

Although constrained by her own sense of class, O'Hare looked with
little regard to women outside the prison walls. About two months into her
term, she wrote, "I am not particularly optimistic concerning the average
middle class woman." Her criticism stemmed from the fact that "not a
woman's club or the women of one church have ever shown one gleam of
interest in this institution."[73] She complained particularly about the wives
of prison administrators as middle-class women who should have felt some
attachment to female inmates.

Despite the reluctance of noncriminal middle-class women to identify
with prisoners, the inmates themselves understood the importance of class
rhetoric in their incarceration. For example, twenty-eight-year-old Dolly
Brady freely admitted working as a prostitute, but called on her "long and
honest residence," affirmed by any man who "ever policed the district in
which she lived," as reason for clemency. Brady, of Cheyenne, Wyoming,
described herself as one with "lax" morals, but never indulging in larceny
and robbery, "for which she . . . had many opportunities."[74] Yet, her attorney told the governor that Brady's petition was "much more difficult than
the ordinary applicant . . . because of the common lack of reputation and
conscience in people of her class."[75] Dolly Brady, no doubt, would have
objected to such a description of herself. Clearly, she had defined standards
for herself that met her understanding of so-called better class and expected the "respectable" men of the community to vouch for her record.

Dolly Brady's claim to executive clemency may have been enhanced
because the crime committed inside her brothel involved an Asian. Clyde
M. Watts, court reporter at Brady's trial, informed the governor that a Japanese customer came to Dolly's house, paid her five dollars, and went to bed
with the woman. Watts remembered that, according to the trial testimony, "she got up and went out in the sitting room and . . . told [them] to
throw the Jap out and take what he had."[76] Dolly's friends in Cheyenne
may have thought it unnecessary for her to serve two years in the penitentiary for a robbery and beating inflicted on a Japanese client. The pardon
and parole board may have recoiled at the thought of a white woman, regardless of her own class definitions, engaging in sexual relations with an
Asian man. However racial and class forces mingled in this case, the governor did not accommodate the petition; Dolly Brady served her full sentence
in the Wyoming penitentiary.

A woman might be able to enhance her own class standing with authorities, if she could demonstrate that the object of her crime ranked lower on
the social ladder than she. Jane Taylor's lawyer used this argument when
seeking a pardon for his client. Although the Winnemucca, Nevada, wom-

an was convicted on a charge of assault with intent to kill, her lawyer argued that "it would have been a blessing to the community if she had been a better shot." Winnemucca citizens joined in the petition, noting that although Jennie was "a woman of the town," she was known for her "strict honesty," "very many redeeming qualities," and "generous contributions for the relief of the afflicted."[77]

The concept of class gave certain women an edge when entangled in criminal matters. In 1909, Herbert S. Hadley, the governor of Missouri, intervened at the local police level when some of his constituency objected to the police treatment of Hildegarde Hallon, a St. Louis woman arrested on charges of forgery. The complaints came to Hadley in letters, immediately heightening the importance of the protest and underscoring the muscle of literate voters. Not only did Hadley inquire about the use of excessive force by police but he challenged the wisdom of disturbing the woman after dark, when the arrest could have been postponed until daylight hours. Particularly, Hadley wanted to know if it had ever been the practice of the St. Louis department "to arrest persons who clearly do not belong to the criminal class."[78]

He might better have asked the forty-three women—eleven whites and thirty-two blacks—at that time incarcerated in the Missouri penitentiary.[79] Their definitions of place and rank inside their own communities certainly did not mesh with the governor's. Within their own cultures and families, women formulated attitudes about position and status that had little or no connection to those of a white male politician or the public agencies surrounding his office.

Not surprisingly, police dropped the forgery charges against Hildegarde Hallon, and she did not need to call on her race and class as bargaining chips in the penitentiary. The few women of the middle class—armed with education, paid legal counsel, and strong political purpose—who entered prison endured great deprivation, but they had sufficient social and economic backing to gain some advantage with prison authorities. Better food, cleaner housing, more access to officials—these were the typical benefits for high profile political prisoners. After prison these women looked to the prospect of reconstructing the fabric of their lives, using their prison time as a badge of courage and a vehicle for public discourse about reform.[80] For western ethnic women, however, dismissed as "low class," a penitentiary sentence reinforced stereotypes held by the dominant society.[81]

While race and class stratified prisoner life for differing groups of women, gender dominated the female experience inside the walls. If anything, it reminded women of their shared dilemma and helped the few housed together in any prison to forge common bonds. Gender ruled as the unspoken vulnerability of all imprisoned women. Seldom did women prisoners overlook that reality.

In 1896, Minnie Snyder, a native of New York, stood trial in Wyoming because her husband shot and killed a rancher, John Rooks. Minnie's husband, Peter, whirled and fired blindly into a fast-pursuing mob, in what appeared to be another clash between newcomer sheep ranchers and local cattlemen.[82] The judge rejected the Snyders' pleas of self-defense, suggested the mob should have lynched the couple, dismissed incriminating evidence given by the cattle vigilantes themselves, labeled the husband and wife the "evil-doers," and sent them off to the penitentiary for terms of ten and six years respectively. Not content with this statement, the judge, aiming his sentencing comments directly at Minnie Snyder, said: "A woman, that is a good woman, is respected in every community, but a woman, when she uses her tongue can stir up more mischief and do more damage in a community than any one. . . . It is one of the saddest of things to sentence a woman to the penitentiary, but my duty is [so] clear."[83]

As the judge finished sentencing Minnie, he declared the country around Lander safe for a "good woman," but that Minnie had "gone too far" in standing by her husband's side during the crisis. Since the notion of standing by one's husband represented a central tenet of marriage in the nineteenth century, one wonders how Minnie could have extricated herself from the court's double jeopardy.

Within a year, friends of the Snyders began to circulate pardon petitions for the imprisoned pair. Countering the censure of Minnie as one who offended gender sensibilities, these petitions placed the inmate back inside the circle of good womanhood as "delicate and kind in disposition . . . and always obedient to her aged parents."[84] Two years later, Minnie's mother wrote to the governor that her daughter's health in prison had deteriorated and expressed fear the young woman would not survive much longer. Despite these appeals, Minnie Snyder, who apparently took no part in the shooting death of John Rooks, did not elude the gender culpability defined by the judge; she received no gubernatorial pardon and remained in the penitentiary at Rawlins, Wyoming, until 29 August 1901, when she was released and moved to Deadwood, South Dakota, to await her husband.[85]

Race, class, and gender outlined the configurations of the woman prisoner profile. Women inmates shared another common element, that of youthfulness. The usual woman prisoner's age fell between eighteen and thirty.[86] For example, from among the extant records for women inmates in Colorado between 1884 and 1909, ages for seventy-two prisoners can be determined. Twenty-two prisoners were over the age of thirty, while fifty women, or nearly 70 percent, were between eighteen and thirty.[87] In Iowa, from 1893 to 1907, from among 107 women prisoners, seventy women or 65 percent showed ages between sixteen and thirty.[88] In Arizona, no woman over thirty was incarcerated at Yuma.[89]

Youthfulness marked the female inmates, imprisoned through their most potentially rebellious years, at ages when society preferred an ordered community of women committed to marriage and motherhood. For young women who challenged that structure, or even thought of doing so, the conditions in the penitentiary suggested the possible consequences.

Those consequences often meant life-changing experiences for young women. Sarah Crook, aged sixteen, escaped from the Texas penitentiary. Crook, sentenced to twelve years for murder, took flight to Louisiana, where Texas officials tracked her in May of 1878.[90] If the authorities apprehended her, Crook certainly faced the same penalty as had Louisiana inmate Alice Dunbar, ten years earlier. In 1868, Dunbar bolted from a prison superintendent's office, after serving almost a full year of an eighteen-month sentence. Authorities captured her in 1871 and returned her to the state prison system. Upon completion of her outstanding six months, Dunbar received her discharge. Officials added no time for the 1868 flight; just as during the recently past days of slavery, this fifty-one-year-old black woman, stripped to the waist and flogged, paid for her escape.[91]

Occasionally, in the cases of very young girls, one or two citizens or attorneys raised a voice of protest on behalf of the child. For example, in Santa Fe, New Mexico, in 1881, a fight between two twelve-year-old girls—one white and one black—resulted in charges, conviction, and jail time for the latter. After the encounter, the father of the white girl, W. H. Gray, secured the arrest of the black child, Mary Elizabeth Washington McKiev. Mary Elizabeth was placed in the county jail and the next day required to appear before justice of the peace García Ortiz.

After listening to Gray and securing the "confession of the . . . little girl," Justice Ortiz found the child guilty and fined her a total of seven dollars and fifty cents. When the child could not pay her fine, Justice Ortiz returned her to the county jail. An attorney, M. S. Breeden, who immediately took the case, wrote in his petition, "considering the respective ages of these *two children* . . . this is a case which calls *loudly* for *Executive Clemency*."[92] The acting governor heard Breeden's call and responded by granting a pardon. The bonding of Hispanics and Anglos against African Americans does not appear to have been confined to the Texas penitentiary but spilled over into New Mexico as well. A local social or political alliance across race lines apparently impelled these adult men to react so vigorously to a quarrel between two children.

New Mexico was not the only jurisdiction willing to punish children with prison time. Other young girls went to penitentiaries as well. In 1880

Henrietta Waideman, "less than sixteen years of age," left the Texas prison system.[93] Four years later, Mary Jane Watson, a fourteen-year-old girl convicted of the theft of a diamond ring, departed, with a reminder that her parole would be revoked for any criminal violation.[94] These teenagers, African Americans, mingled with the general inmate population and worked beside the adults. Although this situation exposed them to violence and sexual abuses, it may also have given them the encouragement and protection of older inmates.

On occasion, local authorities intervened before a child actually entered the penitentiary. Such occurred for Ophelia LeCour, sentenced to the penitentiary at the age of fourteen. Charged with theft, LeCour, who may have been white, received a pardon while still in the county jail.[95] In 1890, in Texas, Susan Bates, "under sixteen years of age," was convicted of perjury and sentenced to five years in the house of corrections. A year and a half later, her attorney, using the written verdict from Bates's trial, demonstrated that the confinement of the inmate at the Huntsville penitentiary violated the judgment of the local court. The lawyer simply placed the embarrassing matter before Governor James Hogg, who signed the pardon two days after receipt of the documents.[96]

Petty theft, "stealing" a diamond ring, perjury—such charges lodged against children and adolescents underscored the controlling purpose of the law. Under what circumstances did officials secure the "confessions" of these children? Certainly intimidation and the desire to frighten children into "good behavior" were among the motivations for placing youngsters inside penitentiaries. These episodes, especially involving children from African American and Hispanic families, again indicated the intention that youngsters learn early about the authority of the state.

Whether adolescent, young woman, or older person, the majority of women committed or faced charges of small crimes against property. A local jail would have been the more appropriate place to serve the brief sentences that should have accompanied such minor offenses. But in high numbers women went to penitentiaries for misdemeanors or nonviolent crimes. For example, in Kansas between 1865 and 1901, forty-six women entered the penitentiary for violent crimes and 105 for nonviolent ones. In Missouri between 1865 and 1871, ten women faced penitentiary time for violent actions and seventy-eight for nonviolent ones. In Arkansas between 1901 and 1906, eighteen women were committed for nonviolent crimes and seven for violent offenses. The nonviolent charges against inmates included grand larceny, accessory to burglary, bigamy, adultery, forgery, slander, perjury, possessing counterfeit coin, and concealing or receiving stolen property.[97]

Grand larceny charges, a common cause for women's imprisonment, often did not meet the usual statutory definition of theft in excess of a twenty-dollar value. Of fourteen former slave women confined to the Huntsville, Texas, penitentiary in 1867, thirteen had been imprisoned on thievery charges (the fourteenth woman gave her husband a pick axe to help him escape from prison). The stolen items included a hog, a night-gown, a pair of drapes, a petticoat, a pair of stockings, and $1.00. Only two women clearly stole an amount to equal a grand larceny charge. One had confessed to her crime after physical torture, and Polly Ann Jennings admitted her theft of eighty dollars, money owed by her white "mistress" who refused to pay the wages due her.[98]

These Texas women came to the attention of William Sinclair, an inspector for the Bureau of Refugees, Freedmen, and Abandoned Lands, who examined the Huntsville penitentiary early in 1867. Sinclair sought executive clemency for approximately 225 former slaves, whom he felt were held against all justice.[99] Sinclair wrote to his superior that the "trivial nature of the crimes charged against them and the severity of the punishment already inflicted . . . should be . . . a sufficient argument for their release."[100]

The case of Caroline Johnson, a free woman from Galveston County, Texas, demonstrated what Sinclair meant. In June 1866, the district court convicted Johnson for the theft of a woman's skirt, valued at three dollars. Nothing in her pardon petition revealed how long Johnson awaited trial in Galveston County before this conviction. William Sinclair, however, noted that most of the Huntsville prisoners had been detained six months to a year in a county jail before trial and that the local time served did not count toward the penitentiary sentence.[101]

Johnson offered Sinclair no particular explanation for the crime, and he recorded only that the prisoner indicated the skirt had been taken from her "mistress." Sinclair hoped he could secure an immediate release for Johnson and the others arguing, "Had they half the funds that many a greater rascal has they would not remain in prison one week."[102]

Despite his goals, Sinclair did not succeed, at least for Caroline Johnson. Not until 20 December 1867 was a pardon petition entered for her. It indicated that the law under which Johnson had been convicted no longer existed. The punishment for her crime had changed from two years in the penitentiary to one year in the county jail, with a possible fine of one hundred dollars. Ten months after William Sinclair interceded for Caroline Johnson and her companions at Huntsville, the Galveston woman received a full pardon.[103] A former slave who eked out a slim living as a domestic worker, Johnson lacked an advocate until this federal officer intervened, and time diminished his success. The impact of her lengthy imprisonment and the questions surrounding her guilt, not only touched her life but rippled through her Texas community.

After all, citizens knew about the court events inside a local jurisdiction. Each person had reason to view the speedy and fickle conduct of the courts with wariness. For example, on 19 November 1866, Amanda Hawkins, a black woman laboring as a farmer in Fayette County, Texas, was indicted for "theft of money," convicted the next day, and sentenced to two years in the penitentiary. In April 1868, in response to a gubernatorial inquiry about Hawkins, a court clerk admitted that no one could find the original indictment, making it impossible to confirm the size of the theft. Hawkins herself had told an investigator at the penitentiary that the amount was $2.50, a sum far below that required for a grand larceny indictment.[104] Charged under vague circumstances for a misdemeanor, Hawkins had virtually no time to assemble a defense, went immediately to the penitentiary, and stayed there almost a year and a half before any official raised questions about her incarceration.

Amanda Hawkins's experience pointed to how rarely major theft accounted for the convictions rendered against women. Rather, women's nonviolent crimes tended to reflect the limited economics of their lives. For women with little education or closed out of western industrial growth, occupational choices stayed narrow. Some jobs were seasonal, none especially lucrative. From region to region, women worked as servants, housekeepers, prostitutes, waitresses, hotel maids, seamstresses, laundresses, cooks, cleaning women, and field hands. Even as the West matured and its economy shifted, the general trend for women to have lower-paying jobs remained steady.

Women with lesser economic options typically associated with men of the same financial standing. Sometimes women's crimes grew out of their connection to these husbands and partners, although which party acted as the instigator of the wrongdoing remained unclear. On one afternoon in Denver, Mary Caffieri and her husband conspired in the theft of oriental rugs from two different establishments. She went to the Colorado penitentiary for two concurrent five-year terms.[105]

Gertie Smith also had connections to Denver crime, where she and her partner Edward Martin operated a shell game. When they moved on to Rawlins, Wyoming, they traveled with Pearl Smith and James Murphy. In Rawlins the two women, who were not related, were charged with distracting store clerks while the men shoplifted. Although the evidence against Gertie and Pearl was circumstantial, they, along with their male companions, went to the Laramie penitentiary for two years.[106]

Frequently, single and married women depended on the economic support of a male partner, whether he obtained it by legal or illegal means. If a husband died or deserted his family, a woman had few opportunities to earn a sufficient income to maintain the home. Poor women, often the only support of several little children, stole food, jewelry, small sums of money. They pilfered a few clothes and household goods. Occasionally they wrote a threatening letter, tried to pass a forged check, or disturbed a church service. When apprehended, they had no money for attorneys and fines, because it was their poverty that made thievery a solution in the first place. Overall, the punishments meted out for these illegalities far surpassed the crimes themselves.

When a woman's transgression included the violation of moral rules, then another layer of social punishment awaited her. Any charge connected to human intimacy—adultery, fornication, bigamy, prostitution—brought strict penalties for women from all cultures. Those penalties often translated into costly fines, the price for sexual misbehavior.

Actually price proved to be exactly what transgressors in morals charges lacked—the price of the fine. Across the era, fines and court costs ranged from $100 to more than $300, handsome fees for women who supported themselves by doing housework or field labor.[107] Without the financial means to pay county fines, prostitutes and poor women, frequently abandoned by the men who were their sexual partners, faced the threat of penitentiary time for carnal offenses.[108]

Even if a woman had not strayed across society's moral boundaries, she might find herself ensnared in charges connected to vice. In 1896 officials in Bonham, Texas, sought remission of a $200 fine for Melia Edwards, a black woman who had worked in the community for years. Edwards's former husband brought the complaint for keeping a disorderly house, a charge for which there appeared to be no foundation. Nonetheless, once she was convicted and could not produce the fine, Melia Edwards went to the county work farm.[109]

The danger of punishment intensified in a morals charge if men and women crossed racial lines, regardless of the gender mix of the couples. In 1881 Sallie Wheeler, an African American mother of four young children and only support for her family, was fined $250 after her conviction for fornication with a white man.[110] The woman had no way to pay a fee of that magnitude and remained incarcerated until county officials wanted her released to care for her children. Nothing in her record indicated whether her male partner had also been charged.

Such was not the case for Texan Ella Anderson, convicted of adultery with a white man and sentenced to a convict labor camp to work off her fine of $300. The camp contractor set the female convict labor rate at thirty dollars per year; Ella Anderson faced a ten-year sentence for adultery. Her partner, a white man, also convicted, served five years, because the same contractor valued male labor at sixty dollars per year. Six years after Ella Anderson went to a work camp, her county attorney filed a pardon petition, arguing that on a misdemeanor the woman had been removed from the local jurisdiction and treated like a state felon.[111] Whatever the circumstances of their union, both Ella Anderson and her white partner gave many years of their lives for ignoring current sexual taboos.

Fifteen years later, eighteen-year-old Dora Meredith, a white woman, went to the Huntsville penitentiary and served seven months of a two-year sentence for an "unlawful marriage to a negro." Attorneys argued unsuccessfully for her immediate pardon on the grounds that her "unnatural white parents" had advised the "girl of very low . . . intelligence" and from a "family . . . of a . . . debasing nature" to enter the marriage.[112] Dora's lawyers determined the only appeal that could be made for a white woman in this situation had to be based on the concept of female stupidity that opened the way for the corrupting influence of others.[113] This gave explanation to the choice of a white woman and a black man to cast aside both popular opinion and legal restrictions against unions across racial lines.

In conclusion, women who came to the penitentiaries of the West often left behind a life that had placed them in an untenable position with local law enforcement officials. Despite the difficulties their public lives generated, these women may have enjoyed some advantage inside the prison because their experiences had forced them to negotiate the rocky road of male authority. The prison world contained new challenges, but public women came equipped with knowledge of their own survival skills and were ready to use them.

Women prisoners who had led private lives, where they resided securely inside the boundaries of acceptable gender conduct, had more lessons to learn in prison. They had to adjust to an unexpected physical environment and to a type of masculine power that they would have liked to deny. Some made the necessary transition; others did not.

Regardless of whether a woman came from a private or public life, few women confronted an evenhanded legal system. Tried in the public press with the language of morality, women had little formal knowledge about the forces that moved quickly to imprison them. Improper court proceedings, excessive sentences for trivial crimes, lengthy time served—all these existed, if they did not indeed prevail. Although their crimes fell largely into nonviolent misdemeanor categories and often reflected the poverty of their lives, women went to male penitentiaries.

The various inequities intensified when the prisoners were women of color. African Americans particularly, in relation to their numbers, went to penitentiaries more often than women from other groups. They served longer sentences and received less leniency through the pardon and parole system.

Class imperatives also influenced the treatment of women prisoners.

Across racial lines, economically disadvantaged women made up the prison rosters. The experiences of middle-class and wealthy women with the criminal justice system seems explained by their near-total exclusion from prisoner records. If women of economic means committed crimes, adjudication was reached for many before they entered western penitentiaries. Women inside the prisons were subjected to arbitrary class assignment by those who supervised them. Within the context of the prison community, women also had their own rules for designating class.

The forces of race, class, and gender shaped the dynamics of penitentiary time. Moreover, these forces cascaded down on the heads of young women, twisting the contours of their adult lives. If they survived the penitentiary, none would forget its special hardships for women. None would want her kith and kin to travel that road. Despite that feeling, women entered male penitentiaries in the West. From the Dakotas to Texas, from Kansas to Idaho, in small cells and on work farms, they became the women of the western prison world.

Notes

1. See Thomas J. Noel, *The City and the Saloon: Denver, 1858–1916* (Lincoln: University of Nebraska Press, 1982), pp. 5, 69, 76, 77, 106, 107, for maps depicting the shifting contours of the Denver saloon district from 1860 to 1915.

2. Ida Jones, Case no. 5267, Sept. 1889, Arapahoe County District Court, Criminal Division, CSA.

3. Ida Jones, Case no. 5751, 22 Apr. 1890, ibid.

4. Ida Jones, Case no. 5802, 5 May 1890, ibid.

5. Ida Jones, Case no. 6043, 14 Oct. 1890, ibid. For more about the Wallace family, see Anne M. Butler, *Daughters of Joy, Sisters of Misery: Prostitutes in the American West, 1865–1890* (Urbana: University of Illinois Press, 1985), photographs following p. 130.

6. See subpoena lists for Cases nos. 5751, 5802, and 6043, Arapahoe County District Court, Criminal Division, CSA.

7. Subpoenas, Ida Jones, Case no. 6054, ibid. In Butler, *Daughters of Joys, Sisters of Misery,* the address of the Wallace Saloon is incorrectly identified as 1937 Market Street.

8. *Denver Express,* 12 Mar. 1917, Denver Police Department Scrapbook, "Excerpts from Crime Records, 1863–1929," microfilmed scrapbook, CSA.

9. See "Officers of the Law," in Butler, *Daughters of Joy, Sisters of Misery,* pp. 74–95.

10. For a discussion of this point and of the fluidity and range of ethnic vice as a response to closed economic avenues across time rather than a cultural manifestation, see Ivan Light, "The Ethnic Vice Industry, 1880–1944," *American Sociological Review* 42 (1977): 464–79.

11. Subpoenas, Ida Jones, Case no. 6054, Arapahoe County, District Court Criminal Division, CSA.

12. See "Legal Entanglements," in Butler, *Daughters of Joy, Sisters of Misery,* pp. 96–121.

13. Judge's Instructions to the Jury, pp. 19 and 20, Ida Jones, Case no. 6043, 14 Oct. 1890, Arapahoe County District Court, Criminal Division, CSA.

14. Sequence of information taken from a largely unmarked scrapbook of newspaper clippings. See "Black Ida" Entries, no. 333, 24 Oct. 1901, Mar. 1902, 3 Aug. 1902, Crime Clippings Scrapbooks, misc., vol. 2, CSA.

15. By 2:00 P.M., the woman had been buried in the prison cemetery (Prisoner no. 1270, Descriptive Records, vols. 1 and 2, roll 1, RG 86, NSA).

16. *Wyoming Reports,* vol. 13, April Term 1904, pp. 96–97, Viola Biggs File, no. 817, Female Inmates File, WSAHD.

17. Ibid., pp. 98–99.

18. Viola Biggs File, no. 817, and Anna E. Trout File, no. 818, Female Inmates File, WSAHD.

19. The appellate court ruled that Viola Biggs was the rightful custodian of Leonard Biggs and that the father had never been in custody or possession of the child, so no kidnapping could occur (*Wyoming Reports,* vol. 13, pp. 97–98). A different situation existed for Nannie Morris, charged by Texas as a fugitive in the kidnapping of her two young sons, whom she took to the Territory of Arizona. Morris, apparently divorced from her husband, W. T. Morton, either took the boys from Morton's residence or fled with the children so the father could not have access to them. The circumstances that led her to take this action were not explained in the court documents (Extradition Application to the Governor of Arizona from the State of Texas on Nannie Morris, 7 Sept. 1899, Nannie Morris, no. 3678 [Extradition Service], State of Texas, Executive Clemency Files, TSA [hereafter Executive Clemency Files, TSA]).

20. Testimony of O. B. Mann, Testimony of John M. Baldwin, State of Wyoming versus Ella Smith, Transcript of Testimony, Big Horn County, District Court Criminal Case Files, Criminal Docket 358, pp. 1–2, 15–16, WSAHD.

21. Smith testified that the previous summer she had to stay on the range almost daily to prevent her herds from being divided and driven off (Ella Smith Testimony, ibid., p. 38, WSAHD).

22. Ibid., pp. 27, 39.

23. Ibid., pp. 22, 23, 30.

24. Ibid., pp. 22–23.

25. Ibid., passim.

26. Ibid., p. 47.

27. For examples in Kansas, see the files of Florence Akers, box 1; Addie L. Amann, box 2; Margaret Baldwin, box 5; Jeanette Johnson, box 69; Georgia Jones, box 70; Jennie Pierce (and Charles Cassida), box 20; and Mary Jane Scales, box 116, all in State of Kansas, Governor's Office, Pardon and Parole Files, 1863–1919, KSHS (hereafter, Pardon and Parole Files, KSHS). For Missouri, see files of Rebecca Boyd, box 21, folder 16; Pernina Jackson, box 21, folder 44; Laura Samuels, box 23, folder 18; Sarah Simpson, box 31, folder 10; Ellen Williams, box 34, folder 14; Jane Young, box 23, folder 42, all in Pardon Papers, RG 5, MSA.

28. George, *Texas Convict,* p. 79.

29. Literacy figures changed gradually across the time period. For example, of the sixty-four black women who entered the Louisiana penitentiary between 1865 and 1872, only five could read and of those five only one could write (Register of Convicts Received, 13 Feb. 1866–29 Dec. 1889, Prisoners nos. 1–9073, LSP). Among twenty-five women imprisoned at the Arkansas penitentiary between 1874 and 1885, nine could read or write, while sixteen were completely illiterate (Register of State Convicts Received at and Discharged from the Arkansas State Penitentiary, 1871–86, ASHC). In Kansas, between 1883 and 1906, of approximately 125 black women prisoners, 109 could read and write (Statement of Convicts, Prisoner Ledger A, KSHS). Hispanic women began to show a common school education by the twentieth cen-

tury. See prisoners Margarita Olivas, no. 2017, and Juana Chacón, no. 2018, Convict Record Book, microcopy roll 1, NMSA.

30. Lewis Wood to Governor L. S. Ross, 26 May 1888, Lizzie Gibson, no. 857, 29 May 1888, Executive Clemency Files, TSA.

31. Pardon Application, Susan Wallace, no. 2872, 6 Dec. 1879, ibid.

32. Citizens' Petition to the Board of Pardons of the State of Nevada, 12 ——— 1877, Maggie Hart File, Nevada State Penitentiary, Inmate Case Files, NSCMA (hereafter, Inmate Case Files, NSCMA).

33. Regardless of how the jury came to its guilty verdict, the district attorney for Washoe County later denied he found anything mitigating in Maggie Hart's case. Calling Maggie Hart the "mistress" of one William Hart and denouncing the pair as "the worst couple of low thieves that Reno could boast of," the district attorney insisted that Maggie "refuses to . . . be respectable," and recommended that if she were released from prison, "although [she is] . . . a Baby Face and can create sympathy in almost any bachelor's breast," she should be shipped "so far beyond the limits of this state under proper escort that she may never come here again" (William Cain to the Board of Pardons of the State of Nevada, n.d., ibid.).

34. ——— to Governor L. S. Ross, 17 Feb. 1888; original petition for Essie Sara from J. S. Hill to Governor L. S. Ross, 7 Feb. 1888, Essie Sara, no. 1108, 28 Feb. 1889, Executive Clemency Files, TSA.

35. George Pendleton to Governor James S. Hogg, 15 July 1892, Sarah Thomas, no. 2474, Executive Clemency Files, TSA.

36. D. R. Pendleton to Governor James S. Hogg, 28 Sept. 1892, ibid.

37. G. I. Turnley to Governor James S. Hogg, 30 Nov. 1892, Kate Stanley and Tal Rogers, no. 2438, 3 Dec. 1892, Executive Clemency Files, TSA.

38. Citizens' Petition, 22 Jan. 1889, Minnie Mitchell, no. 1087, 5 Feb. 1889, Executive Clemency Files, TSA.

39. Pardon, Amanda Roads, no. 3620, 17 Nov. 1883, Executive Clemency Files, TSA.

40. Pardon Declaration, Lena Gayhart, no. 4020, 13 Nov. 1883, Executive Clemency Files, TSA. For other cases of a recent German immigrants with few English skills convicted, one of forgery, the other of unlawful marriage, see Rosa Schmidt, no. 785, 20 Feb. 1888, and Kate Meichmyer, no. 972, 2 Oct. 1888, ibid.

41. The process by which officials obtained confessions came from a long history of unorthodox procedures. In 1866, a former slave, Mary Burns, "confessed" to stealing thirty dollars after she and her daughter were "hung up by the neck" (W. H. Sinclair to Lt. J. F. Kirkman, 26 Feb. 1867, Record of the Bureau of Refugees, Freedmen, and Abandoned Lands, Texas, Assistant Commissioner, Letters Received Register, vol. 1, 1866–67, N-S, box 4, RG 105, NA).

42. Smith did not actually go to the penitentiary for this conviction. The justice of the peace who tried the case asked in the application that Smith's fine be remitted. Her petition to the governor also asked that the costs be remitted to her and this was done (Ellen Smith, no. 919, 7 Aug. 1888, Executive Clemency Files, TSA).

43. Kansas State Penitentiary, Record of Prisoners Received, series 1 and series 2, 1864–1906, KSHS (hereafter, Record of Prisoners Received, KSHS).

44. State of Missouri, Register of Inmates Received and Discharged, vol. C, 1854–71, roll 2, RG 213, MSA (hereafter, Register of Inmates Received and Discharged, MSA).

45. Register of Convicts Received, 13 Feb. 1866–29 Dec. 1889, Prisoners nos. 1–9073, passim, LSP.

46. Record of Convicts: Penitentiary at Anamosa, 30 Apr. 1872–20 June 1907, Prisoners nos. 991–5741, ISA.

47. State of Montana, State Prison Convict Register, 1879–1920 (hereafter, State Prison Convict Register, MtHS); State of Montana, Description of Prisoners, vols. 6–8, 1885–1911, MtHS.

48. *Biennial Report of the Idaho State Penitentiary,* 1903–4, p. 50, ISL.

49. Knepper, "Imprisonment and Society in Arizona Territory," p. 162.

50. This material, drawn from the 1910 census, covers all kinds of penal institutions in the United States (U.S. Department of Commerce, Bureau of the Census, *Negro Population: 1790–1915* [Washington: G.P.O., 1918], pp. 446–47).

51. In 1866 Texan Jane Haynes, a white woman, persuaded Judy Hammer, a former slave, that the two should break into a local store. Haynes participated in the break-in and accompanied Hammer into the store but was not arrested or charged (W. H. Sinclair to J. F. Kirkman, 26 Feb. 1867, Bureau of Refugees, Freedmen, and Abandoned Lands, RG 105, NA).

52. Descriptive Records, vols. 1–3, roll 1, RG 86, NSA; Inmate Record Jackets: Inactive since 1965, project 3087, boxes 77/18–22, NSP.

53. See Prisoners nos. 164, 187, 327, 1797, 2029, 3769, 3938, 4376, 5175, Descriptive Records, vols. 1–3, roll 1, RG 86, NSA.

54. Prisoners nos. 64 and 4376, ibid.

55. Prisoners nos. 1075, 2082, 2359, 2433, 2806, 3116, 3475, 4026, 4165 (second incarceration as 4449), 4583, 5308, ibid.

56. Index to Prisoners, Arkansas Penitentiary, 31 Oct. 1879–June 1933, ADC. Not all letters of the alphabet and all years canvassed. The figures suggest that across time black women constituted more than 90 percent of the Arkansas female prison population. In 1916, black women made up almost 89 percent of the incarcerated females (*Biennial Report of the Arkansas Penitentiary and Reform School,* 1 Nov. 1914–31 Oct. 1916, p. 56, ASHC).

57. All prisoner records since the organization of Arkansas are kept on microfiche in alphabetical order. Under this system the opportunities for misplacing a prisoner's records through filing error are extremely high. Records for some nineteenth-century prisoners apparently no longer exist, and some files consist only of an empty fiche jacket. Prisoner files are stored in the Records Department inside the Arkansas State Penitentiary, Pine Bluff, Ark.

58. "Physician's Report," *Biennial Report of the Board of Penitentiary Commissioners and the Reports of Inspector of Convicts and Penitentiary Physician,* p. 70, State of Arkansas, Penitentiary, series A, RG 4, ASHC.

59. Index to Prisoners, Arkansas Penitentiary, 31 Oct. 1879–June 1933, see Prisoners nos. 2240, 3219, 3505, 4186, 6840, 9304, and the same prisoner numbers, Microfiche Prisoner Records, Records Department, ADC.

60. For a discussion predicated on the concept that to be a white woman means to occupy a "social category" that is "inescapably racialized as well as gendered," see Vron Ware, *Beyond the Pale: White Women, Racism, and History* (London: Verso, 1992).

61. Index to Prisoners, Arkansas Penitentiary, 31 Oct. 1879–June 1933, passim. For pardoned black women, see Prisoners nos. 253, 384, 1326, 1623, 2063, 2399, 3223, 4613, 6127, Microfiche Prisoner Records, Records Department ADC.

62. "Discrimination against Negro Criminals in Arkansas," *Journal of the American Institute of Criminal Law and Criminology* 1 (Jan. 1911): 948.

63. Pardon Application, Caroline Williams, no. 5560, 22 Dec. 1889, Executive Clemency Files, TSA.

64. As early as 1851, prison administrators set the scene for the racism that permeated prison management. In 1851, Catharine Schovenberg received a pardon from the governor of Missouri because the prison had only one cell for women. A black

woman, accused of arson, already occupied this filthy room; the warden argued that a white woman should not be expected to share quarters with a slave. Presumably, if the slave were removed then Schovenberg could inhabit the cell, despite its condition (Catherine Schovenberg File, Pardon Papers, box 5, folder 15, RG 5, MSA). It was unusual for slaves to be imprisoned, as owners usually dealt out punishments, but imprisonment did occur on a few occasions. For example, a fifteen-year-old slave was indicted for the murder of her infant child in 1846. In the same record group, see Citizens' Petitions, Nelly —— File, box 3.

65. Ann Fienup-Riordan comments about a community with an oral tradition that "children were taught that their actions, if performed according to the rules, created a barrier to misfortune and opened a passageway to success in the future. . . . if they failed to live by the rules, illness and death . . . would come to them" (*Boundaries and Passages: Rule and Ritual in Yup'ik Eskimo Oral Tradition* [Norman: University of Oklahoma Press, 1994], p. 158). Robert Park suggested that older women in the African American community held onto family information and were the ones who most forcefully recounted what they knew (*Race and Culture* [London: Collier-Macmillan, Free Press of Glencoe, 1950], p. 73). Michael N. Nagler observed that certain communities used an oral tradition to "encode . . . a learning strategy" for "survival value" ("On Almost Killing Your Friends: Some Thoughts on Violence in Early Cultures," in *Comparative Research on Oral Traditions: A Memorial for Milman Perry,* ed. John Miles Foley [Columbus, Ohio: Slavica Press, 1985], p. 429). For other discussions about the importance of teaching children through an oral tradition, see Deborah Gray White, "Female Slaves," pp. 22–31; and Robin Ridington, *Little Bit Know Something* (Iowa City: University of Iowa Press, 1990), pp. xiii, xv, 213.

66. Mary Godfrey File, 28 May 1867, Pardon Papers, box 23, folder 36, RG 5, MSA.

67. Convict Record Book, 1 and 2, NMSA; Territory of New Mexico Report of the Penitentiary Committee of the House of Representatives of the 30th Legislative Assembly, Santa Fe, Feb. 1893, pp. 55–62, microcopy, Edmund G. Ross, 1885–89, New Mexico Penitentiary, Territorial Archives of New Mexico, roll 122, frame 123, NMSA.

68. Testimony of Inmates Guadalupe Grimsinger, Annie Cordes, and Mary Harrington to the Investigating Committee, 29 July 1909, *Report of the Penitentiary Investigating Committee,* pp. 544–48, TSA.

69. S. M. Robertson to Governor Benjamin Culberson, 19 Oct. 1896, Mrs. W. J. Stewart, no. 4300, 18 Dec. 1896, Executive Clemency Files, TSA.

70. Albert Silas Harris, "Life of Belle Harris Nelson," pp. 56, 66.

71. Kate Richards O'Hare, *Prison Letters* (Girard, Kans.: Appeal to Reason, 1919; History of Women Microfilm, 7648, New Haven, Conn.: Research Publications, 1977), pp. 4, 93.

72. When a friend sent her a large box of soaps, O'Hare distributed them, making it the first time that every woman prisoner—black and white—had a toilet soap instead of the standard issue lye bar (ibid., p. 43).

73. Ibid., p. 31.

74. Dolly Brady to Governor B. B. Brooks, 6 Mar. 1907, Dolly Brady File, Petitions for Pardon, Governor Bryant B. Brooks, WSAHD.

75. Chris Mathison to Governor B. B. Brooks, 21 Apr., 1907, ibid.

76. Clyde M. Watts to Governor Bryant B. Brooks, 19 Mar. 1907, ibid.

77. M. S. Bonnifield, Citizens' Petition, 5 Jan. 1881, Jennie Taylor File, Nevada State Penitentiary, Board of Pardons Files, 1874–1915, NSCMA (hereafter, Board of Pardons Files, NSCMA).

78. Herbert S. Hadley to Benjamin Gray, Chairman, St. Louis Board of Police Commissioners, 10 Mar., 15 Mar. 1909, Herbert S. Hadley Papers, UM.

79. "Warden's Report," *Biennial Report of the Board of Inspectors of the Missouri State Penitentiary,* 1907-8, p. 5, MSA.

80. See the account of Belle Harris in the Utah penitentiary given in chap. 2 above. Emma Goldman and Kate Richards O'Hare, incarcerated in the Missouri state penitentiary at the same time, made prison reform an important issue after their release. See Emma Goldman, *Living My Life,* 2 vols., reprint ed. (New York: Dover, 1970), vol. 1, pp. 483-85, and vol. 2, pp. 625-28; and Sally M. Miller, *From Prairie to Prison: The Life of Social Activist Kate Richards O'Hare* (Columbia: University of Missouri Press, 1993).

81. Of greater importance than the perceived class distinctions among criminal women may have been the class and attitudes of those who controlled the legal process. In 1911 prison reformer George W. Kirchwey argued that the criminal law of the United States was "representative not of the will of the community . . . but rather of class sentiment . . . of those—criminal judges and prosecuting attorneys—to whom the administration of the criminal law is committed" ("Crime and Punishment: The Influence of the Study of the Results of Prison Punishments on the Criminal Law," *Journal of the American Institute of Criminal Law and Criminology* 1 [Jan. 1911]: 719-20).

82. For a discussion of events surrounding the ongoing clash between cattlemen and sheep ranchers, see T. A. Larson, *History of Wyoming* (Lincoln: University of Nebraska Press, 1978), pp. 366-72.

83. Unidentified newspaper clipping, n.d., Peter and Minnie Snyder File, no. 271, Petitions for Pardon, Governor DeForest Richards, WSAHD.

84. Citizens' Petition, n.d., ibid.

85. Mrs. Minnie Snyder to Governor Richards, 12 Dec. 1901, ibid.

86. Women of forty to forty-five years of age were often described as "elderly" and "enfeebled." Some significantly older women did go to the penitentiary. For example in 1878 Sarah Smallwood, age seventy-six, was convicted of assault and battery and described as "tottering on the grave" (Sarah Smallwood, no. 2466, 24 Aug. 1878; also see Polly Mitchell, no. 2171, 6 Oct. 1877, Executive Clemency Files, TSA).

87. Arapahoe County District Court, Criminal Division, CSA.

88. Record of Convicts: Penitentiary at Anamosa, 30 Apr. 1872-20 June 1907, Prisoners nos. 991-5741, ISA.

89. Knepper, "Imprisonment and Society in Arizona Territory," p. 163.

90. Requisition for Mary alias Sarah Crook, 23 May 1878, Mary Crook, n.n., 25 May 1878, Executive Clemency Files, TSA.

91. Alice Dunbar, no. 529, Register of Convicts Received, 13 Feb. 1866-29 Dec. 1899, Prisoners nos. 1-9073, LSP; Asst. Warden Roger S. Thomas interview with author, 22 June 1987, Angola, LSP. Older women were also subjected to imprisonment, although their numbers did not equal the youthful inmates. For examples of women fifty and older, see Julia Anna Mac, n.n., 14 May 1874; Mary Shaw, no. 2913, 22 Dec. 1893; Sarah A. Ware, no. 3873, 25 Mar. 1896, Executive Clemency Files, TSA; and Prisoners nos. 4220, 4654, 4948, 5113, 5281, 5593, Record of Convicts: Penitentiary at Anamosa, ISA.

92. M. S. Breeden to Acting Governor W. G. Ritch, 15 July 1881, Governor's Papers, Lionel A. Sheldon, 1881-85, Territorial Archives of New Mexico, reel 100, NMSA.

93. Pardon Application, Henrietta Waideman, no. 3183, 16 Dec. 1880, Executive Clemency Files, TSA.

94. Pardon Application, Mary Jane Watson, n.n., 1 Sept. 1884, Executive Clemency Files, TSA.

95. Pardon Application, Ophelia LeCour, no. 14, 26 Feb. 1885, Executive Clemency Files, TSA.

96. Pardon Application, Susan Bates, no. 1962, 31 July 1891, Executive Clemency Files, TSA.

97. For Kansas see State Penitentiary, Statement of Convicts, Prisoner Ledgers A, F, G, H, KSHS; for Missouri, Pardon Papers, RG 5, 1865–72, MSA; for Arkansas, *Biennial Report of the State Penitentiary,* 1900–1902, pp. 28–35; ibid., 1903–4, pp. 30–34; ibid., 1905–6, pp. 27–35, ASHC.

98. William N. Sinclair to J. F. Kirkman, 26 Feb. 1867, RG 105, NA. There were, of course, women inmates whose crime exceeded the twenty dollar value required for grand larceny. For examples see Anna Peterson, no. 2959, 6 Feb. 1894, and Julia Slayton, no. 3379, 13 Nov. 1894, Executive Clemency Files, TSA; Cora Stevens, nos. 17758 and 17759, 25 Oct. 1906, Denver County District Court, Criminal Division, CSA; Grace Johnson, no. 2155, Inez Perry, no. 1315, Minnie Farrell, no. 1358, Myrtle Lea, no. ?, and Jennie Williams, no. 1337, State Prison Convict Register, Mar. 1879–Nov. 1910, MtHS.

99. Sinclair referred to the former slave prisoners as "freed people" in his letter. Within a few years, guards and prison administrators living and working inside the penitentiary reserved that term for themselves and their families. Violation of the "free people's" living space brought the severest retribution by prison guards (William H. Sinclair to J. F. Kirkman, 26 Feb. 1867, RG 105, NA; Asst. Warden Roger S. Thomas interview with author, 22 June 1987, LSP).

100. William H. Sinclair to J. F. Kirkman, 26 Feb. 1867, RG 105, NA.

101. Ibid.

102. Ibid.

103. Pardon Application, Caroline Johnson, n.n., 20 Dec. 1867, Executive Clemency Files, TSA.

104. Pardon Application, "Manda," n.n., 18 Apr. 1868, Executive Clemency Files, TSA; William H. Sinclair to J. F. Kirkman, 26 Feb. 1867, RG 105, NA.

105. The People of the State of Colorado versus Charles Caffieri and Mary Caffieri, nos. 17837 and 17840, 10 Nov. 1906, Denver County District Court, Criminal Division, CSA.

106. Pearl Smith File, Inmate no. 680, and Gertie Smith File, Inmate no. 681, Petitions for Pardons, Governor DeForest Richards, WSHAD.

107. For examples of high fines for morals convictions of women described as "poor" and "destitute," see Ann Fitzhugh, no. ?, 23 Aug. 1877; Frances King, no. ?, 6 Nov. 1882; Bertha Spriggs, no. 632, 16 May 1887; Lena Harper, no. 1271, 16 July 1889; Jerry Brown and Fannie Whipple, no. 1279, 19 July 1889; Malinda Mathews, no. 1520, 18 Mar. 1890; Louisa Tunall, no. 2789, 20 Oct. 1893; Elsie Stewart, no. 3203, 5 June 1894; Lizzie Peiarey, no. 5181, 2 Mar. 1899; Alice Cooper, no. 19576, 28 Aug. 1899, all in Executive Clemency Files, TSA.

108. Although Texan Malinda Mathews was convicted of adultery, her partner, Andy Brodus, was acquitted of the same charge (Malinda Mathews, no. 1520, 18 Mar. 1890, Executive Clemency Files, TSA). Each of the following women was to be sent to the Texas penitentiary but received a pardon: Amelia Mantenfel, no. 2091, 7 July 1877; Cora McMahon, no. 3197, 13 Apr. 1881; Henrietta Marble, no. 3630, 28 Dec. 1881; Lida Ryan, no. 2207, 11 May 1892; Mollie Hanson, no. 3393, 15 Nov. 1894, all in ibid.

109. W. W. Ridling to Governor Charles A. Culberson, 16 Nov. 1896; J. W. McKee to Governor C. A. Culberson, 16 Nov. 1896, Melia Edwards, no. 4260, 19 Nov. 1896, Executive Clemency Files, TSA.

110. Sallie Wheeler, alias Sallie Hall, n.n., 21 Sept. 1881, Executive Clemency Files, TSA.

111. Pardon Application, Ella Anderson, no. 826, 25 Apr. 1888, Executive Clemency Files, TSA.

112. Citizens' Petition, n.d., Dora Meredith, no. 4548, 14 Sept. 1897, Executive Clemency Files, TSA.

113. Laws against marriage between whites and persons of color were common until well into the twentieth century. For an example of one state, see Roger D. Hardaway, "Prohibiting Interracial Marriage: Miscegenation Laws in Wyoming," *Annals of Wyoming* 52 (Spring 1980): 55–60.

The Wyoming Territorial Penitentiary reflected the cheerless atmosphere characteristic of nineteenth-century prison architecture. Courtesy of the Wyoming Division of Cultural Resources, Cheyenne, Wyo.

Despite the vigorous defense of her attorney, Ella Smith served time in the Wyoming penitentiary for a conflict with stockmen in her area. Courtesy of the Wyoming Division of Cultural Resources, Cheyenne, Wyo.

Mary Caffieri went to the Colorado penitentiary along with her husband for attempted theft in a Denver rug store. Courtesy of the Division of State Archives and Public Records, Denver, Colo.

Cora Thomas, a twenty-year-old domestic worker, served eighteen months in the Kansas penitentiary for a grand larceny charge. Courtesy of the Kansas State Historical Society, Topeka, Kans.

The inmate in-take card of Mollie Harrison recorded her Bertillon measurements, a practice that gained popular* among American prison administrators. Courtesy of the Nevada State Library and Archives, Carson City, Nev.

Bedecked with a name pin on her collar, Minnie Snyder faced time in the Wyoming penitentiary for an accidental homicide committed by her husband as a mob of ranchers pursued the couple. Courtesy of the Wyoming Division of Cultural Resources, Cheyenne, Wyo.

Although nearly illiterate, Kittie Smith carefully recorded her whereabouts for the Nevada parole board every month for years after her release from the penitentiary. Courtesy of the Nevada State Library and Archives, Carson City, Nev.

After years of scandal, Idaho prison administrators attempted to segregate women inmates at the male prison by building the enclosure shown in the foreground. Courtesy of the Idaho State Historical Society, Boise, Idaho.

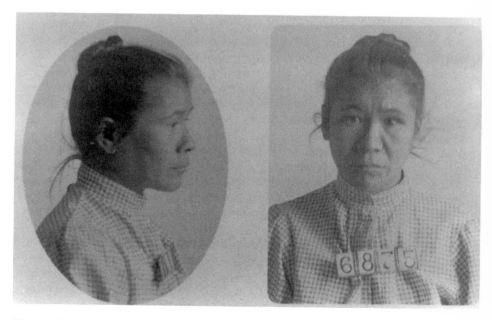

Florence Hague, a Mexican American woman imprisoned in Colorado, shows that officials got double duty from their numbers by turning digits upside down on an inmate's chest. Courtesy of the Division of State Archives and Public Records, Denver, Colo.

Annie Bruce, a teenager from the Mormon community of Smoot, Wyoming, went to prison for the poisoning death of her father, although her culpability remained questionable. Courtesy of the Wyoming Division of Cultural Resources, Cheyenne, Wyo.

Kate Richards O'Hare, shown here several years after her release from the Missouri penitentiary, used her own inmate experience as the basis for her call for prison reform. Detail. Courtesy of the Missouri Historical Society, St. Louis, Mo.

4 Women's Worlds of Violence

i was so Missible [*sic*], Mistreated by my
husband. . . . he beet [*sic*] me and the poor
children like we was dogs.
—Henrietta Cook
Kansas State Penitentiary
1883

Many Kansas neighbors knew that Henrietta Cook and her five children lived in a violent and vicious home. The Cooks' four-month-old baby, left in the care of his father, died after his highchair fell into the fireplace. Later that year, the oft-battered Henrietta apparently asked a local physician to give her a "dose to cure [my] husband of abuse."[1] On that evidence, as well as the testimony of several neighbors about Henrietta's indifferent reaction when Hiram Cook died, the twenty-five-year-old woman was convicted of murder and sentenced to hang. Henrietta Cook, who had married at age fourteen and was pregnant with her sixth child, entered the Kansas penitentiary, where once her death sentence was commuted, she faced life in prison.[2]

Seven years passed before Henrietta Cook and her children began to draw organized public support. Questions about the role of the accommodating

Mary Kafford, Colorado State Penitentiary. Courtesy Division of State Archives and Public Records, Denver, Colo.

family physician, whether anyone deliberately administered the strychnine, and the possibility that Hiram Cook routinely doctored himself with a number of poisons resulted in citizens' petitions for Henrietta's release. It took until 1889 and a change of governors for the prison chaplain, the matron, and the teacher of Henrietta's son to secure a successful conclusion to the campaign for a pardon.[3] Convicted murderess, her children adrift, her health broken from years of childbearing, beatings, and imprisonment, Henrietta Cook had witnessed how violence controlled one's life, overtook a family atmosphere, drew victims to respond in kind, and then punished women who assumed the masculine prerogative of physical force.[4]

For women, violence connected to the penitentiary involved two components. Women's violent behaviors that brought them to the penitentiary constituted the first. These episodes largely stemmed from chronic conditions of verbal and physical abuse in women's workplaces and home environments. The acts of violence that women committed spawned and excused the second, the violent assaults against female inmates once they entered the prison routines.

At first glance, violence and womanhood appeared to be unlikely partners in the West. The ambience of work and war, life and leisure suggested an out-of-doors masculine arena for violence, whether deliberate or accidental. In the eye of the westerner, women of all cultures intruded so seldom onto these fields of action that they possessed little identity as perpetrators of the intentional physical force, mayhem, or murder that violated coded Anglo law. When such occurred, women's violence seemed to be aberrant, completely divorced from female bearing and cultural standards of womanhood.

But women of many hearths and homes resorted to physical assault not so rarely as the larger society thought. Women's violence, however, often lacked craftiness for planned attack, thirst for economic gain, or lust for political advancement. Rather, fear, self-defense, and anger gave birth to the criminal aggression of western women.

Regardless of its origins, women's violence took on a highly public, often emotionally charged, character, as the machinery of the judicial system moved into place. A legal response in cases of assault and death accorded with written and unwritten law. Less obvious in the aftermath was who controlled the subjective elements in prosecution and how the selection of candidates for punishment transpired.

If a woman lived and worked in the vice district and committed a violent crime, she almost certainly went to the penitentiary. Yet both private and public violence surrounded women who followed vice professions, making it difficult for them to remain untouched by its power. In Montana Mattie Lee, a forty-year-old white prostitute, followed a customer, Charles

Hillman, from her house to a saloon, where she demanded three dollars that he owed her. Hillman, a Finn working as a laborer in a nearby wood camp, had come to town for a day of drinking. He spent the afternoon with Mattie, but then lurched off without paying her.

Confronted by the irate Mattie, the drunken client hurled insults at her and refused to pay the debt. Mattie, also intoxicated, fired a single warning shot into the floor. When Hillman continued to ignore her, she placed the revolver against his head and shot him through the eye.[5] Hillman died instantly. Mattie put the gun away, waited for the marshal to arrest her, and made no denial of her guilt. Portrayed in the newspapers as "a dissolute woman and notorious character, better known to her class as 'Dutch Mat,'" Mattie Lee was actually a widow turned prostitute from Augusta, Maine.[6] Mattie Lee entered the Montana penitentiary to serve ten years for manslaughter, while her indigent customer went to a pauper's grave at the expense of the county.

In Montana alone repeated episodes pointed to the fact that prostitutes worked in an environment of frequent and unpredictable violence. In 1880 Belle Watson, Rose Bennett, and Jessie Stuart each went to the penitentiary for violent assaults: Belle, a black woman, for wounding her white male companion and another black prostitute, Rose for the second-degree murder of Frank Graver, and Jessie for a shooting assault on another prostitute.[7] Sixteen-year-old Bertha King, a white prostitute who escaped being drowned by one Montana gambler, accidentally shot and killed another faro dealer only four months later.[8] Described as one whose "winsome face" showed evidence of "vice and crime . . . early revelry and constant dissipation," the teenaged Bertha went to the penitentiary at Deer Lodge for one year.[9] In Butte, Emma Teal, an African American prostitute, stabbed Pauline Foster, also black, as the latter emerged from the Abbey Saloon with Georgia St. Clair, a white member of the demimonde.[10] Although Emma inflicted twelve to fourteen wounds, testimony from a black bartender that before the attack Pauline Foster bragged she had "just gotten through punching one woman" convinced jurors the injured woman was the aggressor; convicted of assault in the second degree, Emma Teal was sentenced to one to five years in the penitentiary.[11] In the same neighborhood, a male customer battered a prostitute so unmercifully over several days that a constable decided to intervene and discovered the woman freshly beaten and tied to a bedstead.[12] Prostitutes lived with violence, felt it, participated in it.[13]

The violence in these women's lives might be dismissed as singular to their profession and not typical of western women generally. Violence, however, sprang into women's lives in many circumstances and often unexpectedly. Episodes that occurred in confusion or by accident metamorphosed into deliberate criminal actions, especially when community sentiment solidified against a woman. Such a chain of events shaped the life of Nevada housewife Carrie Scott.

In 1908 forty-two-year-old Carrie Scott, who possessed an unblemished legal record, inadvertently crossed into the public criminal arena. Carrie and her husband, a nearly indigent couple, lived close to an isolated pump station in rural Nevada. Late one evening, her husband, in an angry exchange, ordered a group of transients milling about the station to move off. As the men started away, one turned back and approached the Scotts in what they thought a threatening manner. Alone, without neighbors to help, husband and wife fired three weapons in the general direction of the intruder, as he continued to advance. The victim, a deaf man, could not hear their warnings, and Carrie, firing her twenty-two rifle wildly into the dark, killed him.

Public agitation against the Scotts ran high. Local prejudice and inflammatory news reports fueled the proceedings.[14] Carrie Scott faced responsibility for the death, accidental or not, but the court turned aside self-defense arguments or the popular western "no duty to retreat" concept.[15] Carrie went to the Nevada penitentiary for a sentence of twenty years.[16] Only the persistence of the court-appointed attorney, who thought the Scotts wrongly charged from the outset, and Carrie's fading health from an abdominal tumor won her a pardon in November 1911.[17]

Carrie Scott lacked the personal finances to buy her way out of the trouble, but she had the advantage of race to lessen her complications. When a disturbance included nonwhite women, chances for an equitable hearing in the courts diminished even further. More disastrous, if a public clash mixed white and black citizens, the African American woman headed for a predictable outcome. In these situations, white aggressors had access to a range of power maneuvers by which they avoided severe penalties. On the other hand, black women had the useful but less formal power of family or community to implore for assistance from white law enforcement and legal officers.

Ada Wade, an African American woman, found herself caught in such an interracial tangle in Cuero, Texas. A group of young white men went into the black community and intruded on a dance for African Americans. The festive occasion quickly turned ugly, for as Ada Wade danced by, one of these men stepped on the back of her dress, tearing it. Wade, with boldness of spirit, accused the interloper of deliberately causing the damage. An angry exchange erupted between the two; Ada produced a knife and struck her adversary a glancing blow. An attack, however slight, of a black woman on a white man brought the expected. Ada Wade went to the penitentiary for four years, convicted of assault with intent to commit murder.

The circumstances did not rest well with the black community and by September local citizens had organized to protest the severity of Ada's sentence. One court officer endorsed the petition, convinced that, rather than a gracious apology the wounded man claimed he offered, Ada Wade had been subjected to the "most opprobrious epithets" by "the injured party or one of his companions."[18] Her sentence was commuted to two years, but Ada Wade still served penitentiary time for her refusal to accept the physical and verbal abuse of a white man.

Annie Carmack of Kansas faced a harsher sentence for her involvement with violence. This episode also centered on a dispute at a dance, with Annie and a friend pitted against an older drunken woman. As the fight escalated, a young man slipped Annie an open knife, and she plunged it into the victim's throat. Annie's antagonist lay dead on the floor.[19] Annie Carmack, aged fifteen, was sentenced to the Kansas penitentiary for fifteen years. Five years later, efforts spearheaded by her father to secure Annie's freedom reached a peak. One attorney informed the governor that the presiding judge agreed to a commutation because "he admits to me that he was severe in his sentences of colored people at that time."[20] Despite the intense lobbying for Carmack, she did not receive a pardon until 1899, after serving more than half her sentence.[21]

By the early twentieth century, incarceration procedures for African American women charged with violence had not changed appreciably. In 1905 Florence Akers, a twenty-year-old "mulatto" cook, entered the penitentiary to serve five to twenty-one years for manslaughter.[22] Arrested at three in the morning and charged with the stabbing death of a black porter from Pittsburg, Kansas, Akers lost out at her trial when a group of black women testified against her. Over the next five and one-half years, the arresting sheriff, the local jailer, a black prison guard, and a lawyer joined in supporting Akers's claim of innocence. The sheriff insisted that he never believed Akers guilty, as the only witnesses against her had been "colored women (toughfs [*sic*])."[23] The undersheriff wrote to the governor that during the time all connected to the crime had been held at the jail, "One solid black negro woman drilled the other negro women time after time as to what to swear when on the stand."[24] Apparently, the police strategy to round up a group of possible murder suspects and hold them until some agreed to turn state's evidence met with success. Florence Akers may have been the unlucky scapegoat for a group of black women who understood exactly the risk they all faced in the courts.

As some court officers demonstrated, the other women probably knew better than the newcomer Akers what to expect from the local authorities.

Five years after the trial, both the prosecutor and the trial judge opposed a pardon for Florence Akers, but not because they found the evidence of her guilt compelling. Instead, they accused Akers of an earlier crime spree through the Kansas towns of Winfield, Arkansas City, Independence, and Cherryvale, although they had no proof of this and it had no bearing on the case at hand. They pronounced Akers "of the worst character" and her associates "of the worst class . . . holding up and robbing people and committing petty thefts."[25] On the basis of testimony from these associates, labeled a criminal gang by the judge and district attorney, the two ascertained Akers's guilt and objected to clemency for her. By their reasoning, Florence Akers deserved to remain in prison because they had heard that she traveled with bad companions, the very source of the damning testimony against her.

Those who had direct contact with Florence Akers disagreed. Sheriff Ogg declared the prisoner had "served long enough for another's crime," and undersheriff Johnson announced, "Florence Akers was 'railroaded.'"[26] These two offered no explanation for their failure to champion Akers at the time of her trial. No matter; the governor turned back the pardon petitions with a terse "unwilling" or "not ready," and Florence Akers remained in the state penitentiary for a murder she possibly did not commit.

Perhaps it was the African American tower and gate guard, J. G. Bowers, who finally wrote the most moving appeal, when he added a note to his petition that he was a Progressive Republican who supported Governor Walter Stubbs "to the end."[27] In September, just in time for the fall elections, Florence Akers received a parole. Her case had completed its purpose. After public altercations, someone in the black community would be punished for the violence.[28] With that message sufficiently conveyed and officeholders searching for ethnic votes, the state reversed its punitive stance and freed Akers.

Enough violence riddled the domestic arenas of the West that the courts did not want for defendants of whom to make examples. In April 1913, a drunken after-hours party in Laramie, Wyoming, took an unexpected violent swing when two African American women quarreled and Mable Clark shot and killed Gertrude Gordon. The women had quarreled throughout the evening, but it was the request of Gertie Gordon that one of the male revelers play "Dixie" on the mandolin that infuriated Mable Clark.[29] Words between the women rose until Gertie Gordon followed Mable Clark to her bedroom and struck her in the face. Presently, Mable returned to the living room, raised a gun and fired, striking Gertie Gordon in the neck, killing her instantly.

On the witness stand, the survivors—eight black men, one other black woman, and one white man—shared a single point of agreement—all had consumed generous amounts of whiskey, gin, and beer for several hours prior to the murder. Not surprisingly, their recollections of the killing differed somewhat, and none had actually seen the shooting. One asserted that an unrepentant, intoxicated Clark stalked up to the just-fallen corpse and said, "I killed the bitch. I'll show you that I'm game," placing her foot on the dead woman's neck.[30] Another insisted Mable did not step on Gertie's neck until after police escorted the killer back to the house for towels to take to jail. Then Mable's comment was reported to have been a much tamer "I'm glad the woman is dead."[31]

These discrepancies did not slow the prosecution. The judge instructed the jury that it could take into consideration the witnesses' "appearance upon the . . . stand . . . their intelligence or lack of . . . their candor or lack of candor."[32] The jury barely hesitated before returning its guilty verdict. Mable Clark went to the penitentiary with a twenty-five-year sentence for the murder of Gertie Gordon, buried at the expense of the county. For these two black women of little means, their lives unraveled along the vectors of western violence.

In this particular case, with its social mingling of blacks and whites, the men involved sidestepped the violence. According to the testimony, they did not initiate the quarrel or taunt the women, egging them on in their argument. They physically separated Mable and Gertie after the first clash, attempted to deflect the mounting tension, and acted in a responsible manner after the killing. Perhaps if one had stayed with Mable, she might have been dissuaded or distracted from grabbing up the murder weapon that brought about her commitment to prison. The women's violence, although perhaps rooted in earlier conflicts, appeared to grow out of the long hours of alcohol consumption, not the immediate actions or antagonisms of the surrounding men. This proved somewhat exceptional, for some women went to the penitentiary because they associated with men who connected them to criminal pursuits and violent lives.

In 1893 Lola Hinesman fled to Trinidad, Colorado, to escape prosecution as an accessory to a brutal murder. The sheriff of Fort Worth, Texas, wanted Hinesman extradited to stand trial in the rape and torture killing of Margaret Twomey, whose body was found nailed to an outhouse.[33] At least three men and one woman agreed to give evidence against Hinesman, although she did not participate in the crime but only concealed the killer. Her motivation—criminal intent, love, jealousy, hatred, fear, ignorance—that might have explained an involvement with an incongruously named murderer, A. Happy, remained the most important and unanswered question in Lola Hinesman's story.

Whether women crafted a criminal plan or cooperated with a male accomplice, violent criminal activity resulted in consequences often heavily weighted against female offenders. The dynamics of crime and punishment centered on the race, class, and gender structures of society. Other details of the proceedings branched from this fundamental framework. Examples of these multilayered factors, including criminal entanglement plotted by a male associate, dominated the experience of two girlhood friends, one Mexican American and one African American, in New Mexico.

In 1907 Valentina Madrid, seventeen, and Alma Lyons, sixteen, were arrested in Hillsboro for poisoning Valentina's thirty-year-old husband, Manuel. Police followed an easy trail to the pair. Alma purchased arsenic the week of the killing, a local physician immediately pinpointed the cause of death, and the two young women "confessed" to the crime. Inquest testimony pointed to Francisco Baca, Valentina's lover, as the originator of the murder plot. In little Hillsboro, Baca refused to stay away from Valentina, and Manuel, the irate husband, threatened murder if he again caught his wife with the other man.[34]

The accused women said that Baca, in a bid to secure the married Valentina for himself, hatched the plan and then vowed to kill his accomplices unless they carried out his directions.[35] New Mexico authorities ignored the enigma of a lovesick Lothario who used threats of deadly attack to force his beloved to commit murder and the impact of this intimidation on the young women, caught between mortal warnings from two older men. Instead, the court separated Baca's case from that of the women and ordered him, by this time denying a connection to the killing, held at the New Mexico penitentiary until his trial.

Officials then moved swiftly forward in the case of Valentina and Alma. The women, who admitted to the deed—Alma purchasing the poison with fifty cents provided by Baca, Valentina placing the poison in her husband's coffee—were indicted early in May. The trial concluded on 9 May 1907; the jury returned a guilty verdict in less than an hour, and the next day Judge Frank W. Parker sentenced the young friends to hang on 7 June 1907.

The expected storm of controversy that erupted over this decision fell on the shoulders of Acting Governor James W. Reynolds. The arguments for and against the sentence of the court ranged across the political spectrum, but most agreed that New Mexico's national reputation would be tarnished by this execution. The scheduled date moved closer and in Hillsboro construction began on the gallows from which the girlhood companions would hang. Two teenagers, who had little or no schooling and could barely sign their own names, stood at the edge of brutal death for a crime, all details of which remained uncertain.[36] Francisco Baca had not yet gone to trial.

On 4 June 1907 Reynolds brought a halt to the macabre proceedings in Hillsboro. Appeasing those calling for "justice" and those arguing for clemency, he declared that the testimony of the condemned women was crucial for Baca's trial. Valentina Madrid and Alma Lyons left Hillsboro, each to begin a life sentence at the Santa Fe penitentiary.

After several delays and a mistrial, Francisco Baca won an acquittal in May 1910 and went free. Valentina and Alma, who testified against Baca, remained in the New Mexico penitentiary for another ten years, bringing their total incarceration time to about thirteen years.[37] The power of Baca's influence, the greater ages of both Francisco Baca and Manuel Madrid, the fear these men inspired in Alma and Valentina, the youthfulness of the women (some accounts put Alma's age at fourteen), the threats and possible physical abuse they endured from both Baca and Madrid, the circumstances of the confessions, the women's general ignorance of their legal rights and constraints against self-incrimination, the decision of the court to charge the pair with a capital offense instead of a lesser crime, the public debates that called for "making an example" of Valentina and Alma, the intention to hang the two before bringing Baca to trial, the freeing of the man widely regarded as the organizer of the crime, the political rather than judicial issues that stopped the executions, the years these women spent in a male penitentiary, the poverty and skin color of the convicted—all these swirled together, revealing the kaleidoscope of race, class, and gender disadvantage for women who collided with the law in the American West.

The plight of Valentina Madrid and Alma Lyons took on "notorious" flavor because it played out in the shadow of the gallows and pandered to a fictional image of "Old West" justice.[38] Other women did not receive a death sentence or the national publicity of Valentina and Alma, but faced an equally unforgiving western legal system when they returned the violence of their lives in kind.[39] Despite the skimpiness of many prison records, case histories demonstrated a reaction to domestic abuse as a central cause for women's violence.[40]

Regardless of whether violence proved spontaneous or ongoing in a woman's life, juries were not generous with acquittals based on self-defense. Caroline Bowman, a black woman living in Belton, Texas, went to the Huntsville penitentiary after she tried to protect herself from a drunken associate, who twice broke into her house and assaulted her. Bowman had lived in Belton all her life and, although illiterate, had an excellent reputation as a solid, hard-working and temperate individual.[41] Nonetheless, after George Ayers interrupted Caroline's card game with Ed Jackson, bashed her on the head with a burning oil lamp, and chased her from her own home, Caroline responded with violence.

Jackson fled, but Caroline returned to her house just as Ayers broke in a second time. As he lunged at her again, Caroline smashed him in the head with a bed slat, a blow that resulted in his death. Caroline Bowman, whose home had been invaded twice, whose person had been wounded and burned, who saw a second assault was imminent, went to the penitentiary; Ed Jackson was released on appeal.[42] It took more than one petition, each of which cited Bowman's advanced age as a reason for clemency, to secure a release for the thirty-nine-year-old woman.[43]

Bowman's experience duplicated that of Mollie Black, an African American woman living in Kansas. Black defended herself against a late night intruder, but was convicted of manslaughter and sentenced to four years in the Kansas penitentiary. This after the prosecution and defense agreed that Black should either be found guilty of murder or freed for a justifiable act of self-defense.[44]

Mollie Harrison's case also mirrored those of Bowman and Black. Harrison, an African American woman who knifed to death a black man in her laundress tent in Winnemucca, Nevada, argued that "I committed that crime in defence of my own life and in my own home."[45] Harrison won her parole, lived by its conditions, went to work in Carson City, Nevada, and repeatedly applied for a full pardon from her conviction.[46] The Nevada pardon and parole panel followed the general trend—African American women who returned violence with violence, even to protect themselves within their homes, could expect little clemency from juries and prison boards.

White women of marginal economic status also had legal problems connected to violence, but the resolution of their cases might differ from those of African American women. In Texas Mrs. Ernest Brown, whose husband worked away from town on the railroad, set out with pistol and horsewhip to confront one Fred O'Neal because he climbed into her bedroom at night, bragged about it to other men, told a neighbor he had a "fix" on the woman, and at the Silver Dollar Saloon made public remarks about her chastity. In response, Brown, fearful of attack from O'Neal hunted the man at his favorite bar where, in a confusing exchange, shots were fired from at least two different guns. O'Neal escaped unscathed by either the gunshots or the law, but Brown was arrested.

Judge F. E. Adams looked on Brown's actions with a sympathetic eye and delivered jury instructions that ought to have guaranteed an acquittal. Despite this, the jury found Brown guilty of unlawfully brandishing a pistol. The court fined Brown thirty dollars, but did not give her prison time, a decision distinctly different than for African American women charged with any crime. Further, after the trial Judge Adams wrote a lengthy petition asking remission of the fine to Brown, whom he referred to as a "lady of good character and of a modest and quiet behavior and demeanor."[47]

Any woman who could tie herself to the prized label of "lady," even if she stormed a saloon with a gun and whip, had some chance of mitigation before the law. Still, claiming personal defense of the abstract concept of "true lady" proved an unreliable legal maneuver for white women, especially poor ones. Mary Frielinger, a fifty-one-year-old housekeeper, was sentenced to life and served fourteen years in the Kansas penitentiary for killing a Dutch immigrant who called her names and "made improper advances" to her.[48] Though the judge presiding at her trial later wrote "she ought to have killed him," Frielinger waited another ten years to be released.[49] In the same penitentiary, Florence Davis served almost the full two years of her sentence for killing a "notorious bad character" who was attacking her with a heavy piece of steel.[50] For these white women, the badge of "lady" failed to deflect punishment.

In Anaconda, Montana, Della Kirk, a white woman who shot and killed a violent companion, was more successful but only because of two fortuitous circumstances. In the summer of 1903, after a ten-month relationship with William Nemo, Kirk decided to leave because of the savage beatings the man gave her. Della packed her trunk, moved to a new boardinghouse, went to the restaurant where Nemo worked as a cook, and announced her plan to leave for Butte the next morning; in response he knocked Kirk to the floor and began to kick her.

Della literally crawled away and returned to her rooming establishment. A few hours later Nemo let himself into the house, saw the trunk, and within moments had set upon the woman again. The enraged Nemo grabbed Della by the throat, they fell to the floor, he yanked her back to her feet and continued to throttle her.

Similar life-threatening attacks had not exonerated other women who entered pleas of self-defense after freeing themselves from such travail. Fortunately for Della Kirk, as William Nemo struggled for his gun while maintaining his death grip on her neck, an eleven-year-old girl, Pearl McGowan, came upon the scene. With Nemo's murderous threats and Della's cries for mercy, Pearl quickly raised the alarm among adults in the house.[51] By the time a policeman arrived, Nemo lay dying on the floor; the officer took Della Kirk into custody.

Although only a child, Pearl proved to be a keen observer and a mature witness.[52] The afternoon following Nemo's death she gave the coroner's jury a clear description of the mortal danger to Della Kirk. Her account verified and strengthened Della's case for self-defense.

Della's second piece of good fortune came from the very severity of the beating Nemo had inflicted. At the inquest, Della's bruised face and chest gave silent proof of the assault, as Nemo's thumb and finger marks remained imprinted on her neck.[53] The jury concluded that William Nemo died from a self-inflicted gunshot wound, although a physician insisted that only a remarkable contortionist could have fired into his own body at such an angle.

Della Kirk can only be described as lucky to have avoided prosecution for defending herself. Poor women of all cultures, especially if unmarried, risked a great deal when they struck back at male tormentors. Even when several witnesses documented the abuse, typically women who protected themselves were regarded as criminals rather than as advocates for their own safety. For example, unlike Della Kirk, Hattie La Pierre, part-time milliner, part-time prostitute, stood before a less amenable Wyoming court system when she responded to the abuse of her companion, Harry Black.

Twenty-one-year-old Hattie met Harry Black, alcoholic, drug user, and gambler, in Denver in the spring of 1905. Their relationship slipped almost immediately into one of constant physical threats and vicious batterings for Hattie.[54] The pair moved on to Lander, Wyoming, where Hattie expected they would marry, but their lives deteriorated into more regular patterns of violence. Black, who at five feet nine inches tipped the scales at one hundred seventy, repeatedly pummeled the one hundred fifteen pound Hattie so severely with his fists and his gun that their landlord asked the couple to leave.[55] They traveled north to Thermopolis, where Black, who gambled badly, continued to live off Hattie's earnings from the brothel.

Black picked up the pace of his abuse, flying into jealous rages over other men, threatening to kill Hattie if she would not come share his rooms.[56] On one occasion, he dragged her to an alley, shouting that "she had better be careful and not get him started because she knew what she would get if he got started."[57] Although Hattie, designated by Black as the party responsible for her own beatings, thought about leaving, both her belief that she loved the gambler and her fear made her decide "she had better submit to his treatment than attempt to escape."[58]

So public became the assaults that the bruised and bloodied Hattie came to the attention of William B. Matheny, town marshal. It was Matheny who investigated an incident above Cover's Saloon, when Hattie sustained a bullet wound to the foot. Black explained away the injury as an "accident," which occurred as he drew his pistol to prepare for two men stalking him as a "piker." Hattie, in the pattern of the abused woman, refused to file any charges in the incident, but Marshal Matheny fined Black for carrying a concealed weapon.[59] Back at his rooms, Black complained "that he did not [intend] to shoot her where it would not count."[60]

Only a few evenings later, Harry Black again dragged Hattie onto the street near the Barr and Wood's Saloon; as he pushed her toward an alley, the woman opened fire, striking the gambler in the neck and the right lung, severing branches of his pulmonary artery. She followed him as he staggered back to the saloon and into the arms of Marshal Matheny. Hattie went directly to the marshal, told him she had thrown the gun into a nearby yard, and asked, "Did I kill him?" The marshal later noted that at eleven o'clock in the evening the beleaguered woman had not eaten, so he left the unsavory Black to the care of others and led Hattie to his boardinghouse to get her some hot supper.[61]

Black's philandering had proved the breaking point for Hattie. As she walked with the marshal toward her late night dinner, she confided that "she loved that man better than any man she ever saw, [but] he was giving money to another woman."[62] She might have learned that news from Black's roommate, to whom Black bragged he wanted to get rid of Hattie because he had a "married woman on the string."[63]

Black lingered long enough to give his own account of the attack, which he thought unprovoked, as he had just given Hattie five dollars and there was "no quarrel" between the two.[64] Hattie La Pierre, however, described a man quite different from Black's magnanimous self-portrayal. She said that just before the shooting Black clenched his fists, abused her verbally, and reached as if going for his gun, screaming "I will kill you and will kill you now."[65] Believing she was about to be shot for the second time in a week, Hattie took the life of her abuser. The dying Black made two truthful comments about his relationship with Hattie when he said, "it was one of the two of us sooner or later" and "the damn bitch was a good shot."[66]

Hattie La Pierre, an example of the battered woman—living in isolation away from friends and family, lacking economic independence, blaming herself for the abuse, fearing attempts to leave meant more brutality, refusing to file legal charges, tolerating violence in the name of love—had her sympathizers, including the marshal and Black's roommate. Nonetheless, the judge rejected a defense jury instruction that if La Pierre had reasonable grounds to believe Black intended to carry out previously made threats or she was about to lose her life or sustain serious bodily harm, she should be acquitted.[67] Arguments of self-defense and honest fear carried no weight; Hattie La Pierre went to the penitentiary for three years on a charge of manslaughter.[68]

An unusual element in Hattie La Pierre's story centered on the support she drew from the town marshal. If, however, law enforcement officers displayed indifference to or participated in violence against women, then abused families had no formal sources for intervention and assistance. In these cases, the one universal agency found in western communities, the law, was closed as a refuge.

For example, Angelina Drouillard, as wife of a Montana sheriff, had no official place to turn for herself and her small children. By 1874 Moses and Angelina Tebeau Drouillard had made their way from Frenchtown, Montana, to Missoula, where Moses began a job as the undersheriff. In 1876 the sheriff resigned; Drouillard stepped into the position and then won election in his own right. Along with Drouillard's wide reputation as a county official came general community knowledge that the Drouillards had a troubled and violent marriage.[69]

In December 1878 an assailant shot Moses Drouillard in the back of the head as he walked past the rooms he and Angelina shared at the jail. The forty-six-year-old Drouillard lived a few hours, but refused to name his attacker. Angelina later claimed that she shot Moses at the encouragement of William McKay, a suitor who had asked her to leave the sheriff and go to Corvallis for a fresh start. The sympathetic McKay indicated he had heard Angelina was "having quite a hard time with Moses." Angelina admitted "it was not only starvation but beating and everything else."[70]

Drouillard came upon this scene and flew into a jealous rage, calling Angelina vile names and telling her to get out of the rooms or he "would beat [her] to death." Making good his threat, Drouillard began to pummel Angelina about the head and threatened to have her and McKay "laid out before sundown." Unable to locate a weapon, Drouillard dashed out to get one at his office. As Moses passed the window, McKay handed Angelina his pistol and told her to shoot. Together McKay and Angelina dragged the one hundred sixty-five pound Drouillard back inside the jail and placed him on a rug. McKay then left, telling Angelina that if she ever revealed his participation, he would kill her.[71]

McKay and Angelina were indicted for murder and tried separately. Despite medical testimony that Angelina could not have moved the dead weight of her husband's body alone, McKay was acquitted. Angelina went to the penitentiary for fifteen years.[72]

Angelina's young children, present during the shooting death of their father, were sent to be raised by family in the Bitter Root Valley. Several months after the murder, the sight of playmates tumbling about in a mock fight caused the five-year-old daughter to explode in hysteria. When calmed, she described the murder scene in an account that matched Angelina's and incriminated William McKay. Whether the child gave this description to her family in French or English was not indicated, but apparently the children had not been questioned at the time of the murder. Perhaps these youngsters only spoke French, which led English-speaking authorities to discount them as witnesses; at least some Missoula residents thought anti-French bias had influenced the outcome of Angelina's case.[73]

Other disturbing events continued to keep the Drouillard family disordered. It was a pregnant Angelina who entered the Montana penitentiary in December 1879, more than a year after she killed her abusive sheriff husband. In May 1880, authorities, silent on the subject of the child's father, released Angelina to St. Joseph's Hospital where on 6 June she gave birth to a daughter.[74]

During her hospital confinement, Angelina managed to conceal chloral hydrate and opium, which she took with her upon her return to the penitentiary. There, after having signed the final adoption papers for her new infant, twenty-four-year-old Angelina used her smuggled drugs and attempted suicide.[75] She recovered and continued to serve her time. In 1882 Angelina was pardoned, almost four years after she had reacted to the relentless violence of "one of the best known . . . and almost universally respected" Missoula County men, said to be "mourned by hundreds" but probably not by Angelina Drouillard.[76]

Marriage itself did not automatically accord women greater favor in the courts. Furthermore, if a married woman undercut her "respectable" status by working as a prostitute, her chances for clemency dipped. Irene Kent, a seamstress running a house of prostitution in Tucumcari, New Mexico, dealt with domestic violence within her own home, but that abuse at the hands of her husband did not strengthen her case in court.

By the time she was twenty, in 1903, this woman had moved from Indiana to Texas to New Mexico, where she dropped her given name of Stella May. Now known as Irene, she married Allen Kent and together they opened a brothel.[77] One afternoon early in June 1910, Irene and Allen joined friends for a picnic, during which everyone consumed copious amounts of alcohol. Returning home at about eight o'clock in the evening, the intoxicated Allen Kent rekindled an old quarrel, demanding money from Irene and punctuating his ferocity with further doses of alcohol.

Later Irene recalled she asked him, "if he would not come to bed and stop drinking[;] he began abusing me and said when he did come he would kill me." "Knowing how quarrelsome and mean he was while drinking," Irene tried to hide her husband's gun, as "he had threatened me many times before." Kent intercepted Irene in the hallway, grabbed her, called her "vile names," and struggled with her for the weapon. Irene remembered nothing beyond that "in the scuffle the gun was discharged."[78] The jury was not impressed with these descriptions, and Irene Kent went to the New Mexico State Penitentiary for a term of three to five years.

After serving the minimum three years of her sentence, Irene Kent secured a chance for the outside employment mandatory for parole. Loretta Batis, a longtime acquaintance, agreed to provide room and board and twelve dollars a month, if Irene came to Raton, New Mexico, to work for the Batis family.[79] Within three months, Irene received a second job offer, this one from El Paso, Texas. Asking permission to leave the state, Irene told the parole authorities she had been invited to take charge of the "Topeka Rooms," described by a local police captain as a "fairly decent" "rooming house for the poor class."[80]

Irene Kent, drawn by the better salary of twenty dollars a month and a chance to leave New Mexico, successfully petitioned to move far from the location of her domestic abuse.[81] In so doing, she exercised that classic western tradition of "moving on," leapfrog fashion, across the West. The west Texas authorities who awaited the paroled woman did not "think Mrs. Kent's associates could be bad or temptations great at this rooming house."[82] Irene Kent, a thirty-three-year-old seamstress/prostitute/madam, sought a new opportunity among the "poor class" of El Paso—a better outcome than that of many women who struggled with domestic abuse and family violence.

As the recipient of abuse, Irene Kent retaliated with violence upon an attacker with whom she was well acquainted, as did other women. In most cases, women knew or lived with the men they killed. For example, of thirty-nine women charged with murder in Denver between 1881 and 1917, twenty-seven killed husbands or male companions. The remaining twelve women killed a neighbor, son-in-law, brothel client, or clients seeking an abortion.[83]

These figures show that the encompassing nature of family violence placed all members of a household in danger. Although husbands and partners became the usual targets, some women turned on the children in their homes. Sarah Bretano went to the Kansas penitentiary on two different occasions for cruelty to a child. On the first occasion in 1878, the thirty-seven-year-old pregnant housekeeper received a sentence of two years for "beating and doing great bodily harm" to her stepson, William Bretano, Jr.[84] Despite her pregnancy and the clemency petition of 145 citizens, Sarah Bretano found the governor unwilling to grant her a pardon.[85] In 1881, on Bretano's second conviction for the same offense, she went to prison for five years.[86] Whether Sarah Bretano used physical force against her own child or a stepchild, this woman repeatedly demonstrated that some factors in her life led her to violence against those weaker than she.

Whether personal or regional disorder explained their behavior, some western women responded to maternal demands with abuse for their children or youngsters left in their care. Amanda Coates injured a child by burning it; Mary Rechtein, an unwed mother turned out of her family home, let her infant die of exposure; Sally Harris, a former slave, gave birth alone by a river and abandoned her newborn on the ferry she boarded immediately afterwards.[87]

When a child died from a mother's assault, conviction was a certainty, but the chances for parole and pardon varied greatly.[88] Mary Ann Taylor, a seventeen-year-old black housekeeper who beat her child to death, served until the earliest release date for good time in Kansas.[89] In the same state, Mary Mork, a twenty-three-year-old white housekeeper with a sixth-grade education, was sentenced to twenty years for taking her two-week-old child to the river and drowning it. Within two weeks a large group of citizens successfully petitioned for her release on the grounds that Mork was "fee-bleminded" and had been deserted by the child's father.[90]

Similarly, Louisa Wood, a young African American woman, served a year and a half in the Missouri penitentiary after the white father of her child had encouraged its destruction. Apparently, she sought an abortion, was arrested for this, and then gave birth to the child inside the peniten-tiary. The warden recommended her release before the onset of winter so that the former slave, alone and without resources, could find support for herself and her child.[91] Bettie Jones served seven years of a life sentence for infanticide before the governor pardoned her because "she has little chil-dren to take care of."[92] How these children had been cared for during the mother's imprisonment and who actually endorsed the idea of this moth-er returning to her children seemed not to be issues in 1880 Texas.

In contrast, Sallie Hill, a fifty-year-old African American woman con-victed of whipping a small boy—her child, stepchild, or grandson—to death, received considerable support for her release from the Texas peni-tentiary. The controversial case was tried three times before the court sen-tenced Sallie to five years in the death of the child, Mack. Black and white citizens joined in seeking her pardon, arguing that "old Aunt Sallie" had no intention of killing the child, there was no proof the child died from the beating, and the witnesses against the woman had been "colored pros-titutes" with a grudge.[93]

Not all in Marion County saw Sallie Hill as innocent in the hideous death of little Mack. An anonymous group of citizens sent a counter peti-tion to Governor Ireland, asserting that the "murder was most brutal" and that "over one third of the jury in the last and final trial were colored."[94] The presence of these jurors, the petitioners argued, showed that the black community wanted Hill imprisoned. Among the intriguing elements in Sallie Hill's case was the role of the black jurors in an era when African Americans were allowed limited exercise of their citizenship. How they se-cured these seats, whether juries commonly included some blacks, and the community impact of the black voice demonstrate that in east Texas the patterns of civil rights may have been more complex than they appeared.

Five years later, in 1890, Alice Vick, a black woman living further west in Eastland County, Texas, experienced the way in which citizenship and rights could yield to circumstantial evidence and result in conviction. Vick, her two pregnant teenage daughters, and several small children moved to a property near Breckinridge in the fall of 1888. The following May, the sheriff and a physician, acting on a strange conversation with Alice Vick about her missing daughters, went to her home to pursue the matter.

Vick led the sheriff to an area in the peach orchard where she thought a baby was buried. When the sheriff finished his search, he had the body of one child and a badly decomposed package of something else.[95] Based on this discovery, Alice Vick, said to have been "uneasy" in the presence of the sheriff and the doctor, was charged with and convicted of the murder of her grandchildren. She went to the Texas penitentiary for five years. An appeal by her attorneys convincingly showed the following: the expected delivery dates for the two daughters made it unlikely that the infants could have been born at the same time; the medical examination of the remains had been done improperly and under poor conditions; the remains in one container could not conclusively be identified as human; Vick's daughter testified that her sister's baby died of natural causes.

An oversight in the court office caused Alice Vick's appeal petition to be filed late.[96] That meant the attorney's various facts about her case did not immediately help her. Alice Vick did not receive a pardon until 1892.

Regardless of what exactly occurred in the Vick household, some type of violence touched that family. When Alice Vick attempted to enlist the aid of the police in resolving that violence, she became the target of their suspicions. What happened, how the infant or infants died, and who bore responsibility, if any, may not have been completely sorted out through the law, where it appears Alice Vick thought she could seek to protect herself and her daughters.

Like the Vicks, other families expressed confusion about violence, how it began, whom it touched.[97] Often the daily routines of violence remained hidden behind family doors. When a sudden murderous act occurred, the surrounding community had little framework for understanding the circumstances. The desire to protect one another, the inability to articulate the passions that grew out of long-standing abuse, pressures to maintain a family's "good name," all jelled into patterns of obfuscation.

For example, eighteen-year-old Annie Bruce from the Church of Jesus Christ of Latter-day Saints community at Smoot, Wyoming, emerged as the central figure in a murky and violent family episode that resulted in her conviction for the murder of her father. Yet many forces within her family and her church connected to the unusual case. In their totality they muddle the events that shaped Annie Bruce's life.

In March 1907 Annie's father, James Bruce, a prosperous and substantial figure in the Mormon church, left the house to work on his ranch. About midmorning Bruce ate a pie cooked the previous day by his daughter and sent to him in the field by his wife. The tasty morsel, laced with strychnine, killed Bruce immediately; in two days, the Uinta County sheriff and prosecuting attorney traveled to the Star Valley area to conduct the inquest at the Bruce family home.[98]

Widespread uneasiness could not be avoided with the arrival of these state officials in the remote Mormon community. A long history of bitter conflict and violent death between Mormons and "Gentiles" had left a legacy of distrust and suspicion for LDS people. Only a few years removed from their legal battles with the federal government, Mormons knew that the cloud of polygamy still hung heavily over their church.[99] In addition, the location of the Smoot group, far from the powerful church headquarters in Salt Lake City, Utah, weakened its bargaining position with the non-Mormon Wyoming government. A family scandal that drew unfavorable state attention to their isolated enclave had to rank among the least desirable of developments for the Smoot Mormons.

After the inquest, the prosecuting attorney said about Annie Bruce, "She was very nervous and agitated, so much so that we decided . . . that she knew more than she was willing to tell us."[100] Young Annie Bruce had many reasons to be "very nervous and agitated." Her father had just died under dreadful circumstances, she baked the poisoned pie, all in her community felt the tension created by the presence of state officials, and she carried the knowledge of whatever prior family difficulty existed in the Bruce home, especially between her parents.[101]

Most damning for Annie was the "confession" she gave to the sheriff and prosecuting attorney, in which she said, "while I was in the act of making the pies a feeling or a wish came over me to kill someone, and this feeling I could not resist."[102] Not surprisingly, Annie, a country girl with a fourth-grade education and raised in a closed religious community, vacillated back and forth between this confession and several other accounts. On the witness stand, to no avail, Annie denied the veracity of her confession.[103]

In April 1908, a jury in Evanston, Wyoming, convicted Annie Bruce of manslaughter and the court sentenced her to the penitentiary. The prosecutor rejoiced, "in our opinion four years is little enough for such an abnormal crime."[104] From back home in Smoot, Annie's LDS bishop Frank P. Cramey and several other church officials joined in denouncing the young woman and her mother's entire family. Declaring that "there is no question of her guilt," and accusing Annie's mother of complicity in the murder, Cramey suggested that "confinement in prison will cause the young woman to divulge the secrets of the atrocious crime."[105]

In the whole twenty-year history of the Smoot community, Cramey contended that only two illegitimate children had been born, both in the family of the widow, Anna Bruce. Warming to the subject of Annie's mother, the bishop praised the deceased James Bruce as an "honorable, God fearing, worthy citizen . . . unhappily married to a woman of vicious habits, bad tempered, and revengeful." He accused Anna Bruce of setting fire to the family barn and giving birth to one of the illegitimate children eleven months after James Bruce left for missionary work, "making his relations with her strained and unhappy." Assuring the governor that the Smoot residents were

"striving to bring up our children [as] God-fearing, law abiding citizens full
of patriotism and love for our great state and union," he closed with an appeal that the governor overlook a petition for clemency circulated by some
local residents. For the bishop, prison could make a "bad girl" into a "good"
one. Cramey implored the governor to recognize that the "leading citizens
do not wish the young woman turned loose . . . until the officers of this state
have had a chance to make an impression . . . on her."[106]

Bishop Cramey, stumbling over himself to convince the governor of the
loyalty and good citizenship of the Smoot folk, revealed bitter divisions that
simmered among the Mormons. Intentionally or not, he outlined powerful family disturbances within the Bruce household. Annie, as the oldest
child, would have possessed at least some knowledge of these contentious
matters. Further, he revealed that, perhaps because of neighborhood witness that placed the Bruce women in a favorable light, not all in the small
community agreed with Annie and Anna's detractors. Smoot Mormons
lined up along the issue of Annie's guilt or innocence. The very night of the
verdict, according to the bishop, "a party of women sympathizers" canvassed house to house with a petition for Annie's pardon.[107]

Annie served her time in Wyoming until 6 October 1909, when the state
transferred her to the penitentiary at Canon City, Colorado.[108] Although
Wyoming officials showed no hurry to parole the young woman, she acquired support at the Colorado penitentiary. Warden Thomas Tynan reported favorably on her conduct record, but declined to make a parole recommendation as an act inconsistent with his duty. Nonetheless, Tynan had
the power to slant his comments against an inmate and he studiously
avoided doing so.[109]

Other prison personnel took up her case with the parole board. The
matron endorsed Annie as a "quiet and faithful prisoner," and J. G. Blake,
the chaplain, said she had a "clear and perfect prison record." Blake
thought the jurors had not felt certain of their verdict and had known of
"circumstances of an extremely mitigating nature."[110]

The chaplain, who may well have learned those circumstances from
Annie Bruce, identified a valid point about the jury. Back in Wyoming,
jurors had circulated a petition for pardon immediately after rendering
their verdict. At least one regretted the jury's rejection of its initial vote of
seven to five for acquittal. Pressured by the argument that we "would make
the county officers out liars if we did not convict her," juror B. F. Bondurant reluctantly changed his vote to manslaughter after seventeen hours of
deliberation. Shortly, he moaned, "Oh it all most [sic] makes me weep bitterly to be one of a jury . . . helped to convict that girl."[111]

Annie's mother, left alone to support nine younger children, also took
up her daughter's case. In 1910, Anna Bruce wrote to the board of pardons

that Annie's incarceration "is quite a worry on my mind," and "[it is] expence [*sic*] . . . as I have to keep sending her clothes . . . I have nothing only what I can work for by going out."[112] When the governorship changed hands, Anna Bruce tried again, this time saying, "my daughter . . . who was deeply wronged of he [*sic*] papa death and humble [*sic*] ask you . . . pardon my innocent child."[113]

The voice of the Smoot community struck a stronger note. In March 1911, another petition circulated among friends, neighbors, and relatives. Among the nearly one hundred signatures were those of at least thirty-one Smoot women, as well as five of the original petitioners against clemency in 1908, including Bishop Frank P. Cramey.[114] Something had changed minds about Annie Bruce inside the Mormon community of Smoot. In April 1911, the young woman, who said "I think I have suffered enought [*sic*] for a crime I never did," received her pardon.[115] Annie Bruce left the penitentiary carrying with her the disorderly and violent secrets of the Bruce family that had led someone to poison her father.[116]

In the nineteenth-century West, society was still building the philosophical infrastructure to address domestic violence. Everywhere families lacked support services to provide education and assistance in these matters. Consequently, women had few community resources to help extricate them from situations of repeated violence. Social taboos against open discussion of family problems and cultural traditions that allowed men unchallenged supremacy within their own homes placed all women in a vulnerable position, one dependent on the balance and decency of the husband/companion.

Certainly many husbands and wives lived together in marital accord or at least domestic truce. Not every woman faced a rampaging mate; not every man inflicted wanton physical harm on his wife and children. But for those women attached to partners who brought violence into the home, avenues for change or escape remained limited. Not every woman viewed separation and divorce as appropriate options. Frequently economic circumstances or maternal responsibilities hindered a woman's chance to leave the place of violence.[117]

The violence committed by women tended to occur within their homes and focused on their spouses, partners, and children. Most acts took place in a family environment of verbal and physical assault. Power dynamics—adults over adults, adults over children—kept families jarred and personal interactions uneven. Women struck back at men suddenly, often out of panic and fear, reacting to experience of earlier abuse to themselves or to their children. On occasion they unleashed their anger on those they could whip, attacking children in cruel ways or emerging as the abusive spouse who attacked the husband.[118] In their assault on child or spouse, women bore the same dark responsibility as the male batterer and descended into the meanest of conduct. Whatever impelled their murderous behavior, when western women were arrested and convicted, they exchanged the violence of their homes for the violence of the penitentiary.

For incarcerated women the second component in their world of violence came from that which they encountered in the male penitentiary. The violence of one abuser multiplied into the violence of many. Few women, even those coming from the most disordered lives, could have anticipated the multifaceted violence that awaited them within the male penitentiary.

Violence inside the prison befell women inmates because of two distinct hardships. The first concerned the care and shelter of female inmates. These inferior arrangements led to and melded with a second aspect of their incarceration, physical abuse disguised as corrective punishment.

The inferior arrangements began with women's transport to the penitentiary. Procedures for male prisoners followed a fairly standard routine. A group of convicts, bound around the neck, wrists, and ankles and from waist to feet, formed a human chain and hobbled along, one behind the other, escorted by a number of deputies. A single prisoner, equally encumbered, stumbled forward in like manner.[119] In some cases prisoners walked or rode in large wagons to the penitentiary, while deputies accompanied them on horseback. As the railroad penetrated more western locations, sheriffs turned to public trains and mixed penitentiary-bound prisoners with other travelers. By any standards, the physical discomfort of the heavy chains taxed the strongest, surpassed only in subjective terms by the embarrassment.

For women, officials made few adjustments, and the opportunities for physical and sexual abuse went unchallenged. In an era before the employment of matrons, how exactly did a county sheriff and his deputies convey female prisoners across hundreds of miles to the state penitentiary? Under what conditions and with how much public humiliation did the eighteen-year-old Annie Bruce cover the more than one hundred fifty miles from the location of her trial in Evanston to the penitentiary at Rawlins and then the nearly four hundred mile trek to the Colorado penitentiary at Canon City? What provisions were made for Irene Kent's journey of more than one hundred sixty miles from Tucumcari to the New Mexico penitentiary? As for African American women, the Mollie Harrisons, Caroline Bowmans, Florence Akerses, Annie Carmacks, and Ada Wades of the West—who saw to the decency of their transport to male penitentiaries? Conveyance of women prisoners from the local jurisdictions introduced women to the realized or potential violence that greeted them inside the walls.

There in-take procedures reinforced the public embarrassment of the recent trip. Women stripped naked for guards or male trusties who examined and measured their bodies. In keeping with the Bertillon fad, jailers recorded every feature of a prisoner. They measured the woman's height and weight, described her eyes, ears, nose, chin, complexion, hair, measured her hands and feet, accounted for her teeth, and noted all her body scars. From this prodding and probing came descriptions that underlined the completeness of the examination: "2 large burn scars on left shoulder"; "bullet scar under right breast"; "lump on left buttock—bullet scar below left shoulder blade"; "large burn on left thigh, birthmark on inside left leg"; "scar from burn inside R. leg"; "scar middle of chest"; "scar from operation on stomach"; "small scar over left breast"; "breast abnormally large"; "small pimples all over body."[120]

Kate Richards O'Hare, in the Missouri penitentiary, wrote of the examination to her family: "one really hard experience . . . it was pretty bad . . . the Bertillon. I am not prudish . . . but it took all my poise and self-control to go through it without breaking. The men . . . were kindness and sympathy and courtesy itself, but they could not rob it of its trying effects."[121]

O'Hare, a woman of national prominence and thus some public protection, described the best circumstances under which the in-take examination might be conducted. Other women, laundresses, cooks, prostitutes, did not receive such considerate treatment.

Perhaps the most humiliating procedure for women inmates concerned the threat of head shaving, a routine practice for male inmates upon entry. Although not a standard requirement for women in American prisons, the possibility of its use was well known by inmates. Well into the nineteenth century England retained this ritual, which brought the greatest protest from new women prisoners. Married women were known to cry out, "It is my husband's hair!"

During the ugly scene, guards at England's Millbank penitentiary forcibly restrained women, handcuffing those who refused to submit. Describing the chaos, a matron observer blamed women's vanity for their reactions and described prisoners as "some stoical, some shiver, some beg, some weep."[122] In the western United States, prison wardens reserved women's head shaving, done in public, as a special punishment.[123]

Once past the initiation into the nonprivate world of the penitentiary, women moved into the inner prison grounds. In most prisons, they continued to wear "citizen's dress," although in a few women wore a regulation striped skirt with an apron. Women laborers at the Texas farm camps went barefoot and wore such skimpy shifts that an investigating committee ordered nineteen inches of fabric added to the hem.[124]

Since little housing had been planned for women, wardens packed all the female prisoners together into the small rooms and cells available. In 1865, following a year of rising female incarcerations, Warden C. A. Swift told the Missouri governor, Charles Fletcher, "anything you can do to reduce the population of the female department of this prison will be a blessing . . . and a benefit to the institution."[125] As the summer of 1866 dragged on and the number of female prisoners continued to rise, Swift appealed again to Governor Fletcher. This time he pointed to the extreme Missouri heat and informed the governor that as many as six women crowded together in one cell. "Its [*sic*] a wonder to me how they endure it," Swift added.[126]

These make-do arrangements, in which women lived in the most filthy conditions, melded with the general disregard with which the system viewed inmates. They also meant that women prisoners had no protected space inside the prison.[127] Their living accommodations were not only pitifully inadequate but always accessible to male guards and often to male prisoners. In this climate, already highly charged by corruption, masculinity, and violence, many men saw no reason to restrain themselves in regard to women prisoners.

Accordingly, they did not. Women prisoners, across the span of this study, endured the same harsh penalties as male prisoners, including the violent physical torture that officials called "punishment" and "discipline." Even after prisons set aside separate quarters for women or kept their work loads less taxing, the threat of the penitentiary's penal regulations hung over women's heads. Any infraction, or the arbitrary report of one, brought dark-cell time, bread and water diet, whipping, or torture devices.

While reformers wrote about punishment that should "qualify the criminal for the resumption of rights,"[128] the notion simply did not apply to women. Since society denied women the processes of full citizenship in general, what rights would women inmates prepare to resume? In command of limited civil prerogatives anyway, what possible difference could their prison treatment make in the future conduct of their already-censured lives? With little civic identity and burdened by negative moral labels, women inmates lived far beyond society's rules for human treatment. In fact, they qualified for any type of abuse, as evidenced by conditions in the Texas penitentiary.

In 1874, Colonel A. J. Ward, manager of the Huntsville penitentiary, assured delegates at the National Prison Congress meeting in St. Louis that the Texas facility operated on a plan for the reformation of convicts through an appeal to self-respect, coupled with religious and educational opportunities, all supplemented by peaceful, cheering visits from family and friends.[129] Granted, Ward had not inherited a prison system in mint condition, but under his management the abuses dropped to new lows.[130] Among them, he allowed women and men to share the bunkhouses, where naked, unwashed inmates slept on corn cob sacks. Women convicts, twelve out of fourteen of them African American, roamed the yard, carrying in their arms the infant children conceived and born inside the penitentiary. One black female prisoner, "Old Jane," gave birth to a mixed-blood child fathered by the white convict doctor, who bragged of his coercive sexual relations with the woman. As punishment for the pregnancy, guards separated Jane from the newborn and placed the mother in the dungeon, but not before subjecting her to the public head shaving.[131]

Indeed, Ward's staff spared women convicts no form of punishment. Guards hung women in the stocks so that the tips of their toes barely touched the ground. Women were beaten, often by more than one guard at a time. Some were forced to "ride" the "wooden horse." Regarded as the worst torture at Huntsville, the horse consisted of a pick-handle embedded partway down into an upright post. In appearance it resembled a high chair with a very narrow seat. Using a step stool, the prisoner mounted this device. Once the inmate was astride, guards removed the stool and, using ropes, fastened the inmate's ankles to rings embedded in the ground. They lashed the prisoner's head to the upright post, or "back of the chair." Forced to dangle from this apparatus without moving, inmates typically passed out, but not before a creeping paralysis moved through the legs, genitalia, and arms.[132]

It might be thought that such punishments occurred only in the formative years of western prisons, when the surrounding social institutions that controlled public behaviors had not yet solidified. Yet, an 1891 national survey about punishment showed the West holding its own in severe penalties for inmates. Arizona, Iowa, Kansas, Minnesota, Missouri, Montana, Nebraska, Nevada, North Dakota, South Dakota, and Texas recorded punishments that included unlimited days in the dark cell, whipping, use of the ball and chain, use of the bat, handcuffing to the wall with the prisoner raised off the floor, and half shaving of the head.[133] Survey respondents reported the punishments set by legislation, not the actual practices inside the walls.

In addition, continued violent attacks on women prisoners showed little amelioration as the West moved into the twentieth century. In 1910, African American women in the Texas prison told of punishment by the lash as the routine of their farm camp. In response to an investigator's questions about whipping procedures, inmate Mary Harrington said of the camp captain that after he threw the women face down on the ground, "he ties their hands and whips them on the naked meat."[134] Jerline Bonds confirmed that Martha Strater's scarred leg came from the lash and that she herself had been whipped on the "rump and legs." Because the captain used a lightweight strap, of her own punishment she said, "he didn't whip me unmercifully."[135] Clearly, based on experience, prisoners ranked the severity of these legalized punishments.

Guards did not limit themselves to the legal punishments but also inflicted extralegal penalties. For example, knocking women to the ground and kicking them never appeared on the list of "approved" punishments, but these deadly attacks were easy for booted guards and captains. These assaults usually came with a torrent of cursing and abusive language, behavior prohibited by regulations for guards.[136] Sometimes a guard developed a particular dislike for a woman prisoner and singled her out for kicking and verbal abuse. In the Nevada penitentiary, Lizzie Woodfolk had repeated encounters with a guard captain who rushed into her cell, kicking her, throwing her against the bed, and generally terrorizing her.[137]

In some cases, jailers devised "special" penalties for women they regarded as recalcitrant. During an investigation into punishments at the Kansas State Penitentiary, matrons of the female ward testified that as late as 1910 guards routinely used strait jackets, handcuffs, and gags as punishments for female prisoners. One warden had "rings . . . placed in the walls . . . of the female ward, for the purpose of extending the arms of prisoners for punishment, the . . . arms being fastened to a ring and extended about the prisoner's head." Male prisoners contributed to this violence, assisting the staff in placing restraints on the women. On at least one occasion, the prison physician bandaged the head of inmate Ada Cross, so that she could not work free of the gag in her mouth.[138]

Ada Cross experienced more than one such episode. The warden ordered that her arm be twisted up into an unnatural position and she be left thus suspended. He also had a special leather harness constructed that contorted the arms and legs into a painful position. This he reserved for use on Ada Cross and another inmate, Lena Davis.[139] Although the harness was destroyed and the warden removed from his position, the matrons who gave this testimony acknowledged that in 1914 the punishments were "less frequent" but still in use.

Determining with accuracy the frequency and extent of women's physical punishments proved elusive. Penitentiary conduct registers provide only the "legal" accounting of how guards handled women's infractions. In addition, guards often carried out disciplinary measures away from the view of other inmates. The few willing to give public witness to such excesses preserved a partial record of the history of violent punishment of women inmates. Again the New Mexico saga of Alma Lyons and Valentina Madrid underscored the direct and indirect violence that circumscribed the lives of women inmates and showed that authorities clouded the documentation of these abuses as much as possible.

In 1914, Alma Lyons's father traveled to the New Mexico penitentiary for a visit. There he discovered Alma, imprisoned for seven years, to be eight months pregnant. She reported to him that when the officials learned of her pregnancy, they confined her to solitary on a diet of bread and water for three weeks. At about the same time, Alma continued, Valentina had become pregnant, but had miscarried due to the harsh treatment.[140] Complaints, investigations, and denials swirled about as the time for Alma's delivery approached. Authorities blamed the pregnancy on an anonymous former inmate, asserted that Alma had never been punished for her condition, insisted that there had been no miscarriage for Valentina. Alma and Valentina, who remained under the supervisors who were being charged with dereliction of duty, recanted many of their statements, and the potential for a political imbroglio for prison administrators faded.

Yet, the New Mexico conduct records reported that both Alma and Valentina were disciplined at a date early in Alma's pregnancy. Officials did not list the offense, the punishment, or the reporting officer for either woman, although they completed these items in the surrounding records for other punished prisoners.[141] Further, authorities removed Alma, a Catholic, to the Saint Vincent Sanatorium of the Sisters of Charity. There she remained from 7 February 1914 until 10 April 1914, which information constituted the complete hospital record of Alma Lyons.[142] Faced with the inmate's irate father and the threat of another prison scandal, authorities arranged for Alma Lyons to give birth under sanitary medical conditions, rarely allowed for women inmates. When the twenty-six-year-old Alma applied for parole in 1918, she listed one child; her son had been adopted by a local family.[143]

Alma Lyons and Valentina Madrid ultimately received pardons and left the prison to take up domestic work. They had spent almost half their lives under the mantle of institutionalized violence. Their release from prison did not necessarily guarantee freedom from that powerful force, as demonstrated in the life of Eliza Jane Thompson.

In 1885, Eliza Jane Thompson, an African American chambermaid from Waco, Texas, accosted her former lover, John Farley, on a street and demanded money from him. Farley had promised for several years to marry Eliza Jane, but after he infected her with venereal disease, he abandoned his former mistress. Enraged and desperate for medicine, Thompson attacked Farley, "a creature utterly devoid of refinement . . . and delicacy of feeling and gentlemanly deportment."[144] Farley escaped injury, but the destitute Thompson was convicted of assault with the intent to commit murder and sent to the Darwin penal farm.

Considerable public sympathy existed for Eliza Jane, perhaps because Farley, the successful owner of a beer and ice business, enjoyed such an unsavory reputation. Buttressed by medical assessments of the gravity of Thompson's condition, the support of the convicting judge, and a citizens' petition, lawyer T. D. Perry succeeded in securing a pardon for the chronically ill woman.[145]

One year later, Eliza Jane was arrested and charged with cursing in public. As she had passed along Austin Street in Waco, Eliza Jane spotted one of John Farley's ice-wagons and murmured some negative comment. Within a moment, without explanation, a local jail guard jumped on her, "seized her by the throat . . . threw her down on the pavement and beat her until he was taken off."[146] One witness to the attack testified that Eliza Jane "resisted and pushed him [the jailer] towards the middle of the street. . . . during all this time . . . [he] used language as 'I'll kill the God d——d bitch!'"[147] Immediately after the attack, the jailer, seeing that Thompson had retreated to the other side of the street, dashed over and renewed his beating. Whether his friendship with Farley explained his behavior or not, the guard nearly killed Eliza Jane before passersby stopped him for a second time.

Influential Waco citizens now lined up to have Thompson's pardon revoked so that she would be returned to the Texas penitentiary. Not surprisingly, John Farley stated that Eliza Jane was a "dangerous woman" and that he feared to appear on the streets.[148] His lawyer, D. A. Kelley, testified that when he encountered Thompson on the street, she fixed him with a "steady fierce glare," muttering, "If I had a cow hide, I'd beat him half to death or whip him all over the street."[149] The sheriff agreed with Farley and Kelley and asked that Thompson be imprisoned immediately.[150] Others joined in the negative descriptions and the local constable told her attorney he would do "nothing to help this woman," although he admitted she was "not at fault in this matter."[151] Thompson's crime appeared to be an attitude that made certain well-placed Waco men uncomfortable.

The violence that surrounded Eliza Jane Thompson captured both the actual physical and the intangible authoritative power women confronted. The penitentiary became the weapon to hold over the former inmate. Thompson, though, refused to accept quietly the constraints against her. Sick and destitute, she managed to make her presence felt among those who wanted her removed from Waco. Nonetheless, she remained a candidate for reimprisonment, despite her failure to commit any significant crime.

Less easy to assess was the mental violence inflicted on all these women through their court experiences, their prison lives, and their subsequent treatment. When they wept, the journalists called them "hysterical and nervous," "devoid of rational sense." When composed, they were "cold and heartless," "lacking in womanly emotion." When they spoke up, they were "bold and sassy," when withdrawn, "cruel and indifferent." Rather they were women with little opportunity to articulate the internal pressures generated by the relentless violence that pursued them both in and out of the prison world.

In conclusion, western violence stalked many areas of western life. It did not exclude women; rather, it directly shaped their lives, as any of them risked finding its ugly presence within the public sphere of their work or the private confines of home. When women acted in a violent manner, their behavior often represented a response to a domestic situation. That situation might be one in which physical conflict was viewed as an acceptable function of daily life or one that caused women to fear for their lives. Women, some of whom tolerated their domestic condition for long periods, often responded with aggressive action to save their own lives or those of their children. Although the violence of some women involved fights with other females, the majority of cases surveyed stemmed from domestic living arrangements and family abuse. Sometimes accidentally, and sometimes deliberately, women returned the violence of their abusers, maiming or killing them.

When the violence of women's lives pulled them in as participants, the western court system stood ready. Self-defense and "no duty to retreat" arguments were often unsuccessful for the defendant; trial and conviction, speedy. Although a woman might receive a pardon or parole quickly, she first passed through the stage of "example," so that others understood the dangers of responding to both the theory and practice of masculine violence.

The arrest, conviction, and imprisonment of women, often on the basis of questionable evidence, delivered powerful social messages throughout communities. In addition, race and class imperatives deepened the formal response of society and burdened women of color with more frequent arrest and longer penitentiary time. In general, the processes that reversed convictions required long periods; while women, innocent or guilty, waited for their cases to be reviewed, they spent their prison time inside a male facility.

These elements brought women into the institutionalized violence of the penitentiary. There women inmates faced a world of violence that officials called "punishment." The violence of the prison world came in both passive and active forms. The inadequate care for women and their lack of protection in male prisons exposed them to the physical assaults of all prisoners. In addition, a less tangible mental violence plagued women's prison time. The threat of punishment, the sounds of the travail of others, the many humiliations, and the time to think about these things had to make an impact, of which women inmates left little clear record.

For women who found themselves learning of society's ungenerous response to female crime, prison life with its many threats to physical and mental safety represented only the beginning of the violence. There remained the violence of women's work and care, as female inmates marked off the days of their time in the penitentiary.

Notes

1. ――― T. Walrond to Honorable Governor, 5 June 1883, Henrietta Cook File, box 25, Pardon and Parole Files, KSHS.

2. For an excellent article that analyzes this case from the perspective of Michel Foucault, see McNall, "'It Was a Plot Got Up to Convict Me.'" McNall argues that the trial served as an arena for the forces of progress and order to defeat social and economic chaos; Henrietta's refusal to play the proper "role" for the jury meant she had to be convicted to affirm the sense of progress in a frontier community. McNall uses the Cook case as a springboard to find larger community notions about power and the need for rational explanations. Some details about the Cook family are drawn from the McNall account.

3. Henrietta Cook to Honorable Governor, 1 Jan., 6 May 1883; J. S. Smith to Governor, 16 May 1883; V. M. Noble to Governor Pouders, 8 Aug. 1886, Henrietta Cook File, box 25, Pardon and Parole Files, KSHS.

4. For violence as a ritual to keep women in a domestic role, see Epstein, *Deceptive Distinctions*, pp. 131–35.

5. *Philipsburg (Montana) Mail*, 25 Dec. 1903.

6. *Philipsburg (Montana) Call*, 23 Dec. 1903; Mattie Lee, Photo no. 1554, State Prison Convict Register, Mar. 1879–Nov. 1910, MtHS.

7. *Anaconda (Montana) Weekly Review*, 28 Feb., 2 May 1880.

8. *Livingston (Montana) Herald*, 4, 5, 6 Oct., 15, 16 Nov. 1893.

9. Ibid., 16 Nov. 1893.

10. *Butte (Montana) Miner*, 22 Jan., 10 Mar. 1896.

11. Ibid., 10 Mar. 1896.

12. Ibid.

13. See also the case of African American prostitutes Mattie Langford and Myrtle Brown in Billings, Montana (*Billings Daily Gazette*, 3 Apr., 25, 28 June 1901). For a more complete discussion of the general violence within prostitution, see Butler, *Daughters of Joy, Sisters of Misery*, pp. 42–46, 110–13, and passim.

14. John M. Breeze, District Attorney, to Mrs. J. W. Scott, 21 May 1910, Carrie Scott File, Inmate Case Files, NSCMA.

15. The concept that one under siege has no legal obligation to withdraw from an altercation is treated extensively in Brown, *No Duty to Retreat*.

16. John M. Breeze, District Attorney, to the Board of Parole Commissioners, 14 Dec. 1910, 27 June 1911, Carrie Scott File, Inmate Case Files, NSCMA.

17. Pardon Record of Carrie I. Scott, no. 1210, 14 Nov. 1911, ibid.

18. Citizens' Petition, Ada Wade, no. 1754, 15 Oct. 1890, Executive Clemency Files, TSA.

19. Frank Howard to Board of Pardons, 12 Dec. 1894, Annie Carmack File, box 20, Pardon and Parole Files, KSHS.

20. W. H. Sears to Honorable Governor, 5 June 1894, ibid.

21. Annie Cormack File, Pardon and Parole Files, box 25, KSHS. This file, with Annie Carmack's name misspelled, represents a clerical error in the alphabetical order, thus information is found in two boxes.

22. Prisoner no. 1629, Statement of Convicts, Prisoner Ledger I, 1901–6, nos. 1–1953, KSHS.

23. M. L. Ogg to Governor Walter Stubbs, 24 Feb. 1910, Florence Akers File, box 1, Pardon and Parole Files, KSHS.

24. O. M. Johnson to Governor Walter Stubbs, 22 Feb. 1910, ibid.

25. Undated brief for Governor, ibid.

26. M. L. Ogg to Governor Walter Stubbs, 24 Feb. 1910; O. M. Johnson to Governor Walter Stubbs, 22 Feb. 1910, ibid.

27. J. G. Bowers to Governor Walter Stubbs, 18 Mar. 1910, ibid.

28. For other Kansas cases involving black women and public disputes, see Ella Anderson File, box 2; Emma Duncan File, box 37; Bessie Hickland File, box 60; Carrie Jefferson File, box 67, all in Pardon and Parole Files, KSHS. For examples in Missouri, see Bettie Smith, box 31, folder 3; Caroline Brown, box 28, folder 10; Mary Ball, box 31, folder 8, Pardon Papers, RG 5, MSA.

29. Testimony of William A. Smith; Testimony of Lillie Yeager, Trial Transcript, no. 1152, Mable Clark File, Albany County District Court Criminal Case Files, WSAHD.

30. Testimony of Elias Pierce, ibid.

31. Testimony of Armstead Corbin, ibid.

32. Instructions of the judge to the jury, n.d., ibid.

33. O. W. Gillespie, County Attorney, to Governor J. S. Hogg, 20 Oct. 1893, Lola Hinesman, no. 9273, Executive Clemency Files, TSA.

34. Valentina B. Madrid, no. 2158, Application of Prisoner for Parole, 27 Nov. 1918, New Mexico Penitentiary Records, Inmate Files, no. 2158, NMSA (hereafter, Inmate Files, NMSA).

35. Alma Lyons, no. 2157, Application of Prisoner for Parole, 9 June 1918, Inmate Files, no. 2157, NMSA.

36. Alma Lyons, no. 2157, Description of Convict, 10 June 1907, and Application of Prisoner for Parole, 9 June 1918; Valentina Madrid, no. 2158, Description of Convict, 10 June 1907, and Application of Prisoner for Parole, 27 Nov. 1918, both in Inmate Files, nos. 2157 and 2158, NMSA.

37. For details of this case not found in the penitentiary records, the author thanks Robert J. Tórrez for his unpublished paper, "Murder at Hillsboro: The Poisoning of Manuel Madrid, 1907," in author's possession.

38. The western courts did not typically sentence women to death. In one other example, Maggie "Sis" Vinegar was sentenced to be hanged in Kansas in 1883, but the execution was not carried out and in 1889 Maggie died in prison of consumption (Maggie "Sis" Vinegar File, 16 Apr. 1883, box 138, Pardon and Parole Files, KSHS).

39. The death penalty, although rarely invoked against women, was always a potential sentence. In 1871 Mary Jane Scales was convicted of the murder of her husband and sentenced to hang. Her sentence was commuted to life at hard labor. Twenty-three years later the almost eighty-year-old African American woman was still in the Kansas penitentiary (Mary Jane Scales File, box 116, Pardon and Parole Files, KSHS).

40. For examples of murder parole petitions without an explanation of the case, see Serena Pace, 19 Sept. 1887; Amanda Pettis, 17 Nov. 1887; Fannie M. Daniels, 5 Nov. 1888, *List of Pardons and Remissions Granted by the Governor of the State of Arkansas for the Years 1887–1889,* ASP. For Kansas see Catherine Friend File, 30 Jan. 1865, box 44; Bessie Hickland File, 26 Nov. 1914, box 60, Pardon and Parole Files, KSHS. Of the states' descriptive registers of prisoners, only New Mexico included an inquiry about the reason for the crime and this column was rarely completed for women. See Convict Record Book, NMSA.

41. Citizens' Petition to Governor James S. Hogg, 12 Dec. 1893, Caroline Bowman, no. 3143, Executive Clemency Files, TSA.

42. Ibid.

43. Caroline Bowman received "a full pardon and [was] restored to full citizenship and the right of suffrage," with the last five words marked out in the pardon document (State of Texas vs. Caroline Bowman, no. 16149, 2 May 1894, ibid.).

44. Mollie Black File, box 10, Pardon and Parole Files, KSHS.

45. Mollie Harrison to the Honorable Board of Pardons, 27 June 1911, Mollie Harrison File, Board of Pardons Files, NSCMA.

46. John M. Chartz to the Board of Pardons, 23 Aug. 1912; John Chartz to the Board of Pardons, 13 Aug. 1913, ibid.

47. Judge F. E. Adams to Governor Charles A. Culberson, 27 Mar. 1895, Mrs. Ernest Brown, no. 17014, Executive Clemency Files, TSA.

48. Mary Frielinger, no. 3052, Statement of Convicts, Prisoner Ledger A, KSHS.

49. Mary Frielinger File, box 44, Pardon and Parole Files, KSHS.

50. Florence Davis File, box 32, ibid.

51. *Butte (Montana) Miner*, 24 June 1903.

52. Pearl McGowan was considered too young to be sworn and was not required to take an oath before her testimony. In 1908, the Montana courts did not allow the testimony of Homer Adams, an adult African American, who would have substantiated Florence Riordan's claims of physical abuse from the spouse she shot and killed (*Billings [Montana] Daily Gazette*, 14 Oct. 1908).

53. Ibid., 25 June 1903.

54. Citizens' Petition to Governor Bryant B. Brooks, n.d.; J. M. Mott, Deposition, Parole Hearing of Hattie La Pierre, 4 June 1906, both in Hattie La Pierre File, Petitions for Pardon, Governor Bryant B. Brooks, WSAHD.

55. For Black's physique, see A. R. Hagar, Preliminary Examination Testimony before Justice of the Peace Charley Allen, [?] Oct. 1905, p. 4, Hattie La Pierre, no. 376, Fremont County District Court Criminal Cases, WSAHD; for Hattie La Pierre see Wyoming State Penitentiary Inmate Register Cards, Prisoner no. 965, Hattie La Pierre File, Petitions for Pardon, WSAHD.

56. A. R. Hagar, Preliminary Examination Testimony, p. 5, Hattie La Pierre, no. 376, Fremont County District Court Criminal Cases, WSAHD; Hattie La Pierre Affidavit, Parole Hearing, 9 July 1906, Hattie La Pierre File, Petitions for Pardon, WSAHD.

57. J. M. Mott, Deposition, Parole Hearing of Hattie La Pierre, 4 June 1906, p. 1, Hattie La Pierre File, Petitions for Pardon, WSAHD.

58. Hattie La Pierre Affidavit; William B. Matheny, Preliminary Examination Testimony, [?] Oct. 1905, Criminal Case File no. 376, ibid., p. 10.

59. William B. Matheny, Preliminary Examination Testimony, ibid., pp. 13–16.

60. J. M. Mott, Deposition, ibid., p. 2.

61. William B. Matheny, Preliminary Examination Testimony, ibid., pp. 9–10.

62. Ibid., p. 10.

63. J. M. Mott Deposition, ibid., p. 2.

64. A. R. Hagar, Preliminary Examination Testimony, ibid., p. 6.

65. Hattie La Pierre Affidavit, ibid., p. 2.

66. A. R. Hagar, Preliminary Examination Testimony, ibid., p. 6; Scott Briggs, Inquest to Harry Black, Hattie La Pierre, no. 376, Fremont County District Court Criminal Cases, WSAHD.

67. State of Wyoming vs. Hattie La Pierre, Instruction Requested by the Defendant and Refused by the Court, Filed 23 Dec. 1905, Hattie La Pierre, no. 376, Fremont County District Court Criminal Cases, WSAHD.

68. On 11 July 1906, the board of pardons commuted the sentence from three years to fifteen months. La Pierre was released 29 Jan. 1907, with sixty-five days good

time (State Board of Pardons to Governor Bryant B. Brooks, 11 July 1906, Hattie La Pierre File, Petitions for Pardon; and Descriptions of Women Inmates, Hattie La Pierre, no. 965, Female Inmates File, WSAHD).

69. *New North-West,* 5 Dec. 1879.

70. "Mrs. Drouillard's Testimony," ibid.

71. Ibid.

72. Ibid., 12 Dec. 1879.

73. Ibid.

74. Ibid., 21 May, 2 July 1880.

75. Ibid., 2 July 1880.

76. Pardon of Mary A. Drouillard, 26 Aug. 1882, Territorial Executive Records, Applications for Executive Pardons, 1875–1890, box 1, folder 25, Record Series 40, MtHS; *Daily Independent,* 21 Dec. 1878.

77. Irene Kent, no. 2754, Territory of New Mexico vs. Irene Kent, no. 381 Transcript of Sentence Statement, 30 Dec. 1910, Inmate Files, no. 2754, NMSA.

78. Irene Kent, no. 2754, Application of Prisoner for Parole, 28 Jan. 1913, ibid.

79. Statement of First Friend or Adviser, Loretta Batis, 14 Feb. 1913; Abe Hixenbaugh, Sheriff, to John B. McManus, Superintendent, 5 Feb. 1913, ibid.

80. Captain W. D. Greet to Captain Fred Fornoff, 17 May 1913, ibid.

81. Irene Kent to J. B. McManus, 14 May 1913; C. E. Morris to Mrs. Irene Kent, 10 Apr. 1913, ibid.

82. Captain W. D. Greet to Captain Fred Fornoff, 17 May 1913, ibid.

83. *Denver Express,* 12 Mar. 1917, "Excerpts from Crime Records, 1863–1929," Denver Police Department Scrapbook, microfilm copy, CSA.

84. Sarah Bretano File, box 13, Pardon and Parole Files, KSHS.

85. Statement of Governor J. H. Prescott, n.d., ibid.

86. Sarah Bretano, 30 Oct. 1878 and 23 Apr. 1881, Statement of Convicts, Prisoner Ledger A, KSHS.

87. Amanda Coates, box 28, folder 20; Mary Rechtein, box 35, folder 47; Sally Harris, box 29, folder 21, all in Pardon Papers, RG 5, MSA.

88. In one case, an eighteen-year-old Irish immigrant was found not guilty by reason of insanity in the beating death of her infant. The woman's history of erratic behavior preceded the birth of her child. At her trial, doctors argued that a long labor and an instrumental delivery could produce insanity (*Anaconda Standard,* 17–19, 21, 22, 24, 26, 28 Feb., 1–4 Mar. 1893).

89. Mary Ann Taylor, 27 Sept. 1879, Statement of Convicts, Prisoner Ledger A, KSHS; and Mary Ann Taylor File, 14 Nov. 1883, box 131, Pardon and Parole Files, KSHS.

90. Mary Mork, no. 9970, Record of Prisoners Received, Prisoner Ledger H, Prisoners nos. 7029–10,000, 6 July 1894–12 Dec. 1901, KSHS; Mary Mork File, box 93, Pardon and Parole Files, KSHS. The fact that Mork was white certainly helped her in the dramatically fast parole process. In 1901 of thirteen women who entered the penitentiary, five were white and two of these, Mork and Cora Frost, were paroled immediately. Annie Spencer, no. 9967, an illiterate black cook sentenced to two years for third degree manslaughter, entered the prison two weeks before Mary Mork but had no record of a parole petition and presumably served her time. See Prisoner Ledger H, Prisoners nos. 9667, 9812, 9824, 9825, 9840, 9841, 9860, 9861, 9900, 9967, 9979.

91. Records are not entirely clear for this inmate (Louisa Wood, no. 1868, Pardon Papers, box 27, folder 28, RG 5, MSA).

92. Pardon, Bettie Jones, no. 3093, 21 Aug. 1880, Executive Clemency Files, TSA.

93. E. W. Taylor to Governor John Ireland, 7 Apr. 1885; B. W. Camp to Governor John Ireland, 7 Apr. 1885; W. T. Armistead to Governor John Ireland, 7 Apr. 1885; Charles F. Todd to Governor John Ireland, 21 Mar. 1885, all in Sallie Hill, no. 111, Executive Clemency Files, TSA.

94. Citizens of Marion County to Governor John Ireland, 26 Feb. 1885, ibid.

95. J. J. Douglas, trial testimony, in Alice Vick, Appellant vs. the State of Texas, Galveston Term, 1891, pp. 2–4, Alice Vick, no. 2329, Executive Clemency Files, TSA.

96. Ibid., pp. 10–16.

97. For other examples involving acts of violence toward children, see Sally Harris, Sept. 1869, box 29, folder 21; Josephine, "A Colored Woman," 15 Sept. 1866, box 22, folder 2; Amanda Coates, 21 Apr. 1869, box 28, folder 20, all in Pardon Papers, RG 5, MSA.

98. State of Wyoming subpoenas to C. H. Peterson, F. P. Cramey, G. W. West, Anna Bruce, Mary Peterson, Annie Bruce, George Bruce, Wilford W. Cramey, O. T. Papworth, W. J. Jensen, Lawrence Bruce, 23 Mar. 1907, Annie Bruce File, Petitions for Pardon, Governor Bryant B. Brooks, WSAHD.

99. There is an extensive literature about the conflicts between the LDS church and the federal government and the emergence of the Mormons in the West and as a religious group. For example, see Thomas F. O'Dea, *The Mormons* (Chicago: University of Chicago Press, 1957); Leonard Arrington, *The Great Basin Kingdom: An Economic History of the Latter-day Saints, 1830–1900* (Lincoln: University of Nebraska Press, Bison Books, 1966); Mark S. Leone, *Roots of Modern Mormonism* (Cambridge: Harvard University Press, 1979); Jan Shipps, *Mormonism: The Story of A New Religious Tradition* (Urbana: University of Illinois Press, 1985).

100. D. G. Thomas to the State Board of Pardons, In the Matter of the Application of Annie Bruce for a Pardon, n.d., Annie Bruce File, Petitions for Pardon, WSAHD.

101. Local Mormon church officials claimed the Bruce marriage was "unhappy" (Bishop Frank P. Cramey to Governor Bryant B. Brooks, 10 May 1908, ibid.).

102. Confession of Annie Bruce, 16 Aug. 1907, ibid.

103. D. G. Thomas to State Board of Pardons, n.d., ibid.

104. Ibid.

105. Bishop Frank P. Cramey to Governor Bryant B. Brooks, 10 May 1908, ibid.

106. Ibid.

107. Ibid.

108. Convicts Discharged or Removed Paper, Annie Bruce, no. 1206, 6 Oct. 1909, ibid.

109. Statement of the Warden Relative to the Application for Parole of Anna Bruce no. 7572, 5 Jan. 1910, ibid.

110. Statement of the Prison Chaplain Relative to the Application for Parole of Anna Bruce no. 7572, 5 Jan. 1910, ibid.

111. B. F. Bondurant to J. H. Ryckman, 1 July [1908?], ibid.

112. Anna E. Bruce to the Honorable Governor and Board of Pardon, 5 July 1910, ibid.

113. Annie E. Bruce to Governor Joseph M. Carey, 21 Mar. 1911, Annie Bruce File, Petitions for Pardon, Governor Joseph M. Carey, WSAHD.

114. Citizens' Petition to Joseph M. Carey, 15 Mar. 1911, ibid.

115. Annie Bruce to Mr. Judge Craig, 5 June 1910, Annie Bruce File, Petitions for Pardon, Governor Bryant B. Brooks, WSAHD.

116. Details of family abuse were often only revealed when court testimony or the possibility of legal charges absolutely forced disclosure. In a Montana murder

trial in 1895, the seventeen-year-old widow of the victim and daughter of the defendants testified that her stepfather had sexual intercourse with her for the previous five years. Her mother, who denied knowledge of such activity, and the stepfather were convicted in the poisoning death of the young woman's husband. Charges against the teenaged widow were dropped (*Daily Missoulian,* 27 Mar., 13, 14 Sept. 1895).

117. On the acceptability of divorce, see Riley, *Divorce,* pp. 4–6. For a discussion of how class influenced divorce, see Paula Petrik, "Not a Love Story: Bordeaux vs. Bordeaux," *Montana the Magazine of Western History* (Spring 1991): 32–46. For an example of the family constraints felt by working women, see Janet Le Compte, ed., *Emily: The Diary of a Hard Worked Woman* (Lincoln: University of Nebraska Press, 1987).

118. Riley, *Divorce,* p. 82, 90.

119. George, *Texas Convict,* pp. 60–65, 103–7; *Sweet Smell of Sagebrush,* pp. 66–67.

120. Physical descriptions of women's bodies can be found in any prison register used in this study. For specific examples cited (seven African American and three white inmates), see Blanche Williams, Photo no. 1200; Emma Bell, Photo no. 1270; Emma Yamer, Photo no. 1272; Inez Perry, Photo no. 1315; Minnie Farrell, Photo no. 1358; Nellie Scanlon, Photo no. 1670; Myrtle Lea, Photo no.?; Lea Carlisle, Photo no. 3166, in State Prison Convict Register, MtHS; Inmate Examination, 21 Dec. 1908, Mollie Harrison File, Board of Pardons Files, NSCMA; Description of Convict, Alma Lyons, no. 2157, 8 June 1907, Inmate Files, no. 2157, NMSA.

121. O'Hare, *Prison Letters,* p. 9.

122. Robinson, *Female Life in Prison,* pp. 19–23.

123. Board of Commissioners of Public Institutions, *Second Annual Report,* 1874, pp. 349, 351, UKKC.

124. Testimony of Inmates Annie Cordiss, Louisa Reed, Dora Thompson to the Investigating Committee, *Report of Penitentiary Investigating Committee,* pp. 983–84, TSA.

125. Warden C. A. Swift to Governor Thomas Fletcher, 2 Oct. 1865, Pardon Papers, box 20, folder 23, RG 5, MSA.

126. Warden C. A. Swift to Governor Charles Fletcher, 31 July 1866, Pardon Papers, box 21, folder 48, RG 5, MSA.

127. Rafter, *Partial Justice,* pp. 3–21, 177–79.

128. Thomas Hill Green, "Anglo-American Philosophies of Penal Law," *Journal of the American Institute of Criminal Law and Criminology* 1 (May 1910): 42–43.

129. Ward, Dewey, and Company, Lessees, "The Texas State Penitentiary," from the Transactions of the Prison Congress, 1874; reprinted in Board of Commissioners of Public Institutions, *Second Annual Report,* 1874, pp. 340–42, UKKC. Colonel Ward may have been the same A. J. Ward who leased convicts from Arkansas from 1860 to 1863 but abandoned the penitentiary as Union troops approached Little Rock (Jane Zimmerman, "The Convict Lease System in Arkansas and the Fight for Abolition," *Arkansas Historical Quarterly* 8 [Autumn 1949]: 172; Garland E. Bayliss, "The Arkansas State Penitentiary under Democratic Control, 1874–1896," *Arkansas Historical Quarterly* 34 [Autumn 1975]: 195–96).

130. Crow, "Political History of the Texas State Penal System," pp. 77, 96.

131. Board of Commissioners of Public Institutions, *Second Annual Report,* 1874, pp. 346, 349, 351, UKKC.

132. Ibid., pp. 343, 346–47.

133. *Report of a Committee . . . to Investigate the Matter of the Punishment of Convicts at the Minnesota State Prison,* 25 July 1891, pp. 20–23, MnHS.

134. Testimony of Inmate Mary Harrington to the Investigating Committee, 29 July 1909, *Report of the Penitentiary Investigating Committee*, p. 548, TSA.

135. Ibid., p. 561.

136. Testimony of Inmates Ennis Carlisle, Hannah Steele to the Investigating Committee, ibid., pp. 556–57, 559, 563. The captain testifying to the same committee denied that he permitted his staff to use vulgar language to the women inmates (pp. 574–75).

137. Transcript in the Matter of the Inquiry as to the Sanity of Lizzie Woodfolk, an Inmate of the Nevada State Prison, Carson City, Nev., 8 Mar. 1915, Lizzie Woodfolk File, Board of Pardons Files, NSCMA.

138. Affidavit of Mary Fitzpatrick, 22 May 1914, Governor's Papers, George Hodges, Correspondence, 1913–15, Board of Corrections: Investigations of Punishments, box 33, KSHS.

139. Affidavit of Elizabeth C. Simpson, 23 July 1914, ibid.

140. Tórrez, "Murder at Hillsboro," p. 11.

141. Punishment Record Book, Prisoners nos. 2157 and 2158, p. 7, Inmate Files, NMSA.

142. Sister Frances de Chantel to John B. McManus, 1 Dec. 1938, Alma Lyons, no. 2157, Inmate Files, no. 2157, NMSA.

143. The length of Alma's stay at St. Vincent's suggests that she remained with the child until a home was found. That time surely gave her the opportunity to bond with her infant. In 1938, after her release, Alma and her son, Frank, returned to the hospital to request his birth certificate. Neither the hospital nor the penitentiary could provide documentation. Both agencies assisted Alma and her son, examples of the power of family, to secure a delayed certificate of birth from the Department of Public Health (Sister Frances de Chantal to John B. McManus, 1 Dec. 1938; Superintendent to Mr. Frank R——, 22 Dec. 1938, ibid.).

144. T. D. Perry to Governor John Ireland, 18 May 1885, Eliza Jane Thompson, no. 103, Executive Clemency Files, TSA.

145. R. W. White, M.D., to Governor John Ireland, 19 May 1885; B. W. Rivers to Governor John Ireland, 21 May 1885, Citizens' Petition to Governor John Ireland, 18 May 1885; Thomas J. Goree to James W. Baines, 22 June 1885, ibid.

146. Pearré Boynton to Governor John Ireland, 19 July 1886, ibid.

147. R. O. Johnson Deposition, 20 July 1886, ibid.

148. John Farley Deposition, 9 July 1886, ibid.

149. D. A. Kelley Deposition, 8 July 1886, ibid.

150. W. T. Harris Deposition, 9 July 1886, ibid. Thompson's penitentiary record does not say whether she was returned to the prison.

151. Pearré Boynton to Governor John Ireland, 21 July 1886, ibid.

5 Women's Health inside the Walls

I expect within two or three weeks to become a Mother and as it is a matter of life and death for me and my child . . . I . . . ask you . . . as an act of common humanity to grant my pardon.
—Mrs. R. M. Lister
Texas State Prison System
1891

Convicted of adultery in September 1890, Mrs. R. M. Lister did not have the five hundred dollar fine and went to the county jail. Approximately five months pregnant, Lister entered prison alone for "influential friends of the man bailed him out," and he abandoned his codefendant, "taking no interest in the woman . . . or the fruit of their joint crime."[1] Although women unable to pay local fines often went to penitentiary work farms, Lister spent the remainder of her pregnancy at the local poorhouse. Authorities transferred her there on the recommendation of a physician who examined Lister once during the early part of her pregnancy.[2]

As her delivery time approached and her health deteriorated, Lister became an increasing worry to local officials, who hoped to get rid of her before the birth. Even W. H. Brooker, the attorney who filed her appeal for remission

Ellen Smith, Colorado State Penitentiary. Courtesy Division of State Archives and Public Records, Denver, Colo.

148

of the fine, showed cold concern for his client, saying, "in her present position and surroundings there is great danger of her death as well as that of her offspring—whether that would be better for the county and mankind is not for us to consider."[3] Brooker couched his strongest pardon argument, certainly not in humanitarian terms, but in those of political gain for the governor, embroiled in administrative charges against his appointees. On 17 January, Governor Ross signed the papers that released the destitute woman to have her child outside prison.

Among the areas that suffered from the overall managerial malaise and added to the violent atmosphere of the penitentiaries, the physical health and well-being of the prisoners ranked among the most critical. Prisoners lived, not only in squalor, but without basic nutrition to help sustain them in the unsanitary environment. In addition, minimal, near barbaric, medical care encouraged contagious disease and rapid death.[4]

For women inmates, the neglect of health meant another aspect of prison magnified under the lens of gender. Four elements adversely affected the physical well-being of women prisoners. These were the prison diet, the treatment of chronic illnesses, the absence of available medical facilities, and the impact of all these on pregnancy and child care inside the prison. Ultimately, these factors reinforced yet another dimension to the violence women prisoners confronted.

Health topics merited only a small amount of space in annual penitentiary reports aimed at emphasizing the budget efficiency of state custodial care. Wardens insisted that prisoner health improved from year to year, but stumbled over their own contradictory information. For example, in 1871 A. J. Bennett reported that 112 prisoners (excluding twenty-one presidential pardonees and eight escapees) left Huntsville the previous year. Eight of these had died and an unspecified number from among the forty-six pardoned had been released due to chronic infirmities. Bennett judged another thirty-one remaining inside the prison unfit to work. Ten of the thirty-one Bennett labeled "insane or permanently diseased."[5] These numbers did not include illness and death figures for the work camps outside the walls, statistics that would have greatly inflated the totals.

Just within the main prison, the Texas penitentiary housed a significant number of prisoners with health problems so severe the administration grudgingly acknowledged them. But Bennett boasted that "seldom does the 'sick report' account for the same person many days together."[6] No doubt the watchful eye of the prison physician, H. C. Oliphant, kept prisoners wary of the sick list. Oliphant said inmates knew he tested their "representations of disability" and that "censure and exposure are sure to follow deception."[7]

Only three months after Bennett and Oliphant delivered these reports, an investigative committee described a somewhat different health situation at the penitentiary. The committee found one wing of a main building "so damp and unhealthy as to be unfit for use."[8] While the annual report called inmate illness only negligible, now Oliphant admitted "the ratio of sickness was two-thirds larger among the convicts confined in that part of the prison than any other of the buildings."[9] By 1872 Oliphant was complaining "a very large percentage of those received . . . came here crippled and permanently disabled, or laboring under incurable constitutional diseases," and in the next breath reporting "the health of the convicts has been remarkably good."[10]

Other states also claimed that a healthy clime prevailed at the prison. In 1874, the Kansas board of commissioners eloquently noted that "the hospital is a haven of rest for the suffering convict, from which he is soon returned to the working ranks, cured of all his bodily ailments."[11] Yet, in 1874 dietary provisions were so inferior at Kansas that how the ill recovered or the well stayed healthy remained curious.

For more than six months of 1874, the beef delivered to the penitentiary fell far below the standard outlined in the agreement with the meat contractor, John Volz. The spoiled meat and shortfall deliveries would have gone undocumented except for the attention of the inmate steward assigned to the kitchen. He began his own daily ledger describing the condition of the meat at arrival. His records showed "very poor," "tenderloin taken out," "bruised and scarred up," or "short" for most days.[12] For particularly bad batches, the inmate refused to sign the receipt invoice, deferring to the warden, who typically accepted the meat. The attentive steward suffered an "accident" in late August 1874; officials removed him from kitchen duty and thus halted the daily delivery accounts. His departure left records about the quantity and quality of beef delivery in administrative confusion for the remainder of the year.[13]

By 1890, inmates still reported that Kansas offered little in the way of a decent diet. Prisoner John N. Reynolds, assigned to arduous labor in the mines, described breakfast as unsweetened coffee and hash made from bread and the meat of the previous day. The midday dinner, eaten in the mine, consisted of a slice of corn bread, a piece of meat, and a quart of water. The inmates considered it dessert when the meal included cold cabbage, turnips, or cracked corn. Once inmates returned above ground, they looked forward to a supper of two tablespoons of sorghum molasses, a piece of bread, and a cup of unsweetened tea.[14]

These incidents illuminated a central reason for the ill health of convicts—prison diet was remarkably poor, while prison labor was extremely taxing. Administrators and contractors allocated food monies reluctantly, seeking to feed inmates on the smallest possible budget. In addition, prison civil servants found food contracts an easy way to bilk the state by diverting deliveries to private homes or charging exorbitant amounts for rotten food.[15]

Given the chance, inmates recounted how these bureaucratic thieveries translated into daily realities at the prisoners' table.[16] A Wyoming prisoner recalled that at his first penitentiary meal of boiled beef and bread each inmate received an empty tomato can to be used for drinking water and an "abundance of a dark colored mixture, which for a better name was called coffee." During his incarceration, he knew that "hash or stew would constitute the bill of fare on any given date," a diet that resulted in an inmate leaving prison "usually in poor physical condition even after a stay of only ten months."[17]

Prison inspectors and administrators took an opposite stance about the food, generally arguing that inmates grumbled unnecessarily and ate better than they deserved. In Minnesota in 1907 the published prison menu for the first week of January presented a varied selection, such as one might find in a public hotel. Prisoners were said to have beef liver, potatoes, roast pork with dressing, roast beef, turnips, prunes, vegetable soup, cheese, and cake. Only some inmates actually received this nourishing food, as officials reserved the "nicer items" for the "better grade" prisoners.[18]

In 1910 a Texas penitentiary inspector assured an investigating committee that all inmates enjoyed plentiful amounts of good quality food. While he conceded that at most work farms rats and ants infested the meat storage, he thought other dietary items adequate, with ground cornmeal and regular servings of potatoes, beans, dried apples, and coffee.[19] Texas inmates testifying to the same committee outlined a less attractive diet. On a work farm, inmates received biscuits, bacon, and "stuff called coffee" for breakfast. But of the biscuits, one inmate remarked, "cooked about Saturday and we got them about Monday. . . . You couldn't smash them with your hand."[20] Inmates transferred from work farms to the walls regarded the "inside" diet, which included one slice of white bread a day, soured milk, and coffee doctored with copperas, as vastly superior to the food at the camps.[21]

One Wyoming inmate wryly recalled that whenever he heard a man express a wish to lose weight, he was reminded of that "fat reducer . . . old Grahams" (Otto Gramm, prison lessee), who did not want "his men to get fat and sluggish." According to the inmate the penitentiary doctor maintained that a man in prison "should be given just as small an amount of food as possible, just enough to keep the undertaker away." Concluded the inmate, "some days the cook would count the beans one short and some poor fellow would fall by the wayside before the next meal."[22]

Limited selection and meager quantity marked the diet of many nineteenth-century people, but generally most would have expected food free from spoilage or infestation by maggots. Convicts regularly received such food. Federal prisoners removed from the Texas penitentiary testified: "the meat . . . could not be eaten"; "they gave us meat that the buzzards would not eat"; "the scraps from the table were made into . . . soup that gave the men a diarrhea"; "the beef was so tainted that we could smell it before coming into the dining room."[23]

In many penitentiaries, some survived only because their families sent supplemental packages or the funds for extra food purchases. Although not permitted to cook in the cells, inmates, especially those in "good behavior" categories, could request other edibles delivered to them.[24] In Texas, one inmate testified that he regularly sent to town for sugar, molasses, and chickens.[25]

In all circumstances connected to diet, women prisoners faced added disadvantages. Kate Richards O'Hare said of the Missouri penitentiary, "Food is a problem." Since the staff transported meals three blocks from the kitchen to the women's dining hall, all food for the female prisoners arrived "stone cold and . . . uneatable."[26] Hot or cold, meals built around stale bread, lard, potatoes, and some sugar to give laboring men energy for the day's work were not conducive to women's good health. Fresh milk, wholesome bread, butter, and cheese—health staples of the nineteenth century and important for child-bearing and lactating women—simply did not appear on daily menus. Women often entered prison in less than excellent physical condition and the steady diet of starches and pork fat did not help them to improve.

Officials maintained that female prisoners received better food than the male inmates, but at least some women disagreed with that claim.[27] Some described the quantity as ample, but the quality as unfit. In 1902 Laura Reed asserted that women inmates in Texas got plenty of food, but "the cats or something have been eating on the meat and we have to eat it."[28]

Mexican American Guadalupe Grimsinger insisted to a later investigating committee that women inmates enjoyed ample amounts of good food and that the sick could request all the milk, eggs, rice, and oatmeal they desired.[29] Guadalupe, however, lived in special housing with the Anglo women prisoners, the committee addressed her as a white woman, and obviously her prison arrangements differed from those of the African American women at the same camp.[30] The committee members seemed to doubt twenty-one-year-old Guadalupe, imprisoned for over seven years on an accessory to murder conviction, and thought her afraid to reveal actual conditions.

Since all her testimony endorsed the prison management, Guadalupe may not have felt it in her best interests to be completely forthcoming with the committee. After all, prisoners remained behind with their jailers when investigating committees departed, a reality designed to cool the candor of many a witness.[31] Even with her positive assessment of food and care, Guadalupe, who said she had a thirteen-year-old daughter, admitted that, "I used to be just as healthy as I could be; I never did suffer, but my health broke down about a year and a half ago."[32] An undiagnosed painful breast complaint had left the woman "fretted" and unable to work for more than occasional short periods.

Guadalupe's African American colleagues gave committee members other information to consider about diet. Mary Harrington, in response to a question about whether Captain Brabham and his staff fed the women, replied, "Sometimes they do and sometimes they don't." Her answers about the recent appearance of generous quantities of meat and bread and "plenty of vegetables" suggested the farm managers had prepared for the arrival of the committee.[33] Lulu Lane, another African American prisoner, didn't think the diet better and reported that the usual meal included some but not all of the following: biscuits, bacon, grits, potatoes, rice, corn bread, beef, and syrup, occasionally butter and milk. Further, Lulu maintained that she went to bed hungry regardless of the menu, "because sometimes the grub is cooked so you can't eat it."[34]

In addition to coping with the limited and poorly prepared diet, white women and many African American and Mexican American women rarely followed the heavy work regimen of men and had no regular programs of physical exercise. At most, officials allowed them a walk in the prison yard, and this on an irregular basis. Boredom added to the sedentary existence and encouraged lethargy.[35] Thus, inactivity compounded the ailments caused by a woman's earlier nutritional history and worsened by the consistently bad prison diet.

Even in an era where social standards of beauty allowed women latitude in weight, female prisoners came to the penitentiary carrying more pounds than medically advisable for their height.[36] Of sixty-four black women remanded to Louisiana officials between 1866 and 1872, only eight stood taller than five feet four inches, while more than thirty measured five feet two inches or less. On these diminutive frames, the women carried weights that averaged between 120 and 140 pounds. Blindness in one eye, the absence of a few or all teeth, heads, arms, and bodies covered with the scars of burns, disease, and wounds—these were the common descriptions of young women who had not yet reached their twenty-fifth birthday.[37] Had the women arrived in the best of health, a year in the penitentiary would have drained the strongest, but these female inmates began their prison terms with a medical disadvantage from the outset.

In addition, many entered prison manifesting the symptoms of serious illnesses. Heart disease, epilepsy, rheumatism, asthma—the ordinary medical problems of many people turned life threatening after months on starvation rations in drafty damp prisons, where the unwell seldom saw a licensed physician who provided supervised care. Even when a doctor offered a prompt diagnosis and recommended immediate release, the slowness of the bureaucracy left sick women without hospital or nursing care for long periods. Alice Faulkner spent five months in the Missouri penitentiary, until officials justified her pardon on the grounds the woman was "almost incapable of guilty intent in consequence of physical and mental weakness caused by epileptic fits."[38]

Other women caught in drug and alcohol abuse, neither recognized as an illness, struggled without assistance for their problems. Official recognition of these conditions usually took the form of a single brief notation recorded during the in-take process. Several registers included tobacco, alcohol, and drug use under a "Habits" entry of "irregular" or "intemperate," making it difficult to assess the type of addiction from which a woman suffered when she came to the penitentiary.[39]

As prison record keeping improved, officials demonstrated more interest in the addictive habits of inmates. By the 1880s, Texas queried inmates on alcohol and tobacco use. The latter officials divided into users (397) and nonusers (48). In reference to alcohol, the survey took a more sophisticated approach, using four categories: strictly temperate (39), moderate (103), spasmodic drinkers (127), and admittedly intemperate (176).[40]

In the early twentieth century, New Mexico also canvassed its inmates on this topic. The survey showed that of 324 prisoners, five of whom were women, 140 admitted an addiction to alcohol and 294 to tobacco.[41] Methods for determining the statistics, standards of measurement, changing definitions of addiction, and inmate veracity all served to make the results only suggestive, but they do point to alcohol and tobacco dependency as an ingredient in prisoner demographics.

Alcoholics had few resources, other than religious temperance programs, to assist them through their imprisonment. Perhaps their first lessons concerned the ease with which one could secure alcohol in prison. Inmates used a variety of recipes, such as cutting shellac or adding lemon extract to alcohol from the dispensary to brew crude spirits; whether they endured more agony from its poison or from the guards who found them inebriated could be debated.[42] Those unwilling to risk probable illness and possible death from the denatured alcohol concoctions relied on accommodating guards and trusties to smuggle whiskey inside the walls.

In any event, the alcoholism of women prisoners stood outside the realm of professional concern. In part, this stemmed from an entrenched social refusal to recognize that alcoholism crossed gender lines. Yet, many women inmates' personal histories revealed that their crimes occurred within an atmosphere of heavy alcohol use, and they themselves were intoxicated at the time of their criminal actions. In prison, the woman who used alcohol or was ill with alcoholism might try to find some spirituous drink, despite the resulting punishments. Mollie Forsha's conduct record said only that she "obtained liquor surreptitiously and became drunk and insolent, for which she was put in the dungeon."[43]

Drug use also plagued many convicts and did not necessarily cease at the gates of the penitentiary. Inside the walls prisoners, calling on both internal and external sources, devised ways to secure a variety of drugs. According to the historian Paul E. Knepper, in 1893 the Arizona penitentiary physician ordered close to 10,000 prescriptions for a prison population that hovered around two hundred inmates, suggesting a high level of substance dependency among the inmates. By 1905 officials acknowledged the use of drugs, including cocaine, opium, hashish, and marijuana, as a common problem at the Arizona prison.[44]

In the same period, similar conditions existed in the Idaho penitentiary, where Warden E. L. Whitney called the increasing opium trade "a great deal of annoyance." He found it nearly impossible to control the smuggling of "spirituous liquors" and cocaine along with other "dope." Whitney feared that success with this contraband would make "degenerates of the users" and encourage them to widen their illegal operation to include firearms for mutiny and jail break. He hoped to eradicate drug traffic by establishing harsh new penalties for the smugglers, a strategy historically proven ineffective.[45] Although Whitney voiced concern about the "health and morals of the inmates," the physician's report for the same year made no assessment of the seriousness of illicit drug usage among Idaho prisoners.[46] But for female inmates at several different prisons, jailers' entries such as "confirmed opium eater," "Health good—is an opium smoker," "Scars from use of Morphine needle thick on legs and arms," "Morphine and Hop Fiend," and "morphine eater" hinted at the number of women drug abusers found inside penitentiaries.[47]

Women prisoners in advanced stages of venereal disease constituted another unwell group of female inmates. In Texas, Lillie St. Clair, a twenty-year-old white woman convicted of aggravated assault, lay near death from venereal disease and consumption. In making the case for Lillie to the governor, James H. White, sheriff of El Paso, explained that Lillie, the "confirmed opium eater" above, had entirely ceased the habit since her confinement and was believed "cured."[48] Although Lillie's conviction should have sent her to the penitentiary, both her illness and her race helped to keep her at the county jail. After seven months of incarceration, her health had failed so much that officials wanted Lillie out of the jail and returned to her parents' home. "Her mind and body wrecked," Lillie, whom the county declared "sufficiently punished," received her pardon eleven days later and returned home to die from the combined impact of drug abuse, venereal disease, and consumption.[49]

Lillie St. Clair garnered some local attention because she was white and known in her community. At the penitentiaries, lower-class women with venereal disease received only minimal care, even given the limited treatment available to the medical community. Physicians, who did not always address the widespread venereal disease among prisoners, used a prescription of oil and calomel, quinine, or a compound fashioned after a patent medicine called "S.S.S."[50] Beyond that, doctors did not initiate quarantine measures or seek administrative support for special care for the diseased.

Kate Richards O'Hare called the practice of mixing the "clean women" with the "frightfully syphilitic" "criminally stupid." She complained bitterly that she used the same bathtub as an Alaskan native woman in the last stages of venereal disease, whose throat was "one mass of open sores." She thought it wrong that "clean, healthy girls," by whom she meant African American prisoners, had to scrub the tubs and that no one disinfected or kept separate the food dishes.[51] Despite distaste for the circumstances, O'Hare could not ignore the agony of the sick women around her, writing to her family, "The poor Indian girl who . . . [has] syphilis is finding it so terribly hard to die."[52]

Other kinds of disabilities, apart from addictions and venereal disease, placed some women at even greater risk in the penitentiary because their physical circumstances made them nuisance cases for the prison staff. In 1903, Lida Gould, a deaf black domestic, went to the Montana penitentiary for the theft of $500.[53] Although literate, exactly how much did this woman understand, in an era prior to public use of sign language interpreters, about her trial, conviction, and imprisonment? According to another deaf inmate, Sarah Davies, very little. In 1897, Davies appealed to the governor of Kansas for a pardon, because her deafness prevented her from understanding the courtroom proceedings on her charge of using abusive language. Almost certainly part of Davies's problems stemmed from the inability of the hearing people around her to comprehend deaf speech, often articulated at loud and nonmodulated levels.[54]

Inside the prison, the special needs of disabled prisoners generated very little interest among wardens and guards. The labored communication with the deaf or the assisted mobility for the blind required an investment of time, patience, and kindness few officials appeared willing to expend.[55] Disabled prisoners, confused by their surroundings, hampered by narrow societal perceptions, and removed from even the semblance of care, must have yielded to fear, anger, and depression. Such demonstrations only further alienated a disinterested administration.

In 1902 Mary Conery, a fifty-six-year-old blind woman from the Oklahoma Territory, entered the Kansas state penitentiary sentenced to life for murder. Eighteen months later, officials in Kansas judged Conery to be insane and returned her to the sheriff of Lincoln County in the Oklahoma Territory. Whether the woman was insane at the time of her conviction, or lost her mental stability inside the Kansas penitentiary, providing for her physical needs seemed less important than the practical matter of removing her from the prison routines.[56] If Kansas moved her to its insane asylum before the transfer to Oklahoma, then Mary Conery went to a ward one floor above the women's quarters at the penitentiary. There the round-the-clock lockup conditions, which included hours spent chained to a wall, surpassed even the stark arrangements in the prison section.

In most cases, officials seemed to believe that mentally ill prisoners "misbehaved" or "acted queerly" out of spite. Although prisoners were not above such motivation, that dynamic did not explain the behavior of all "disruptive" women.[57] Margaret Hardy, who entered the Idaho penitentiary in 1895 on a life sentence, evinced many disturbing symptoms, but she elicited little compassion from prison officials. They viewed Hardy as willfully unpleasant. Her conduct, which ranged from promises of obedience to fits of rage, included anguished cries, abusive language, and arson. These might have been the behaviors of any angry prisoner, but Hardy also repeatedly tried to kill herself, usually by eating grass. Hardy's crime—poisoning a young black child whom she had adopted—and extreme behavior swings, complete with the suicide attempts, suggested a woman with serious mental imbalance. In response to her fluctuating conduct, her jailers retaliated with harsher and harsher punishments, even constructing a special windowless boxlike cell for her. Hardy, closed in total suffocating darkness, responded by setting fire to the contraption; Idaho penitentiary administrators decided she was "hopeless," a prisoner who would never learn how to "behave." Seven months after her arrival, officials declared Hardy insane and transferred her to the state asylum.[58]

Within this story lies a strange tangle of logic. If Margaret Hardy was insane, why did officials act as if she were not? Did Idaho officials recognize that Hardy had always been mentally ill, and that therefore their responses were harmful? Or did they decide that, since the prisoner refused to conform to penitentiary regulations, they would ship her to some other agency with more provisions for women? Or did they concede that their treatment exacerbated the instability that surrounded Margaret Hardy's crime in the first place?

Hardy's problems appeared to predate her entrance to prison, but for some women the penitentiary itself prompted the descent into mental illness. After authorities moved Rachel Springer from the penitentiary to the Missouri State Lunatic Asylum, the superintendent there took up the case of the "quiet and rational" young woman. Rachel's "insanity," he declared, "began during imprisonment" at the male penitentiary. He urged her pardon because the "same causes will exist in prison on her return."[59] Given the conditions in the Missouri penitentiary for men in 1865, the superintendent could have referred obliquely to a range of physical and emotional circumstances that taxed Rachel Springer's mental balance. She appeared to suffer from a "situational" insanity, perhaps caused by sexual assault, a particularly vicious guard, or privation of every sort. Such circumstances might have produced personal distress and emotional instability in any number of prisoners.

Many women never benefited from a doctor's concern about their stability, but nonetheless mental torment infused their prison lives. Kate Richards O'Hare perceived this stress and anxiety that women felt after months and years in the penitentiary. A woman two cells from O'Hare, whom the political activist described as a "mental, spiritual, and physical wreck," anguished in such a way that she would "sob and moan and weep for hours and hours at a time." Many of the other women O'Hare also saw as "not strong enough to stand alone" and she thought they sustained themselves by the belief that "their dead comrades in misery come back to care for and protect them." The women's cells, O'Hare asserted, were "peopled by . . . kindly comfortable amiable ghosts, who flit about all night on errands of mercy and love."[60]

The kindness of inmate spirits—whether disembodied or living—represented close to the best that sick women could hope for in male penitentiaries. Staff physicians who pushed too aggressively for inmates did not last long at the prisons. They were easily replaced by political appointees more willing to endorse the unclean conditions. Even the most attentive physicians recognized the limits of their influence in a system where as few dollars as possible were allocated for inmate maintenance. Regular medical care and decent facilities for the sick did not exist, and states responded sluggishly to appeals for improved conditions. When appropriated, funds for hospitals were just as likely to go astray as any others amidst the general fiscal mismanagement.

In the 1870s the doctor at the Texas penitentiary demonstrated how physicians mixed their medical standards and their political sense. From 1870 to 1873 Dr. Oliphant requested the construction of a separate hospital building. In the absence of a designated infirmary, he used a "narrow alley between two buildings" for his hospital, a passageway through which the working prisoners moved on their way to and from the shops. Oliphant hoped for a "roomy and comfortable hospital" and finally enthused in 1873 that, thanks to the prison lessees, convicts now enjoyed the "full benefit of a well regulated hospital system."[61] But a former military prisoner, working as a hospital steward for Oliphant at the Texas prison, told of health care far from well regulated.

Guards brought wounded and sick prisoners from the camps to the infirmary weeks after an injury or the onset of illness. Once at the main hospital, prisoners lingered a few days, often with the inmate steward as their only medical attendant. Oliphant himself visited the facility about once every two weeks and rarely saw a patient on a regular basis. As for his hospital records, Oliphant certified that convict deaths from gunshots and whippings resulted from secondary hemorrhage and constitutional syphilis.[62]

By 1880, the medical facility at the Texas prison continued to be substandard for the era. In that year, a new prison physician, R. H. Bush, performed nine amputations and reset three fractures, but conceded he performed the surgeries under less than acceptable conditions. He reported the hospital "practically destitute," with one "very small case of instruments" and no modern medical books.[63] This only seven years after Bush's predecessor, Dr. Oliphant, claimed the hospital system excelled as a modern facility.

Twenty-five years later, similar conditions prevailed at the Idaho penitentiary, where annually the physician reminded administrators of the need for a hospital at the prison.[64] Emergency surgical procedures and the care of the chronically ill demanded a facility, according to Dr. George Collister. Finally, in 1910, the warden renovated an existing building, transforming it into a prison hospital. A new concrete floor and a few other refinements and Dr. Collister, who recognized this was the best he would get, terminated his annual requests.[65] Despite its limitations, Collister's small clinic may have surpassed what was available in Wyoming. Inmates at that prison called the hospital the "butcher room," and reported that an inmate taken there never returned to the cell house.[66]

As medical facilities limped along from inhumane to primitive, women had no separate medical area for treatment. The make-do prison housing arrangements for women spilled over into medical care. In systems that had little or no provision for sick and wounded male prisoners, women did not paradoxically assume priority status. Even when administrators endeavored to provide for women's medical needs, the results could be ludicrous. In 1877 the matron at the Missouri penitentiary pointed out that with the number of female inmates at forty-nine, the prison desperately needed a women's hospital. She noted that the prison used an abandoned community room for its sick women. This unheated room, with poor lighting and limited ventilation, authorities declared unfit for male recreation time, but designated it as the infirmary for women.[67]

Prison doctors, surrounded by disgusting filth, contaminated food and water, and unthinkable violence, did little to upgrade the prisoners' well-being. Physicians' annual reports boasted of sanitary conditions, good health, and low mortality rates. Only rarely did doctors formally protest the desperate circumstances around them. Instead, they treated the prisoner as a malingerer and complained about the time spent with sick convicts. At times, physicians allowed themselves to sink to a low level of behavior and developed their own fearsome reputations with inmates.

In 1880 the Texas physician for inmates reported that he "prescribed for at least 400 at the prison dispensary, and have listened to the imaginary complaints of many."[68] In the early 1900s, a Wyoming doctor, bored by one inmate's repeated requests for help with a sore foot, ordered the man restrained on a kitchen table and used pliers and a pocket knife to rip out an ingrown toenail.[69] At the New Mexico penitentiary, from 1914 to 1915, the physician, Dr. Massie, wrote the same medical order—work—for almost every diagnosis.[70]

Within such an environment, basic medical care eluded women prisoners as well. In an atmosphere where physicians hardened themselves against their medical charges, doctors dismissed women as whining and weak. Kate Richards O'Hare reported after she went to the prison doctor for severe soreness in her neck and shoulders that "his remarks and treatment would be high comedy if it were not for the bitter tragedy that lies underneath."[71]

Even when a woman found medical support, the poor facilities and an indifferent system kept care minimal. For instance, E. K. Smith, doctor for Etta Cole during her incarceration at the county jail, thought the state should never have transferred the woman to the Nevada penitentiary. He diagnosed the thirty-year-old Etta, a drug abuser, as stricken with an "intense pelvic inflammation involving the internal generative organs." While Etta remained with the county, this doctor tried without success for an authorization to have her hospitalized. Even the local sheriff vouched for the woman's poor health.[72] Despite Etta's condition, she went on to the penitentiary, where the Nevada prison physician agreed with Dr. Smith. He confirmed that Etta suffered from a "growth affecting the organs peculiar to her sex," but she received no pardon and was discharged at the expiration of her sentence.[73]

Struggling against a bias that tended to dismiss female illness as imaginary, sick women needed an advocate within the system to help them get medical attention or release from the illness-inducing conditions of imprisonment. Georgia Monroe, a twenty-five-year-old African American woman, drew the attention of the superintendent of state penitentiaries, L. A. Whatley, because she worked in his residence. Whatley took the unusual action of speaking to Governor Hogg about Monroe. In a letter marked

"Personal, Important," Whatley even asked the Texas governor to act on Monroe's pardon before departing on a trip to the East.[74] Monroe, serving a twenty-five-year sentence for murder, suffered from chronic bronchitis and asthma. At Whatley's request, prison physician R. H. Bush supplied the necessary medical certification, stating that Monroe's asthma attacks were so severe "you can hear her wheezing before you enter the room."[75] Despite her deteriorating health, Monroe, without the personal intervention of the superintendent, apparently would have died at Huntsville.

Monroe suffered from a severe form of a common prison illness, for respiratory disorders ran through the penitentiary, as bronchitis, asthma, "wasting" disease, "bloody flux," or consumption invaded the cells and work farms of the West. Whatever its label, tuberculosis proved a fearful scourge. With its penchant for dark, unsanitary breeding grounds, this nineteenth-century killer found easy targets in the greatly weakened prisoners. The recommended treatment of the era—rest, healthful diet, and dry climate—did not conform to penitentiary routines. Women with consumption either died in prison or were released during the last stages of their illness.

In 1897 Irene Moore, an African American cook convicted of theft, entered the Texas prison system for a term of four years. Less than three years later, Moore's consumption had advanced so drastically that the twenty-two-year-old woman lay near death. Officials considered her case pressing when they filed in August, but it was December before the dying Moore received her pardon.[76]

The pardon process moved ahead more quickly for a white woman confined to the Huntsville prison in 1887. By 1891, Lillie Gibson, sentenced to five years for second degree murder, suffered from acute consumption. During the four years she spent in solitary confinement, her weight dropped from 150 pounds to 108 pounds and she coughed blood. The prison physician, R. H. Bush, convinced that Gibson would not live much longer, asked for her immediate release, action he apparently would not take on his own initiative for the black inmate Georgia Monroe. Thomas Goree, the prison superintendent, endorsed this request because he only held two women in the female department, reserved for white women, and if Lillie and Georgia Lewis both left, he could close those quarters.[77] Lillie Gibson's plight showed that unwell white women did not receive much medical care, but, segregated from the work details, they certainly lived under conditions different from the black women sent to the farms. Lillie herself said that she had "never been punished or had a cross word spoken" to her during her prison confinement, a circumstance unheard of for African American women inmates.[78]

The procedures by which authorities released Irene Moore and Lillie

Gibson from the prison pointed to a common problem for all women inmates. With the absence of facilities for female inmates, wardens and doctors made little effort to separate women with contagious diseases from other prisoners. Instead, women inmates, regardless of their health, were jammed into small quarters together.[79]

In 1910, Dr. George Collister of the Idaho penitentiary remarked in his report that in the event of contagious diseases, medical policy called for the sick inmates to be isolated from the rest of the prison population. But in his next report, Collister asked that "some provisions . . . be made for prisoners suffering from tuberculosis and syphilis, so they may be isolated and still have fresh air and sunlight." Collister explained that he had no different cells for well and sick inmates due to overcrowded conditions at the prison. He feared the spread of contagious illnesses and expressed concern over the well-being of sick prisoners never allowed the benefits of the out-of-doors.[80] By 1916, six years after Collister first advocated a policy of attending to contagious diseases, five women prisoners lived together in one room at the Idaho penitentiary. Two of the five suffered from tuberculosis or syphilis.[81] Collister's report for that year made only a one-sentence reference to the desirability of isolating the inmates with these diseases.[82]

Contagious diseases placed all convicts closed in the dirty, stench-filled prisons in a precarious medical situation. Women, however, with their own peculiar health concerns, were particularly neglected by penitentiary practices. With all illness suspect to the authorities, the gender-specific physical difficulties of women became just one more way in which administrators saw women prisoners as bothersome.

In a system that provided almost nothing in the way of sanitary toilet facilities, women's monthly menstruation added both physical and emotional hardship to incarceration. This important component in the life of women received no attention in the official records of penitentiary life. Doctors, who might be expected to be alert to the problems of menstruation under the particularly primitive conditions of the penitentiary, maintained a studious silence on the subject. Yet, all men knew the monthly period to be a factor in the care of women prisoners.

Members of a 1910 Texas investigating committee did not hesitate to address the most personal questions to the black women prisoners (but not the Mexican American or the whites) brought to testify. White businessmen and politicians asked African American women about the regularity of their menstruation, the care provided during menses, and whether at the onset of their monthly period guards still drove them into the fields to work. The women described a world of "no sanitary conveniences," in which protests about getting wet and chilled in the fields meant nothing; they told of occasionally receiving "a little medicine for cramps," and of the guard captain who assured women their sickness "didn't amount to anything" and "they would feel better after they got on the outside."[83]

But the attitude of guards went beyond simple male ignorance about the discomforts of menstruating women. Jerline Bonds claimed that when she was fifteen years old and sick with cramps, Captain Brabham climbed onto her bed and stood on her stomach, after which he kicked her down the stairs. Other prisoners and the committee viewed Jerline's account of the attack as unlikely because a man could not have stood upright in the small space between the top bunk and the ceiling of the prisoners' barracks. Although the other women hesitated to corroborate the story about the bunk, they had watched the guard booting Jerline down the stairwell. Regardless of the sequence of events, by age seventeen, broken in health and unfit for work, Jerline Bonds suffered from periodic swelling in her groin, a residue from the brutal beating that others had witnessed.[84]

Brabham himself denied that any such events had transpired. He insisted that when the women had their "monthly sickness" he often left them in the barracks, instead of marching them to the fields. Brabham admitted that if "satisfied in my own mind there is nothing the matter," he made the women go to work. He claimed that sometimes in the field he allowed menstruating women to sit out for an hour or so. When queried as to how he could tell if the women were ill, Brabham replied, "I can't tell," and acknowledged he just guessed.[85]

Along with menstruation, pregnancy and childbirth added to the particular medical concerns of women inmates. Pregnancy interfered with the implementation of a penitentiary sentence and kept some women detained in local jails, while authorities tried to decide what to do with them. As county officials stewed over the fate of Lottie Belmont, they continued to hold the pregnant woman for five months without providing medical care. As the time of her confinement grew close, the county stepped up its campaign to have Lottie, suffering from severe bronchitis, pardoned. Now arguing that the young woman, an "unfortunate victim" of the "excessive use of morphine," deserved medical attention for her pregnancy, citizens and court officers lobbied for her release.[86] Petitions for Lottie called her pregnancy "advanced" in November, but the unwell woman did not secure her pardon until March of 1890, possibly just before she delivered her baby.

On some occasions, officials did not act promptly enough and found themselves with a newborn in the county jail. In 1896 Drucilia Pinkston, sentenced to two years in the penitentiary, gave birth in the county jail of El Paso, Texas, before the courts there decided what to do with the prisoner. When the attending doctor saw that the baby could not survive in confinement, he joined with several other county officers to expedite Pinkston's release.[87]

Although pregnancy made officials reluctant to send a woman from the county jail to the penitentiary, expectant mothers did enter prison. For example, between 1866 and 1870, Ellen Fox, Jennie Davis, Laura Wood, Catharine Hickey, Augusta Hanna, and Matilda Hershey all received pardons from the Missouri governor because they were about to deliver babies or had just done so inside the penitentiary.[88] In Texas Effie Willson, Chlora Manning and Mary Ann Shepard won pardons because of pending births.[89] All three were poor women, "an elephant on our hands," in the view of officials.[90] Officials also noted that the children of Manning and Shepard were about to be placed on the county paupers' list and so wanted the poverty-stricken pregnant women released to support their families. The added economic burden to the state that came with these prison births, plus the poor circumstances of parentless children on the outside, prompted decisions to release pregnant women, regardless of the crime they had committed.

In none of these prisoners' files was it clear where in the penitentiary and under what medical arrangements the births occurred. In addition, penitentiary records and pardon applications often blurred information about whether a woman entered prison pregnant or became so during incarceration. In some cases officials could not deny that the pregnancy had occurred inside the penitentiary.[91]

In 1897 Texas officials began to promote the pardon case of Jennie O'Neill, an African American prisoner. At age eighteen, the indigent O'Neill was charged with horse theft for taking a ride to visit friends. As she had no means to hire an attorney, a local judge assigned her two young attorneys who accepted her "confession" at face value, entered no defense, and convinced her to plead guilty. Not until O'Neill had served two and a half years of a five-year term and was in an "advanced stage of pregnancy" did officials begin to act on the pardon initiative launched immediately after her conviction.[92]

Once the state machinery moved into action, O'Neill had her pardon within two weeks. Such was not true for all pregnant women prisoners. For example, Sarah Jonican, an African American prostitute, entered the Texas prison system at the age of twenty, convicted of murder and sentenced to life. More than five years later the prison doctor endorsed a pardon for Jonican because he thought she might be suffering from severe ulcers with excruciating pain and frequent hemorrhages.[93] Given the tendency of prison physicians to label life-threatening injuries inflicted at the camps as routine sickness, the actual source of Sarah's ills could not be determined. Although the physician expressed little hope that Jonican would survive, his main concern was that the disabled prisoner would prove to be "a great trouble and expense." Nowhere did he mention, as did Jonican's conduct record, that in prison Jonican cared for her child, "four or five years of age."[94] Whether she was pregnant when she entered the penitentiary or after her arrival, Sarah Jonican gave birth to and raised her baby on a state work farm until either illness or injury made her too great a liability for the camp manager.

The provisions made for these youngsters confined to state penitentiaries with their mothers appeared to be negligible. Some wardens worried about the lack of heat for newborn infants, but small children stayed with their mothers under starkly adverse conditions. Occasionally, however, a glimmer of enlightened direct action guided decisions about inmate mothers. For example, in 1892, when Eliza Rearick entered the South Dakota penitentiary, she brought her nine-month-old nursing infant. Faced with the question of fiscal responsibility for the child, the board of charities entered into negotiations with Rearick's home county. The final agreement authorized the warden to keep the child with the mother at the cost of one dollar a week to Sanborn County.[95]

Despite this one case, the possibility that male penitentiary officials would recognize and address issues of motherhood and child care among women prisoners did not materialize. Seventeen years after South Dakota tried to confront the realities of imprisoning mothers, other states continued to ignore this critical subject. In Texas, Annie "Cora" Morgan, a black woman, testified before the investigating committee with one of her two prison-born children, four-year-old daughter Corrine, standing at her side. The child, born eight years after Cora entered the penitentiary, had been fathered by the son of the white camp manager, Captain Bowden. Young Jerry Bowden, who "called out" the women inmates from their work details to the bushes, denied his parenthood and left employment at the camp shortly after Corrine's birth. To protect herself because "if I had told him . . . he would have punished me so severe I would not have lived," Cora told Captain Bowden, her child's grandfather, that a "yellow negro" prisoner was Corrine's father.[96]

Little Corrine and her younger half-brother must have been hardy children to survive their infancy inside the work camp.[97] The events surrounding another birth at the farm suggested the bare harshness with which women inmates saw their children come into the world. Several women inmates testified with exquisite detail as to the experiences of one of their company.

According to the testimony, the pregnant inmate, Elvira, told Captain Brabham early in the day that she had started her labor. Brabham replied to Elvira that she would feel better if she went along to the field to do her work. Only shortly thereafter, the woman, without medical attention, lay under a white-blossomed magnolia tree and delivered her child onto the ground. Another inmate, Queen Bess, hearing the mother's cries, ran to her, picked the sand-covered infant from the dirt, wiped the blood and grime from its body, and tore a piece from her skirt to make a swaddling for the infant.[98]

Guards hurried the other women away from the scene, while the mother and child stayed under the magnolia tree. After a lengthy time, Captain Brabham had the woman loaded into a wooden wagon and carried to the barracks. Dr. J. P. Westmoreland, the penitentiary physician, who testified that he departed for the prison when notified of the birth, did not arrive until late evening to examine the newborn, which shortly died of pneumonia. The inmate mother of this sorry tale did not speak before the committee, for she had finished her time and returned to Trinity, Texas, where she no doubt always remembered the white magnolia tree of the Eastham Camp.[99]

Unquestionably, officials reacted to pregnant inmates with complex attitudes. In pardon requests, they obliquely referred to a prisoner's "delicate condition" or discreetly mentioned that a woman was "in a family way." Notions about propriety and social retreat for pregnant women clashed with the public exposure of prison routines and further fueled distaste for women prisoners.[100] Male administrators and doctors appeared unwilling to demand decent medical attention for women who gave birth inside male prisons. At the same time they did little for infants and children who lived inside the walls with their mothers.

Men showed themselves quite baffled by the merging of motherhood and criminality, almost unable to comprehend that women prisoners retained parental feelings. In 1866, Warden Swift, a generally compassionate administrator at the Missouri penitentiary, described Margaret Davis as an "inoffensive Negro woman" in his pardon application for her. Swift sought Davis's release because she, "was sent with a deformed child of about four years of age. . . . I have never separated the mother and child owing to a peculiar attachment existing between them."[101] Locked into a rigid imagery for criminal women, male prison officials had great difficulty transcending their perception of female inmates as deviants.[102]

Perhaps nothing underscored this male dilemma more clearly than the experience of Mary Wiley. In October 1869, Benjamin Wiley, Mary's father, received a seven-year sentence to the Missouri penitentiary, convicted on a charge of incest.[103] In October, when Benjamin Wiley began his prison term, Mary Wiley, also entered the Missouri penitentiary. Mary, nursing a three-month-old infant, the child of her own father, had also been convicted of incest and sentenced to two years in the state prison.

The evidence showed that nineteen-year-old Mary had been subjected to "this circumstance," according to neighbors, for several years before the age of fifteen. Citizens' petitions collected on her behalf described Mary as the "unconscious agent" in the commencement of the Wileys' incestuous lives. Despite the complex circumstances, the governor, in a burst of paternalistic enthusiasm, cited the need to be sure that Mary and her child went to a home with the "proper influences" and delayed the release of the young mother for ten months.[104]

All the gender forces that swirled through the western legal system, the prisons, the nature of violence, and masculine thinking about women fused in this pathetic tale. Judge and jury held Mary Wiley, a child, accountable for the sexual violence of her father. Her maternity inverted and reinverted a madonna/whore image until society lost its sense both of justice and of compassion. Missouri officials, cognizant of the prison's long record of unfit provisions for women and infants, could not justify releasing these two. The battered teenager was left to care for her infant inside a male penitentiary. Women such as Margaret Davis and Mary Wiley, struggling with the constraints of an unforgiving social system and trying to care for small children inside penitentiaries, gave new meaning to family and the endurance of mothers.

At the same time, the practice of allowing women prisoners to keep their children with them provided prison administrators with a remarkable opportunity to advance gendered care within the western penitentiary system. That opportunity withered and died. Other than the example in South Dakota, western officials failed to explore the ways in which a maternal component could alter prison life for women or influence children's upbringing in a positive manner.

Women prisoners struggled to survive in an environment that sapped their mental and physical strength. The daily diet could destroy the most fit, of whom there were few among the women inmates. The poor health care of their earlier lives, coupled with their illnesses and substance addictions, meant that women prisoners came into the system in less than excellent health. Denied even a modicum of proper nutrition, women further had to contend with a generally filth-ridden environment that increased their chances of disease and death. The illnesses of the prison imposed themselves on the already weakened women. Instead of dank cells and unfit food, women prisoners needed careful medical supervision. In penitentiaries lacking even basic hospital facilities, such was not forthcoming. In addition, most prison physicians failed as allies in this struggle. Many among them dismissed women as just another group of complaining inmates, giving little or no attention to the peculiar gender health needs they might have.

In that area, the women had no chance for assistance or understanding about matters of monthly menstruation, pregnancy, and childbirth. In fact, prison officials allowed these to be additional reasons for punishment of women prisoners. Monthly discomforts or labor pains represented another way to abuse women and to further humiliate them individually and collectively. Ultimately, women's health matters added more patterns to the continuum of violence. Forced work situations and inappropriate birthing conditions, both highlighted by the absence of gender dignity, gave male overseers yet another form of violence to make a woman's prison time distinctive.

Notes

1. District Attorney George Paschal to Governor L. S. Ross, 14 Jan. 1891, Mrs. R. M. Lister, no. 1862, Executive Clemency Files, TSA.

2. J. M. Hays, M.D., to Governor Lawrence S. Ross, 15 Jan. 1891, ibid.

3. W. H. Brooker to Governor Lawrence S. Ross, 16 Jan. 1891, ibid.

4. For example, in 1880, almost 150 convicts died in the Arkansas penitentiary after measles, followed by pneumonia and typhoid fever, broke out among the prisoners (Ford, "History of the Arkansas Penitentiary to 1900," p. 97).

5. *Report of the Superintendent of the State Penitentiary,* 1871, pp. 12–13, 35–39, TSA.

6. Ibid., p. 18.

7. "Physician's Report," ibid., pp. 15–16. Dr. Oliphant typically gave reports with mixed messages. On the one hand, he wanted to praise the health conditions at the prison; on the other, as a doctor, he recognized the disastrous conditions. In 1870 he had protested that inmates were fed "beef and corn bread . . . without any change whatever" and that "scurvy and diarrhea" had been the "most prevalent and obstinate diseases" at the prison (H. C. Oliphant to Col. N. A. M. Dudley, 31 Jan. 1870, *Report of the Condition of the State Penitentiary,* Huntsville, 1870, p. 31, TSA). For another account of a physician's unwillingness to excuse sick prisoners, see George, *Texas Convict,* p. 138.

8. *Report of Special Committee on Penitentiary,* 1871, p. 4, TSA.

9. Ibid.

10. H. C. Oliphant to the Board of Directors, 31 Dec. 1872, *Report on the Condition of the State Penitentiary,* 1871–72, p. 11, TSA.

11. Board of Commissioners of Public Institutions, *Second Annual Report,* 1874, p. 316, UKKC.

12. Ibid., p. 324.

13. Ibid. For an account of similar food problems in the twentieth century, see the testimony of inmate Jap L. Clark to the investigating committee ("Removal of Arthur Trelford, Superintendent of the Penitentiary, 1907," Governor's Papers, George Curry, 1907–10, special issues, reel 178, frames 177–291, NMSA).

14. Reynolds, *Twin Hells,* pp. 63, 65–66.

15. Penitentiary inspector Sam Hawkins admitted to the investigating committee at Huntsville, Texas, that there was no system to record the quantity or quality of the food delivered to the prison farm, nor any check on whether it was actually served to inmates (Sam Hawkins to the Investigating Committee, 22 July 1909, *Report of the Penitentiary Investigating Committee,* pp. 321, 324, TSA).

16. Assistant Warden Roger S. Thomas of the Louisiana State Penitentiary esti-

mated that the combination of unsanitary conditions, poor diet, disease, work regimens, and brutality made it unlikely that any nineteenth-century prisoner could live longer than ten years (Roger S. Thomas to author, 22 June 1987, Angola, La.).

17. *Sweet Smell of Sagebrush*, pp. 9, 17.

18. Heilbron, *Convict Life at the Minnesota State Prison*, p. 87.

19. Testimony of Inspector Sam Hawkins to the Investigating Committee, 22 July 1909, *Report of the Penitentiary Investigating Committee*, p. 321, TSA.

20. Testimony of Inmate H. H. Bullock to the Investigating Committee, 21 July 1909, ibid., p. 263. In Wyoming a prisoner said of the bread, "I don't think that a diamond cutter could make a scratch on the softest one [bread crust] in that box" (*Sweet Smell of Sagebrush*, pp. 75–76).

21. Testimony of Inmates W. A. Parks and Sam Tubb to the Investigating Committee, *Report of the Penitentiary Investigating Committee*, pp. 273, 276, TSA. Copperas is a green sulfate of iron. Its uses include making inks and dyeing. See also the description of the Texas diet in George, *Texas Convict*, pp. 130, 133–34, 137–38.

22. *Sweet Smell of Sagebrush*, p. 68.

23. Testimony of U.S. Military Prisoners Thomas Morris, Francis Miner, William H. Moorehouse, and James H. Taylor to Officials of the Kansas State Penitentiary, Board of Commissioners of Public Institutions, *Second Annual Report*, 1874, pp. 343, 344, 345, UKKC.

24. O'Hare, *Prison Letters*, p. 4; in Wyoming the practice was allowed with strict limitations (*Sweet Smell of Sagebrush*, p. 84).

25. Testimony of Inmate H. H. Bullock to the Investigating Committee, 21 July 1909, *Report of the Penitentiary Investigating Committee*, pp. 265–66, TSA.

26. O'Hare, *Prison Letters*, p. 4.

27. Heilbron, *Convict Life at the Minnesota State Prison*, p. 101.

28. Tomlin, *Henry Tomlin*, pp. 74–75.

29. Testimony of Inmate Guadalupe Grimsinger to the Investigating Committee, 29 July 1909, *Report of the Penitentiary Investigating Committee*, p. 545, TSA.

30. The one white woman interviewed answered in German and gave little testimony, insisting that everything was "all right." She was, however, a domestic for and friends with the wife of the sergeant of the guards at the camp (Testimony of Inmate Annie Cordes to the Investigating Committee, 29 July 1909, ibid., pp. 547, 571).

31. Seven months after this investigation, the follow-up testimony of nine women indicated that at least one had been whipped for giving information to the investigators ("Report of Special Subcommittee," 16 Feb. 1910, ibid., pp. 983–84).

32. Testimony of Inmate Guadalupe Grimsinger to the Investigating Committee, 29 July 1909, ibid., p. 546.

33. Testimony of Inmate Mary Harrington to the Investigating Committee, 29 July 1909, ibid., p. 548.

34. Testimony of Inmate Lulu Lane to the Investigating Committee, 29 July 1909, ibid., pp. 554–55.

35. The monotony of prison life at the Utah penitentiary proved one of the greatest hardships for Belle Harris. See Albert Silas Harris, "Life of Belle Harris Nelson," pp. 44–45, 51, 71, 78.

36. See Blanche Williams, Photo no. 1200; Emma Bell, Photo no. 1270; Minnie Farrell, Photo no. 1358; Jennie Williams, Photo no. 1337; Nellie Kremey, Photo no. 1965, State Prison Convict Registers, 1899–1920, MtHS.

37. See especially Prisoners nos. 61, 94, 150, 217, 300, 301, 460, 726, 954, 1074, 1549, 1716, 2261, 2265, 2288, and 2289, Register of Convicts Received, 13 Feb. 1866–29 Dec. 1899, Prisoners nos. 1–9073, LSP.

38. Alice Faulkner File, 25 May 1869, Pardon Papers, 1844–72, box 28, folder 36, RG 5, MSA. Missouri had precedents for this case; an earlier inmate, Virginia Rurke, who had such severe epileptic seizures that she required the "constant attention of a guard," received a pardon (ibid., box 8, folder 14); and a few years later Elizabeth Walaschmidt, of whom the warden said, "frequent and terrible attacks of epilepsy have broken her health," also received a pardon (Elizabeth Walaschmidt File, 23 May 1864, ibid., box 17, folder 42).

39. For examples, see Prisoners nos. 1391, 8171, 1390, 769, 2604, 1872, 2129, 6685, 6840 (of whom seven were black and two white), Arkansas Department of Corrections, Inmate Files, 1865–1915, ADC; Prisoners nos. 321, 322, 458, 1272, 1345, 1716, 2082, 2277, 2359, 2418, 2433, 2979, 3057, 3348, 3448, 3475, 3882, 3909 (twelve black, six probably white), Descriptive Records, vols. 1 and 2, roll 1, RG 86, NSA.

40. *Biennial Report of the Directors and Superintendent of the Texas State Penitentiary,* 1880, p. 65, TSA.

41. Reports of Superintendent of the Penitentiary, 1910–11, Governor's Papers, William J. Mills, 1910–12, Reports, reel 188, frame 733, NMSA.

42. *Sweet Smell of Sagebrush,* p. 119; Testimony of Inmates John Lenz and W. J. Dent to the Investigating Committee, 22 July 1909, *Report of the Penitentiary Investigating Committee,* pp. 230, 281, TSA; Testimony of Arthur Trelford before the Penitentiary Investigating Committee, 28 June 1907, p. 2, "Removal of Arthur Trelford, Superintendent of the Penitentiary, 1907," Governor's Papers, George Curry, 1907–10, special issues, reel 178, frames 177–291, NMSA.

43. Warden D. C. Hyman to Board of Pardons, 28 Aug. 1875, Mollie Forsha File, Board of Pardons Files, NSCMA. Mollie, a prostitute convicted of murdering a man she testified was attacking her, had been sentenced to twenty-seven years in the Nevada penitentiary. She applied for a pardon in 1875, after giving birth to twins more than three years after she entered prison. Warden Hyman may have had good reason to write Mollie a favorable conduct report for the pardon board, since according to local legend, the warden fathered Mollie's twins (Rafter, *Partial Justice,* p. 98).

44. Knepper, "Women of Yuma," p. 241.

45. E. L. Whitney to the Board of State Prison Commissioners, 1 Dec. 1906, *Biennial Report of the Idaho State Penitentiary,* 1905–6, p. 11, ISL.

46. Dr. Collister did make a statement opposing the use of tobacco and recommended daily rations be curtailed or eliminated (George Collister, Prison Physician, to the Board of State Prison Commissioners, ibid., pp. 13–14).

47. James H. White to L. S. Ross, 17 Nov. 1888, Lillie St. Clair, no. 1050, Executive Clemency Files, TSA; Ellen Smith, no. 1165, 9 Jan. 1885, State of Colorado, Penitentiary Records, Record of Convicts, 1871–95, CSA; Lillie Heartly, Photo no. 1998; Grace Johnson, Photo no. 2155; Lea Carlisle, Photo no. 3166, State Prison Convict Register, Mar. 1879–Nov. 1910, MtHS.

48. James H. White, Sheriff, to Governor L. S. Ross, 17 Nov. 1888, Lillie St. Clair, no. 1050, Executive Clemency Files, TSA.

49. Lillie St. Clair, Application for Pardon, no. 12475, 28 Nov. 1888, ibid.

50. Testimony of Dr. J. P. Westmoreland to the Investigating Committee, 24 July 1909, *Report of the Penitentiary Investigating Committee,* pp. 521–22, TSA.

51. O'Hare, *Prison Letters,* p. 9. By the time of O'Hare's incarceration, treatment for venereal disease had improved over nineteenth-century practices. For an example of earlier care, see Florence Brady and Rose Bennett entries for treatment of disease by the prison physician at the Montana State Penitentiary in 1891, table E, p. 25, in *First Annual Report of the Board of State Prison Commissioners of the State of Montana,* 1892, MtHS.

52. O'Hare, *Prison Letters*, p. 70.

53. Lida Gould, Photo no. 1510, State Prison Convict Register, Mar. 1879–Nov. 1910, MtHS.

54. Sarah A. Davies File, 20 May 1897, box 31, Pardon and Parole Files, KSHS.

55. In Texas as early as 1870 the prison physician suggested other state facilities would be better suited to care for the one blind male, two male "idiots," three insane males, and two insane females (H. C. Oliphant to Col. N. A. M. Dudley, 31 Jan. 1870, *Report on the Condition of the State Penitentiary*, 1870, p. 32, TSA).

56. Mary Conery, Prisoner no. 178, Statement of Convicts, Prisoner Ledger I, 1901–6, KSHS.

57. Virginia Gregory's attorney, physician, and family argued she was insane before she attempted robbery in 1868 and had that defense been used, the woman would have been acquitted (Virginia Gregory File, 20 July 1868, Pardon Papers, box 27, folder 7, RG 5, MSA).

58. Robert Waite, "Necessary to Isolate the Female Prisoners: Women Convicts and the Women's Ward at the Old Idaho Penitentiary," *Idaho Yesterdays* 29 (Fall 1985): 3–4.

59. Statement of Dr. R. Abbott, 15 Mar. 1865, Rachel Springer File, 7 Apr. 1865, Pardon Papers, box 19, folder 33, RG 5, MSA.

60. O'Hare, *Prison Letters*, pp. 71, 10. O'Hare may have been using some coded way to explain to her family that women prisoners found ways to conduct illicit relationships or minister to each other during the night hours.

61. H. C. Oliphant, M.D., to Governor E. J. Davis, 1 Dec. 1870, *Report of the Superintendent of the State Penitentiary*, 1871, p. 17, and H. C. Oliphant, M.D., to Board of Directors, Texas State Penitentiary, 31 Dec. 1872, *Reports on the Condition of the State Penitentiary*, 1873, p. 10, TSA.

62. Testimony of U.S. Military Prisoner Levi Crockett to Officials of the Kansas State Penitentiary, Board of Commissioners of Public Institutions, *Second Annual Report*, 1874, pp. 348–49, UKKC.

63. R. H. Bush, Prison Physician, to Directors of the Texas State Penitentiary, 1 Nov. 1880, *Biennial Report of the Directors and Superintendent of the Texas State Penitentiary*, 1880, pp. 73, 75. TSA.

64. George Collister, Prison Physician, to the Board of Prison Commissioners, in *Biennial Report of the Idaho State Penitentiary*, 1903–4, p. 52; 1905–6, p. 14; 1907–8, p. 11, ISL.

65. George Collister, Prison Physician, to the Board of Prison Commissioners, 5 Dec. 1910, ibid., 1909–10, p. 13, ISL.

66. *Sweet Smell of Sagebrush*, p. 16.

67. *Biennial Report of the Board of Inspectors of the Missouri Penitentiary and the 30th General Assembly*, 1877–78, pp. 151–52, 161, MSA.

68. R. H. Bush, Prison Physician, to Directors of the Texas State Penitentiary, 1 Nov. 1880, *Biennial Report of the Directors and Superintendent of the Texas State Penitentiary*, 1880, p. 73, TSA.

69. *Sweet Smell of Sagebrush*, p. 16.

70. Physician's Record Book, 1914–15, New Mexico State Penitentiary Records, NMSA.

71. O'Hare, *Prison Letters*, p. 30.

72. E. K. Smith, M.D., to George W. Keith, 3 Jan. 1909; J. J. Owens to George W. Keith, 6 Jan. 1909, Etta Cole File, Inmate Case Files, NSCMA.

73. A. Huffaker, M.D., to George Keith, 6 Jan. 1909; "Is This Woman Wanted" Circular, 24 July 1909, both in ibid.

74. L. A. Whatley to Governor James S. Hogg, 7 June 1894, and envelope addressed to Governor J. S. Hogg, Georgia Monroe, no. 16505, Executive Clemency Files, TSA.

75. R. H. Bush, Prison Physician, to L. A. Whatley, Superintendent of the Penitentiary, 7 June 1894, ibid.

76. J. G. Smithers to the Penitentiary Board, 2 Aug. 1899; Application for Pardon, no. 19786, 22 Dec. 1899, Irene Moore, no. 5559, Executive Clemency Files, TSA. In the same records see also pardon application for eighteen-year-old Clara Wilson, dying of consumption (Clara Wilson, no. 3552, 20 Apr. 1895).

77. R. H. Bush, M.D., to Captain J. G. Smithers, 25 Mar. 1891; Superintendent Thomas J. Goree to Governor J. S. Hogg, 27 Mar. 1891, both in Lillie Gibson, no. 1896, Executive Clemency Files.

78. Lillie Gibson to Governor J. S. Hogg, 24 Mar. 1891, ibid.

79. Arizona barely averted an epidemic in 1902 when a new inmate, Jesús Chacón, broke out in smallpox and exposed the four other women in the cramped female quarters (Knepper, "Imprisonment and Society in Arizona Territory," p. 161).

80. George Collister, M.D., to the Board of Prison Commissioners, 5 Dec. 1910, *Biennial Report of the Idaho State Penitentiary,* 1909–10, p. 12; ibid., 1911–12, pp. 11–12, ISL.

81. *Idaho Daily Statesman,* 19 Feb. 1916, p. 10.

82. George Collister, M.D., to Board of Prison Commissioners, *Biennial Report of the Idaho State Penitentiary,* 1915–16, p. 16, ISL.

83. Testimony of Inmates Ennis Carlisle, Jerline Bonds, and Hannah Steele to the Investigating Committee, 29 July 1909, *Report of the Penitentiary Investigating Committee,* pp. 557–64, TSA. Conditions at the women's camp had been revealed publicly as early as 1908 by a San Antonio newspaper reporter (George Waverly Briggs, *The Texas Penitentiary: A Study of the Texas Convict System and Suggestions for Its Betterment,* reprint of a series of articles from the *San Antonio Express* [n.p., 1910], p. 42, UTBC).

84. Testimony of Inmate Jerline Bonds to the Investigating Committee, 29 July 1909, *Report of the Penitentiary Investigating Committee,* p. 559, TSA.

85. Testimony of Captain I. L Brabham to the Investigating Committee, 30 July 1909, ibid., p. 572.

86. Citizens' Petition to Governor Lawrence S. Ross, 22 Nov. 1889; P. M. Johns, M.D., to District Attorney George Paschal, n.d.; Certification of Health by John V. Spring, M.D., 8 Feb. 1890, all in Lottie Belmont, no. 1501, Executive Clemency Files, TSA.

87. W. N. Vilas, M.D., to Governor C. A. Culberson, n.d., Drucilia Pinkston, no. 3998, Executive Clemency Files, TSA.

88. Ellen Fox, 31 Jan. 1866, box 21, folder 2; Jennie Davis, 29 Oct. 1867, box 24, folder 41; Laura Wood, 13 Oct. 1868, box 27, folder 28; Catharine Hickey, 18 May 1870, box 31, folder 13, all in Pardon Papers, RG 5, MSA; Augusta Hanna, 19 Feb. 1865, p. 361; Matilda Hershey, 13 June 1866, p. 106, Register of Inmates Received and Discharged, vol. C, RG 213, MSA. For other inmates pardoned because of a probable pregnancy, see the cases of Belle Halstead, no. 1263, State Penitentiary, Prisoner Case Files, June 1878–Nov. 1891, SDSA (hereafter, Prisoner Case Files, SDSA); and Jennie Smith, no. ?, 24 Sept. 1875; and Lucy Childs, no. 12036, 7 Jan. 1888, both in Executive Clemency Files, TSA.

89. Effie Willson, no. 3101, 12 June 1875; Chlora Manning, no. ?, 9 Oct. 1877; Mary Ann Shepard, no. ?, 4 Dec. 1880, all in Executive Clemency Files, TSA.

90. M. B. Plewrons[?], County Judge, to Governor O. W. Roberts, 12 June 1880, Effie Willson File, no. 3101, Executive Clemency Files, TSA.

91. Historians of Arizona suggest that Pearl Hart, a white woman of some local criminal reputation, won release from the Yuma prison because officials wanted to avoid the scandal that would result when her pregnancy was announced (Knepper, "Imprisonment and Society in Arizona Territory," pp. 178–79; Jeffrey, *Adobe and Iron,* p. 83).

92. Judge J. R. Burnett to Governor C. A. Culberson, 25 Apr. 1895; John I. Moore and Citizens' Petition to Board of Pardons, 11 June 1895, both in Jennie O'Neill, no. 4567, Executive Clemency Files, TSA.

93. R. H. Bush, M.D., to Captain B. E. McCulloch, 24 June 1886, Sarah Jonican, no. 351, Executive Clemency Files, TSA.

94. Certificate of Prison Conduct, Sarah Jonican, no. 351, Executive Clemency Files, TSA.

95. Eliza Rearick, no. 525, Prisoner Case Files, SDSA.

96. Testimony of Inmate Annie Morgan to the Investigating Committee, 29 July 1909, *Report of the Penitentiary Investigating Committee,* p. 567, TSA.

97. In 1881, Texas pardoned Malinda Wilmore, a destitute black woman convicted of stealing beef, because she was "weakly and sick," and had a four-month-old child (Malinda Wilmore, no. ?, 22 Sept. 1881, Executive Clemency Files, TSA).

98. Testimony of Inmates Rosa Brewing and Hannah Steele to the Investigating Committee, 29 July 1909, *Report of the Penitentiary Investigating Committee,* pp. 552, 563, TSA.

99. Testimony of Dr. J. P. Westmoreland to the Investigating Committee, 24 July 1909; Testimony of Inmate Rosa Brewing to the Investigating Committee, 29 July 1909, ibid., pp. 525–26, 552, TSA.

100. For a discussion of how society stigmatizes all pregnant women, see Shelley E. Taylor and Ellen J. Langer, "Pregnancy: A Social Stigma?" *Sex Roles* 3 (1977), 27–35. For examples of sociologists' work demonstrating that attitudes toward pregnancy in modern America are the result of a long history of male ambivalence and hostility toward female sexuality, see Edwin Schur, *Labeling Women Deviant: Gender, Stigma, and Social Control* (Philadelphia: Temple University Press, 1983), p. 93.

101. Pardon Request of Warden Swift, 26 Sept. 1866, Margaret Davis File, box 22, folder 10, Pardon Papers, RG 5, MSA.

102. On the role of criminal women and society's uses of the madonna/whore imagery, see Clarice Feinman, *Women in the Criminal Justice System* (New York: Praeger, 1986), pp. 3–6, 19, 34–36. For a discussion of the importance of mothering to society, the use of the so-called maternal instinct in social control, methods of upholding the maternity ideal, and violations of the norms of motherhood, see Schur, *Labeling Women Deviant,* pp. 81–82, 88–92.

103. Incest convictions could be hard to sustain. Bartholemew Charpentier, a native of France who claimed he did not know the law, sought and received a pardon for an incest conviction ten years earlier. Charpentier had been charged with having sexual relations with his deceased wife's daughter, no age given in the record (Bartholemew Charpentier, no. 1155, 26 Mar. 1889, Executive Clemency Files, TSA). In the same records, see the case of S. S. Wharton, whose supporters noted that he only had one witness, "the woman," against him. A pardon, they believed, would "not only be of benefit to him but to his family" (Citizens' Petition, 1 Oct. 1908, S. S. Wharton, no. 24421, 17 Nov. 1908). The board originally declined Wharton because he presented no statement of the circumstances.

104. Citizens' Petition, 10 Oct. 1869; Governor J. McClung to Secretary of State Francis Rodman, 30 Sept. 1870, Mary Wiley File, box 32, folder 15, Pardon Papers, RG 5, MSA.

Valentina Madrid, seventeen years old when sentenced to hang for the poisoning death of her husband, spent thirteen years in the New Mexico penitentiary, although the male mastermind of the murder plot was never brought to trial. Glass plate neg. #2158. Courtesy of the New Mexico State Records and Archives, Santa Fe, N.M.

Originally sentenced to hang, sixteen-year-old Alma Lyons faced a life term in the New Mexico penitentiary, where she gave birth to a son eight years after her incarceration. Glass plate neg. #2157. Courtesy of the New Mexico State Records and Archives, Santa Fe, N.M.

A Wyoming judge refused to instruct the jury to consider self-defense for Hattie La Pierre, although the young prostitute shot and killed an abusive male companion after he began beating her on the street. Courtesy of the Wyoming Division of Cultural Resources, Cheyenne, Wyo.

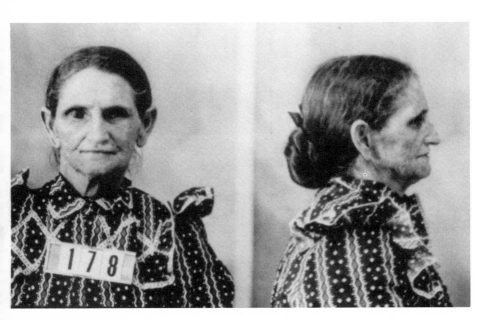

The blind fifty-six-year-old Mary Conery, judged by officials at the Kansas penitentiary to be insane one year after her imprisonment for murder, was returned to a sheriff in the Oklahoma Territory. Courtesy of the Kansas State Historical Society, Topeka, Kans.

Lida Gould, a deaf domestic, went to the Montana penitentiary for the theft of five hundred dollars, although there was little evidence that the woman could understand the court proceedings against her. Courtesy of the Montana Historical Society, Helena, Mont.

This earliest building of the Montana penitentiary captures the first attempts to construct an imposing edifice for the territory. Courtesy of the Montana Historical Society, Helena, Mont.

The Montana cellblock built in the 1890s dwarfs a log building from the territorial era and shows how officials used an assortment of structures to house growing inmate populations. Courtesy of the Montana Historical Society, Helena, Mont.

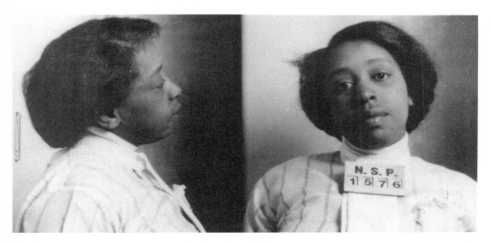

Nevada prisoner Lizzie Woodfolk defied her jailers to such an extent that she earned a sanity hearing in which she made her claims of abuse clear to the board of medical examiners. Courtesy of the Nevada State Library and Archives, Carson City, Nev.

A Cheyenne prostitute, Dolly Brady argued that her record of decency was well known among local law enforcement officers and deserved consideration in her clemency plea. Courtesy of the Wyoming Division of Cultural Resources, Cheyenne, Wyo.

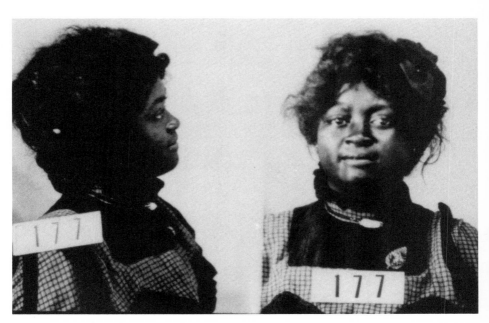

At age twenty-three, Sarah Phillips left behind a husband and child in the Oklahoma Territory when she was sent to the Kansas penitentiary on a charge of shooting to kill. Courtesy of the Kansas State Historical Society, Topeka, Kans.

Viola Biggs and her mother went to the Wyoming penitentiary convicted of kidnapping Viola's infant son, although the appeals court later overturned the conviction. Courtesy of the Wyoming Division of Cultural Resources, Cheyenne, Wyo.

When her son-in-law brought a spurious kidnapping charge against his wife, Anna E. Trout found herself implicated as well and served time with her daughter in the Wyoming penitentiary. Courtesy of the Wyoming Division of Cultural Resources, Cheyenne, Wyo.

6 Women and Prison Work

> Of course, nine hours a day at a sewing machine is no light task, but I am perfectly well and quite efficient, so manage very nicely.
> —Kate Richards O'Hare
> Missouri State Penitentiary
> 1917

In 1919, Kate Richards O'Hare, Socialist, labor activist, and convict penned these confident words in her second letter from the Missouri penitentiary.[1] Hardly representative of the female prison population, O'Hare, through letters with a decided political message, provided a rare, articulate assessment of the meaning of prison life for women.[2]

Despite the optimistic tone with which O'Hare began her term, within less than three months the extreme physical demands of the shop exacted their toll. O'Hare, suffering from chronic swollen feet and severe soreness in her neck and shoulders, complained that the constant vibrations of the sewing machine press striking against her knee had caused varicose veins.[3] Increasingly, her letters spoke of the fatigue, the strain of the work, the callousness of the matron, the unbearable

Rose Burns, Colorado State Penitentiary. Courtesy Division of State Archives and Public Records, Denver, Colo.

heat.[4] Work, as Kate O'Hare learned, defined life in the penitentiary for women prisoners.

This, of course, was as penitentiary managers intended. Nineteenth-century prison officials, as well as their antagonists, the social reformers, agreed that idle hands, especially those of criminals, became the devil's workshop.[5] Prison work, whether as a punitive measure or as a reforming agent, served as the principle around which nineteenth-century society structured penitentiary life.

Despite this importance, prison administrators, preoccupied with supervising the labor of male inmates in quarries, mines, and factories, rarely devised any well-organized program for the woman prisoner. As a result, women either languished in the tedium of complete idleness or worked grueling jobs. Whether confronted by ill-formed work plans or excessively strenuous industrial and agricultural conditions similar to those of male prisoners, female inmates found few chances to benefit physically, emotionally, or financially from their prison labor. In general, the work of women prisoners fell into two main categories: domestic chores and sexual service. Authorities adapted both to the work programs devised for male prisoners.

In the West, convict work assumed a range of forms including hard labor within the prison walls, the private contractor plan in which state authorities turned over control of the penitentiary to an individual businessman, and the lease program that jobbed out prisoners to private citizens.[6] Western states manipulated these general categories into an array of plans, always trying to fit prison work into an economic equation based on and beneficial to the region. So diverse were the labor plans across the country that in 1911 Sir Evelyn Ruggles-Brise, president of the English Prison Commission and International Prison Committee, commented after surveying the U.S. prison labor force, "There are as many systems in America as there are states, and even in the same state, we find many different systems."[7]

Hard labor, a ubiquitous prison image in the popular imagination, meant backbreaking work at the behest of the state for the state. The fundamental intent of hard labor rested on the notion that criminals should both be self-sustaining and produce profit for the jurisdiction that incarcerated them. Central to this proposition lay the unlikely assumption that exhausting physical work, performed as a result of coercion and brutality, led to personal reformation and a cheerful spirit. Even if prison work did not result in an individual metamorphosis, society generally wanted the satisfaction of knowing that it was not strapped with the bed and board expenses of its criminal population.[8]

Each state expected the warden or private contractor to strive for such a goal in prison management. For example, in 1867, the inspector for the

Missouri State Penitentiary indicated that the state looked to realize a return of about $80,000 on inmate labor contracted out to various shops. He further estimated that Missouri could anticipate the figure would increase to $114,000 a year and "hence, the institution will become self-sustaining, if not a source of income to the state."[9] Similarly, in 1874, a report on the unsavory conditions of the Kansas State Penitentiary reviewed the fiscal soundness of all U.S. prisons and pointed to Maine's penitentiary, the only one to show "an excess of receipts over expenditures," as the model for all others to emulate.[10]

The hard labor geared to self-maintenance philosophy generally fueled the management of the Arizona territorial prison at Yuma. Built mainly by prisoner labor, the facility opened in 1876 and for the next three decades it operated as a work in progress. Inmates, under a series of politically appointed superintendents, quarried rock, constructed the main wall, installed drainage and electricity, laid roads, tended gardens, and put up buildings. Except for a brief flirtation with a private contractor who wanted inmates to work for his irrigation company, Arizona officials, with their differing opinions about prison management, retained control of labor at the Yuma prison.[11]

Despite intentions that penitentiaries should remain under the direct supervision of civil officials, it quickly became evident that warehousing prisoners represented a costly expenditure, one that economically immature western states felt ill-prepared to shoulder. The second work program, contract labor, sought to deflect these financial problems, as it wedded the state penal program to private business interests. Under this plan, legislatures authorized local entrepreneurs to establish workshops and factories inside penitentiary walls. In a contract agreement, a business owner purchased convict labor at a per diem rate, and the state continued to manage the prison routines. This allowed those with business expertise to run industry, while the warden devoted his time to penitentiary management. The arrangements generally soured quickly, as disputes arose between business managers who demanded more and more matériel from the state and wardens who thought contractors interfered with effective penology. In these controversies, western legislators, reluctant to assume full financial responsibility for prisoners, vacillated about the limits of private control. As a result, they made the history of contract labor notable for its seesawing regulations and patronage politics.

For example, the original Arkansas penitentiary opened in 1841. For the next twelve years, management of the penitentiary, twice beset by fire, bounced back and forth between state officials and contractors before it finally became the province of private business.[12] Similarly, Missouri's 1833 plan to establish its Jefferson City penitentiary as a center for reformation faltered by 1839. Only three years after the first prisoners entered the facility, heavy operational costs led politicians to agree to a work contract with a private businessman.[13]

Regardless of whether the state or a private party supervised the work program, the intentions remained the same—demand and extract the greatest possible amount of work from the prisoners for the least possible financial outlay. Thus, legislatures, burdened by prison expenditures, distracted by other public needs, and hostile to criminal populations, slid from state-supervised hard labor to widening the prison management role of private entrepreneurs. In the least successful contracts, the contractor not only agreed to provide food, clothing, and shelter to the inmates but also to maintain the security of the institution with private guards.[14]

Such a shift represented a disaster for prisoners, as they lost even a rudimentary governmental system of checks and balances in regard to judicial administration, work expectations, or their physical well-being. Professional concern for corrections and accountability to the electorate vanished as state officials backed away from direct prison management. Private contractors who assumed control of prisons came with little interest or expertise in penal philosophy and regarded their commitment as a personal financial investment. Participating officials and business owners rarely cared to enhance the lives of prisoners, but rather wanted to relieve the state of an odious responsibility. All contracting parties hoped to expand the largesse to private industry, which benefited from its access to the cheap supply of prison laborers.[15]

That fact alone raised a furor in the West, where labor organization and union disputes ranked as some of the most volatile in the nation's history. Labor activists decried the uneven profit equation established by pitting the inmate laborer against the free worker. The matter of prisoners' wages and business's profit versus employment of the "honest worker" gained strength as a rallying cry for laborers.[16]

As early as 1874 Kansas officials deflected a portion of this protest. In defense of the contract system the board of commissioners suggested the convict should be given a "small percent of his earnings," but balked at going to "the extreme that a penitentiary should be a grand co-operative establishment, where the net profits should be divided among the workmen."[17] The commissioners accepted the principle of business profit with minimal inmate compensation, but ignored the delicate matter of economic competition between enforced laborer and free worker. In Texas, Superintendent Thomas Goree thought the problem could be diffused by using inmates for work that free laborers eschewed.[18]

Only a few years later, prison officials stepped even more gingerly when discussing the issue. Conceding that "No system of labor will be tolerated by the community today which may destroy the earning power of honest working men and women," the Colorado board of charities and corrections defended continuation of the contract system.[19] It concluded that the "only valid objection to convict-made goods is the low price at which . . . these articles have been placed on the market."[20] The very next year, Colorado duly noted the "contract labor system is being year by year driven from the field."[21] It suggested introducing a plan where inmates had a certain number of "free" hours, during which they could devote their time to manufacture of a product of their own choosing, with a shared profit arrangement with the prison. It offered, however, no solution to the main complaints of labor organizers that prison-made products sold at greatly cheaper rates, prisoners earned only ten or fifteen cents per day, and some business owners made substantial profits on the open market.[22]

When yet another twenty years passed and Kate Richards O'Hare took up the issue, she saw it as a matter for women workers, both as inmates and free employees. With her keen sense of political justice, O'Hare complained bitterly that for nine hours each day the women prisoners were "driven to . . . produce wealth of which we are robbed of every penny by organized society."[23] At the same time, she fretted because "I know my unpaid labor is being used to drag down the wages of every girl who works in an overall factory."[24]

Debates and protests aside, various forms of contract labor enjoyed great currency with prison administrators in the West. Among a collection of western states that chose the contract plan, Minnesota compiled one of the more financially successful endeavors for the investors. Between 1851 and 1853, the Minnesota Territory, with funding from the federal government, constructed a twelve-cell prison surrounded by a fourteen-foot wall. The warden personally owned the $8,000 worth of sash-, door-, and shingle-making machinery in the prison and, by an act of 1853, was given complete control of the institution. Since the territory's lawbreakers filled the cells only slowly at the outset, by 1858, the same year Minnesota entered the Union, the legislature decreed that the warden should receive all persons from counties without suitable jail facilities.[25] This move, which ignored distinctions between major and minor felonies, quickly swelled the ranks at the penitentiary, solved the prison's labor shortage, and led to an ever-expanding relationship between the warden and private business owners.

By 1868, the manufacturing interests of Seymour and Sabin had secured the prison labor contracts and parlayed the initial investments into a massive business. George M. Seymour, a promoter of the Stillwater and St. Paul Railroad, oversaw the employment of about eighty workers—forty convicts and forty local citizens—in an operation that included the making of doors, sashes, tubs, buckets, and barrels. In only six years, Seymour and Sabin mushroomed to such a degree that a joint stock company was formed and the venture took on the production of farm engines, office equipment, and furniture.[26]

Few states replicated the prosperity of Minnesota and Seymour and Sabin, and even the best-walled factories could not elude the impact of the national economy. Prison industry slumped with sluggish markets caused by economic depression as much as any other. In addition, the shallow fiscal integrity of all prison systems and the prisoners' willingness to sabotage production, especially through arson, impeded the hope of solid economic returns. Nonetheless, the contract system retained its popularity as a labor system suited to the West.[27]

In some western areas drawing on neighborly connections to the South, a third work system, the lease program, gained a foothold.[28] In this arrangement, the warden or superintendent leased or sold the labor of inmates to private businesses or individuals located outside the prison walls. The prison itself encompassed shops, generally reserved for skilled workers. Increasingly, the main penitentiary functioned as a receiving center from which officials sent able-bodied inmates, usually persons of color, to work on roads, mines, levees, cotton plantations, or in citizens' homes. Private business owners and individual families paid a fee to the state for a lease period and took over full responsibility for the convicts. Under these conditions, as prisoners moved beyond the confines of the penitentiary, state oversight further eroded. Lessees invested little in care of the inmates and used dogs, chains, and guns to retain control in the camps. Sanitation proved a particular difficulty in rural work areas that had never been prepared to house three or four hundred inmates. The death rate in the camps often ran to almost 10 percent a year.[29]

These conditions were guaranteed to provoke further prison controversy. Administrators tended to accentuate the supposed benefit and benevolence of any of these work situations,[30] while reformers and prisoners themselves told a different story.[31] The point of departure among officials and reformers, and some prisoners who considered these issues,[32] lay not so much in an argument about the state's expectation of labor but rather in what constituted an inhumane and crippling work environment.[33] State and territorial penitentiaries in the American West frequently allowed cruel treatment to permeate daily work conditions, undercutting any redeeming features that labor supposedly possessed.[34]

Nonetheless, for some male inmates prison work programs offered job training and educational opportunities otherwise not accessible. Kansas, by law, mandated that prisoners be taught trade skills that would open employment possibilities after prison. In their 1874 report, prison commissioners emphasized the absolute necessity of implementing that provision, pointing out that of 245 new inmates that year, only fifty-six demonstrated any trade skills. Arguing that literacy rates among the inmates far exceeded industrial skills, the commissioners called for more rigorous manual training to prepare men for employment when they returned to society. They saw prison industrial training as an important component in the overall educational program of Kansas.[35]

By 1912 Kansas boasted of a rich selection of courses available for prison inmates. The curriculum had expanded beyond the industrial arts and included, among other subjects, shorthand, music, history, penmanship, and Spanish. Although seventeen women were enrolled, they attended classes separate from the men, who on school nights ate at a special dining table where conversation was permitted.[36] Kansas had underwritten an extensive program geared to elevate the literacy of prisoners, along with their social sense and job opportunities. It had included women, even as it segregated them.

Penitentiary work opportunities for men also diversified as the age of industry wore on in America. For example, by the 1890s production at the Huntsville, Texas, penitentiary included blacksmith, paint, wheelwright, and foundry departments, and shops for making boilers, wagons, furniture, shoes, and clothing, as well as a cloth factory. The machinery for all these enterprises was available to the prisoner worker, who received any needed training from civilian employees or the more-skilled inmate foremen.[37]

Contractors tended to reserve foreman jobs for white inmates who curried favor with the civilian bosses. Competition for the limited slots was high, since the job carried more prestige and the inmate foreman had the authority to punish other convicts for work infractions. Although a cherished assignment, management of the shop placed a convict in an adversarial relationship with other inmates. Still, it was an important opportunity for an inmate who wanted to advance in a trade.[38]

Texas convict A. L. George, an itinerant laborer, understood these practicalities and determined to get the best work advantage out of his prison time as possible. Convicted of murder, George spent over five years inside the Huntsville prison, where he learned shoemaking. After about seven months as a novice working at a cobbler's bench, George won a promotion to one of the machines, where he stitched shoe parts together. Within a few months, he moved on to convict foreman, a job he held for two years, "diligently trying to master the trade in all its branches."[39] Eventually, he became the assistant foreman of the shoe department machinery. Each promotion brought less taxing physical labor, increased skills and authority, and more contact with the civilian foreman, less with prisoners. Upon his release from prison, George moved to Brownwood, Texas, where he purchased a shoe shop and established a successful business.[40] Thus he advanced economically because of skills he learned as a prisoner.

With an eye to these sorts of success stories, male administrators continued to overhaul work programs for men. In 1909 Colorado reorganized its work routines for prisoners under the administration of Warden Thomas J. Tynan. A prisoner who learned architecture inside the penitentiary designed a hospital built by prison labor. In addition, inmates installed new electric lighting and heating systems.[41] Each of these jobs prepared prisoners to assume new and improved work roles when released.

Other prison activities also encouraged the learning and maintenance of artisan skills that would benefit men after incarceration. At the penitentiary in Yuma, Arizona, men passed their free time making an assortment of articles that showcased their individual talents. Prisoners turned out leather bridles, jewelry, scrimshaw, and finished cabinets, all crafted with fine detail. Authorities allowed them to display these items at a prison market place, attended by civilians willing to pay the twenty-five-cents admission. The outsiders both bought the finished products and sold the prisoners fresh fruit and additional craft supplies. The prison retained one-third of the proceeds, and prisoners could bank their money as a nest egg for the future.[42] Wyoming permitted a similar market. Once a month civilians could wander through the prison, purchasing a range of articles manufactured by the inmates.[43] Thus, male inmates had two possible avenues for employment improvement that might significantly alter their job opportunities once they had served their time.

In addition to providing male prisoners with job training opportunities, officials began to adjust their thinking about the place of education in the prison. Despite the Kansas opinion that literacy rates posed no significant concern in 1874, the prison administration's attitudes toward education changed as the nation moved into the twentieth century. Having relied in the past on the chaplain or the warden's wife to conduct a few evening classes, administrators now wanted basic educational skills formalized. More and more prisons searched for trained educators to instruct male prisoners.

By 1899 the superintendent of public schools had been employed to teach three nights a week at the Stillwater, Minnesota, penitentiary.[44] In 1903, the warden of the Idaho penitentiary reported that the prison library had grown from 100 volumes in 1886 to 1,700 for the current year. Given the high rate of illiteracy, as well as the numbers of those who secured an education through correspondence courses, the warden recommended the establishment of a prison school.[45]

While male prisoners could extract occupational and educational benefits while incarcerated, women accrued few similar benefits. From the outset, any of the three labor categories placed women prisoners at a disadvantage. No system had been designed to include work by women prisoners. Planning for women, regardless of the existing work procedures, hardly entered the thinking of those who managed the daily routines. Men devised penitentiary work for the male transgressor whose problematic return to the societal fold turned on a firm policy of physical punishment. Women prisoners simply did not figure in prison industrial programs. As a result, little prison work existed for women, leading to uneven policies and unequal opportunities. In specific ways, women were closed off from the chance to learn a skill, earn prison wages, or advance educationally.

For women, who often worked without pay and had fewer educational opportunities, the frequent loss of "good time" further distanced them from realizing tangible benefit from their prison work. "Good time" referred to a credit rating, by which a prisoner could reduce the number of days in a prison sentence. Formalized by law in the nineteenth century, the good time policy took shape as a weapon to be used cavalierly by officials to control convict behavior.[46] For any infraction, prisoners, especially women, found an arbitrary number of previously accumulated release days subtracted from their records. Any guard, without corroboration, could report a woman guilty of violations—talking in line, cursing, staring at male inmates—and her good time deductions were entered in the punishment register. Whether the woman had actually broken the rule or whether she had resisted some form of physical, sexual, or psychological coercion remained unimportant. Even when prison work existed for women, these discipline policies served to dilute its benefits. As male prisoners learned a trade, earned a wage, went to school, and accumulated good time, their post-prison prospects greatly surpassed those of women.

Regardless of which strategy, or combination of strategies, officials pursued, the results for women were the same; prison work became one more negative in an experience that robbed women of their health, placed them in positions of sexual vulnerability, and reinforced their status as outcasts in the larger society. As a result, women criminals, who faced an impressive array of gender disparities within the judicial system, encountered a distinct handicap in the matter of prison work. Further, the ill-devised work programs for women, which persisted into the early twentieth century, reinforced the definition of female inmates as a "nuisance" within male penitentiaries. Idleness marked the time of many women in prison; this inoccupation intensified the sexual atmosphere in an environment of extreme gender imbalance. As a consequence, wardens and contractors allowed sexual vulnerability for females and physical gratification for males to become the defining feature of a woman's prison work.

For example, in 1890, twenty-one-year-old Manuela Fimbres, the mother of an eight-year-old child, entered the Arizona Territorial Prison, which had no facilities for women. In the first days of her sentence, Manuela, a prostitute convicted as an accomplice in the murder of an Asian customer, remained segregated from the prison population. When management of the inmates fell to superintendent John Behan, matters changed for Manuela.

Behan moved Manuela to an open thatched shack in the prison yard and made her available to the men of the Yuma prison. Manuela spent her time wandering about the prison interior, where both guards and inmates had sexual access to the young woman. Whether through consensual or coercive encounters, she quickly bore one child and became pregnant with a second. These circumstances, coupled with charges of brutality and malfeasance, brought about the removal of Behan, but only after the reports of his generally disreputable administration had spread beyond the isolated penitentiary town.[47] Authorities blamed Manuela for demoralizing the discipline of the penitentiary and granted her a pardon on the condition that she remove herself from the Arizona Territory.[48]

Other jurisdictions used women's sexuality for prisoner gratification as well. In Louisiana, between 1869 and 1894, Major Samuel Lawrence James held an exclusive state lease contract, which permitted him control over more than 15,000 convicts. In the 1880s, he moved large numbers of inmates, including the women prisoners, to Angola, an out-of-the-way plantation located along Mississippi River swampland. The women, all African American, worked as servants to the James family and as field hands. At the conclusion of a successful harvest, James sent female convicts into the camp areas as "rewards" for male convicts and, thus, extracted both heavy agricultural labor and sexual service from women prisoners.[49]

This practice also worked its way through the Texas system. Following nineteenth-century scandals that resulted from mixing male and female prisoners, Texas established a separate female agricultural camp. The assigned work meant that African American women labored in the fields, plowing, planting, and cleaning ditches. The unassigned work meant they acquiesced to the sexual demands of white guards.

Women prisoners in Texas had few opportunities to report such situations and officials showed a reluctance to leave clear documentation about sexual violations. Despite these obstacles, when asked, several women explained the sexual realities for female inmates. In the Texas penitentiary, sexual incidents, both forced and consensual, formed a regular part of women's experiences from 1865 through 1915.

Although administrators intended gender segregation at the Eastham Camp, owned by Delha Eastham, to end the sexual scandals and prison births of the nineteenth century, women continued to be guarded by men and have contact with some male prisoners. The very location of the camp, more than twenty miles from the Huntsville penitentiary, created problems. Camp guards, far from the view of the central administration or visiting inspectors, conducted themselves as they wished. Male inmates used their assignments at the camp as an opportunity to engage women in sex. Women prisoners assessed their circumstances with these two groups of men and made the sexual decisions that seemed appropriate to each as an individual.

When queried by a prison investigating committee, African American female inmates told of spontaneous and scheduled sexual liaisons. Some reported occasions of overt force, others of implied threat. Still others explained the small rewards to be gained through physical cooperation for anyone selected as a "special" woman to a guard. All conveyed the uneven power inherent in sexual relationships at the camp.

Guards singled women out by color, seeking the "bright women" and the "yellow women," but avoiding the "dark women."[50] While women worked in the field, a guard, said Rosa Brewing, would "ride up . . . look at you right hard and give . . . a signal where to go."[51] Women "stepped out" from the row into the weeds as if to "answer the call of nature" for the assignation. Watch guards made no comment about the length of time missed from the field.

When women returned to the bunkhouse at night, guards sent to the officer in charge for a particular inmate and met her at the hospital building. Guards came into the dormitory and awakened sleeping women, taking them outside to the wood pile. They required some women to act as lookouts for the captain, while they engaged others in sex.[52] They produced odd medical concoctions to thwart pregnancy. In return for cooperation, guards gave a dollar, promised favors, or offered to assist in a release.

The men also used threats of every kind and the women understood the difficult nature of their position. Rosa Brewing resisted the proposition of the picket guard because she knew the head sergeant would give her a whipping if the pair were caught.[53] On the other hand, Lulu Lane, trying to elude a field guard, said, "I don't want to bother with you nohow [*sic*] . . . you haven't anything for me but a dime or fifteen cents and I don't need it." The rejected guard reported that Lulu "sassed" him; the captain whipped Lulu Lane, telling her, "you are a liar; I don't believe Mr. Baines was after you."[54]

Women who turned to the captain for protection found themselves ignored or the object of punishment as well. Amy Payne, forced into sex by a picket guard who caught her in the fields, afterwards tried to raise an alarm to the captain when women were led from the barracks at night. Those taken also sent up a cry together.[55] Some women inmates watched the futility of all this and decided not to acknowledge the prevalent sexual activity. Mary Harrington insisted that she didn't know anything about nocturnal events, saying, "There was a woman whipped not long ago here about noticing things."[56]

The ill-matched power relationships required that women make practical sexual decisions. They literally had their lives to lose if they did not cooperate. When the investigating committee asked Annie Morgan what reply she had given to the proposition of Jerry Bowden, son of the camp manager, she responded, "He asked me to stay with him, and I was a convict and I told him I was a convict and I could stay with him if he said so."[57]

As women recognized the greater power of the male guards, they also tried to secure a few privileges and accommodate their own sexuality. For women who worked barefoot and wore only skimpy shifts, the weekly two dollars earned from a guard for sexual cooperation meant the chance to buy stockings or send a little money to families on the outside. Guards might have women whipped for resistance, but in exchange for compliance, they could protect them from beatings. With a nod to pragmatism, Rosa Brewing said of her more than two-year relationship with a sixty-year-old guard, "I thought he could do me some good."[58]

As the committee pressed Rosa on whether she had consented to the picket guard's attentions, she replied forthrightly, "I was a convict and in prison and . . . I thought if I got that chance I would do it." When the obtuse committee members asked of what chance she meant, Rosa told them, "Of being with a man; you asked me for the truth and I am going to tell you."[59] But the committee persisted, surely it was not Rosa's habit to "go with white men" outside the penitentiary. The bluntly direct woman responded, "I like white men, on account of my father was a white man, is the reason I like them."[60]

Rosa Brewing, a black woman who did not even know her own age, articulated what prison officials did not want to acknowledge. Women prisoners suffered from sexual deprivation, as well as male inmates, and physical attractions transcended racial lines. Women, as well as men, had established sexual habits when they entered prison. Cut off from the gender interaction of their own cultures, women prisoners made the best of a bad circumstance.[61] While physical force characterized much of the sexual labor women performed in prison, their own choices and needs played a role as well. Some chose same-sex relationships, although authorities tended to cloak the evidence about these.[62] In Texas, Rosa Brewing assessed her situation, perceived there were some fearful ingredients in prison sex, and considered a partnership with a "pretty old and pretty gray" white guard better than brutal rape, constant whipping, or total abstinence.[63]

When called to testify about these episodes, Captain I. L. Brabham gave predictably vague answers about connections between male guards and women prisoners. Assuring the committee that he did not tolerate illicit behavior from the staff, Brabham conceded that it was an important function of his office to make sure certain liaisons did not occur. Guards who leaned toward intimacy with the women, including the sixty-year-old picket guard with a family in Huntsville, Brabham reprimanded. Brabham dismissed the childbirths as episodes that occurred before his watch. As for the women, he asserted he maintained a vigilant charge over them. If any guards bothered them, he felt sure the women would report to him. The committee remained unimpressed, and one member grumbled to the captain that he was "responsible for the shame of the nation resting upon us through your conduct."[64] Brabham's protests of professional surveillance aside, the committee considered the evidence of sexual misconduct at the Eastham Camp too shocking for inclusion in its final report.[65]

Of course, some prison officials made an effort, or at least said they did, to keep women prisoners carefully separated from males. After years of allowing women the freedom of the prison until 10:30 at night,[66] Idaho officials decreed in 1905 that females should be permanently segregated from the rest of the prison population and, for the first time, supervised by a matron.[67] A small stone building, surrounded by a wall seventeen feet high and two and a half feet thick and located outside the main prison, became the quarters for the women.

Removing female inmates from the easy reach of male prisoners, although not from that of male guards, inspired officials to develop a separate schedule of work activities for women. Officials quickly assigned the women to a domestic program of cleaning the new building, washing, and cooking for themselves. Future plans called for the women to make shirts for the male prisoners.[68] Idaho, having weathered a number of penitentiary scandals, decided it could no longer condone the blatant sexual use made of its women prisoners and cast the inmates into the only other work role that seemed appropriate—that of domestic workers.

By instituting a program of household chores, Idaho fell into step with other western prisons, where domestic labor, along with sexual coercion, dominated work assignments for prison women.[69] In a discussion of women prisoners in Missouri, the historian Gary R. Kremer indicated that in 1876 approximately 87 percent of all labor performed by about forty women in the Missouri prison fell under the heading of domestic work. In addition to those sent as servants to private homes, other women inside the walls cooked, mended and sewed prison clothing, and washed the men's laundry. Women working for private citizens accumulated more than 9,000 days of domestic labor, while comparable chores inside totaled well over 3,000 days of work for the state.[70]

In 1892, the warden of the Minnesota penitentiary reported that his six women inmates were "quiet and orderly and submissive." None had been punished for at least two years, apparently because they had been kept busy with "sewing, . . . darning, cleaning, scrubbing," and caring for the officers' quarters.[71] At the New Mexico penitentiary, officials employed women prisoners in the same manner. Incarcerated women, usually African Americans and Mexican Americans, cleaned the warden's quarters, washed windows, and prepared food in the prison kitchen.[72]

It simply did not occur to administrators that women prisoners could take up work other than domestic service upon their release from prison. In 1892 women prisoners in Colorado did cooking, sewing, and mending, and little else.[73] Eighteen years later, women prisoners in Colorado spent their days doing the exact same tasks. Dorothy S. Lowell, the matron at the Colorado State Penitentiary, reported in 1910 that she instructed the women prisoners in cooking, cleaning, laundry work, mending, darning, plain sewing, fancy drawn work, lace making, and knitting. These skills, along with neatness of person and cleanliness, would prepare the former inmate to "make an honorable living for herself, or an excellent house and home keeper." As these twenty-two prisoners scrubbed and stitched under Lovell's watchful eye, she constantly "held before them that in this domestic work is woman's highest realm."[74]

Most inmates must have looked on this work as predictable, for the women who entered prison came largely from the ranks of domestic workers. At the Kansas State Penitentiary, between 1865 and 1901, 110 of 151 women committed gave their occupation as housekeeper, servant, or washerwoman. The others called themselves laborers and dressmakers, or professed to be without occupation. Indeed, of the total number of women, only one, a native of Spain, listed a nondomestic profession—that of trapeze artist.[75]

Generally, then, women's prison work replicated female labor performed outside the walls, but within an intensified context and with severe consequences for shoddy or delinquent performance. In New Mexico, authorities sent Dolores Jaramillo to the dark cell for three days for fighting at her job in the kitchen. At the same prison, Juana Chacón accumulated a long list of violations in the punishment register. Most of her misbehavior occurred while she worked in the kitchen or the warden's quarters. Among her punishments, she was locked in a closet for one day through the work hours and lost at least twelve days of good time toward her release.[76]

For prison authorities, the use of women for domestic chores inside male penitentiaries seemed a practical solution to an awkward situation. As long as they had to house females in facilities that had little or no provision for gender differences, officials felt they might as well take advantage of the domestic support services women could give. The day-to-day operation within penitentiaries, virtually self-contained communities, depended on arrangements for cooking, cleaning, and sewing. Women prisoners represented just the right number of workers needed for the domestic categories of the prison. There were, after all, few social or economic indicators from society to guide prison officials to any different program for women.

Despite the women who aggressively refused to buckle to rule inside the walls, prison officials felt comfortable about female inmates as a "docile," perhaps even pathetic, class having access to domestic work areas, such as the kitchen and the officers' living quarters. With the exception of a relatively few prisoners convicted of murder or manslaughter, women seldom rated special treatment as dangerous criminals who required maximum security precautions. In fact, even women convicted of murder and assault usually mingled with the rest of the female population, unless their prison behavior took a violent turn.[77] Thus, women in prison, regarded as more of an aggravation than a security risk, could contribute through domestic labor to the desired goal that the prison be a self-sustaining, self-perpetuating institution.[78]

In some states, prison officials decided to expand women's domestic skills to an entrepreneurial scale comparable to the common uses of male labor. The environment Kate Richards O'Hare found at the Missouri penitentiary resulted. There, sixty of eighty women prisoners worked nine hours a day Monday through Friday and half a day on Saturday, making overalls and jackets for a manufacturer who had contracted with the state for prison labor. O'Hare estimated that at the 1919 wage scale, the women "earned" from twelve to twenty dollars a week, although they received no compensation. She noted that the shop's seven half windows, positioned ten feet above the floor, were useless and that the one full window had been nailed shut and painted over because, according to prisoner legend, a woman had once looked out at a male inmate. O'Hare complained that the matron directed all three of the ancient fans at her own desk, leaving the inmates to swelter at their machines.

Despite O'Hare's rather privileged status as a political prisoner, nothing spared her from the grueling daily routine that usually began after a fitful two hours of sleep, followed by a bleak and silent breakfast, included hours of sitting in one position, and ended with a so-called exercise period where women huddled against the yard wall trying to avoid the vicious summer heat radiating from the pavement. No high-placed political friend intervened for Kate O'Hare when she ran a sewing machine needle through her finger. The matron simply doused it with turpentine and sent the prisoner back to her machine. O'Hare soon understood that despite her education, her middle-class background, and her high profile as a political detainee, she, as a prisoner, should fear the black hole or the bread and water punishment as much as her companions, many of whom had long criminal histories and far greater experience with prison procedures.[79]

O'Hare learned to assess the length of a woman's prison tenure by the level of the inmate's mental and physical deterioration. She came to perceive that the prison regimen stripped a woman of her individuality, her judgment, indeed, her mind. In one letter, she wrote, "I have no more control over the amount of work . . . I must do than my sewing machine. . . . the law of the shop is the absolute limit of human endurance and to that law I must bow."[80]

In addition to the work assignments inside the walls and the contractual arrangements made with manufacturers and businessmen, officials had another use for women's labor: leased domestic service into local homes. Although this policy removed the inmate from within the walls, tenuous situations resulted, for at any moment, for real or imagined infractions, the woman could be sent back inside. Above all, racism drove this domestic service leasing practice, which flowered almost immediately at the end of the Civil War.

In October 1865, Rebecca Boyd, incarcerated in the Missouri penitentiary since August, received a letter from her former owner, Bettie Boyd. In this missive, Bettie Boyd reached out to the seventeen-year-old young woman with a tangle of language that foreshadowed the dim future for the former slave. Bettie Boyd, in a letter dripping with smugness, wrote to Rebecca: "altho you have been tried by the laws of the land, we cannot forget the ties that once bound us . . . we are assured we were in every particular kind, indulgent & forbearing. I feel assured that you can never complain of your treatment. My conscience will never reproach me for our treatment to any under our care. I know not the circumstances that have so soon closed your career of freedom & brought you to the dingy gloomy cell of a prison . . . you . . . got what you deserved."[81]

Bettie Boyd did not conclude on such a harsh note but continued that she wrote to "soothe your anguish & if you desire to *come home*—come back to those who have been your friends."[82] The Boyds offered to support a pardon for Rebecca, on the condition that she would leave Missouri and return to their home in Kentucky. The former slave owner closed with a request that Rebecca, sentenced to three years, have the jailer write for her and send the Boyds news of "what you know of the rest of the freed ones of the family," all of whom may have doubted that claim of kinship.

Rebecca's "crime" consisted of passing money of a large denomination she received from one former slave to another. None of the three involved could read and thought they were using a five-dollar bill, until one presented it to a merchant. On this evidence, grand larceny charges were leveled against Rebecca. Bettie Boyd didn't care about these particulars and just wanted her "trustworthy" illiterate black domestic servant restored to her. Although Rebecca Boyd did not receive her pardon until five months later, her records seem to suggest that to secure it, she had to accept the unappealing invitation to Kentucky.[83]

Although this case did not exactly represent local domestic leasing, it exposed the roots of the plan. White families arranged with wardens to hire convict women for domestic work for a lease period, during which the inmate worked off her fine or prison time. Such was the circumstance in which Belle Ragsdale found herself in the 1860s.

In May of 1866, Ragsdale, a former slave from Paris, Missouri, was sentenced to two years in the penitentiary for grand larceny. Shortly after, the warden released Ragsdale to the home of George McIntire to do domestic work. In December of 1867, Mrs. McIntire decided to travel to Fulton, Missouri, for the winter, and she desired that Belle Ragsdale should go along to care for the McIntire children. George McIntire, in an appeal to the governor, noted that Belle was "a very smart girl, a good girl to take care of children . . . her conduct has been good. She has been at my house for nearly twelve months. . . . my wife is anxious . . . to obtain her pardon."[84]

The decision about Belle's fate fell to Warden H. A. Swift and Governor Thomas Fletcher, who together compiled one of the few fairly positive nineteenth-century prison administrative records, especially in regard to women inmates.[85] Warden Swift forwarded McIntire's letter, along with his own, to the governor. He said of Belle, "She is an apt Negro. . . . The opportunity for a home . . . may not occur again and under the circumstances I . . . recommend her for clemency."[86] Belle Ragsdale received her pardon on 7 December 1867 and presumably left to winter in Fulton, although one wonders what sort of life this former slave ever enjoyed. Perhaps the McIntires brought some measure of well-being into Belle's existence, but as one who had lived as slave, prisoner, lessee, and pardoned inmate, Belle Ragsdale probably watched freedom pass by in the lives of other people but never grasped it for herself.

Despite the opportunity for abuse, the lease system continued. In 1867, J. W. Cox interceded on behalf of Catherine Mulleny and stated that she had been living with his family for several months as a "trusty house servant," and he wanted her pardoned before the warden turned all the women back inside.[87] In 1868, a Missouri employer sought release for Jane Brooks, who had spent the majority of her term leased out and had distinguished herself, he said, as a "good, obedant [sic] and fathful [sic] girl."[88] By 1877, the matron at the Missouri penitentiary reported that working outside the walls had been "abolished, with a few appropriate exceptions."[89]

Those few appropriate exceptions allowed Missouri and other states to cling to the lease system as a way to secure income for the penitentiary and favors for some citizens.[90] Nonetheless, for some women this system provided a possible avenue for permanent release from the penitentiary, if the contracting family remained agreeable. In 1893 Maria Mingo of Texas was hired out to William Hynes to work off her conviction for the theft of $8.50 and court costs assessed at $331.50. After serving sixty days' jail time, Maria went out on a lease for the two-year term it would take to satisfy the remainder of her exorbitant fines.[91] Thirteen months into this indenture, Maria benefited in the one way the lease could help a convict woman. The lease family assisted in recommending her pardon, thus freeing her from one year of her hire. The attorney writing on her behalf called Maria "a *Good Negro*—she is not a Sunday School schollar [*sic*] nor an example for them to follow but *all Nigger*. . . . She is nothing but a Negro woman, trifling as any Negro woman and as good as any Negro woman, with one child (I suppose illegitimate)."[92]

Confronted with an array of legal and social biases, Maria Mingo extricated herself from the lease system, but not from the racism that surrounded the whole incident. At least her record gave no evidence of the sexual vulnerability that continued to haunt women convicts even under the lease program. In 1880, Governor O. M. Roberts of Texas waived ninety dollars of a one hundred dollar fine levied against Ann Cushman, convicted of adultery. Cushman had already served a "hired out" contract of one and a half years for this minor charge. A pregnancy that began while she was in private service, coupled with her general poverty and the uncertain fate of her other children, seemed to be the factors that moved the governor to act.[93] Nine years later, Julia Grant received a pardon because she also had four small children and officials felt they could not hire her out for the reason no one would be willing to "pay anything for her."[94]

As late as 1901, E. T. McConnell, the superintendent of the Arkansas penitentiary, testified to an investigating committee that he permitted prisoners to work outside the walls for private citizens and that he had an inmate woman working in his own home. When asked if he knew that the action was against the law, McConnell defiantly replied that the penitentiary board was his law. He then boasted that, after all, his administration represented an improvement in the treatment of prisoners. He explained that when he first arrived at the penitentiary *all* the black women prisoners were hired out for a monthly pittance. For reducing the number of leased convicts, he felt quite pleased.[95]

The lease system helped to freeze African American women in their role as domestic workers. With its ragged contours, it pressured black women to feign a passive manner when they worked for white families or face returning to the penitentiary. Overall, it reinforced the fundamental use of women prisoners as domestics. The prison work arena particularly accentuated this fact in several ways.

First, society excused the lack of planned work for women in the nine-teenth and early twentieth century on the basis of the small population of female prisoners and the fact that male penitentiaries had no means to accommodate women inmates. Actually, no appropriate facilities existed for women because tightfisted legislatures failed to allocate funds for pris-on renovation or construction. Crowded facilities and small numbers of convicted "deviant" women mingled in the minds of the public to trivial-ize the significance of the female prisoner. Once dismissed as a person of no social consequence, the woman prisoner had a slim chance of captur-ing the attention of policy makers or the public funds needed to establish a reasonable work program.

Second, turmoil, hardship, and degradation filled the prison work en-vironment for women. Officials did not plan work programs carefully and, when faced with a female population, they simply yielded, allowing wom-en to be used for sexual gratification, agricultural labor, or domestic service. Both hard labor within the walls and the private contractor arrangement exploited women in specific gender terms.

Women either stayed in their cells in forced inactivity, provided sexu-al diversion for male officials and inmates, cleaned and cooked for officers, plowed and planted, or worked merciless hours in the prison industry. Leas-ing to private families, despite declarations of good intention by citizens and possible opportunities for a better physical environment, really meant that prisoners entered into bondage with that family. Many situations reeked of human baseness, but all paid scant attention to women's rights, played on women's sexual vulnerability, accentuated the role of women as domestic workers, and brought about a decline in women's health; none assisted women in changing their lives upon release. All in all, prison work was just one more gender disadvantage for women—one where, in an aura of continuing violence, authorities abused both the physical and emotional well-being of female inmates.

In May of 1920, almost fourteen months after her arrival at the Missouri penitentiary, O'Hare left prison, her sentence commuted by her political foe, President Woodrow Wilson. When she arrived at the Jefferson City prison, she must have seemed privileged to herself and the other women inmates. She enjoyed greater access to the warden, her prison companions deferred to her, and loving friends and family sustained her. As a woman prisoner, however, her experiences closely paralleled those of other females. Like many of the women with whom she served, O'Hare, tried and convict-ed on questionable legal grounds, burdened with an excessively severe sen-tence for the crime charged, entered an antiquated western prison to be absorbed into the hideous conditions of work inside the walls.[96] She turned her back on prison to reenter an economic and political world that allowed her to use her penitentiary time as evidence of the importance of social reform. The gender constraints O'Hare faced in prison strengthened her voice as a reformer.

Such was not likely to be the case for other women inmates as they walked away from the penitentiary gates. For them, prison, especially in its poorly designed work programs, only tightened society's rigidly applied rules of race, class, and gender. They departed—laundresses, servants, seamstresses, cooks—as the unfortunate heirs to a prison legacy created by a negligence in work provisions and an exclusive focus on sexual and domestic matters. Work at the penitentiary, on the satellite farms, through the lease system had introduced them to more violence—physical, sexual, intellectual. In the American West, penitentiary work did little to expand the horizons of opportunity for convicted women.

Notes

1. O'Hare, *Prison Letters*, p. 7.

2. For more detailed information about O'Hare's entire career, see Sally M. Miller, *From Prairie to Prison.*

3. O'Hare, *Prison Letters,* pp. 30, 69, and 70.

4. Ibid., see pp. 69, 70, 80, 84.

5. For the nature of prisons and prison labor, see Sullivan, *Prison Reform Movement,* pp. 1–16; Gary R. Kremer and Thomas E. Gage, "The Prison against the Town: Jefferson City and the Penitentiary in the Nineteenth Century," *Missouri Historical Review* 74 (July 1980): 414–32; Kroll, "Prison Experiment"; and Martin B. Miller, "At Hard Labor," pp. 79–88. For a sociologist's perspective see Georg Rusche, "Labor Market and Penal Sanction: Thoughts on the Sociology of Criminal Justice," in Platt and Takagi, pp. 10–16.

6. These labor classifications should only be regarded as general divisions. Note that the terminology is overlapping. The contractor was often referred to as the "lessee," one who has "leased" the work at the prison. The "lease system" referred to hiring prisoners, as individuals or in groups, out to work.

7. Ruggles-Brise, "English View of the American Penal System," p. 356.

8. "Report of the Warden," *Biennial Report of the Idaho State Penitentiary,* 1913–14, p. 3, ISL; M. F. Johnston, "The Life of a Woman Convict," *Fortnightly Review* 69 (Mar. 1901): 566; Timothy P. Donovan and Willard B. Gatewood, Jr., *The Governors of Arkansas: Essays in Political Biography* (Fayetteville: University of Arkansas Press, 1981), p. 76.

9. "Inspector's Report," *Missouri General Assembly, House Journal with Appendix/Index,* 24th General Assembly, Regular Session, 1867, p. 502, MSA.

10. Board of Commissioners of Public Institutions, *Second Annual Report,* 1874, p. 296, UKKC.

11. Knepper, "Imprisonment and Society in Arizona Territory," pp. 267–88; Jeffrey. *Adobe and Iron,* pp. 25–27, 52, 60–61, 100–101, 109.

12. Bayliss, "Arkansas State Penitentiary under Democratic Control, 1874–1896," p. 194.

13. Kremer and Gage, "Prison against the Town," pp. 416–17.

14. The arrangements between the state and the contractor varied from state to state and contractor to contractor. Missouri originally charged the state with appointing the warden and deputy warden, who maintained disciplinary control. In a cost saving measure, the latter position was eliminated and the authority of the warden reduced (Board of Commissioners of Public Institutions, *Second Annual Report*, 1874, p. 294, UKKC). In 1873, Arkansas handed carte blanche control of the penitentiary to the contractor. Although the arrangement called for state oversight, supervision often faltered during the ten year contract. See Bayliss, "Arkansas State Penitentiary under Democratic Control," pp. 198–200.

15. At the turn of the century, Arkansas's Governor Jeff Davis clashed with his own penitentiary board about an illegal convict lease arrangement that favored a local businessman. The board insisted on honoring a ten-year contract that turned over one-third of the state's inmates to W. W. Dickinson of the Arkansas Brick Manufacturing Company (Donovan and Gatewood, *Governors of Arkansas*, pp. 115–20).

16. For an example of western labor rhetoric, see Elizabeth Gurley Flynn, "The I. W. W. Call to Women," *Solidarity* 31 (July 1915): 9.

17. Board of Commissioners of Public Institutions, *Second Annual Report*, 1874, pp. 300–301, UKKC.

18. Walker, *Penology for Profit*, p. 67.

19. *Third Biennial Report of the State Board of Charities and Corrections*, p. 10, CSA.

20. Ibid., p. 11.

21. *Fourth Biennial Report of the State Board of Charities and Correction*, p. 30, CSA.

22. Texas convict A. L. George indicated that business was always brisk for convict goods, because the quality was excellent and the cost low (*Texas Convict*, p. 187).

23. O'Hare, *Prison Letters*, p. 15.

24. Ibid., p. 92.

25. Neill, *History of Washington County and the St. Croix Valley* and Williams, *Outlines of the History of Minnesota*, p. 533.

26. Willard E. Rosenfelt, gen. ed., *Washington: A History of the Minnesota County* (Stillwater, Minn.: Croixside Press, 1977), pp. 184, 297. In 1911, the prosperous binding-twine industry at the Minnesota penitentiary caught the envious attention of Wisconsin ("Notes on Current and Recent Events," *Journal of the American Institute of Criminal Law and Criminology* 1 [Jan. 1911]: 803–4).

27. Other states enjoyed sporadic success with the contract system. After a long struggle to establish a productive work system, Missouri, between 1876 and 1884, added seven factories to existing industries inside the walls and by 1891 the penitentiary was self-supporting. See Kremer and Gage, "Prison against the Town," pp. 426–29.

28. For a thorough discussion of the lease system, see Walker, *Penology for Profit*, esp. pp. 13–77.

29. After the Civil War, Louisiana, Arkansas, and Texas leased out their entire prison populations. This use of prisoner labor, especially on public roads, helped to introduce the chain-gang system in the South. See Kroll, "Prison Experiment," p. 9; John Vodicka, "Prison Plantation: The Story of Angola," *Southern Exposure* 4 (1978): 34; and Jane Zimmerman, "The Penal Reform Movement in the South during the Progressive Era, 1890–1917," *Journal of Southern History* 17 (1951): 466–69.

30. An excellent example of the administrator's assessment of salutary prison work conditions is found in a speech by Colonel A. J. Ward, prison manager of the Texas penitentiary at Huntsville in the 1870s. For a description of his address to the 1874 National Prison Congress in St. Louis, Missouri, see Anne M. Butler, "Still in

Chains: Black Women in Western Prisons, 1865–1915," *Western Historical Quarterly* 20 (Feb. 1989): 27.

31. Thomas Hill Green, "Anglo-American Philosophies of Penal Law"; Kirchwey, "Crime and Punishment"; Reynolds, *Twin Hells,* pp. 63–64, 73–78; and Gordon L. Olson, ed., "'I Felt like I Must Be Entering . . . Another World': The Anonymous Memoirs of an Early Inmate of the Wyoming Penitentiary," *Annals of Wyoming* 47 (Fall 1975): 160–63, 166. Olson's article is an edited version of *Sweet Smell of Sagebrush,* cited in earlier chapters. Green and Kirchwey addressed the issues of power abuse and the need for professional behavior and reform of public attitudes. Reynolds and the Wyoming inmate described episodes of ill-treatment and torture connected to prison work.

32. The anonymous Wyoming prisoner complained about the way other inmates did or did not do their work. See "I Felt like I Must Be Entering . . . Another World," pp. 167–68, 169–70, 176, 179, 182.

33. In 1911, the *St. Paul Press* reported that twenty-eight out of forty-two governors had sent messages to their legislatures about prisons. All agreed that idleness must not be tolerated and all prisoners must be provided with appropriate employment so they could earn money for themselves and their families ("Notes on Current and Recent Events," *Journal of the American Institute of Criminal Law and Criminology* 2 [Sept. 1911]: 319).

34. For example, for descriptions of conditions in Arkansas see "Discrimination against Negro Criminals in Arkansas" and "The Convict Leasing System in Arkansas," *Journal of the American Institute of Criminal Law and Criminology* 1 (Jan. 1911): 947–49; for Iowa, see Governor's Office: series 8, Reports, boxes 11 and 13, Commissions, Investigations, Penitentiaries: Anamosa, 1876–78, ISA; for Kansas, see Legislature Records, State Penitentiary Investigation, 1895: box 15, Investigation of the Warden of the State Penitentiary, Seth W. Chase, 1895, Affidavits of Elizabeth C. Simpson and Mary Fitzpatrick, 23 July 1914, Governor George Hodges Papers, Correspondence, 1913–15, Board of Corrections, Investigation of Punishments, box 33, KSHS; for Minnesota, see *Report of a Committee . . . to Investigate the Matter of Punishment of Convicts at the Minnesota State Prison,* 1891, MnHS; for New Mexico, see Punishment Record Book, NMSA; for Texas, see Board of Commissioners of Public Institutions, *Second Annual Report,* 1874, pp. 343–51, UKKC; Charles Shirley Potts, *Crime and the Treatment of the Criminal,* Bulletin of the University of Texas 146 (Austin: University of Texas, 1910), pp. 71–73; *Report of the Penitentiary Investigating Committee,* TSA.

35. Board of Commissioners of Public Institutions, *Second Annual Report,* 1874, p. 292, UKKC.

36. "Notes on Current and Recent Events," *Journal of the American Institute of Criminal Law and Criminology* 2 (Jan. 1912): 932.

37. George, *Texas Convict,* pp. 186–88.

38. Ibid., pp. 143, 144, 164, 184; *Sweet Smell of Sagebrush,* pp. 11–12.

39. George, *Texas Convict,* p. 143.

40. Ibid., p. 231; a Wyoming inmate, whose early life was spent as a ranch worker, graduated from tying brooms to bookkeeper of the factory office. After his release, it is believed he worked for an industrial company in Rawlins, Wyoming (*Sweet Smell of Sagebrush,* pp. 12, 152, 154).

41. Stone, *History of Colorado,* p. 820.

42. John M. Jeffrey, "The Bizarre Bazaar," *Journal of Arizona History* 11 (Autumn 1970): 202–17.

43. *Sweet Smell of Sagebrush,* p. 85.

44. *Fourth Biennial Report of the State Board of Charities and Correction*, p. 30, MnHS.

45. "Report of the Warden," *Biennial Report of the Idaho State Penitentiary*, 1903–4, pp. 11–12, 14, ISL.

46. See Martin B. Miller, "At Hard Labor," p. 82.

47. *Arizona Republican*, 24 Aug. 1890; Manuscript, Yuma Territorial Prison; John Behan File, AHS. In addition, see a description of this episode in Butler, *Daughters of Joy, Sisters of Misery*, pp. 79–81.

48. Pardon Proclamation, 4 Sept. 1891; Certificate of Release by M. M. McInernay, 25 Sept. 1891, Manuela Fimbrez, no. 572, box 25, folder 383, Secretary of the Territory, Yuma Prison, ASA.

49. Roger S. Thomas, Assistant Warden, to Frank C. Blackburn, Warden, "History of Angola: Major Samuel Lawrence James," 27 Dec. 1985, pp. 1, 3, 4, LSP.

50. Testimony of Inmate Rosa Brewing to the Investigating Committee, 29 July 1909, *Report of the Penitentiary Investigating Committee*, p. 550, TSA.

51. Ibid., p. 551.

52. Testimony of Inmates Rosa Brewing, Lulu Lane, Ennis Carlisle, Jerline Bonds, Hannah Steele, Annie Morgan to the Investigating Committee, 29 July 1909, ibid., pp. 548–69.

53. Testimony of Inmate Rosa Brewing to the Investigating Committee, 29 July 1909, ibid., p. 549.

54. Testimony of Inmate Lulu Lane to the Investigating Committee, 29 July 1909, ibid., p. 556.

55. Testimony of Inmates Ennis Carlisle, Jerline Bonds to the Investigating Committee, 29 July 1909, ibid., pp. 558, 560.

56. Testimony of Inmate Mary Harrington to the Investigating Committee, 29 July 1909, ibid., p. 548.

57. Testimony of Inmate Annie Morgan to the Investigating Committee, 29 July 1909, ibid., p. 565.

58. Testimony of Inmate Rosa Brewing to the Investigating Committee, 29 July 1909, ibid., p. 550.

59. Ibid., p. 549.

60. Ibid., p. 553.

61. Joseph F. Fishman, *Sex in Prison: Revealing Sex Conditions in American Prisons* (n.p.: National Library Press, 1934), pp. 21, 28.

62. Ibid., pp. 129–30.

63. Testimony of Inmate Rosa Brewing to the Investigating Committee, 29 July 1909, *Report of the Penitentiary Investigating Committee*, pp. 549, 550, 553, TSA. For a discussion of the way that black women shaped helpful environments for themselves, see Linda Williams Reese, "Race, Class, and Culture: Oklahoma Women, 1890–1920" (Ph.D. dissertation, University of Oklahoma, 1991), pp. 107–65.

64. Testimony of Captain I. L. Brabham to the Investigating Committee, 30 July 1909, *Report of the Penitentiary Investigating Committee*, pp. 572–74, TSA.

65. Crow, "Political History of the Texas Penal System," p. 178. A brief discussion of women at the Eastham Camp appears in Walker, *Penology for Profit*, pp. 135–36.

66. Old notes, n.d., Idaho State Penitentiary, Women Prisoners' File, ISP.

67. "Warden's Report," 1905–6, Women Prisoners' File, ISP.

68. Ibid.

69. Typically, domestic labor has represented the employment of most women, whether criminals or not. This subject is treated somewhat for English female prisoners in Russell P. Dobash, R. Emerson Dobash, and Sue Gutteridge, *The Imprisonment of Women* (Oxford: Basil Blackwell, 1986).

70. Kremer, "Strangers to Domestic Virtues," pp. 303–4.

71. *Biennial Report to the Governor of Minnesota,* July 31, 1894, p. 37, MnHS.

72. Punishment Record Book, pp. 119, 153, 164, 176, 178, 180, 181, NMSA.

73. Letchworth, *State Boards of Charities,* p. 19.

74. "Matron's Report," *Seventeenth Biennial Report of the Colorado State Penitentiary,* 1910, p. 65, CSA.

75. Statement of Convicts, Prisoner Ledgers A, F, G, H, 1864–1901, passim, KSHS.

76. Punishment Record Book, pp. 119, 176, 178, 180–81, NMSA.

77. Generally, society assumed that women were naturally more passive than men; women criminals were not seen as "dangerous," especially in comparison to men (*The American Prison from the Beginning: A Pictorial History* [n.p.: American Correctional Association, 1983], p. 172).

78. Dobash, Dobash, and Gutteridge, *Imprisonment of Women,* pp. 8–12, 21–23, 39–40, 65–72; Sullivan, *Prison Reform Movement,* p. 20.

79. O'Hare, *Prison Letters,* esp. pp. 15, 19, 35, 43, 51, 69, 71, 80, and 84.

80. Ibid., p. 15.

81. Bettie Boyd to Becca, 22 Oct. 1865, Rebecca Boyd File, Pardon Papers, box 21, folder 16, RG 5, MSA.

82. Ibid.

83. Citizens' Petition, 9 Mar. 1866, ibid. Discharge records show Rebecca Boyd received ten dollars for clothing and ten dollars for discharge on 22 Mar. 1866 (Missouri State Penitentiary, Detailed Statement of Cash Disbursements, 5 Dec. 1865–31 Dec. 1866, Rebecca Boyd, 22 Mar. 1866, "Report of the Inspectors of the Penitentiary," *Appendix, Missouri Twenty-fourth General Assembly,* 1867, MSA).

84. George McIntire to Governor Thomas Fletcher, 5 Dec. 1867, Belle Ragsdale "Colored" File, Pardon Papers, box 25, folder 10, RG 5, MSA.

85. Thomas Fletcher, a Radical Republican, assumed the office of governor on 2 Jan. 1865. He found conditions in Missouri tumultuous after the Civil War and the penitentiary overcrowded and archaic. He expected to use the penitentiary to suppress "lawlessness begotten of treason" and responded favorably to Warden Swift's requests to lease out or pardon women convicts. See Swift's letters to Fletcher and notations on pardon applications, 1865–72, passim, Pardon Papers, RG 5, MSA. Also see Floyd Calvin Shoemaker, *Missouri and Missourians: Land of Contrasts and People of Achievements,* 5 vols. (Chicago: Lewis Publishing, 1943), pp. 934, 954.

86. George McIntire to Governor Thomas Fletcher, 5 Dec. 1867, Belle Ragsdale "Colored" File, Pardon Papers, box 25, folder 10, RG 5, MSA.

87. Catherine Mulleny File, Pardon Papers, box 23, folder 17, RG 5, MSA.

88. Jane Brooks File, Pardon Papers, box 25, folder 26, RG 5, MSA. For other examples of this system in Missouri in the same records see files for Rebecca Boyd, box 21, folder 16; Josephine, box 22, folder 2; Cornelia Mitchell, box 22, folder 37; Mary Weber and Hanora McMara, box 23, folder 7.

89. "Matron's Report," *Biennial Report on the State Penitentiary,* 1877–78, pp. 151–52, MSA.

90. L. A. Whatley, superintendent of the Texas penitentiary, interceded for Bertha Sampson because she had worked as a servant in his house and his nieces were interested in her service (L. A. Whatley to Governor C. A. Culberson, 11 Jan. 1899, Bertha Sampson, no. 5112, Executive Clemency Files, TSA).

91. J. M. Hathaway to Governor J. S. Hogg, 20 Dec. 1894, Maria Mingo, no. 3475, Executive Clemency Files, TSA.

92. Ibid.

93. Ann Cushman, no. 3171, 17 Dec. 1880, Executive Clemency Files, TSA.

94. A. J. Rigsby et al. to Governor L. S. Ross, n.d., Julia Grant, no. 1407, 10 Dec. 1889, Executive Clemency Files, TSA.

95. *Report of the Penitentiary Joint Committee of Arkansas,* 1901, p. 240, ASHC. For a general assessment of the Arkansas penitentiary see Thomas O. Murton, "Observations on the Correctional Needs of the State of Arkansas: A Proposal Prepared for the Arkansas Prison Study Commission." Murton said, "The Arkansas Penitentiary System can best be described as archaic. It remains an isolated remnant of an ancient philosophy of retribution, exploitation, corruption, sadism, and brutality. The sordid history of this penitentiary is indelibly recorded on the bodies of these citizens who had the misfortune to be committed to penal servitude in this barbaric system" (p. 48). Murton, a criminologist, was the subject of the commercial film *Brubaker.* A photocopy of his report is at the Arkansas State History Commission.

In 1919, C. B. James of the Trinity and Brazos Railroad Company applied to hire Lizzie Williams (Colored) for household domestic service in Teague, Texas. Although part of a modernized parole system, the direct hiring of African American women out of the penitentiary for domestic service retained elements of the old lease system in both form and spirit (C. B. James to Judge J. D. Moore, 25 Apr. 1919; Proposed Employer Application, 17 Apr. 1919; J. Willis Pierson to Governor W. P. Hobby, 23 Apr. 1919, Lizzie Williams, no. 568216, Executive Clemency Files, TSA).

96. Kate Richards O'Hare's biographer reported, "The prosecutor told the jury that O'Hare was not a criminal but a dangerous woman, dangerous because she was 'shrewd and brainy'" (Sally M. Miller, *From Prairie to Prison,* p. 150).

7   *Women Prisoners Respond*

I'll fight for my rights if [I] am a lone women.
　　—Eliza Jane Thompson
　　Texas State Penitentiary
　　1885

In 1889, after an imprisonment of seven years, Annie Peterson applied for a pardon on the grounds that, as the only female prisoner in the Nevada penitentiary, she could not "participate in any of the pastimes that the other prisoners enjoy." It is hard to imagine what pastimes any Nevada inmates, male or female, "enjoyed," but two years later Peterson continued to hope for a pardon based on that argument.[1] Her appeal attests to the fact that women prisoners strove to be their own advocates, as they tried to manage their lives in the violent prison world that surrounded them.

Women, using forms of compliance and resistance, fashioned strategies to respond to the conditions they encountered inside male penitentiaries. Their efforts arched across the entire masculine power structure, from guards to governors. Women inmates succeed-

Mollie Ford, Colorado State Penitentiary. Courtesy Division of State Archives and Public Records, Denver, Colo.

199

ed in varying degrees, but they found agency in seemingly small ways. In the main, these efforts allowed women to survive and gave them some measure of control in an environment that offered them little. The responses of women inmates divided into two areas: (1) their direct and indirect participation in legal procedures, which took place outside the penitentiary; and (2) their personal action inside the prison. In concert these two elements demonstrate the way in which women prisoners carved a sliver of gendered space within western penitentiaries.

Women's legal maneuvers faced certain impediments. First, requests for a new trial, a pardon, or a parole took place within the realm of the judicial system. Both literally and figuratively, this legal arena remained beyond the reach of women prisoners. Although many women participated in the preparation of their pardon or parole requests, their incarceration placed them beside rather than in the path of the legal trajectory.

The law required that applications for pardon and parole be submitted to the governor's office. There a secretary assigned each inmate a file number and placed the forms in numerical order for presentation to the board. To have an application moved ahead in the queue entailed sending a special letter of justification to the governor, who might consent to a change in the docket.[2] This cumbersome bureaucratic procedure understandably took months, with governors interested in matters more pressing and politically advantageous than prisoners' paroles. In the meantime, anxious inmates waited months and years for their paperwork, just one request among many, to wend its way through the governor's office and other agencies.

Second, most female inmates were women of color or recent European immigrants, both groups with slim monetary resources. Hindered by pecuniary circumstances, many women had little choice but to rely on the court-appointed defense attorney. Although some lawyers acted in a diligent and professional manner, others undercut a woman's insistence of innocence by urging abandonment of a not-guilty plea and acceptance of the court's sentence.[3] Once the woman had withdrawn her plea and been convicted, her uninterested counselor dropped from sight, and the woman's first attempt to work through the system's procedures had collapsed.

In 1874, when Judge Augustus Cook took up the case of Rosetta Cook, a former slave, he told the Texas governor, "I assigned her counsel . . . and she was (after a fashion) defended." Perhaps the defense counsel found little merit in his client not only because she was an indigent African American woman but because an all-black jury heard her case. Judge Cook had no quarrel with the jury, which acted on the case as presented. He objected, however, to the prosecution's evidence.

The judge thought the convicting testimony tainted, for he considered the state's witness a "vicious old negress who pursues the business of fortune telling . . . conjuring and curing . . . charms" and believed she had been "lying by the whole cloth." Nonetheless, Judge Cook had no proper grounds for granting a new trial, "a motion to that effect having been *neglected*," he grumbled. Based on the laxity of the defense counsel, the judge asked that on "behalf of humanity and the just administration of the law" a pardon be granted, which Rosetta received eleven days later.[4]

Legal intervention by a white judge aided Rosetta Cook, but not every poor woman could depend on such assistance. Maggie Patillo, an African American girl of less than sixteen, served more than four years for infanticide before the district attorney initiated a pardon request for her. T. D. Rowell claimed he had known at the trial that Bettie Patillo, the grandmother, enraged by her young daughter's pregnancy, had left Maggie's newborn by a creek to perish.

According to Rowell, another prosecutor prevailed on Maggie to plead guilty in return for dismissing charges against her mother. Now, with the girl four and a half years into a five-year penitentiary sentence, Rowell took up Maggie's cause, "unknown and unsolicited by any member of her family or friends." He defended Maggie, saying she was "nothing but a common illiterate negro girl and her parents are like her, illiterate and poor." Though Rowell conceded he chose a "late day to write" he felt his "conscience" would be "clear on the subject when it [the pardon] is done."[5]

Rosetta Cook and Maggie Patillo demonstrated the limitations faced by poor women, especially those of color, who asserted their innocence but were pushed through a trial and then could only hope for renewed legal action, either through the appeals court or by a pardon. Those could occur, if a court officer felt keenly about the injustice of a particular case and possessed enough perseverance to direct the matter through the appropriate channels.

Better for the woman inmate if she had some leverage she could use for herself. Annie LeRoy bargained her way to a pardon because the county attorney needed her testimony in a murder trial. The prosecutor called LeRoy an "indispensable witness" for the state and asked for her pardon "as speedily as possible." LeRoy understood the importance of her position and, in an effort to protect it, requested that her discharge papers be returned directly to her.[6]

Rather than wait for a thoughtful judge, a guilt-ridden prosecutor, or a needy district attorney, wise women inmates looked for help in the outside world among those who cared most about them. When twenty-year-old Pearl Smith, a cigar maker, entered the Wyoming penitentiary in 1902, her Denver family, friends, and husband knew nothing of her whereabouts. Pearl, who had disappeared from Denver the previous spring, had simply slipped from sight. Yet, within a month after Pearl's incarceration, the Denver relatives heard of the Wyoming difficulties, and Pearl declared her intention to return to her kin upon release.[7] Immediately, her relatives, a white family of limited education, mounted a letter-writing campaign on her behalf. Pearl's mother, Mrs. B. F. Wade, told the governor, "I plead as only a Mother can," and promised to "send many letters from Good Respectfully [*sic*] people."[8] Neighbors, a local pharmacist, Pearl's former employer, a Denver police officer, and the family doctor inundated Governor DeForest Richards with appeals for the youthful offender.[9]

Although Wyoming officials held a slight opinion of Pearl and her connection to a group of Rawlins shoplifters, they responded with unusual alacrity. For them, releasing Pearl and sending her back to Denver meant Wyoming's burden of a woman inmate became Colorado's headache with a possible thief. Regardless of her earlier relationships with her kinfolk, Pearl made an advantageous move when she enlisted their aid. They did for her what she herself could not organize within the prison. In December, Pearl Smith left Wyoming to return to her family in Denver.[10]

Other women estranged from their relations made decisions similar to Pearl Smith's. In 1902, Kittie Smith, a twenty-eight-year-old black woman with a vagrancy record in California, entered the Nevada penitentiary at Carson City to serve a five-to-eight-year sentence for robbery.[11] Facing hard time in a penitentiary, far different from her jail time in California, Kittie began to work on parole possibilities. Although nearly illiterate, Kittie managed to contact her sister in Portland, Oregon, and ask for family support. In turn, Kittie's sister, Mrs. G. Williams, wrote to Warden Denver S. Dickerson, promising to send fare for her sibling inmate to return to the family in Portland. Before Williams's letter arrived in Carson City, however, Kittie had won the favor of Warden Dickerson's wife, secured her parole, and gone to work in the warden's home.[12] Within a month, Kittie had moved to Reno, Nevada, shortly after to Sacramento, California, on to Klamath Falls, Oregon, and back to Sacramento.

Over nearly a four-year period, Smith, who could barely scratch out two written sentences, religiously sent her monthly parole reports to the Nevada board of pardons. With absolute regularity, Smith informed the board of her ever-changing address, work situation, and health. At the same time, her little letters chronicle a life of menial jobs—work in a laundry, a dry cleaning establishment, scrubbing in private homes, domestic service in a roominghouse—and declining health—arthritis, loss of mobility in her left arm, and finally a major stroke at about the age of thirty-three.[13]

During her wanderings, Kittie Smith, essentially a homeless transient, scrupulously observed the conditions of her parole, thereby protecting herself. Lacking a formal education, she nonetheless understood exactly how to make certain Nevada officials had no reason to rescind her parole and demand the remainder of her eight-year sentence. Although Kittie did not go to Portland to live with her family, she had counted on relatives when an eight-year term in the Nevada penitentiary threatened to overwhelm her. Her sister had assured Warden Dickerson that once Kittie was safely back in Portland, her siblings would "look after her and give her a good home."[14] In that statement, Williams alluded to an important element in the response strategies of black women prisoners.

Black families may not have enjoyed wealth and status by white standards, but they raised a persistent voice to the dominant community for incarcerated family members. After Annie Carmack went to the Kansas penitentiary for murder in 1891, her father endeavored to secure her a pardon, in part because she was under sixteen at the time of the crime. Five years later, with the pardon process at a standstill, Annie's father had the Carmack family Bible notarized to prove his daughter's age.[15] He stayed closely involved in the legal maneuvering and kept informed about the status of Annie's case with the governor. Finally, in 1899, his persistence was rewarded and Annie Carmack received her pardon.

Black families, like Annie Carmack's, that had conformed to the constraints of white society called on their carefully cultivated reputations when daughters, sisters, wives, and mothers faced penitentiary time. They may have recognized the civic limitations placed on their rights, but they knew how to circumvent those and extract support from authorities in the legal community.[16] In 1902 Clara Ewing's husband, "an industrious colored man," generated official and citizen support for her release from the Kansas prison, and Clara wrote the necessary letter to the parole board, expressing her remorse for stealing a child's skirt valued at $2.50.[17]

For several years, William Jordan made appearances before the parole board for his sister, Ella Buckner, a prisoner in the Kansas penitentiary. Ella, sentenced to eleven years for a robbery, contributed her part to the process, writing her own letter to the parole board, promising to "do right."[18] In the same state, Colonel Richard Boyd, a retired Topeka policeman, and his wife, "very estimable old colored people" and "highly respected," represented the main reason their daughter Rose Sullivan should have clemency, according to Kansas governor E. W. Hoch.[19] Well aware that candidates looked for black votes at election time, Boyd had reminded Governor Hoch of the family's past political loyalty. Hoch's expressed admiration for the Boyds did not extend to daughter Rose; two years later, in 1910, Rose Sullivan remained in the Kansas penitentiary.

Although African Americans in all western locations walked an uneasy road, others besides family members stepped forward for those who had clashed with the white power structure. Often at great risk, the black community, demonstrating its fundamental belief in the theory of democracy, pursued measures it hoped would result in relief for African American inmates. Particularly as the distance between slavery and freedom expanded, African Americans widened and deepened the use of their civil rights, even though they often had to depend on white officials to carry out the mechanics of their demands.[20]

In 1887, when Jane Burrell went to the penitentiary for two years on a charge of stealing fifteen dollars, her black neighbors in Palestine, Texas, rallied to her support. They did so using several white residents, most especially Jane's attorney, F. M. Hanks, as their conduits for moving through the legal system. Hanks appealed for Jane on the slanted reasoning that "tho black (she can't help that) she is nevertheless a *woman*."[21] He noted that "like most of her race, she is very poor and . . . unable to employ any counsel for her defense."[22]

Blacks in Palestine, equally poor, joined the effort for Burrell, exercising the right of petition, a bold statement of citizenship in a world aggressively hostile to their culture. All these black men, identified as "colored farmers" on the petition, had their names inscribed by attorney Hanks; thirteen other names, all written in one hand, appeared with the "x" of an illiterate citizen.[23] In addition, several women, restaurant workers without a racial designation, signed the petition. In Palestine race and gender obstacles to citizenship had been suspended in this particular case.

Another voice for release came from Colonel Martin Hinzie, who retained the attorney Hanks for Jane's legal needs. In addition, Hinzie personally wrote to the governor that Jane, "entirely honest and trustworthy in every respect," worked as his house servant for many years. Hinzie, present in Jane's cabin the night of the robbery, declared he had seen the woman sick in bed, unable to carry out the crime.[24]

Jane Burrell's case contained many unanswerable and intriguing questions: why did Hinzie and Hanks insist she was fifty years old, when the prison record listed her age as thirty-five; where and who was the father of Jane's two daughters, ages twelve and nine; for what reason was Hinzie, a "zealous friend" to the governor and a "gentleman of wealth and influence," inside Jane Burrell's cabin the night of the robbery; why was Hinzie willing to hire the attorney F. M. Hanks for a black woman who "had not a cent"; how did it come about that blacks and women in Palestine signed the petition for Jane's release? Less mysterious was the quickness with which blacks and women engaged the instruments of governance when those in control made them accessible.

Twelve years after the struggle of Jane Burrell and her friends to make the system function for a black woman convict, another Texas female confronted similar difficulties. Susie Black, a twenty-two-year-old mother, entered the Texas penitentiary for five years on a charge of second degree murder. Susie, an uneducated cook, had left behind three daughters, ages seven, five, and three, living on "the cold charities of the world" because her husband had deserted the youngsters.[25] With her children's welfare in a precarious state, Susie needed to explore possible avenues for release. In September 1898, Susie wrote to Carthage, Texas, lawyer H. N. Nelson, "I was proud to here [sic] from yo [sic] I am the house girl at Mrs. and Mr. J. S. Price the finantiane [sic] agen [sic] of the Penn [sic] and he sayes [sic] that he will help me so pleas [sic] ask my Jeurre [sic] to have mercy on me and help me pleas [sic]."[26] How Susie made the contact with Nelson remained unclear, but her attempt to engage his services was not.

Attorney Nelson undertook the application, but met with little success. Three months after she had written him, Susie received a discouraging letter in which Nelson said, "Susie, this is the best I can do. . . . it looks like all your friends have forsaken you. I send you Judge Graham's letter so you will see what to do. He will help you in the right way. I hope you will get out—all your jury signed the application."[27] Despite Nelson's suggestion that he had exhausted his efforts, by the spring of 1899 he continued to work on Susie's case.

At that time, three men from the black community filed a citizens' petition, asking that the governor advance Susie Black's place on the pardons docket and restore her quickly to her children. Almost thirty-five years after the end of slavery, the petition of these black citizens depended on validation from white citizens; the county clerk, district clerk, and sheriff vouched for the three African American men as "respectable colored men and . . . worthy of belief."[28] Susie Black, confined within the Texas penitentiary, undertook the action she could from inside the prison, but that action was reinforced by members of her community.

Granted, the outcome, the pardon Susie received in October 1899, depended on the persistence of a white attorney and the support of county officials.[29] That state of dependency changed for black inmates as African Americans gained a greater professional foothold in the twentieth century, and prisoners began to look inside their own culture for legal help. In 1903 a prosecutor in Kansas noted that an extremely ill black prisoner, Jane Williams, had "hired a colored attorney."[30]

The oppressive features of the prison system evoked individual and collective resistance among African Americans. The many inequities in imprisonment for black women, the hardship placed on their children, and the sense of injustice that permeated the community prompted a tenacious response to an overwhelming system. G. McNeal, pastor of the black congregation at the Pleasant Green Baptist Church in Kansas, wrote for Ella Bradfield, describing her family background and promising to find her "permanent and suitable employment . . . freed from criminal influences."[31] In the same state, J. G. Bowers, a black guard in charge of the tower and the gate, wrote about Florence Akers that "her being of my race," he and his wife wanted to help the young woman.[32]

Basically, women inmates of all cultures wrote whatever was expected of them to comply with notions of "reformation" and "remorse" that parole boards wanted to hear. In Missouri, Johanna Smith, supporting three youngsters after her husband left for the Civil War, told the governor, "I confess I did wrong, but if you . . . pardon me so I could go to my poor children, I am certain I would never offend the law again."[33] Mary Deter of Kansas, mother of a fifteen-month-old son, simply took an oath promising never to violate the liquor laws again.[34] In Texas, Mary Jane Profit told the board, "please help me to go home for the 4th of July. . . . And I will never give the state any more trouble."[35] Those with writing skills composed their own letters, hoping to include circumstances that would make their cases irresistible to an invisible parole board. In addition to the expected declaration of a desire to live without further legal troubles, women generally built the rationale for their petitions around one of two notions.

The first of these concerned their health. Given the unsavory conditions in all prisons, a woman usually did not have to stretch the truth when she argued in her petition that her health was rapidly deteriorating. Mollie Forsha told the Nevada governor she could not live long with what she had to endure.[36] Carrie Scott, another prisoner in the Nevada penitentiary, sought clemency from her murder conviction, explaining that two doctors "say . . . I have a tumor in my stomach as large as a man's head and . . . I can never get well unless I have a serious operation."[37] Despite medical documentation of her failing health and legal opinions that Carrie was only a bystander at the murder, she received no pardon until 1911, three years after she came to the Nevada prison.

Women's second rationale involved making a specific gender appeal and announcing the intention to return to "correct" womanly behavior. Jennie Taylor, sentenced in 1880 to the Nevada penitentiary on a charge of assault with intent to kill, called on her earlier good reputation as a "remarkably kind, generous woman to the poor destitute and needy," in her petition for a pardon.[38] That claim, supported by signatures from two hundred of the "best citizens of Humboldt County," helped to earn Jennie a pardon less than four months after she entered prison.

Minnie Haywood, convicted of keeping a disorderly house in Austin, Texas, turned to the members of a local women's society for endorsement of her reformation. In so doing she selected an outspoken organization, striving to "rescue women from a life of shame and to lift them to a better life."[39] Minnie, with the assistance of the rescue society, won a release from jail and agreed to try a different life path. On the advice of the treasurer of the rescue society, Mrs. J. L. Vendenburgh, Minnie took work managing a roominghouse in San Antonio, Texas. Despite this good turn of events, fines of more than $200 from her conviction in Austin still hung over Minnie's head.

Minnie faced the loss of everything, as well as reimprisonment, unless the board of pardons granted a remission of her fines. Alone in San Antonio and uncertain of how to bring about the needed pardon, Minnie turned to her friend, Vendenburgh. Minnie wrote, "I am working very hard and doing all I can to try to . . . do right. Poor girls are to be pitied. I am glad you say you have confidence in me."[40] In another letter, she agonized over whether she should tell her new pastor in San Antonio about her troubled past and wondered why the minister who headed the parole board never bothered to contact her.[41]

At this point, Vendenburgh, who vehemently opposed "confessing all" to the new associates in San Antonio, moved into action. She sent a blistering letter to the Reverend W. C. Denson, whose board had the last say in requesting the remission of fines from the governor. In her letter, Vendenburgh remarked: "'*Justice delayed* is *justice denied*' and it seems to me it is putting a premium on non-reformation to put no confidence in a person's . . . struggling as this poor woman is doing. Is it *Christian* like? It *is* man like. . . . Let her bury her past and tell no one—*men* don't have to confess their past. . . . I am getting full of righteous indignation at the delay. . . . what more do you . . . men need?"[42]

Vendenburgh's pointed remarks apparently lit a fire under the slow-moving Reverend Denson. Minnie Haywood's pardon from fines came from the governor's office on 9 July 1896. Although Minnie had not quite known how to expedite the legal process and though poor health, work demands, precarious finances, and loneliness weighed on her, she perceived that she could use the resources of the rescue society. To guarantee Vendenburgh's support required that Minnie act in accord with the moral expectations of the rescue society, or at least appear to do so. Those moral standards may indeed have become her choice, as when she told Reverend Denson, "I am living a different life. I never expect to go back to that wicked life any more."[43]

Regardless, Minnie Haywood knew how to frame the language of her letters to conform to the standards of those granting the pardon. She lacked, however, the added consideration a woman could request if she had dependent children. In 1899, Mrs. M. L. Loveless wrote to the Texas governor asking him to "hear the prayer of a friendless woman . . . a widow and mother of three children."[44] Loveless owned a small bakery where she sold sweets and cider, a combination that led her to about a dozen violations of the liquor laws. In a state where pro- and anti-prohibition forces engaged in heated battle, Loveless brought down a torrent of local political wrath on her head. Among a series of letters written against her, one claimed, "She has caused more trouble than any other half dog out-laws in this county. . . . Her children are better off with her in jail. . . . She is known to be wholly depraved by the best citizens . . . and not entitled to any consideration."[45]

Loveless admitted to the charges against her, but cloaked her actions in motherhood, telling the governor, "I want to go home to my children. Penury and want drove [me] to *do for them what no* mother can refrain from doing for her children crying for bread."[46] Further, she invoked her status as a widow and her "duty" to her deceased husband to "care for and support" his children.

After Loveless had been incarcerated for almost six months, Governor Sayers approved her pardon for remission of fees. She joined those women who successfully engaged the petition process and won release from prison. Not all women saw their appeals brought to a positive resolution. Many were turned back or earned their freedom only after several petitions. Whatever the outcome, the process of formulating appeals and writing letters involved women in the legalities from which most had been excluded at the time of trial. Some wrote letters dictated by attorneys, while others composed their own words. Doing so forced even those with limited literacy to write out the events of the crime, to explain their actions. The pardon and parole procedures, though imperfect and acted on far from the penitentiary, engaged women's minds and filled a part of the seemingly endless time in a prison day. In a system where women had little power, parole applications helped to restore some sense of personal agency, often lost after a trial and imprisonment. Above all, the process gave women hope—the promise of release from the male penitentiary world and for many a deserved legal vindication.

Women did not only focus their responses to prison life on the outside world and the procedures by which they might be freed. Day to day routines inside the penitentiary demanded strategies for survival. Inside the walls, women prisoners took action designed to control their lives. They did this by cultivating an attitude of compliance or one of resistance. Each offered women prisoners benefits and risks.

Women inmates found some advantage to accepting prison routines without overt complaint. When confined to small "female apartments," a practice that became more widespread as prisons entered the twentieth century, women could improve several aspects of their lives. Inside women's quarters, rules about inmates talking among themselves tended to be relaxed. If officials assigned women inmates the task of cooking their own meals, rather than eating whatever came from the main kitchen, the diet became more palatable. Women found sewing and mending for themselves boring, but far less arduous than the quarry and factory labor of the men.[47] Although deprived of regular physical exercise, women with good behavior ratings were more likely to be allowed an evening walk than male inmates.[48]

In Utah the warden told Belle Harris to choose which two hours of the day she preferred for a stroll about the grounds. On a particularly beautiful Sunday afternoon he permitted Belle to walk along the prison wall and look down on the male prisoners.[49] Compliance was the price for these privileges, and such did not come easily to Belle. She remarked: "I have a perfect war with myself to keep quiet and be calm with the insulting humiliation to which I am subjected."[50]

What Belle and other women tried for were the larger benefits they could secure through compliance. In Texas, Delia Goodwin, sentenced to seven years for murder, "conducted herself very well; so much so that she has been trusted by the officers to go outside of the prison limits."[51] In her petition to the governor, Delia, who stabbed a man in self-defense, wrote from the Huntsville penitentiary, "I can get some of the most influential citizens of this place . . . to approve of my pardon."[52] Delia's decision to follow a path of absolute conformity brought her personal advantages not usually enjoyed by convicted murderers.

In addition, compliance allowed women to avoid physical abuse. A Missouri matron spoke of the "absolute obedience" expected from women inmates and the effectiveness of a sharp word.[53] Verbal corrections carried the implied threat of more severe measures from guards. Kate Richards O'Hare told her family, "I can never forget the feeling of sick horror that swept over me when I was reprimanded for saying, 'Good morning' to a woman who nodded to me as we were forming in line."[54] Wardens who reported, as did Minnesota's in 1892, that women prisoners were "quiet and orderly, submissive to all the rules and regulations" overlooked the way inmates used docility to soften daily life and avoid harsh punishments.[55]

Women also used gender cooperation as a method of securing benefits for themselves. When Josie Kensler, advanced in pregnancy, entered the Idaho penitentiary in 1897, she cultivated her image as a middle-class "lady" who passed her time doing fancy needlework. A clever and independent thinker, Josie carefully constructed a persona that would suggest that criminal activity was utterly foreign to her. Several years after her confinement, Josie exuded motherly concern for a new cellmate, sixteen-year-old Ida Laherty, and spoke of the good example she hoped to be for the younger inmate.[56] Faced with a life sentence for the murder of her husband, Josie may have originally deduced the value of docile conduct after the warden invited her to take her first prison meal in the comfort of his private quarters.

This civil start aside, difficulty marked Josie's imprisonment. A daugh-

ter, born in July, was taken away and placed up for adoption; five years later Josie became pregnant a second time. As a complex prison scandal unfolded, Josie used the interest of newspaper reporters to charge that her
former dining companion, the warden, had forced her to allow the prison
doctor to perform an abortion.[57]

The explosive case took more twists as Josie, alluding to further intimidation by authorities, withdrew her charges and then recanted the retrac-
tion. Through several months of investigation, Josie Kensler did her best to
negotiate this embarrassing situation for prison officials into a release for
herself. Although that did not occur until 1909, Josie Kensler relied on her
wits to improve each crisis of the moment during her imprisonment.

Josie Kensler used both intellectual strategy and physical compliance as
tools to help herself in prison. Other women did so as well, always with an
eye to bettering nearly intolerable living conditions. To do so they aligned
themselves when possible with the most powerful of the men at a prison—
the warden and the guards. Other male personnel, especially penitentiary
physicians and chaplains, proved less helpful as advocates inside the walls.
Both were not only gubernatorial political appointees but dependent on
cordial relations with wardens and superintendents to retain their positions.[58] By and large they confined themselves to pedestrian annual reports
that either ignored or barely hinted at the disastrous conditions for wom-
en prisoners.[59] On more than one occasion their disinterest declined to
such a degree of professional compromise that they earned only the distrust and scorn of the inmates.[60] Kate Richards O'Hare wrote of the chaplain at the Missouri penitentiary: "The dislike I feel towards the chaplain
here is . . . because he is unfaithful to his trust. He is hired . . . to look after
the moral and spiritual welfare of the women . . . and they are absolutely
neglected. . . . Not the slightest personal interest, not a word of help or sympathy or comfort to the soul-sick and heartbroken."[61]

Women could not depend on the peripheral officials, who visited the
prison on an irregular basis. They needed to connect with those with whom
they had daily contact. These alliances promised both physical protection
and material goods. Barbara Jones, a cook in the home of the prison lessee,
Colonel L. A. Ellis, had so much favor with Huntsville prison authorities
that one penned her letter to the Texas governor. With its elaborate phras-
ing and elegant penmanship, the letter, an unlikely product for a young
black woman in 1881, added to the supporting petitions from Ellis and his
spouse, as well as the prison superintendent Major Thomas J. Goree and his
wife.[62]

These alliances, although useful, had the potential to compound a
woman's problems and place her in an awkward position. In New Mexico,
inmate Ada Hulmes found herself caught in a penitentiary investigation

that centered on a former warden, Thomas P. Gable. Gable had stepped down in 1887 amid charges that he falsified payroll reports, inventories, and financial accounts. Further, his opponents said that as there were no female inmates incarcerated during his administration, Gable imported women and ran the prison as "a common bawdy house."[63] Four years later, by which time had Ada Hulmes and several other women had entered the prison, Gable, who had gone on to serve in the territorial house of representatives, continued to be under fire for instigating an unfavorable report against the assistant superintendent, José Manuel Montoya.

Central to the many charges was the role of Ada Hulmes, a thirty-one-year-old Anglo inmate. Montoya's foes maintained that she traded sexual favors for special privileges from the superintendent. Around Santa Fe, Gable and his associates helped to spread a rumor that Ada had her own private room, furnished with a piano.

Under questioning Ada denied both privileged rank and sexual misconduct. She insisted she had no piano in her quarters and she had not been intimate with Montoya and a guard, Luis Alarid. Her testimony about her prison accommodations seemed less convincing, for she asserted that women inmates shared the female apartments equally, two to a room. She explained her private room as a choice made by the Spanish-speaking prisoners who didn't care to associate with an Anglo and seemed "to want to stay together."[64] The superintendent, E. W. Wynkoop, described the crowded arrangement for the other inmates as a "privilege" for the Hispanic women.[65]

Whatever Ada Hulmes's experiences, she appeared to be in the midst of a political triangle that included the ousted Thomas P. Gable, the present administration, and several Anglo prisoners who wanted Montoya, the assistant superintendent, removed.[66] Gable referred to the Hispanic employees of the prison as "damned . . . sheepherders," who would never let Hulmes out of prison.[67] Apparently, Gable tried to have a letter, in which he outlined his plan against Montoya, slipped to Hulmes during prison visiting hours. Hulmes, he expected, as the sole Anglo female inmate, would see the benefits of aligning with a member of the house of representatives, who would be able to advance the ever-desired pardon. Hulmes had to decide which camp offered the best for her. With no guarantee of release, Ada Hulmes took the prudent course and denied any intimate involvement with prison staff. She safely calculated that authorities would not want her around for long after all the public attention.

In Arizona, Pearl Hart, a twenty-eight-year-old Canadian native, handled her involvement with prison men a bit differently. Sentenced to five years in the Arizona penitentiary at Yuma, Hart was released in 1902 after three years of confinement. That it was many years before a former territorial official admitted the early release avoided a pregnancy scandal suggests Pearl had indicated forcefully she was ready to implicate penitentiary personnel.[68] Although Arizona aficionados like to chuckle about the fact that no one bothered to seek a medical confirmation of the pregnancy, some prison official must have known Pearl's claim was a possibility.[69]

An intentional pregnancy could serve as one way to freedom for women prisoners, but the long-range difficulties for an inmate were enormous. The strategy could backfire, and then the inmate looked ahead to a daunting experience of pregnancy and childbirth inside the penitentiary. Should the child survive, separation and adoption were the options for the inmate mother.

Opposite the Josie Kenslers, Pearl Harts, and Ada Hulmeses, other women inmates took more aggressive action to counter the male authority surrounding them. Although escapes did not include the glamorized "jail breaks" of fiction, women did manage to slip away from their jailers. Their departures appeared to have been spontaneous events, where they took advantage of official neglect. Women walked away from work farms, bolted through poorly maintained walls, disappeared from domestic service. Between 1897 and 1914, six women prisoners, all African Americans, escaped from the Arkansas system; none were reported as recaptured.[70]

Not all women succeeded in eluding the authorities when they escaped, a measure taken after other strategies had failed. In Texas, Lizzie Plummer, a young black woman, originally found herself ensnared by the law when she was questioned concerning an unlawful abortion. Lizzie maintained she had not been pregnant and thus could not have had an abortion.

The root of Lizzie's case lay within the black community. Although the charges and counter charges seem trivial one hundred years later, at stake were issues of power, status, and the search for common values for black Americans. As rumor of pregnancy spread through the black church and local social club, the lodge to which Lizzie belonged formed a committee to investigate the situation.[71] Without warning, the women of the committee went to the home of Martha Banton, Lizzie's mother. Later the unannounced visitors swore that they found Lizzie in labor.[72] The lodge members had agreed that, if they discovered Lizzie, recently installed as secretary, to be pregnant, she would have to resign or be expelled.

The intrusion of this zealous group into the home of Lizzie's mother generated understandable resistance from all who lived there. One committee member pleaded with Lizzie's mother, who also held office in the club, to understand that the visitors were "merely trying to protect the lodge."[73] The committee failed to explain why the lodge allowed Lizzie to take office late in May, if by 15 June she was at least six months pregnant, as her accusers appeared to claim.

Citizens for the defense noted that puzzle as well. Family members, neighbors, and a mélange of white citizens came to Lizzie's defense, including her dressmaker, her mother's employer, and a piano merchant and his clerk. Each of these testified that she or he could determine pregnancy by appearance and that Lizzie had not been enceinte when seen about Austin in the spring of 1894.[74] No clear evidence was produced that an abortion had occurred or a premature infant had been born. Lizzie claimed that she had suffered from a severe headache the night of the committee visit. Even the sheriff and constable, who admitted they had searched the Banton home and torn up floorboards without a search warrant, testified they found nothing of a birth or a deceased child.[75] Despite the weak case against her—no physical evidence was ever recovered—Lizzie was convicted of perjury and sent to Huntsville for five years.

Lizzie, who had languished in the county jail for over nine months, had little reason to believe she would be released from the penitentiary in a speedy fashion. The pardon and parole process moved forward at its usual pace. Petitions included the arguments that the grand jury had possibly failed to advise Lizzie Plummer of her protection against self-incrimination and the jurors' assessment that "it is not unlawful for a woman to produce an abortion of herself."[76]

No doubt Lizzie, "a member of one of the best negro families in Travis County," distraught by the public humiliation of the trial testimony and a gynecological examination performed in the county jail, felt panic at the long prison sentence.[77] Before her pardon documents could be delivered to the penitentiary, Lizzie Plummer, who had served eleven months in a male penitentiary, escaped. Her pardon was revoked, and she was recaptured and returned to the penitentiary for another three months.[78]

Lizzie Plummer endured physical and emotional violence over a period of many months. Finally she struck back and took flight. Once she was apprehended, she lost access to the instrument of pardon that exonerated her from the fanciful court proceedings. The governor's office agreed the original imprisonment was faulty but determined Lizzie Plummer should now be punished for violation of prison regulations, which she should never have had to follow in the first place.

The patent unfairness of such episodes fueled the defiance of women. As prisoners lived through these experiences and watched other female inmates around them treated accordingly, their resistance to the blistering constraints rose. While not everyone had the opportunity or wherewithal to escape physically, many knew how to make verbal resistance their chief weapon.

In 1915, Lizzie Woodfolk, an African American cook serving seven to ten years for manslaughter, created havoc in the Nevada penitentiary and appeared to know exactly why she was doing that. Lizzie Woodfolk stood up for herself. First, she sent word to the warden that she was pregnant, but when that was disproved, her strategy turned physical and hostile. Her behavior became so erratic that the warden arranged an insanity hearing for her at the first judicial district court. Testimony from both the officer in charge of the women's department and Woodfolk herself indicated that she had thrown food out of her window, tried to kick down her door, struck a guard, and attacked another woman inmate with a stick.

Lizzie's remarks before the district court judge and medical panel hardly seemed to be the wanderings of a mentally unstable person. She described her "bad behavior" as a response to the rough treatment she received from guards. Lizzie complained that certain guards swore at her, brought her dirty water and filthy food, harassed her sexually, knocked her down, and terrorized her. She told her examiners, "I have showed respect to these people here, but I won't have them sass at me." She particularly objected to guards' remarks about her moral standards, saying, "I am a woman in prison, but I am kind of half way respectable." Looking to her future, Lizzie added, "My name has been scattered and slandered all over town . . . and I have to work for my living."[79]

The clash with her cellmate Lizzie attributed to the woman's practice of making remarks to the guards about Lizzie's sexuality. Insulted, Lizzie defended her throttling attack on the other female inmate, expressing her expectations of the correct comportment of a white woman by saying, "Any woman of her race that will go around and holler things about a colored woman needs killing."[80]

Ultimately, Lizzie Woodfolk gave words to the simple expectation of all prisoners that a penitentiary should have its limits when she told the judge, "if you mistreat a prisoner, you can't get no good out of them." Woodfolk did not claim that she was perfect or innocent, but she did insist on a prisoner's right to dignity. Nevada resolved the case by transferring her to the insane asylum, where she lived without incident until she secured a parole in November 1917.[81]

As for Lizzie's much-hated cellmate, the woman apparently utilized her own plan for survival inside the Nevada penitentiary. That white inmate clearly decided to protect her interests by teaming up with the all-Anglo male staff against Woodfolk. In an "us against her" environment, the second prisoner had a chance to capitalize on Lizzie's disruptive behavior as a measure of her own better conduct, a circumstance that might bring her improved food, warmer blankets, or longer recreation time. Indeed, the guards at the Woodfolk hearing presented the second inmate as the "injured" party in the brawl, without mention of how she might have added to the ill will. This prisoner had, at least temporarily, deflected the negative attention of her jailors to Lizzie Woodfolk.

Living arrangements and the small number of women did not allow for a great deal of group action. Still those opportunities did arise on occasion. In January 1894 twenty African American women and one white woman, prisoners at the Missouri penitentiary, banded together and refused to work or return to their cells. Their punishments included as many as seven lashes and several days on a diet of bread and water. One woman, Jane Hunter, added "swearing" to her part in the demonstration, which officials labeled as a "riot." The lash and bread and water aside, two days later, another inmate joined two of the rioters as the three continued the protest.[82]

Typically, punishment registers gave witness to the ways in which women inmates expressed their distaste for the conditions in male penitentiaries. Unjust experiences in the courts did not put women into the most agreeable frame of mind when they encountered yet another layer of male authority. Individually and collectively they found ways to strike back at the prison system.

While women might not always have had the physical strength to tangle with male guards, they made good use of their vocal skills to express protest. A sarcastic answer, a shouted curse, a murmured insult—these shot forth quickly, disrupted prison routines, and were often difficult for guards to pinpoint. Women inmates knew how to wage a verbal war.

During the six years Ella Bradfield spent inside the Kansas penitentiary, she accumulated a lengthy disciplinary record for just such vocal offenses. She violated prison rules in a number of ways—quarreling in her workplace or at table, speaking up to guards and directly disobeying their orders, refusing to keep the silence rule after the evening lockup.[83] Such women, identified as "troublemakers," went to the dark hole and lost precious days of "good time," thereby hurting their chances for early release, but perhaps buoying their spirits.[84]

Those gains may have hurt in the long run for a favorable parole hearing depended on a good conduct record or the willingness of the warden to agree that one existed. Annie Carmack did not have such a clean slate. Received at the penitentiary in January of 1891, Carmack refused to settle into the mode of the docile prisoner. By March she had been punished for threatening an assistant matron who refused to excuse an inmate friend from punishment. Over the next three years, Annie Carmack resorted to insolence, quarreling, work slowdowns, and violence to press back against the conditions around her.[85]

These acts of resistance came with heavy penalties. In the 1880s, Sarah Johnson, who entered the penitentiary at the age of sixteen, used "insolence and impudence" and fighting, as well as writing a note, to circumvent regulations. She paid with four whippings of twenty-five, twenty, fifteen, and twenty strokes.[86] Also in Texas, Caroline Williams received ten, fifteen, and ten lashes for her three occasions of "impudence" and "laziness."[87]

In New Mexico, the penitentiary seethed with defiance and misconduct. Although inside the walls at New Mexico cultural antagonisms could run high,[88] the establishing of friendly and romantic relationships between men and women prisoners crossed Mexican American/Anglo lines. Invigorated by these attachments, at every opportunity women inmates joined with men in making the prison a center of constant rule violation.

Prisoners P. J. O'Donnell and F. Butler both went to the dark cell for delivering illicit mail to and from the women.[89] Jim Black and Cabe Adams were confined in their cells for waving their hands and making faces at the women prisoners, instead of concentrating on their task of peeling vegetables. José Romiro and Prudencio Trujillo were chained to the door for five days for laughing and making motions at the women during chapel services.[90] Francesco Romano lost his trusty status and went to solitary for two days for talking with the women prisoners at night.[91] John Smith served as a regular Cupid's messenger, carrying notes to all women and contributing his own, "writing loving and vulgar notes to the female convicts." He brought cigarettes and matches to Juana Chacón; she allowed him to hug and kiss her, as others distracted the matron.[92]

Women engaged in these illegal interactions with vigor and imagination. Female inmates cut holes in the kitchen screens to pass out locks of their hair to be woven into chains and accepted contraband tobacco, paper, and pencils. They wrote notes to the men and to each other every chance they got—in the dining hall or the chapel, in the yard or at the privy.

Every place, every moment was an opportunity. Magdalena Cabalbos lost her tobacco and other privileges for two weeks because she stood in the prison yard and stared at some visitors.[93] Juana Chacón was confined in the closet for one day and lost two days good time for receiving a note hidden at the slop bucket; Anna Freeman went to the closet for three days and lost thirty days good time for sending the missive.[94] Juana quickly found other ways to break the rules, hauling a knife tied to a piece of string into the women's ward through a window. Perhaps she wanted to treasure it as a love-token, hide it as a weapon, cut a piece of fruit, or simply refuse obedience.

These actions gave prisoners the sense that they did not totally yield to the shackles of prison regulation. Women, in their small numbers, developed community and perhaps even an occasional touch of merriment. In this they employed long-held traditions of humor used by groups that face oppression or alienation.[95] Their witticisms were for a small audience—just themselves—but they offered comfort drawn from shared experience. When women banded together to laugh about their circumstances or, more likely, the men who oversaw them, they vented at least some of the anger and frustration that came with penitentiary time.[96]

They needed humor to offset the grim punishments with which guards greeted their offenses. Further, prisoner bonding through defiance gave them all courage when the more dreary styles of resistance surfaced. These came unexpectedly and threatened to depress the spirit of all.

They took the form of self-mutilation or suicide, unpleasant reminders of the kinds of choices women were prepared to make to retain control of their lives. Anna Freeman managed to slow her work by claiming a leg ailment that was found to be self-induced. Freeman tied a strip of gingham tightly around her calf, stopping circulation and causing swelling and discoloration. For her action and her pain, Anna Freeman lost thirty days good time and thus lengthened her sentence.[97]

For those who could no longer think of ways to thwart the environment or endure another round of whipping and dark cell torture, suicide offered the ultimate resistance.[98] Prisoner no. 1270 of the Nebraska penitentiary made the most forceful, if desperate, statement about women's penitentiary time. Only nine months into her sentence for manslaughter, she managed to secrete a weapon, cut her throat, and move forever beyond the prospects of twenty-five years inside a male prison.[99]

Within this difficult atmosphere women found their voice and in small ways, sometimes at a painful price, responded to the prison system and its grueling routines. Some turned to the judicial system they had stumbled over and strengthened their minds by engaging the legal procedures that might free them. Some negotiated with officials and carved out the best possible penitentiary time for themselves. Others, through individual resistance, open defiance, and conspiracy, demonstrated their contempt for the unmitigated regimentation and brutality.

Of course, some of their best ploys must be those never to be known. These included the ignored regulations, sexual trysts, petty arsons, slowed work, silent glances, ruined sewing, stolen materials, coded gestures, broken dishes, pilfered food, swiped cigarettes, and contraband liquor that were never detected by prison officials. These daily subterfuges did not make their way into the disciplinary register. Nor did prison officials really want to admit how successfully prisoners could elude detection and how relentlessly they refused to accept prison conditions. Perhaps these invisible victories gave women, not so tractable as officials wanted to boast, their greatest feeling of personal action, thus infusing them with the needed spirit to survive.

When they chose to and they could, women protected each other, and they forged conspiratorial friendships with male inmates. They returned violence with violence, both verbal and physical. It was certainly a human exchange with which they were well acquainted. Although such behavior gave them the satisfaction of challenging the oppressive circumstances, the subsequent punishments could be fierce.

Overall, women's responses should not be exaggerated. Very real constraints, including chains and whips, kept the actions of women prisoners limited. The most aggressive respondents—those who fought back or exposed prison corruption to outside investigators—risked the most severe retaliation from the authorities. Often female inmates had only their sexual availability as a bargaining chip within the prison world, as so graphically described in 1910 by the African American women inmates in Texas.[100] In such an environment, a vast range of attractive choices did not surround women inmates.

The weeping and broken women who lived with Kate Richards O'Hare in the Missouri penitentiary gave witness to the inflexible power wielded by the state in western penitentiaries. Even the informed, strong-minded O'Hare herself faltered after months in the constricting atmosphere. That less-privileged women prisoners raised a protest in any form and for any amount of time speaks to the great resilience in the human spirit.

Notes

1. Annie Peterson File, 1 May 1891, Board of Pardons Files, NSCMA.

2. N. A. Cravens to H. N. Nelson, 8 Mar. 1899, Susie Black, no. 5455, Executive Clemency Files, TSA.

3. Women's poverty placed them at a disadvantage in securing legal representation. In 1896 Emma Banta, sentenced to six months for shoplifting, wrote to the governor that her lawyer asked for twenty-five dollars if he was to represent her, but she, the mother of eight children, said, "[I] havte [*sic*] a sent [*sic*]" (Emma Banta to Governor ——, 21 Mar. 1896, Emma Banta File, box 6, Pardon and Parole Files, KSHS).

4. Judge Augustus Cook to Governor Richard Coke, 5 Jan. 1874, Rosetta Cook, no. 1370, Executive Clemency Files, TSA. Rosetta Cook's pardon is dated 16 Jan. 1875. There could have been a lapse of a year between Judge Cook's letter and her release, but that seems unlikely, since Judge Cook had instructed the sheriff to postpone sending Rosetta Cook to the penitentiary until the governor could respond. Apparently, Judge Cook, writing at the start of a new year, misdated his letter to the governor.

5. T. D. Rowell to Governor J. S. Hogg, 28 Nov. 1893, Maggie Patillo, no. 16091, Executive Clemency Files, TSA.

6. Edward D. May to the Honorable Joseph D. Sayers, 10 July 1899, Annie LeRoy, no. 5324, Executive Clemency Files, TSA.

7. Mrs. G. S. Sayton to Governor DeForest Richards, 8 Sept. 1902; Warden J. P. Hehn to Governor DeForest Richards, 23 Nov. 1902, Pearl Smith File, Petitions for Pardon, Governor DeForest Richards, WSAHD.

8. Mrs. B. F. Wade to Governor Richards, 8 Sept. 1902, ibid.

9. Mrs. M. V. Benson to the Governor of Wyoming, n.d.; Mrs. R. R. Bronley to Mr. Richards, 7 Sept. 1902; L. L. McMahan to Mr. Governor Richards, 8 Sept. 1902; Thomas Lambie to Governor Richards, 9 Sept. 1902; A. A. Bodine to the Governor of Wyoming, 9 Sept. 1902; Officer Grant to Governor Richards, 4 Sept. 1902, notarized statement of N. D. Estes, M. D., 12 Sept. 1902, all in ibid.

10. Apparently Pearl Smith's criminal difficulties continued in Denver. In 1905, a Maggie Raymond, whose court file also shows the name "Pearl Smith," was arrested on a charge of stealing four dollars and released on her husband's collateral of his "tools and carpenter utensils" (Defendant's Recognizance, 16 Aug. 1905, Maggie Raymond File, no. 17164, 21 Aug. 1905, Arapahoe County District Court, Criminal Division, CSA).

11. Criminal History Record of Kittie Smith, a.k.a. Katie Smith, Department of Justice, Bureau of Criminal Identification, 5 Feb. 1913; Commitment Papers, Kitty Smith, no. 9221, 20 Nov. 1912, Kittie Smith File, Board of Pardons Files, NSCMA.

12. The Dickersons were prominent in Nevada politics. Denver S. Dickerson, a native of California, served in the Spanish-American War, and held several political offices in Nevada before being elected lieutenant governor. When the governor died in 1908, Dickerson was acting governor until 1911. In 1913, he accepted a post as warden of the penitentiary, where he was committed to prison improvement (James G. Scrugham, ed., *Nevada: A Narrative of the Conquest of a Frontier Land,* 3 vols. [Chicago: American Historical Society, 1935], vol. 1, p. 437; *Biennial Report of the Warden of the Nevada State Prison,* 1913–14, p. 32, NSL.

13. Kittie Smith to the Board of Pardons, Monthly Reports, 1 Oct. 1913–10 May 1917, Kittie Smith File, Board of Pardons Files, NSCMA.

14. Mrs. G. Williams to Warden Dickson [*sic*], 14 Dec. 1913, ibid.

15. Cormack Deposition, 22 Aug. 1896, Annie Cormack [correct spelling Carmack] File, box 25, Pardon and Parole Files, KSHS.

16. Certainly other ethnic families lobbied for their imprisoned family members, despite difficulties caused by governmental barriers. In 1915, Valentina Madrid's brother wrote in Spanish his request that his sister be released from the New Mexico penitentiary. Attributing her crime to her "ignorance and bad companions," the brother promised the parole board that Valentina could join him and their father at the family ranch and perform domestic service (R. L. Barelá to Miguel Otíro, 22 Feb. 1915, Valentina Madrid, no. 2158, Inmate Files, no. 2158, NMSA; trans. James Feldman).

17. Citizens' Petition; Clara Ewing to Parole Board, 1 May 1903, Clara Ewing File, box 41, Pardon and Parole Files, KSHS. For other husbands pleading for wives, see files of Mary Wash, box 13, folder 51, and Mary Higgins, box 17, folder 1, Pardon Papers, RG 5, MSA.

18. Warden Haskell to Governor E. W. Hoch, 9 Apr. 1907; Ella Buckner to Governor E. W. Hoch, Ella Buckner File, box 17, Pardon and Parole Files, KSHS.

19. Governor E. W. Hoch Re: Case of Rose Sullivan, 23 Dec. 1908, Rose Sullivan File, box 130, Pardon and Parole Files, KSHS.

20. Clearly, the enfranchisement of African Americans moved at a disjointed pace in the West. Even as blacks attained political place, white forces countered their gains by backhanded tactics. In 1898 a Texas attorney, Ben S. Rogers, undertook the application of a destitute German woman, Ernestine Falk, convicted of keeping a disorderly house. Rogers told the governor, "I have prepared her petition gratis and secured the signatures of the County officers, including the Commissioners of the County (except the 'darkey' [*sic*])" (Ben S. Rogers to Governor Charles A. Culberson, 17 Dec. 1898, Ernestine Falk, no. 5145, Executive Clemency Files, TSA).

21. F. M. Hanks to Governor L. S. Ross, 26 May 1887, Jane Burrell, no. 642, Executive Clemency Files, TSA.

22. F. M. Hanks to Governor L. S. Ross, 26 May 1887, and F. M. Hanks in Citizens' Petition to Governor L. S. Ross, n.d., ibid.

23. Ibid.

24. Martin Hinzie to Governor L. S. Ross, 26 May 1887, ibid.

25. Petition of Sam Flake, Sid James, and Cash Black to Governor Joseph D. Sayers, 4 Apr. 1899, Susie Black, no. 5455, Executive Clemency Files, TSA.

26. Susie Black to H. N. Nelson, 10 Sept. 1898, ibid.

27. H. N. Nelson to Susie Black, 14 Dec. 1898, ibid.

28. Citizens' Petition, n.d., ibid.

29. Pardon Statement of Susie Black, no. 19140, 13 Oct. 1899, ibid.

30. Statement from County Attorney ———, 9 May 1903, Jane Williams File, box 146, Pardon and Parole Files, KSHS.

31. Parole application form and letter, Pastor G. McNeal, 16 Oct. 1904, Ella Bradfield File, box 13, Pardon and Parole Files, KSHS. Other clergy with a prison mission also assisted women inmates, both black and white. See Margaret Russell File, box 115, and Bertha Draper File, box 36, Pardon and Parole Files, KSHS.

32. J. G. Bowers to Governor Walter Stubbs, 18 Mar. 1910, Florence Akers File, box 1, Pardon and Parole Files, KSHS.

33. Johanna Smith to Governor Thomas Fletcher, 14 Feb. 1865, Sarah Fleming, Johanna Smith, Elizabeth Woolman File, box 19, folder 8, Pardon Papers, RG 5, MSA.

34. Mary Deter File, 14 Apr. 1890, box 34, Pardon and Parole Files, KSHS.

35. Mary Jane Profit to Mr. Fritz Smith, 20 June 1920, Mary Jane Profit, no. 57675, Executive Clemency Files, TSA.

36. Mollie Forsha to Governor Bradley, Apr. ? [1874], Board of Pardons Files, NSCMA.

37. Carrie I. Scott File, 14 Nov. 1911, Board of Pardons Files, NSCMA.

38. Appeal for Pardon Document, n.d., Jennie Taylor File, Board of Pardons Files, NSCMA.

39. Citizens' Petition to Governor Charles Culberson, Minnie Haywood, no. 4071, Executive Clemency Files, TSA.

40. Minnie Haywood to Mrs. J. L. Vendenburgh, 13 May 1896, ibid.

41. Minnie Haywood to Mrs. J. L. Vendenburgh, 25 May 1896, ibid.

42. Mrs. J. L. Vendenburgh to Brother Denson, 30 May 1896, ibid.

43. Minnie Haywood to Reverend W. C. Danson, 8 June 1896, ibid.

44. Mrs. M. L. Loveless to Governor J. D. Sayers, 8 Mar. 1899, Mrs. M. L. Loveless, no. 5215, Executive Clemency Files, TSA.

45. W. A. Brooks to Governor C. A. Culberson, 10 Jan. 1899, letter received by Governor J. D. Sayers and sent to the Board of Pardons, 27 Jan. 1899, ibid.

46. Mrs. M. L. Loveless to Governor J. D. Sayers, 8 Mar. 1899, ibid.

47. Letchworth, *State Boards of Charities,* p. 19.

48. Heilbron, *Convict Life at the Minnesota State Prison,* p. 101.

49. Albert Silas Harris, "Life of Belle Harris Nelson," pp. 45, 77, CLDS.

50. Ibid., p. 64.

51. Citizens' Petition, n.d., Delia Goodwin, no. 1275, Executive Clemency Files, TSA.

52. Delia Goodwin to Governor E. J. Davis, 4 June 1874, ibid.

53. Kremer, "Strangers to Domestic Virtues," p. 305.

54. O'Hare, *Prison Letters,* p. 84.

55. *Biennial Report of the Warden of the Minnesota Prison,* 1892–94, p. 24, MnHS.

56. For a full account of Josie Kensler in the Idaho penitentiary, see Waite, "Necessary to Separate the Female Prisoners."

57. Ibid., pp. 4–6.

58. Those physicians and chaplains who made a significant attempt to alter prison conditions or protest inhumane treatment were regarded as a nuisance and often dismissed. For a doctor who clashed with the warden over punishments and

lost his job, see "Attorney General's Report in the Matter of the Charges of Cruel Treatment of Convicts under the Present Management of the New Mexico Penitentiary, 28 June 1907," p. 4, and testimony of Dr. David Knapp, "Removal of Arthur Trelford, Superintendent of the Penitentiary, 1907," Governor's Papers, George Curry, 1907–10, special issues, reel 178, frames 177–291, NMSA. Donald R. Walker points out the frustration for chaplains, stymied by prison routines and hampered by a lack of funds from the state and the outside congregation (*Penology for Profit*, pp. 182–84). For a chaplain who intervened on issues ranging from a prison school, to labor routines, to unjust punishments, to limited supplies and met with resistance from every prison administrator, see the papers of Rev. S. M. Tenney, chaplain at the Rusk, Texas, penitentiary from 1911 to 1914. For the range of his efforts on behalf of prisoners, see, among others, Governor O. B. Colquitt to Rev. S. M. Tenney, 5 Jan., 1912; Oscar F. Wolff to Rev. S. M. Tenney, 20 Feb. 1913; Rev. S. M. Tenney to Warden J. A. Palmer, 3 June 1913; Oscar F. Wolff to Rev. S. M. Tenney, 26 Aug. 1913; W. O. Murray to Rev. S. M. Tenney, 24 Nov. 1914; Louis W. Tittle to Rev. S. M. Tenney, 26 Nov. 1913, all in Samuel M. Tenney Family Papers, HFPRC. For another chaplain who refused to remain quiet about prison abuses, see Donald R. Walker, *Penology for Profit*, pp. 183–84.

59. "Report of Chaplain," *Report on the Condition of the State Penitentiary*, 1871–72, pp. 11–12, TSA. For good examples of the tertiary role of the chaplain see the wardens' reports in the *Biennial Reports of the Idaho State Penitentiary*, 1903–16, ISL; and James P. Sanford, "Chaplain's Report to the Warden, 1865," Reports of the Penitentiary at Fort Madison, 1860–72, Governor's Office: series 8, Reports, box 82, ISA. For pious attitudes of chaplains see Harriette B. Gunn, *In the Shadow of the Wall* (Boston: Christopher Publishing House, 1922), esp. pp. 20–23, 121–30, 207–15.

60. For examples, see the testimony of Dr. A. B. J. Merrill in *Report of a Committee . . . to Investigate the Matter of Punishment of Convicts at the Minnesota State Prison*, 1891, pp. 42–50, MnHS, and the testimony of Dr. J. P. Westmoreland, *Report of the Penitentiary Investigating Committee*, pp. 520–26, TSA.

61. O'Hare, *Prison Letters* p. 49.

62. Barbara Jones to Governor O. M. Roberts, 14 Sept. 1881. The letter appeared to be in the hand of one Haywood Broham, who also signed Jones's conduct record (undated Barbara Jones conduct statement of Major T. J. Goree, Barbara Jones, no. 3373, Executive Clemency Files, TSA).

63. Report of the Special Committee to Investigate the Penitentiary, 29th Legislative Assembly, Dec. 1890–Feb. 1891, Territorial Records, reel 9, frames 431–78, p. k, NMSA.

64. Testimony of Ada Hulmes, ibid., reel 9, frames 431–78, p. 18. A Mexican American convict, Rafaél Baca, testified that an Anglo inmate tried to coerce him into swearing to the relationship (pp. 10–11); José Montoya denied he had been intimate with Ada Hulmes (p. 19), and the superintendent E. W. Wynkoop supported that statement (p. 3). The committee concluded the charges were false (see p. g).

65. Testimony of E. W. Wynkoop, ibid., reel 9, frames 431–78, p. 3.

66. Testimony of Rafaél Baca, ibid., reel 9, frames 431–78, p. 10.

67. Testimony of H. G. Davis, ibid., reel 9, frames 431–78, pp. 8–9.

68. Knepper, "Imprisonment and Society in Arizona Territory," pp. 177–78.

69. Jeffrey, *Adobe and Iron*, p. 83.

70. Ledger: Escaped Arkansas State Penitentiary, 1887–1972, ADC.

71. Deborah Gray White explains the importance of group action among African American women, saying "the female gossip network, the means by which community members are praised, shamed, and coerced, is usually found in societies

where women are highly dependent on each other and where women work in groups and form female associations" ("Female Slaves," p. 27).

72. Testimony of Patsy Lewis, Fannie Moore, Viney Duncan, Geneva Starks, Jennette White, Copy Statement of Facts, State of Texas versus Lizzie Plummer, no. 10663, Lizzie Plummer, no. 3860, 13 Mar. 1896, and no. 4009, 16 June 1896, Executive Clemency Files, TSA.

73. Testimony of Martha Banton, Copy of Statement of Facts, ibid.

74. Testimony of Kate B. Eggleston, Mrs. M. E. Brown, L. Schoerding, and Willie Rancow, ibid.

75. Testimony of R. E. White and J. M. Davis, ibid.

76. Judge F. G. Morris, Application for Pardon, 18 Mar. 1896; Jurors' Petition to Governor C. A. Culberson, n.d., ibid.

77. Citizens' Petition, n.d.; Statement of A. N. Denton, M.D., 28 Mar. 1895, ibid.

78. Proclamation of Pardon, no. 3860, 23 Mar. 1896; Addendum by Governor C. A. Culberson for no. 17404, 13 June 1896, ibid.

79. Testimony of Lizzie Woodfolk, Transcript in the Matter of the Inquiry as to the Sanity of Lizzie Woodfolk, an Inmate of the Nevada State Prison, Carson City, 8 Mar. 1915, pp. 2, 6, 7, Lizzie Woodfolk File, Inmate Case Files, NSCMA.

80. Ibid., p. 9.

81. Ibid., p. 3. Also John J. Sullivan, M.D., to the Board of Pardons, 12 Nov. 1917; John J. Sullivan to Homer Mooney, 17 Nov. 1917; Lizzie Woodfolk Discharge Certificate, Nevada Hospital for Mental Diseases, 17 Nov. 1917. The violence in Lizzie's life did not end with her parole and eventual pardon. In 1927 she was arrested in Reno, Nevada, for assault with intent to kill, and in November 1932, in the same city, arrested for shooting to death another African American woman, Mary Fowler (J. E. Hoover to Chief of Police, Reno, Nev., 1 Dec. 1932; Melvin E. Jepson to Warden M. R. Penrose, 16 Jan. 1933, ibid.).

82. Punishment Register, 22 Jan. 1894, p. 333, RG 213, MSA.

83. Prison Record of Ella Bradfield, Ella Bradfield File, 19 Mar. 1898, box 13, Pardon and Parole Files, KSHS.

84. For example, see undated brief, Florence Akers File, box 1, Pardon and Parole Files, KSHS.

85. Prison Record of Annie Carmack, Annie Carmack File, box 20, Pardon and Parole Files, KSHS.

86. Certificate of Prison Conduct, 8 Dec. 1899, Sarah Johnson, no. 5558, Executive Clemency Files, TSA. The previous August two other women serving life sentences were reported to the penitentiary board for four punishments each of "insolence, impudence, and fighting." Presumably they had been punished with the lash as well (J. G. Smither to Penitentiary Board, 2 Aug. 1899, Irene Moore, no. 5559, 22 Dec. 1899, Executive Clemency Files, TSA).

87. Certificate of Prison Conduct, 8 Dec. 1899, Caroline Williams, no. 5560, Executive Clemency Files, TSA.

88. For example, inmate Howard Ringo deliberately struck the coffeepot carried by an inmate waiter and said, "you pour to [sic] much, you Mexican son of a bitch." Inmate Charles McFarland used the same epithet to José Montoya, who was in charge of the cell house, and threatened to throw him off the cellblock tier (Punishment Record Book, pp. 162, 188, NMSA).

89. Ibid., pp. 45–46.

90. Ibid., pp. 153, 157, 158.

91. Ibid., p. 214.

92. Ibid., pp. 164, 180.

93. Ibid., p. 8.

94. Ibid., p. 178.

95. Regina Barreca, *They Used to Call Me Snow White . . . But I Drifted: Women's Strategic Use of Humor* (New York: Penguin Books, Viking, 1991), pp. 111–13; Linda A. Morris, *Women Vernacular Humorists in Nineteenth-Century America: Ann Stephens, Frances Whitcher, Marietta Holley,* Garland Publications in American and English Literature, ed. Stephen Orgel (New York: Garland Publishing, 1988), p. 2.

96. Nancy A. Walker, *A Very Serious Thing: Women's Humor and American Culture* (Minneapolis: University of Minnesota Press, 1988), pp. 105–6.

97. Punishment Record Book, p. 176, NMSA. In Texas, a male inmate cut off two of his fingers to impede plans to ship him from the Huntsville prison to one of the outside camps, because he considered the farms so untenable. He received a severe whipping for his actions (Donald R. Walker, *Penology for Profit,* p. 132).

98. For an example of a prisoner hanging himself after harsh treatment, see *Sweet Smell of Sagebrush,* p. 140.

99. Prisoner no. 1270, Descriptive Records, vol. 1, roll 1, RG 86, NSA.

100. For a discussion of this, see chap. 6, "Women and Work."

Conclusion

If my stay here has not satisfied the ends of justice[,] if all that I have suffered dose [*sic*] not satisfy the law that sent me here, then gentlemen, I can offer no other plea[,] only that . . . I shall strive in every sense to live the life of a law abiding citizen.
—Kittie Smith
Nevada State Penitentiary
1913

Kittie Smith had learned the right lessons in the Nevada penitentiary. She knew it best for an indigent African American woman seeking a parole to couch her request in terms of law and order. Yet, this nearly illiterate woman could barely refrain from asking "What has this had to do with justice?" The answer that reverberated across the West for Kittie Smith and other women inmates was "very little." If society, through its politicians and civil servants, wanted to convert women lawbreakers into good citizens, they simply selected the wrong institution. If, on the other hand, society sought to punish women, not only for legal transgressions, but especially for gender violations, the male penitentiary proved an excellent choice. Justice had little connection to the western penitentiary, ordained as the state agency to implement legal directives, particularly as

Annie Crowe, Colorado State Penitentiary. Courtesy Division of State Archives and Public Records, Denver, Colo.

they applied to men. Accordingly, wardens, superintendents, and lessees rarely considered themselves civic mentors or guardians of prisoners. Rather, they acted as the disciplinarians of the state, whose legal power was vested in the hands of a few.

Those few, in the main but not exclusively Anglo males, shared common values about the social order and the place of gender in an emerging West. The often trivial criminal charges, the hurried court procedures, and the brutish imprisonment practices directed against women indicate that dynamics beyond felonious behavior influenced how the male establishment perceived female crime. The experiences of women before the bar and inside western prisons suggest that a generalized female acquiescence superseded concerns about broken statutes. Women's case files rarely expressed an official opinion that an incarcerated female offender represented a threat to society. Instead, parole boards denied a woman freedom because she "had not been sufficiently punished," or she "traveled with bad companions in the past," or she "broke the hearts of her respected parents."

Why then did women from western cultures spend time, often long periods, inside male penitentiaries? The answer lies not only in the absence of facilities for women but also in the race by western states to keep institutional development apace with social growth. It rests as well in a poorly articulated but deeply felt fear about the need to impose order on a region with a changing social, economic, and political base. Although such fears might drive a social order in any location, might account for women in prisons in many places, the American West wrestled with its own set of problems. In a turbulent West, if the new body politic could not control women, the least of its citizens, what hope did it have for regional domination?

At the same time, the states within the West overlapped culturally, allowing neighborly attitudes about race and gender to inform regional thinking. Arkansas, Louisiana, Missouri, Texas, once committed to black slavery, butted against more western locales where bondage had no legal history. Differing geography didn't necessarily produce differing cultural values; intraregional boundaries blurred more than a map marks. Social custom, often in its least attractive features, wafted across plains and mountains to infuse thought and action. A prison cell in Nebraska mirrored a work farm in Texas more closely than westerners cared to admit. The cultural barriers between a Louisiana and a Montana, an Arkansas and an Iowa proved not so high after all.

Widely diverse peoples populated these nineteen states of the West, but a strikingly common racial thinking lurked in their midst. The South may have honed the most overt practices of racism, but throughout the West residents from many points of origin showed themselves willing to set the concepts in place. It was as if bitter sentiments unleashed by national civil war would not abate. The homicidal passions that set region against region, brother against brother, sister against sister, did not so easily evaporate in the post–Civil War West. Instead they rearranged and twisted into new forms of hatred. They took on an expanded vitality, ready to be hurled at whomever "offended" in the region that emerged as the arena for shaping the modern American identity. A vigilante lynching, a train robbery, a saloon shoot-out—they have distracted us from examining the underlying complexities of western violence and their connection to patterns of life in other national regions.

The social roots of violence that scholars Richard Maxwell Brown and Richard White saw bonding South and West found themselves another niche in western prisons. In everyday society, violence grounded in racism wormed its sullied way through the decisions about whom to charge, convict, and imprison. Inside the prisons, the same force accounted for treatment of prisoners and attitudes of some inmates toward each other.

Paradoxically, the racial mix of men and women brought together to the courts, the cohabitation crimes with which they were charged, the testimony at their trials, and the cross-racial alliances that formed in prisons all point to the ludicrous irony and inherent weakness in racist thinking. Even the most meanspirited policies could not deter those who chose to defy racial constraints. In the course of this study, personal alliances of many cultural arrangements and racial mixes surfaced, including woman-to-woman relationships, as well as man-to-man, and across gender lines. Prisoner aligned with prisoner, warden with inmate, doctor with convict, guard with trusty. Some were friends, some were lovers. Some situations were coercive and included their own ugly twist of racism. Others, involving prison personnel and women inmates, reflected the worst in a power imbalance.

Nonetheless, all people of the West did not adhere to formal declarations of the importance of racial separation. In fact, there emerges a suggestion that, even with the blatant linguistic racism of the written records and the unpredictable physical dangers, in daily life sharp ethnic divisions were less forcefully observed than in modern society. African Americans, Mexican Americans, Anglo Americans constructed their own interactions with each other, sometimes at great risk, but usually with personal choice. At least among some westerners, a strain of cultural pluralism diluted the formal structures of political and economic segregation. The racial mosaic of the American West continues to unfold as a contradiction between theory and practice, policy and reality.

In this mix of humanity, a small number of women inmates proved critical to the evolving penitentiary design. While we have tended to dismiss groups with few members as unimportant, in this case scant numbers strengthened the impact of the social message to all women. Women who entered western penitentiaries served as a fearful example for those who would never cross those forbidden thresholds. Poor women watched what happened to their mothers, daughters, sisters inside prisons. Middle-class and wealthy women heard about the "pitiful wretches" from their church groups, reform organizations, and politically connected husbands; they witnessed for themselves at prison band concerts, chapel services, or the monthly bazaar day. The sequestered prison world was a known commodity to those beyond the walls, despite the indifference society feigned. For women, even among those culturally sheltered, the penitentiary symbolized the most extreme penalty for breaking the covenants of society in regard to gender place.

When those covenants ruptured, women charged with committing a crime lost social ballast. Whether women of a public life or the private realm, whether women of color or not, entrance into the judicial system placed each in jeopardy. The connection to crime somehow lessened a woman's link to womanhood and placed her outside the boundaries of the "acceptable" society. Within days, a community stripped a woman of her gender status, even as she confronted an array of legal complexities.

Criminal women, typically from society's poorest groups, were hurled into a court network for which they were ill prepared. An arsenal of social disapproval surrounded them, they lacked political allies, and their economic status limited their choice of legal advocate. Their experiences with trial procedures and the withdrawal of support from the community, especially as trumpeted in the newspapers, confirmed their changing identity. Women shifted from the world of freedom to the world of incarceration literally overnight. When convicted, these women entered penitentiaries that belonged to men, in every sense of the word.

There they found slim evidence of a female presence, as their numbers remained small. In fact, had penitentiaries accommodated many women, the value of the social lesson, making an example of the woman lawbreaker, would have been diluted. The presence of many female inmates in male prisons would have forced legislators and administrators to construct a place for criminal women. Two cells here, a cleaning assignment there would not have sufficed. This is not to say that the results would have been humane, rehabilitative, or uplifting, since they rarely were for male inmates, but women might have entered the criminal justice system of the West as a normal constituency rather than an aberrant minority. The burgeoning West, with its galloping development, wanted to expend neither the time nor the money on arranging for that provision.

Between 1865 and 1915, incarceration of women in a prison planned exclusively for male inmates was not the uncommon event we have thought. In these institutions, women inmates entered into a maleness labyrinth, built by administrators and prisoners. The practice of hiring a matron—often the warden's wife—gained ground only slowly in western prisons. Since women's inmate numbers stayed low, matrons appeared to be an unnecessary salary drain on limited state resources. Hired to supervise the daily routines of the women and act as quasi chaperons, the matrons brought limited improvement. Their presence did not automatically guarantee a happier circumstance for women prisoners. Whether of gentle touch or rigid discipline, matrons, as state employees, worked at the pleasure of the prison administration, which remained under the umbrella of male authority. Like male guards, many adjusted their personal compass until the routines of the prison seemed ordinary. For those who could not tolerate the environment, prison employment was understandably brief.

With or without matrons, women inmates encountered a community driven by corruption, violence, and masculinity. The men who lived and worked inside a penitentiary had little reason to think of it as other than their world. Few women were prepared for such total immersion into this community of men, especially one where power fragmented along so many different lines. While in some aspects of the western experience, women capitalized on societal growth to enlarge their opportunities, the atmosphere inside the penitentiary did not facilitate an expanded female role. Women prisoners, literally as a matter of life and death, had to fashion responses that gave them a chance to survive in a largely untenable environment. Within various forms, women acted through strategies of compliance and resistance to make a gendered place in a world that did not welcome females.

In maneuvering their way through the judicial system and carving a space inside the penitentiary, women never lost sight of the fact that race and class compounded all the elements of their prison time. From arrest to trial to imprisonment to release, nonwhite women discovered greater difficulties, more injustice. Often hindered by poverty and illiteracy, they nonetheless demonstrated the power of family and community in their negotiations with the legal hierarchy.

All in all, the experiences of women in western male penitentiaries reinforce the importance of race, class, and gender as components in our understanding of the past. Unfortunately, what remains clouded is a clear statement about the nature of women's criminality. The questionable arrests, unlikely confessions, shoddy trial procedures, the desire to punish womanhood rather than illegality, the emphasis on incarcerating women of color—all these compromise the issue of women's crime in the emerging West. Certainly some women broke the law and intended to do so; not every imprisoned woman was innocent of wrongdoing. In letters and appeals, all prisoners hoped to put the best face on past criminal actions. Yet, even if the words of female convicts are reduced by half, even if skepticism undercuts the veracity of their pardon petitions, a stunning account of legal discrimination against women persists. In a collection of women convicted by emotion rather than justice, by rhetoric rather than evidence, the true criminality of western women remains almost totally obscured.

It has been tempting to refer to the most wretched days of prison history as exceptional, examples of a time before the "West was won." Popular conventions of the West have typically asserted that those who oversaw a morass of prison brutality represented only a small percentage of superintendents and wardens. In fact, the opposite was true.

John Behan, the notorious 1889 warden of the Arizona territorial prison, hardly walked alone in prison mismanagement. Among a long list, New Mexico had its Thomas P. Gable; Texas claimed Colonel A. J. Ward, I. L. Brabham, and Marian Ezell; Iowa its Martin Heisey and three years later, Seth Craig; Montana its Frank Conley; Wyoming its Otto Gramm. When reformers drove them out, those who followed offered little change and shortly toppled in their own investigations or resigned in frustration. Those administrators who halted torture or instituted sensible work programs did not last long. Even the best minded could not eliminate the massive fiscal dishonesty that kept every prison a bastion of poverty, an arena of corruption, a center of cruelty. In essence, the penitentiary as a locus of institutionalized negativism satisfied societal expectations. Reform was acceptable, with stringent limitations; punishment was not supposed to be pleasant.

Frequently, the former prison officials did not slink away in disgrace or embarrassment but assumed positions of power and respect in the community. Horace A. Smith, warden at the Missouri penitentiary at the end of the Civil War, served eight years as a judge of a county court. When John Behan died in 1912, the Arizona Historical Society oversaw his funeral, at which he was eulogized for his commitment to public service. Major Samuel Lawrence James, who kept prisoners in virtual slavery, amassed a fortune and power in post–Civil War Louisiana. In a later era, Frank Conley of Montana, a former prison guard, acquired great wealth by questionable means and rose to the inner circle of influence. The men responsible for prison management and conditions circulated widely among the most "respectable" of a community. They connected the heinous world of the penitentiary and the comfortable society of the movers and shakers of new western communities.

As they traveled between these two disparate arenas, the men connected to prison management did not shed their perceptions of gender in either space. Accordingly, they carried into both of those worlds deeply rooted attitudes. In one environment they witnessed and endorsed the violence inflicted on women prisoners; in another they thought in terms of "ladies" and womanhood. They accepted for one group of women what they rejected for another. Yet their acceptance of violence for criminal women enhanced its place as a social component of the West and suggested how easily women might experience physical assault in any environment. Although many of these men would never have indulged in direct violence against wives and daughters in their families, they formed the bridge between the few females of the male prisons and the many women of the larger society. Men of respected rank—politicians, civil servants, parole board members, prison employees, penitentiary investigators, contractors, physicians, chaplains—by their silence, helped to spin the invisible web of violence that engulfed women in the West. Simple citizens or community leaders, they had a unique opportunity in which they might have spoken publicly against the physical assault of the prisons, but most let the chance pass and watched violence against women become more firmly woven into the fabric of the West.

For over five decades in western prisons women found little provision made for their incarceration. In the early years considered here, unfit circumstances awaited women inmates. Prison administrators settled for makeshift accommodation in every aspect of prison life for women. Because of that policy, women inmates confronted poor housing, debilitating health conditions, and few work opportunities outside of domestic and sexual service. Although certain inappropriate practices changed across time—women did not continue to share cells with men, some states eliminated the most shocking punishments, a staff of matrons replaced male guards—substantive advances remained elusive. In fact, as prison reformers successfully lobbied for improvements in the care of male prisoners, discrimination against women inmates actually increased. Traditions of poor provision for women inmates in the nineteenth century slid into different forms of disadvantage in the twentieth. States continued to consider women convict numbers insignificant and deny that female inmates warranted financial investment.

Early practices, such as those that barred women from regular chapel services or excluded females from the penitentiary band, evolved into differences in visitation rights, school access, mail privileges, job training, library materials, medical care, lock-down procedures, and parole guidelines. In each instance, women inmates lost ground as the twentieth century moved forward and the number of females incarcerated in the West rose steadily. Those few women prisoners of the formative years of western penitentiaries truly illuminate the genesis of female incarceration; their experiences, like an old lantern, cast a long shadow across the faces of modern women prisoners. The years of discrimination directed at western women prisoners marked a path that leads to a West where the numbers of female inmates are no longer few, but the legacy of the past is large.

The American West energized the hearts and the imaginations of the women and men who lived there. Its distinctive regional appeal generated individual and collective emotion from the peoples of the many cultures who came together within its embrace. Something in those differing lived experiences transmuted into intellectual language that launched an uncommon merger of geography, people, and American scholarship. Like most marriages, this one traversed a rocky road and has demanded constant critical examination and reassessment.

Perhaps its single most vexing component has been the place of violence within the history of the West. Despite many efforts to understand violence in western experiences, this troubling element continues to dominate the historical debate and the popular imagination. Western violence remains a powerful ingredient in the national consciousness. Whether a subject of scholarly concern or the gimmick of scriptwriters and musicians, violence as a western theme shows no inclination to retreat from our public thinking. Since we are, as a nation, so committed to the West and its accoutrements, it is time to answer the challenge of Richard Maxwell Brown and reorganize our definitions of violence. In so doing, intense male-centered legends of battles and gunfights need to be set aside. With their out-of-doors athletic cast, they add to the misconception that western violence remained the noble romp of gallant men of many cultures.

We have, as a nation, turned away from the evidence that documents the reality of violence for western women. Behind the closed doors of the West, in homes and boardinghouses, in saloon rooms, in cabins and hotels, on ranches, in brothels and dark alleys, in mansions and humble abodes, alone and in the presence of their children, women confronted violence on a regular basis. What remains unclear in the historical record are the numbers of western women who lived silently with spouse abuse, marital rape, and domestic violence. The tendency of wives to be secretive about a physically aggressive husband, the inclination to exclude such matters from the public record, the limitation on cross-culture communication, and the failure of law enforcement officers to intervene in family disputes all contributed to an unrealistic impression about women's lives and violence. Furthermore, if we add several other groups of women not considered in this study—those never arrested, those who escaped charges because an inquest panel found for self-defense, those acquitted of murder or manslaughter charges, and those wounded or killed during domestic altercations—the possible instances of violence in the lives of western women escalates dramatically.

When all these factors coalesce within our national protective attitude toward heroic images of western men, it is not surprising that we grossly underestimate the subject of violence and women in the American West. It may never be possible to unravel the full extent of violence for women in the land of purple sage and great spaces. Yet it is a gender dimension that promises to augment our perceptions of this complex region. Across our western horizon, the long-silent voices of women prisoners ask us to re- member their lives, the circumstances that brought them to prison, and the violence they endured inside male penitentiaries.

Selected
Bibliography

Primary Materials

Manuscript Collections

Arizona Historical Society, Tucson, Ariz.
    Manuscript, Yuma Territorial Prison, John Behan File
Arizona State Archives, Department of Library, Archives, and Public Records, Phoenix, Ariz.
    Secretary of the Territory, Yuma Prison
    Yuma Territorial Prison Register and Descriptive List of Convicts, 26 May 1875–26 Jan. 1918
Arkansas Department of Corrections, Pine Bluff, Ark.
    Handbook Register of Convicts, 1910–20
    Index to Prisoners, Arkansas Penitentiary, 31 October 1879–June 1933
    Inmate Files, 1865–1915
    Ledger: Escaped, Arkansas State Penitentiary
    List of Pardons and Remissions Granted by the Governor, 1887–89
    Pardons and Remissions, 1887–88
    Register of Prisoners, July 1912–Dec. 1913, 1915–20
Arkansas State History Commission, Little Rock, Ark.
    Biennial Reports of the State Penitentiary, 1890–1906, 1910–14
    Daybook, Secretary, Board of Penitentiary Commissioners, 7 May 1884–26 Aug. 1884
    George W. Hays Papers, Correspondence
    Thomas McRae Papers, Correspondence
    Observations on the Correctional Needs of the State of Arkansas: A Proposal Prepared for the Arkansas Prison Study Commission by Thomas O. Murton, 1967
    Proceedings of the Board of Commissioners of the State Penitentiary, Arkansas, 16 Apr. 1873–4 Apr. 1893
    Register of State Convicts Received and Discharged from the Arkansas State Penitentiary, 1871–86
    Report of the Committee to Investigate the Management of the Arkansas State Penitentiary, 1895
    Report of the Penitentiary Joint Committee of Arkansas, 1901
Church of Jesus Christ of Latter-day Saints, Historical Department, Salt Lake City, Utah

Index to Mormons Incarcerated in the Utah Territorial/State Prison, 1889–1908

Journals

    William Grant, Autobiography and Diary

    Albert Silas Harris, "Life of Belle Harris Nelson"

    Isabella Maria Harris Nelson, Journal

    Joseph Parry, Autobiography

    Harrison Sperry, Autobiography

Colorado Division of State Archives and Public Records, Denver, Colo.

    Biennial Report of the Attorney General of the State of Colorado, 1909–10

    Biennial Reports of the State Board of Charities and Corrections, including the Commissioner, Warden, and Physician, 1878–90

    Crime Clippings Scrapbooks, vols. 1–3

    Denver/Arapahoe County District Court, Criminal Division, Inverse Index

    Denver Police Department Scrapbook

    Penitentiary Records

        Inmate Photographs

        Miscellaneous Publications, Reports, Studies

        Record of Convicts, 1871–95

        Prisoners Index to no. 20183

Historical Foundation of the Presbyterian and Reformed Churches, Montreat, N.C.

    Tenney Family Papers, Samuel Miles Tenney

Idaho State Library, Boise, Idaho

    Biennial Report of the Idaho State Penitentiary, 1903–14

Idaho State Penitentiary, Boise, Idaho

    Women Prisoners' File

Iowa State Archives, Des Moines, Iowa

    Governor's Office: series 2, Correspondence; series 8, Reports

    Record of Convicts: Penitentiary at Anamosa, 1870–1907

    Record of Convicts: Penitentiary at Fort Madison, 1870–1907

Kansas State Historical Society, Topeka, Kansas

    Governor's Office

        Criminally Insane Ward

        Pardon and Parole Files, 1863–1919

    Governor's Papers

        George Hodges

        Lorenzo D. Lewelling

        Edmund N. Morrill

        Thomas A. Osborn

    Lucy B. Johnston Papers

    Prison Investigation Minutes, 1914

    Prisoner Photographs

    Record of Prisoners Received, 1864–1905

    State Penitentiary Investigation, 1895

    Statement of Convicts, Prisoner Ledgers A, F, G, H, I, 1864–1906

Library of Congress, Washington, D.C.

    Report of the Commissioners on the Penal Code, with the Accompanying Documents. Harrisburg: S. C. Stambaugh, 1828.

    Report of the Committee Appointed to Investigate and Recommend the Best Means of Employment of the Prisoners in the State Penitentiary to the 47th General Assembly, Jefferson City, Mo.

Report of Committee on Contracts on the Subject of Their Visit to Penal and Reformatory Institutions, 1874. Boston: Rockwell and Churchill, 1875.
Louisiana State Penitentiary, Angola, La.
    Convict Record, 11 Jan. 1901–16 Sept. 1907
    Interview, Asst. Warden Roger S. Thomas, 22 June 1987
    Register of Convicts Received, 13 Feb. 1866–29 Dec. 1889
    Unpublished Historical Reports, Office of Asst. Warden
Minnesota Historical Society, St. Paul, Minn.
    Annual Reports of the Warden and Inspectors of the State Prison, 1862–78
    Biennial Reports, Minnesota State Board of Control of State Institutions, 1902–10, 1922
    Biennial Reports of the Warden and Inspectors of the State Prison, 1881–1900
    A Conditional Pardon System: Governor William R. Merriam, 1892
    Fifth Annual Report of the Warden of the Territorial Prison, 1858
    Handbook of the Minnesota State Prison, 1903, 1908, 1909
    Minnesota Executive Documents, 1871, 1887–88
    Report of a Committee . . . to Investigate the Matter of Punishment of Convicts at the Minnesota State Prison, 1891
Missouri State Archives, Jefferson City, Mo.
    Index of Penal Records, vol. 1, A–F
    Missouri General Assembly Journals and Appendices, 1865–67, 1879, 1893, 1895, 1909
    Missouri State Penitentiary Register of Inmates, 1836–1911
    Punishment Register, Mar. 1871–Dec. 1896
    Register of Inmates Received and Discharged
    Sentence and Judgment Papers, July 1871–July 1873
    Secretary of State, Pardon Papers, 1844–72
Montana Historical Society, Helena, Mont.
    Annual Reports of Prison Commissioners, 1891
    Descriptive List of Prisoners Received
    Laws, Rules, and Regulations Relating to the Government and Management of the State Prison
    State Prison Convict Register
    Territorial Executive Records, Applications for Executive Pardons, 1875–90
Nebraska State Archives, Lincoln, Nebr.
    State Penitentiary, County Record, vol. 1, nos. 2143–11518
    State Penitentiary, Daily Journal, vol. 1 and 2, 1887–95
    State Penitentiary, Descriptive Records
Nebraska State Penitentiary, Lincoln, Nebr.
    Inmate Record Jackets: Inactive since 1965, project 3087
Nevada State, County, and Municipal Archives, Carson City, Nev.
    Nevada State Prison, Board of Pardons Files, 1874–1915
    Nevada State Prison, Inmate Case Files
Nevada State Library, Carson City, Nev.
    Biennial Report of the Attorney General, 1899–1912
    Biennial Report of the Warden of the Nevada State Prison, 1867–1914
    Journal of the Senate and Appendices to the Journal, 1867–1915
New Mexico State Records Center and Archives, Santa Fe, N.M.
    Territorial Records
        Executive Records, Governor's Papers, Penal Papers
            George Curry

William J. Mills
J. W. Raynolds (Acting Governor)
Edmund G. Ross
Lionel A. Sheldon
Penitentiary Records
    Annual Records, 1885–1915
    Business Journal, 1885
    Convict Record Books, 1884–1917
    Governor's Notebooks re Prisoners, 1884–1915
    Inmate Files, nos. 1873–3078
    Parole Book, no. 1, 1907–14
    Physician's Record Books, 1898–1906, 1913–15
    Punishment Record Book, 1885–1917
South Dakota State Archives, Pierre, S.D.
    State Penitentiary, Prisoner Case Files, June 1878–Nov. 1891
Texas State Library, Austin, Tex.
    Biennial Reports of the Directors and Superintendent of the Texas State Penitentiary, 1878–80
    Executive Clemency Files
    Record of Evidence and Statements before the Penitentiary Investigating Committee, 1911–12
    Report of the Penitentiary Investigating Committee, 1910
    Report of Special Committee on Penitentiary, 1871
    Report of the Superintendent of the Penitentiary, 1871–74
    Reports of the Condition of the State Penitentiary, 1869–74
University of Kansas, Kansas Collection, Lawrence, Kans.
    Biennial Reports of the Kansas State Board of Corrections, 1912–16
    Biennial Reports of the Women's Industrial Farm at Lansing, 1912–16, 1920–22
    Board of Commissioners of Public Institutions, *Second Annual Report,* 1874
    General Rules and Regulations of the State Penitentiary of Kansas, 1883
    Girls' Industrial School at Beloit, Report, 1916–18
    Tenth Annual Report of the Bureau of Labor and Industry, Kansas, 1894
University of Missouri, Western Historical Manuscript Collection, Columbia, and
    State Historical Society of Missouri Manuscripts, Columbia, Mo.
    Herbert S. Hadley Papers
University of Texas, Barker Center for American History, Austin, Tex.
    Information Booklet, Texas State Penitentiary
    Miscellaneous Files, Prison
    Scrapbooks, Prisons, 1939–67
    Texas Department of Corrections
Wyoming State Archives, Museums and Historical Department, Cheyenne, Wyo.
    Description and History of Wyoming Convicts, vol. 1
    District Courts Criminal Case Files
    Petitions for Pardon
        Bryant B. Brooks
        Joseph M. Carey
        DeForest Richards
    Special Report of the U.S. Grand Jury, 1886
    Wyoming Penitentiary Records, Female Inmates File

U.S. Government Documents and Publications

Graham, Hugh Davis, and Ted Robert Gurr, eds. *Violence in America: Historical and Comparative Perspectives.* Vol. 1: *A Report to the National Commission on the Causes and Prevention of Violence.* Washington: G.P.O., 1969.

U.S. Department of Commerce. Bureau of the Census. *Negro Population: 1790–1915.* Washington: G.P.O., 1918.

U.S. Department of Commerce. Bureau of the Census. *Prisoners in State and Federal Prisons and Reformatories, 1926.* Washington: G.P.O., 1919.

U.S. Department of Interior. Records of the Office of the Secretary of the Interior. Territorial Papers. Colorado, 1861–68. Letters Received Relating to the Penitentiary at Canon City and Miscellaneous Subjects. Microcopy 431, roll 1, RG 48.

U.S. Department of Justice. Bureau of Justice Statistics. *Sourcebook of Criminal Justice Statistics: 1993.* Edited by Kathleen Maguire, and Ann L. Pastore. Washington: G.P.O., 1994.

U.S. Department of Justice. General Records. Chronological Files, Colorado. Microfilm. Box 280, RG 60.

Newspapers

Anaconda (Mont.) Standard
Anaconda (Mont.) Weekly Review
Arizona Republican
Avant Courier (Bozeman, Mont.)
Billings (Mont.) Daily Gazette
Butte (Mont.) Inter Mountain
Butte (Mont.) Miner
Daily Independent (Helena, Mont.)
Daily Missoulian (Mont.)
Idaho Daily Statesman (Boise)
Jefferson City (Mo.) Republican
Livingston (Mont.) Herald
New North-West (Deer Lodge, Mont.)
Ogden (Utah) Daily Herald
Philipsburg (Mont.) Call
Salt Lake Daily Herald (Utah)
Sheridan (Wyo.) Daily Enterprise

Books and Journals

Barrows, Samuel J. "The Delinquent." "European Prisons." *Charities and the Commons* 19 (Oct. 1907–Apr. 1908): 1276–77, 1183–90.

Blackmar, Frank Wilson. "Penology in Kansas, 1893." *Kansas University Quarterly* 1 (Apr. 1893): 155–77.

Booth, Maud Ballington. *After Prison—What?* New York: Fleming H. Revell, 1903.

Briggs, George Waverly. *The Texas Penitentiary: A Study of the Texas Convict System and Suggestions for Its Betterment.* Reprint of a series of 1908 articles from the *San Antonio Express.* N.p., 1910.

Faithfull, Emily. *Female Convicts: Discharged without Protection, Consignment to Ruin.* London: Victoria Press, 1864[?].

Flynn, Elizabeth Gurley. "The I. W. W. Call to Women." *Solidarity* 31 (July 1915): 1.
Folwell, William W. "The Disposal of City Cleanings, a Presentation to the Eleventh Annual Session of the State Historical Society Meeting." In *Executive Documents of the State of Minnesota, 1887–8,* vol. 2. St. Paul, Minn.: J. W. Cunningham, 1888.
Heilbron, W. C. *Convict Life at the Minnesota State Prison, Stillwater, Minnesota.* 2d ed. St. Paul: Heilbron, 1909.
Johnston, M. F. "The Life of a Woman Convict." *Fortnightly Review* 69 (Mar. 1901): 559–67.
Journal of the American Institute of Criminal Law and Criminology, 1910–12.
Letchworth, William P. *State Boards of Charities.* Boston: Geo. H. Ellis, 1892.
Lombroso, Cesare. *The Man of Genius.* New York: Charles Scribner's Sons, 1896.
Lombroso, Cesare, and William Ferrero. *The Female Offender.* New York: D. Appleton, 1900. Reprint ed. New York: Philosophical Library, 1958.
M'Kinney, Mordecai. *The Pennsylvania Justice of the Peace: The Law Relative to the Jurisdiction of Justices of the Peace. . . .* 2 vols. 1839. 4th ed. Philadelphia: T & W Johnson, 1887.
Myron, Angel, ed. *Reproduction of History of Nevada, 1881: With Illustrations and Biographical Sketches of Its Prominent Men and Pioneers.* Berkeley, Calif.: Howell-North, 1958.
National Prison Association. *Proceedings of the Twenty-third Annual Congress.* Saint Paul: n.p., 1894.
Neill, Edward D. *History of Washington County and the St. Croix Valley.* Minneapolis: North Star Publishing, 1881.
Norcross, Frank H. "The Crime Problem." *Yale Law Journal* 20 (June 1911): 599–603.
O'Connor, Richard. *The Police Promoter.* 3d ed. New York: T. A. McGahren, 1912.
Potts, Charles Shirley. *Crime and the Treatment of the Criminal.* Bulletin of the University of Texas 146. Austin: University of Texas, 1910.
Robinson, Frederick William. *Female Life in Prison.* 4th ed. rev. London: Ballantyne Press, 1888[?].
Stopes, Marie Carmichael. *Married Love: A New Contribution to the Solution of Sex Difficulties.* 18th ed. London: G. P. Putnam's Sons, 1927.
Williams, J. Fletcher. *Outlines of the History of Minnesota.* Minneapolis: North Star Publishing, 1881.
Willoughby, W. W. "Anglo-American Philosophies of Penal Law II: Punitive Justice." *Journal of the American Institute of Criminal Law and Criminology* 1 (Sept. 1910): 354–77.

Memoirs and Reminiscences

Arnold, Carl. *The Kansas Inferno.* Wichita, Kans.: Wonderland Publishing, 1906.
Campbell, Charles C. *Hell Exploded: An Exposition of Barbarous Cruelty and Prison Horrors.* Austin: n.p., 1900.
George, A. L. *The Texas Convict: Thrilling and Terrible Experience of a Texas Boy.* Austin: Ben C. Jones, 1893.
Goldman, Emma. *Living My Life.* 2 vols. Reprint. New York: Dover, 1970.
Gunn, Harriette B. *In the Shadow of the Wall.* Boston: Christopher Publishing House, 1922.
It's Hell in a Texas Pen: The Barbarous Conditions as Told by the Ex-Convicts and Unearthed by the Legislature. [Dallas?]: n.p., 1925.
Le Compte, Janet, ed. *Emily: The Diary of a Hard Worked Woman.* Lincoln: University of Nebraska Press, 1987.

Murphy, Patrick C. *Shadows of the Gallows.* Caldwell, Idaho: Caxton Printers, 1928.
O'Hare, Kate Richards. *Prison Letters.* Girard, Kans.: Appeal to Reason, 1919. History of Women Microfilm 7648. New Haven: Research Publications, 1977.
Olson, Gordon L., ed. "'I Felt like I Must Be Entering . . . Another World': The Anonymous Memoirs of an Early Inmate of the Wyoming Penitentiary." *Annals of Wyoming* 47 (1975): 152-90.
Reynolds, John N. *The Twin Hells: A Thrilling Narrative of Life in the Kansas and Missouri Penitentaries.* Atchison: Bee Publishing, 1890.
The Sweet Smell of Sagebrush: A Prisoner's Diary, 1903-1912; Written Anonymously in Wyoming's Frontier Prison, Rawlins, Wyoming. Rawlins: Friends of the Old Penitentiary/Old Penitentiary Joint Powers Board, 1990.
Tomlin, Henry. *Henry Tomlin, the Man Who Fought the Brutality and Oppression of the Ring in the State of Texas for Eighteen Years and Won. The Story of How Men Traffic in the Liberties and Lives of Their Fellow Men.* Ennis, Tex.: n.p., 1906.

Secondary Materials

Theses and Dissertations

Boom, Aaron M. "History of Nebraska Penal Institutions, 1854-1940." M.A. thesis, University of Nebraska, 1931.
Craddock, Amy. "The Imprisonment of Women as Formal Social Control: A Constructive Critique of Theoretical Perspectives and Empirical Research." M.A. thesis, University of North Carolina, 1985.
Crow, Herman Lee. "A Political History of the Texas Penal System, 1829-1951." Ph.D. dissertation, University of Texas, Austin, 1964.
De Grave, Kathleen R. "Swindler, Spy, Rebel: The Confidence Woman in Nineteenth-Century America." Ph.D. dissertation, University of Wisconsin, Madison, 1989.
Filo, Barbara Ann. "Reclaiming Those Poor Unfortunates: The Movement to Establish the First Federal Prison for Women." Ph.D. dissertation, Boston University, 1982.
Ford, Hiram U. "A History of the Arkansas Penitentiary to 1990." M.A. thesis, University of Arkansas, 1929.
Knepper, Paul Eduard. "Imprisonment and Society in Arizona Territory." Ph.D. dissertation, Arizona State University, 1990.
Reese, Linda Williams. "Race, Class, and Culture: Oklahoma Women, 1890-1920." Ph.D. dissertation, University of Oklahoma, 1991.

Articles and Pamphlets

Antler, Joyce. "Was She A Good Mother: Some Thoughts on a New Issue for Feminist Biography." In *Women and the Structure of Society,* ed. Barbara J. Harris and Jo Ann K. McNamara, pp. 53-66. Durham, N.C.: Duke University Press, 1984.
Banner Associates. "Wyoming Territorial Penitentiary: Historic Structure Report, Penitentiary Structure." Author's possession.
Bayliss, Garland E. "The Arkansas State Penitentiary under Democratic Control, 1874-1896." *Arkansas Historical Quarterly* 34 (1975): 195-213.
Brenzel, Barbara. "Lancaster Industrial School for Girls: A Social Portrait of a Nineteenth Century Reform School for Girls." *Feminist Studies* 3 (1975): 40-53.

———. "Domestication as Reform: A Study of the Socialization of Wayward Girls, 1856–1905." *Harvard Educational Review* 50 (1980): 196–213.

Brooks, Edward C. "Prison Chaplain." *Colorado Magazine* 41 (Summer 1964): 253–60.

Brown, Richard Maxwell. "Violence." In *The Oxford History of the American West,* ed. Clyde A. Milner II, Carol O'Connor, and Martha A. Sandweiss, pp. 393–425. New York: Oxford University Press, 1994.

Butler, Anne M. "Still in Chains: Black Women in Western Prisons, 1865–1915." *Western Historical Quarterly* 20 (Feb. 1989): 18–35.

———. "Women and Work in the Prisons of the American West." *Western Legal History* 7 (Summer/Fall 1994): 201–21.

Chesney-Lind, Meda. "Women and Crime: The Female Offender." *Signs* 12 (Autumn 1986): 78–96.

Conley, John A. "Beyond Legislative Acts: Penal Reform, Public Policy, and Symbolic Justice." *Public Historian* 3 (1981): 26–39.

———. "Prison Productions and Profit: Reconsidering the Importance of Prison Industries." *Journal of Social History* 14 (1980): 257–75.

———. "Revising Conceptions about the Origins of Prisons: The Importance of Economic Considerations." *Social Science Quarterly* 62 (1981): 247–58.

Degler, Carl N. "What Ought to Be and What Was: Women's Sexuality in the Nineteenth Century." *American Historical Review* 79 (Dec. 1974): 1467–90.

Edgerton, Keith. "Power, Punishment, and Poverty: The United States Penitentiary at Deer Lodge City, Montana Territory, 1871–1889," *Western Historical Quarterly* 28 (Summer 1997): 161–84.

———. "Power, Punishment, and Work: The Montana Prison, 1889–1921," paper delivered at the Western History Association, Denver, Colo., 12 Oct. 1995.

Engelstein, Laura. "Combined Underdevelopment: Discipline and the Law in Imperial and Soviet Russia." In "An *AHR* Forum," *American Historical Review* 98 (Apr. 1993): 338–81.

———. "Reply." In "An *AHR* Forum," *American Historical Review* 98 (Apr. 1993): 338–81.

Feinman, Clarice. "Sex-Role Stereotypes and Justice for Women." In *Women and Crime in America,* ed. Lee H. Bowker, pp. 383–84. New York: Macmillan, 1981.

French, Laurence. "An Assessment of the Black Female Prisoner in the South." *Journal of Women in Culture and Society* 3 (1977): 483–88.

Goldstein, Jan. "Framing Discipline with the Law: Problems and Promises of the Liberal State." In "An *AHR* Forum," *American Historical Review* 98 (Apr. 1993): 338–81.

Graff, Harvey J. "Crime and Punishment in the Nineteenth Century: A New Look at the Criminal." *Journal of Interdisciplinary History* 7 (Winter 1977): 477–91.

Green, Rayna. "The Pocohontas Perplex: The Image of Indian Women in American Culture." In *Unequal Sisters: A Multi-Cultural Reader in U.S. Women's History,* ed. Ellen Carol DuBois and Vicki L. Ruiz, pp. 15–21. New York: Routledge, 1990.

Haft, Marilyn G. "Women in Prison: Discriminatory Practices and Some Legal Solutions." In *Women, Crime and Justice,* ed. Susan K. Datesman and Frank R. Scarpitti, pp. 320–21. New York: Oxford University Press, 1980.

Hahn, Nicolas Fischer. "Female State Prisoners in Tennessee: 1831–1979." *Tennessee Historical Quarterly* 39 (Winter 1980): 485–97.

Hardaway, Roger D. "Prohibiting Interracial Marriage: Miscegenation Laws in Wyoming." *Annals of Wyoming* 52 (Spring (1980): 55–60.

Highfill, Robert D. "The Effects of News of Crime and Scandal on Public Opinion." *Journal of the American Institute of Criminal Law and Criminology* 17 (May 1926–Feb. 1927): 40–103.

Hine, Darlene Clark. "Rape and the Inner Lives of Black Women in the Middle West: Preliminary Thoughts on the Culture of Dissemblance." In *Unequal Sisters: A Multi-Cultural Reader in U.S. Women's History,* ed. Ellen Carol DuBois and Vicki L. Ruiz, pp. 292–97. New York: Routledge, 1990.

Hirata, Lucie Cheng. "Chinese Immigrant Women in Nineteenth Century America." In *Women of America: A History,* ed. Carol Berk and Mary Beth Norton, pp. 224–44. Boston: Houghton Mifflin, 1979.

Holden, W. C. "Law and Lawlessness on the Texas Frontier, 1875–1890." *Southwestern Historical Quarterly* 44 (Oct. 1940): 188–203.

Hougen, Harvey. "The Impact of Politics and Prison Industry on the General Management of the Kansas State Penitentiary, 1883–1909." *Kansas Historical Quarterly* 43 (1977): 297–318.

———. "Kate Barnard and the Kansas Penitentiary Scandal, 1908–09." *Journal of the West* 17 (1978): 9–18.

Jeffrey, John M. "The Bizarre Bazaar." *Journal of Arizona History* 11 (Autumn 1970): 202–17.

Kent, Philip. *History: Montana State Prison.* Edited by James R. McDonald. Deer Lodge, Mont.: n.p., 1979.

Knepper, Paul Eduard. "The Women of Yuma: Gender, Ethnicity, and Imprisonment in Frontier Arizona, 1876–1909." *Criminal Justice Review* 17 (Autumn 1992): 236.

Koshar, Rudy. "Foucault and Social History: Comments on 'Combined Underdevelopment.'" In "An *AHR* Forum," *American Historical Review* 98 (Apr. 1993): 338–81.

Kremer, Gary R. "Politics, Punishment, and Profit: Convict Labor in the Missouri State Penitentiary, 1875–1900." *Gateway* 13 (Summer 1992): 28–41.

———. "Strangers to Domestic Virtues: Nineteenth-Century Women in the Missouri Prisons." *Missouri Historical Review* 84 (Apr. 1990): 293–310.

Kremer, Gary R., and Thomas E. Gage. "The Prison against the Town: Jefferson City and the Penitentiary in the Nineteenth Century." *Missouri Historical Review* 74 (July 1980): 414–32.

Kroll, Michael A. "The Prison Experiment: A Circular History." *Southern Exposure* 4 (1978): 6–11.

Light, Ivan. "The Ethnic Vice Industry, 1880–1944." *American Sociological Review* 42 (1977): 464–79.

Mancini, Matthew J. "Race, Economics, and the Abandonment of Convict Leasing." *Journal of Negro History* 63 (1978): 339–52.

McKelvey, Blake. "A Half Century of Southern Penal Exploitation." *Social Forces* 13 (1934–35): 112–23.

McNall, Scott G. "'It Was a Plot Got Up to Convict Me': The Case of Henrietta Cook Versus the State of Kansas, 1876." *Qualitative Sociology* 9 (Spring 1986): 26–47.

Miller, Martin B. "At Hard Labor: Rediscovering the Nineteenth Century Prison." In *Punishment and Penal Discipline: Essays on the Prison and the Prisoners' Movement,* ed. Tony Platt and Paul Takagi, pp. 79–88. Berkeley, Calif.: Crime and Social Justice Associates, 1980.

Nagler, Michael N. "On Almost Killing Your Friends: Some Thoughts on Violence in Early Cultures." In *Comparative Research on Oral Traditions: A Memorial for Milman Perry,* ed. John Miles Foley. Columbus, Ohio: Slavica Press, 1985.

Petrik, Paula. "If She Be Content: The Development of Montana Divorce Law, 1865–1907." *Western Historical Quarterly* 18 (July 1987): 261–91.

———. "Not a Love Story: Bordeaux vs. Bordeaux." *Montana the Magazine of Western History* 41 (Spring 1991): 32–46.

Pierce, Virgil Caleb. "Utah's First Convict Labor Camp." *Utah Historical Quarterly* 42 (Summer 1974): 245–57.

Ridington, Robin. *Little Bit Know Something.* Iowa City: University of Iowa Press, 1990.

Rusche, Georg. "Labor Market and Penal Sanction: Thoughts on the Sociology of Criminal Justice." In *Punishment and Penal Discipline: Essays on the Prison and the Prisoners' Movement,* ed. Tony Platt and Paul Takagi, pp. 10–16. Berkeley, Calif.: Crime and Social Justice Associates, 1980.

Shelden, Randall G. "From Slave to Caste Society: Penal Change in Tennessee, 1830–1915." *Tennessee Historical Quarterly* 38 (1979): 462–78.

Shover, Neal, and Stephen Norland. "Sex Roles and Criminality: Science or Conventional Wisdom." *Sex Roles* 4 (1978): 111–25.

Simon, Rita James. "Women and Crime." In *Encyclopedia of Crime and Justice,* ed. Sanford H. Kadish, vol. 4, pp. 1664–69. New York: Macmillan, Free Press, 1983.

Smart, Carol. "Criminological Theory: Its Ideology and Implications concerning Women." In *Women and Crime in America,* ed. Lee H. Bowker, pp. 6–16. New York: Macmillan, 1981.

Smith, Sherry L. "Beyond Princess and Squaw: Army Officers' Perceptions of Indian Women." In *The Women's West,* ed. Susan Armitage and Elizabeth Jameson, pp. 63–75. Norman: University of Oklahoma Press, 1987.

Steffensmeier, Darrell J., and John H. Kramer. "The Differential Impact of Criminal Stigmatization on Male and Female Felons." *Sex Roles* 6 (1980): 1–8.

Taylor, Shelley E., and Ellen J. Langer. "Pregnancy: A Social Stigma." *Sex Roles* 3 (1977): 27–35.

Tórrez, Robert J. "Murder at Hillsboro: The Poisoning of Manuel Madrid, 1907." Unpublished paper, in author's possession.

Tydeman, William E. "The Landscape of Incarceration: Idaho's Old Penitentiary." *Idaho Yesterdays* 38 (Summer 1994): 10–11.

Vodicka, John. "Prison Plantation: The Story of Angola." *Southern Exposure* 4 (1978): 32–38.

Waite, Robert. "Necessary to Isolate the Female Prisoners: Women Convicts and the Women's Ward of the Old Idaho Penitentiary." *Idaho Yesterdays* 29 (Fall 1985): 2–12.

White, Deborah Gray. "Female Slaves: Sex Roles and Status in the Antebellum Plantation South." In *Unequal Sisters: A Multi-Cultural Reader in U.S. Women's History,* ed. Ellen Carol DuBois and Vicki L. Ruiz, pp. 22–31. New York: Routledge, 1990.

White, Richard. "Outlaw Gangs of the Middle Border: American Social Bandits." *Western Historical Quarterly* 12 (Oct. 1981): 387–408.

Wilson, James A. "Frontier in the Shadows: Prisons in the Far Southwest, 1850–1917." *Arizona and the West* 22 (Winter 1980): 323–42.

Witt, Shirley Hill. "Native American Women Today: Sexism and the Native American Woman." *Civil Rights Digest* 6 (Spring 1974): 29–35.

Yoshioka, Robert B. "Asian American Women: Stereotyping Asian Women." *Civil Rights Digest* 6 (Spring 1974): 44–45.

Zimmerman, Jane. "The Convict Lease System in Arkansas and the Fight for Abolition." *Arkansas Historical Quarterly* 8 (Autumn 1949): 171–88.

———. "The Penal Reform Movement in the South during the Progressive Era, 1890–1917." *Journal of Southern History* 17 (1951): 462–92.

Zumbrunner, Wanita A. "The White Palace of the West." *Palimpsest* 59 (May/June 1978): 88–97.

Books

Adler, Fred. *Sisters in Crime: The Rise of the New Female Criminal.* New York: McGraw-Hill, 1975.

Allen, Harry E., and Clifford E. Simonsen. *Corrections in America: An Introduction.* 4th ed. New York: Macmillan, 1986.

The American Prison from the Beginning: A Pictorial History. N.p.: American Correctional Association, 1983.

Arrington, Leonard. *The Great Basin Kingdom: An Economic History of the Latter-day Saints, 1830–1900.* Lincoln: University of Nebraska Press, Bison Books, 1966.

Barreca, Regina. *They Used to Call Me Snow White . . . but I Drifted: Women's Strategic Use of Humor.* New York: Penguin Books, Viking, 1991.

Bowker, Lee H., ed. *Women and Crime in America.* New York: Macmillan, 1981.

Brown, Richard Maxwell. *No Duty to Retreat: Violence and Values in American History and Society.* Norman: University of Oklahoma Press, 1991.

Butler, Anne M. *Daughters of Joy, Sisters of Misery: Prostitutes in the American West, 1865–1890.* Urbana: University of Illinois Press, 1985.

Cerveri, Doris. *With Curry's Compliments: The Story of Abraham Curry.* Elko, Nev.: Nostalgia Press, 1990.

Connell, R. W. *Masculinities.* Berkeley: University of California Press, 1995.

Coolidge, Dane. *Fighting Men of the West.* New York: Dutton, 1932.

Cunningham, Eugene. *Triggernometry: A Gallery of Gunfighters.* Caldwell, Idaho: Caxton Printers, 1956.

Datesman, Susan K., and Frank R. Scarpitti, eds. *Women, Crime and Justice.* New York: Oxford University Press, 1980.

de Beauvoir, Simone. *The Second Sex.* New York: Alfred A. Knopf, Bantam Books, 1970.

D'Emilio, John D., and Estelle B. Freedman. *A History of Sexuality in America.* New York: Harper and Row, 1988.

De León, Arnoldo. *They Called Them Greasers: Anglo Attitudes toward Mexicans in Texas, 1821–1900.* Austin: University of Texas Press, 1983.

Dilulio, John J. *Governing Prisons: A Comparative Study of Correctional Management.* New York: Macmillan, Free Press, 1987.

Dobash, Russell P., R. Emerson Dobash, and Sue Gutteridge. *The Imprisonment of Women.* Oxford: Basil Blackwell, 1986.

Donovan, Timothy P., and Willard B. Gatewood, Jr. *The Governors of Arkansas: Essays in Political Biography.* Fayetteville: University of Arkansas Press, 1981.

Douglas, Ann. *The Feminization of American Culture.* New York: Alfred A. Knopf, 1979.

Drago, Harry Sinclair. *Wild, Woolly and Wicked.* New York: Clarkson N. Potter, 1960.

El Saadawi, Nawal. *Memoirs from the Women's Prison.* Translated by Marilyn Booth. Berkeley: University of California Press, 1994.

Emrich, Duncan. *It's an Old Wild West Custom.* New York: Vanguard Press, 1949.

Epstein, Cynthia Fuchs. *Deceptive Distinctions: Sex, Gender, and the Social Order.* New Haven: Yale University Press and the Russell Sage Foundation of New York, 1988.

Feinman, Clarice. *Women in the Criminal Justice System.* New York: Praeger, 1986.

Ferguson, Ann. *Blood at the Root: Motherhood, Sexuality and Male Dominance.* London: Pandora Press, 1989.

Fienup-Riordan, Ann. *Boundaries and Passages: Rule and Ritual in Yup'ik Eskimo Oral Tradition.* Norman: University of Oklahoma Press, 1994.

Fishman, Joseph F. *Sex in Prison: Revealing Sex Conditions in American Prisons.* N.p.: National Library Press, 1934.

Fletcher, Beverly R., Lynda Dixon Shaver, and Dreama G. Moon, eds. *Women Prisoners: A Forgotten Population.* Westport, Conn.: Praeger, 1993.

Foucault, Michel. *Discipline and Punish: The Birth of the Prison.* Translated by Alan Sheridan. New York: Pantheon Books, 1977.

Freedman, Estelle B. *Their Sisters' Keepers: Women's Prison Reform in America, 1830–1930.* Ann Arbor: University of Michigan Press, 1981.

Gard, Wayne. *Frontier Justice.* Norman: University of Oklahoma Press, 1949.

Giallombardo, Rose. *Society of Women: A Study of a Women's Prison.* New York: John Wiley & Sons, 1966.

Glueck, Sheldon, and Eleanor T. Glueck. *Five Hundred Delinquent Women.* New York: Alfred A. Knopf, 1934. Reprint. New York: Kraus Reprint, 1971.

Goffman, Erving. *Stigma: Notes on the Management of Spoiled Identity.* Englewood Cliffs, N.J.: Prentice-Hall, 1963.

Griswold, Robert L. *Family and Divorce in California, 1859–1890: Victorian Illusions and Everyday Realities.* Albany: State University of New York Press, 1982.

Hall, J. A., and L. T. Hand. *History of Leavenworth County, Kansas.* N.p.: n.p., 1921.

Haynes, Fred E. *The American Prison System.* New York: McGraw-Hill, 1939.

Hibbert, Christopher. *The Roots of Evil: A Social History of Crime and Punishment.* Boston: Little, Brown, 1963.

Hollon, W. Eugene. *Frontier Violence: Another Look.* New York: Oxford University Press, 1974.

Ignatieff, Michael. *A Just Measure of Pain: The Penitentiary In the Industrial Revolution.* New York: Columbia University Press, 1978.

Jeffrey, John Mason. *Adobe and Iron: The Story of the Arizona Territorial Prison.* La Jolla, Calif.: Prospect Avenue Press, 1969.

Jordan, Philip D. *Frontier Law and Order.* Lincoln: University of Nebraska Press, 1970.

Larson, T. A. *History of Wyoming.* Lincoln: University of Nebraska Press, 1978.

Leonard, Eileen B. *Women, Crime, and Society: A Critique of Criminology Theory.* New York: Longman, 1982.

Leone, Mark S. *Roots of Modern Mormonism.* Cambridge: Harvard University Press, 1979.

Lewis, Orlando F. *The Development of American Prisons and Prison Customs, 1776–1845.* Patterson Smith Reprint Series in Criminology, Law Enforcement, and Social Problems 1. Montclair, N.J.: Patterson Smith, 1967.

Macey, David. *The Lives of Michel Foucault: A Biography.* New York: Pantheon, 1993.

Mandarak-Sheppard, Alexandra. *The Dynamics of Aggression in Women's Prisons in England.* Aldershot, Eng.: Gower Publishing, 1986.

McGrath, Roger. *Gunfighters, Highwaymen and Vigilantes: Violence on the Frontier.* Berkeley: University of California Press, 1984.

McKelvey, Blake. *American Prisons: A Study in American Social History Prior to 1915.* Patterson Smith Reprint Series in Criminology, Law Enforcement, and Social Problems 17. 1936. Montclair, N.J.: Patterson Smith, 1968.

Miller, James. *The Passion of Michel Foucault.* New York: Simon and Schuster, 1993.

Miller, Sally M. *From Prairie to Prison: The Life of Social Activist Kate Richards O'Hare.* Columbia: University of Missouri Press, 1993.

Milner, Clyde A., II, Carol A. O'Connor, and Martha A. Sandweiss, eds. *The Oxford History of the American West.* New York: Oxford University Press, 1994.

Mirandé, Alfredo, and Evangelina Enríquez. *La Chicana: The Mexican-American Woman.* Chicago: University of Chicago Press, 1979.

Morris, Linda A. *Women Vernacular Humorists in Nineteenth-Century America: Ann Stephens, Frances Whitcher, Marietta Holley.* Garland Publications in American and English Literature, ed. Stephen Orgel. New York: Garland Publishing, 1988.

Moynahan, J. M., and Earle K. Stewart. *The American Jail: Its Development and Growth.* Chicago: Nelson-Hall, 1980.

Murton, Thomas O. *The Dilemma of Prison Reform.* New York: Holt, Rinehart, and Winston, 1976.

Naish, Camille. *Death Comes to the Maiden: Sex and Execution, 1431–1933.* New York: Routledge, 1991.

O'Dea, Thomas F. *The Mormons.* Chicago: University of Chicago Press, 1957.

O'Neal, Bill. *Encyclopedia of Western Gunfighters.* Norman: University of Oklahoma Press, 1979.

Park, Robert. *Race and Culture.* London: Collier-Macmillan, Free Press of Glencoe, 1950.

Peiss, Kathy, and Christina Simmons, eds., with Robert A. Padgug. *Passion and Power: Sexuality in History.* Philadelphia: Temple University Press, 1989.

Penrose, Matt R. *Pots o'Gold.* Reno, Nev.: A. Carlisle, 1935.

Platt, Tony, and Paul Takagi. *Punishment and Penal Discipline: Essays on the Prison and the Prisoners' Movement.* Berkeley, Calif.: Crime and Social Justice Association, 1980.

Rafter, Nicole Hahn. *Partial Justice: Women in State Prisons, 1800–1935.* Boston: Northeastern University, 1985.

Ray, Grace Ernestine. *Wily Women of the West.* San Antonio, Tex.: Naylor, 1972.

Riley, Glenda. *Divorce: An American Tradition.* New York: Oxford University Press, 1991.

Sawicki, Jana. *Disciplining Foucault: Feminism, Power, and the Body.* New York: Routledge, 1991.

Schur, Edwin M. *The Americanization of Sex.* Philadelphia: Temple University Press, 1988.

———. *Labeling Women Deviant: Gender, Stigma, and Social Control.* Philadelphia: Temple University Press, 1983.

Scrugham, James G., ed. *Nevada: A Narrative of the Conquest of a Frontier Land.* 3 vols. Chicago: American Historical Society, 1935.

Sheldon, Wilmon H. *Woman's Mission to Humanity.* Boston: Christopher, 1968.

Shipps, Jan. *Mormonism: The Story of A New Religious Tradition.* Urbana: University of Illinois Press, 1985.

Shirley, Glenn. *Belle Starr and Her Times: The Literature, the Facts, and the Legends.* Norman: University of Oklahoma Press, 1982.

Shoemaker, Floyd Calvin. *Missouri and Missourians: Land of Contrasts and People of Achievements.* 5 vols. Chicago: Lewis Publishing, 1943.

Simon, Rita James. *Women and Crime.* Lexington: D. C. Heath, 1975.

Smith-Rosenberg, Carroll. *Disorderly Conduct: Visions of Gender in Victorian America.* New York: Oxford University Press, 1985.

Sprague, William F. *Women and the West: A Short Social History.* New York: Arno Press, 1972.

Stone, Wilbur Fisk, ed. *History of Colorado.* Vol. 1. Chicago: S. J. Clarke Publishing, 1918.

Sullivan, Larry E. *The Prison Reform Movement: Forlorn Hope.* Boston: Twayne Publishers, 1990.

Van Kirk, Sylvia. *Many Tender Ties: Women in Fur Trade Society, 1670–1870.* Norman: University of Oklahoma Press, 1980.

Walker, Donald R. *Penology for Profit: A History of the Texas Prison System, 1867–1912.* College Station: Texas A&M University Press, 1988.

Walker, Nancy A. *A Very Serious Thing: Women's Humor and American Culture.* Minneapolis: University of Minnesota Press, 1988.

Ward, David A., and Gene G. Kassebaum. *Women's Prison: Sex and Social Structure.* Chicago: Aldine Publishing, 1965.

Ware, Vron. *Beyond the Pale: White Women, Racism, and History.* London: Verso, 1992.

Weeks, Jeffrey. *Sexuality.* Chichester: Ellis Horwood, 1986.

West, Elliott. *Growing Up with the Country.* Lincoln: University of Nebraska Press, 1989.

White, Richard. *"It's Your Misfortune and None of My Own": A New History of the American West.* Norman: University of Oklahoma Press, 1991.

Whitfield, Dick, ed. *The State of the Prisons: Two Hundred Years On.* London: Routledge, 1991.

Index

Lowell, Dorothy S., 187
Lyons, Alma, 119–20, 137–38, 147 n. 143
Lyons, Frank, 147 n. 143

Mac, Julia Anna, 109 n. 91
Madden, Rose, 78 n. 90
madonna/whore image, 16, 42 n. 14, 167, 173 n. 102
Madrid, Manuel, 119
Madrid, Valentina, 119–20, 137–38, 219 n. 16
Maine penitentiary, 176
Manning, Chlora, 164, 172 n. 89
manslaughter convictions, 69, 114, 116, 121, 124, 130, 131
Mantenfel, Amelia, 110 n. 108
Marble, Henrietta, 110 n. 108
Marion County, Tex., 128
Martin, Edward, 101
masculinity, 5–6, 12, 51, 103; among homosexual men, 80 n. 114; among prison community, 50. *See also* violence, masculinity of
Mason, Steward D., 77 n. 81
Massachusetts: prison administration in, 12; probation in, 8
Massie, Dr., 160
Matheny, William B., 123
Mathews, Malinda, 110 nn. 107, 108
matron, 27, 174, 186, 229
McConnell, E. T., 191
McCoy, James, 22, 37, 40
McCoy, Rose, 23, 26, 40
McFarland, Charles, 222 n. 88
McGowan, Pearl, 122, 143 n. 52
McGrath, Roger D., 3
McIntire, George, 190
McKay, William, 125
McKelvey, Blake, 14
McKiev, Mary Elizabeth Washington, 98
McMahan, Rosa, 75 n. 45
McMahon, Cora, 110 n. 108
McMara, Hanora, 197 n. 88
McNall, Scott, G., 141 n. 2
McNeal, G., 205
Meichmyer, Kate, 106 n. 40
Meredith, Dora, 103, 111 n. 112
Merrill, Clarence, 49
Metz (W. S.) and Sackett (C. L.) (attorneys), 34
Mexican War, 13
Millbank Penitentiary. *See* penitentiaries, Millbank

Mills, E. B., 77 n. 81
Miner, Francis, 169 n. 23
Mingo, Maria, 191
Minnesota: female prisoners, 18; legislature, 10–11; Territory, 178. *See also* penitentaries, Minnesota State
Missoula, Mont., 124, 125, 126
Missouri, 226; female prisoners, 34, 91, 99, 166, 186–87; pardons of female prisoners in, 78 n. 91, 107–8 n. 64, 189; prisons in, 58, 59, 66, 75 n. 39, 78 n. 90, 94, 96. *See also* penitentiaries, Missouri State
Missouri State Lunatic Asylum, 157
Mitchell, Cornelia, 197 n. 88
Mitchell, Minnie, 90
Monroe, Georgia, 160–61
Montana, 4, 226, 230; African American female prisoners in, 91, 156; Deer Lodge, 10, 13, 64, 114; female prisoners, 18; murder trial in, 145–46 n. 116; prison management in, 230; Territory, 13; trusty system, 64. *See also* penitentiaries, Montana State
Montoya, José Manuel, 211, 221 n. 64, 222 n. 88
Moore, Fannie, 222 n. 72
Moore, Irene, 161–62, 172 n. 76
Moorehouse, William, H., 169 n. 23
Morgan, Annie (Cora), 165, 173 n. 96, 185, 196 nn. 52, 57
Morgan, Corrine, 165
Mork, Mary, 127–28, 144 n. 90
Morland, Emily, 78 n. 90
Mormon(s), 4, 49, 72–73 n. 2, 94, 129–32; church, 145 n. 99
Morris, Nannie, 105
Morris, Thomas, 169 n. 23
Morton, W. T., 105
Mulleny, Catherine, 190
murder convictions, 69, 92, 112, 118, 125–29, 152, 161, 180, 206, 209. *See also* infanticide
Murphy, James, 101
Murton, Thomas O., 198 n. 95

Nagler, Michael N., 108 n. 65
Naish, Camille, 16, 17
National Conference of Charities and Correction, 56
National Prison Congress, 135, 194–95 n. 30
Native Americans, xiv, 5, 20 n. 21, 29